TITLE VII
PROGRAM 1992

THE LINGUISTIC MOMENT

THE LINGUISTIC MOMENT

From Wordsworth to Stevens

by J. Hillis Miller

Princeton University Press
Princeton, New Jersey

Copyright © 1985 by Princeton University Press

Published by Princeton University Press, 41 William Street,
Princeton, New Jersey 08540

In the United Kingdom: Princeton University Press, Oxford

All Rights Reserved

Library of Congress Cataloging in Publication Data will be
found on the last printed page of this book

ISBN 0-691-05442-8
    0-691-01439-6 (pbk.)

This book has been composed in Linotron Baskerville

Princeton University Press books are printed on acid-free paper,
and meet the guidelines for permanence and durability
of the Committee on Production Guidelines for Book Longevity
of the Council on Library Resources

Printed in the United States of America

9   8   7   6   5   4

In Memory
of
Paul de Man

CONTENTS

ACKNOWLEDGMENTS

The writing of this book has extended over a good many years. I have incurred many obligations along the way, and take pleasure in acknowledging them here.

Most of all I thank the many colleagues, students, and audiences at Johns Hopkins, at Yale, and at many other colleges and universities, who have listened patiently and constructively to various versions of parts of this book. Work on this book began originally during my tenure of a Fellowship from the John Simon Guggenheim Memorial Foundation. It has continued, along with other work, during a Fellowship at the Center for the Humanities, Wesleyan University, a Fellowship from the Council of Humanities at Princeton University, a Senior Fellowship from the National Endowment for the Humanities, a Carnegie Fellowship at the University of Edinburgh, and a month at the Bellagio Study and Conference Center of the Rockefeller Foundation. I am deeply grateful for the free time provided by all of these and for the generous allowance of research leaves by The Johns Hopkins University and Yale University.

Early versions of parts of this book, since extensively revised, have been published in various journals and books. Part of chapter 1 was published as "Theoretical and Atheoretical in Stevens" in Frank Doggett and Robert Buttel, eds., *Wallace Stevens: A Celebration*. Copyright © 1980 by Princeton University Press. Revised by permission of Princeton University Press. Reprinted (in revised form) by permission of Princeton University Press. Part of chapter 2 was published in an earlier version as "The Still Heart: Poetic Form in Wordsworth" in *New Literary History* ii, 2 (Winter 1972). Another part of chapter 2 was published as "The Stone and the Shell: The Problem of Poetic Form in Wordsworth" in *Mouvements premiers: études critiques offertes à Georges Poulet*

ACKNOWLEDGMENTS

(Paris: Librairie José Corti, 1972). Parts of chapter 5 have been published as "The Linguistic Moment in 'The Wreck of the Deutschland' " in *The New Criticism and After*, ed. Thomas D. Young (Charlottesville: University Press of Virginia, 1976), as part of "Nature and the Linguistic Moment" in *Nature and the Victorian Imagination*, ed. U. C. Knoepflmacher and G. B. Tennyson (Berkeley, Los Angeles, London: University of California Press, 1977), as part of "Theology and Logology in Victorian Literature" in *Journal of the American Academy of Religion* XLVII, 2, supplement (June 1979), and as part of the same essay reprinted in *American Critics at Work: Examinations of Contemporary Literary Theories*, ed. Victor A. Kramer (Troy, NY: The Whitston Publishing Co., 1984). Part of chapter 8 has been published in an earlier form in the "Preface" to *William Carlos Williams: A Collection of Critical Essays*, ed. J. Hillis Miller. Copyright © 1966 by Prentice-Hall, Inc. Published by Prentice-Hall, Inc., Englewood Cliffs, NJ 07632. Another part of chapter 8 has been published in an earlier form as "Williams' *Spring and All* and the Progress of Poetry" and is reprinted or reproduced by permission of *Daedalus*, Journal of the American Academy of Arts and Sciences IC, 2 (Summer 1970), Boston, MA. An earlier version of chapter 9 was published as "Stevens' Rock and Criticism as Cure: I" in *The Georgia Review* XXX, 1 (Spring 1976). I thank the editors of these publications for granting me permission to regather this material for revision and inclusion here.

I thank also the various publishers and persons for permission to make citations from the following copyrighted books. I am grateful to Donald H. Reiman for permission to make citations from his definitive edition of Shelley's "The Triumph of Life" in Donald H. Reiman, *Shelley's "The Triumph of Life": A Critical Study* (Urbana: University of Illinois Press, 1965). Copyright © 1965 by the University of Illinois Press, Urbana; copyright now held by Donald H. Reiman. Permission was granted by Oxford University Press on behalf of the Society of Jesus to make citations from Gerard Manley Hopkins, *Poems*, 4th ed., ed. W. H. Gardner and N. H. MacKenzie (London, Oxford, New York: Oxford University Press, 1970). © The Society of Jesus 1967, 1970. I am grateful to Macmillan Publishing Company for permission to make citations from *The Complete Poems of Thomas Hardy*, edited by James Gibson (New York: Macmillan Publishing Co., Inc., 1978) (Copyright © Macmillan London, Ltd, 1976). I thank Macmillan Publishing Company for permission to quote from *The Variorium Edition of the Poems of W. B. Yeats*, ed. Peter Allt and Russell K. Alspach (New York: Macmillan Publishing Co., Inc., 1977) (Copyright 1957 by Macmillan Publishing Co., Inc.), W. B. Yeats, *Essays and Introductions* (© Mrs. W. B. Yeats, 1961), and *Explorations* (Copyright © Mrs. W. B. Yeats, 1962). I thank also Michael B. Yeats and Macmillan London, Ltd, for permission to make citations from *Collected Poems of W. B. Yeats* and *Essays and Introductions* and *Explorations* by W. B. Yeats. Grateful acknowledgment is made to New Directions Publishing Corporation for permission to make citations from the following books: William Carlos Williams: *Collected Earlier Poems*. Copyright 1938 by New Directions Publishing Corporation. William Carlos Williams: *Imaginations*. Copyright © 1970 by Florence H. Williams. William Carlos Williams: *In the American Grain*. Copyright 1933 by William Carlos Williams. William Carlos Williams: *Many Loves*. Copyright 1948 by William Carlos Williams. William Carlos Williams: *Pictures from Brueghel*. Copyright © 1954, 1955, 1962 by William Carlos Williams. William Carlos Williams: *The Collected Later Poems*. Copyright 1944, 1948, 1949, 1950 by William Carlos Williams, © 1963 by the Estate of William Carlos Williams. William Carlos Williams: *Paterson*. Copyright © 1946, 1948, 1949, 1951, 1958 by William Carlos Williams © 1963 by Florence Williams. For all of the above: Reprinted by Permission of New Directions Publishing Corporation. I am also grateful to Random House, Inc. and Alfred A. Knopf, Inc. for permission to reprint excerpts from the following: *The Col-*

ACKNOWLEDGMENTS

lected Poems of Wallace Stevens (New York: Alfred A. Knopf, Inc., 1954). Copyright 1954 by Wallace Stevens. Wallace Stevens, *Opus Posthumous* (New York: Alfred A. Knopf, Inc., 1957). © 1957 by Elsie Stevens and Holly Stevens. I thank, finally, the Paul Klee-Stiftung, Kunstmuseum Bern, for permission to reproduce Paul Klee's *Tanzspiel der Rotröcke*, 1924.119. © 1984, Copyright by COSMOPRESS, Genève & ADAGP, Paris. The painting is in a private collection in Zollikon, Switzerland. It is in oil and paper on panel and measures 35 x 44 cm. I am grateful to Dr. Dimiter Daphinoff for helping me obtain permission to reproduce this painting.

J. H. M.

PREFACE

Between Theory and Practice

> . . . perhaps one is a philologist still, that is to say, a teacher of slow reading [*ein Lehrer des langsamen Lesens*].
>
> Friedrich Nietzsche, "Preface" to *Daybreak*[1]

The odd status of prefaces, as of titles, epigraphs, dedications, and footnotes, has frequently been observed of late.[2] Prefaces are like thresholds, frontiers, gates, or doorways to the infolded text within. Marginal, fencing, framing, liminal, or januarial, they are neither quite inside the work they introduce nor quite outside. They are neither quite part of the work—a contribution to its working, its effective energy of the production of meaning—nor quite not part of it. They may even inhibit or block that working. Prefaces are, precisely, *parerga*, like those "pamphlets—or 'Parerga' as he called them—by which [Mr. Casaubon, in *Middlemarch*] tested his public and deposited small monumental records of his march."[3] A preface, however, is a peculiar sort of *parergon*, extra-work beside the work, hors d'oeuvre, not in the sense of being preliminary to the work,

---

[1] Friedrich Nietzsche, "Preface," *Daybreak: Thoughts on the Prejudices of Morality*, trans. R. J. Hollingdale (Cambridge: Cambridge University Press, 1982), p. 5, trans. slightly altered; German: Friedrich Nietzsche, *"Vorrede,"* *Morgenröte, Werke in Drei Bänden*, ed. Karl Schlechta, I (Munich: Carl Hanser Verlag, 1966), p. 1016. Further citations will be from these editions.

[2] See Jacques Derrida, *"Parergon," La vérité en peinture* (Paris: Flammarion, 1978), pp. 21-168, and *ibid., "Hors livre: Préfaces," La dissémination* (Paris: Les Éditions du Seuil, 1972), pp. 9-67.

[3] George Eliot, *Middlemarch*, II, *Works*, Cabinet Edition (Edinburgh and London: William Blackwood and Sons, n.d.), chap. 29, p. 12.

anticipatory of it, or adjacent to it while it is being written, but first and last at once.

A preface can only be written after the book, and it can only be written by someone with full knowledge of where the book leads the reader, the goal it reaches. On the other hand, a preface is almost the first thing the reader encounters. It is the first step in the journey that will lead her or him to the goal of finishing the book. A preface is both foretaste and aftertaste. Insofar as one must have read the book through in order to understand it, to take that panoramic view of it the preface claims to have, the preface will by definition be incomprehensible or at least partially opaque to the reader who encounters it first, at least until she or he has read the book, at which point she or he will not need the preface. If a preface is like a sign to a bridge, it is simultaneously at both ends of the bridge, or it is like a sign that has *Enter* on one side and *Exit* on the other. A preface is magically encountered again and seen in a new light when the reader gets to the other side. A preface is two-faced, like Janus, guardian of portals and patron of beginnings and endings.

Poems may also contain in one way or another *parerga*. This is a book, or at any rate, before it was written or while it was being written it was intended to be a book, about moments of suspension within the texts of poems, not usually at their beginnings or ends, moments when they reflect or comment on their own medium. I call this suspension the linguistic moment. It is a form of parabasis, a breaking of the illusion that language is a transparent medium of meaning. As my chapters attempt to show, through a variety of examples from Wordsworth to Stevens, the linguistic moment in poetry may take a wide diversity of forms, but in all the cases studied here it has such momentum that it tends to spread out and dominate the functioning of the whole poem.

That, or something like it in different versions at different times, was the conscious focus guiding my choices of examples and my procedures of interpretation during the process of writing the various chapters of this book. In the course of writing, not surprisingly, other recurrent and related foci have emerged. If I had known already from the beginning where I was going to arrive through the act of writing the book, I would not have needed to write it. It gradually dawned on me in the course of writing the various chapters that each of my poems constitutes a different version of a spatial emblem of human temporality. My interpretation of the poems has led me to follow out as much this pathway of reading as the initial guiding thread of the linguistic moment. At any rate I have been led to explore the nodes of intersection between these two topics. Though poetry is, like music, a temporal art, and the words must be read one by one through time in order to make sense of them, and though exploration of the mysteries of human temporality is one of the primordial themes of lyric poetry, time itself, as Martin Heidegger has observed in *Sein und Zeit*, can only with great difficulty be expressed in other than spatial terms. Our ordinary expressions for time are spatial, as in the movement of the clock's hands across its face, or as in the linear image of movement along a row or pathway of words for the temporality of the act of reading.[4]

There exists a surprising variety of such spatial emblems of time in poetry. Each has its own implications and its own problematic. Though I do not claim that my poems represent an exhaustive repertoire, they nevertheless cover a lot of ground, from the image in Book V of *The Prelude* of the Arab riding across the desert fleeing from the deluge and toward the "something evermore about to be" of the

[4] See Martin Heidegger, "Within-time-ness and the Genesis of the Ordinary Conception of Time," II, 6, sec. 81, *Being and Time*, trans. John Macquarrie and Edward Robinson (London: SCM Press Ltd., 1962), pp. 472-480; German: *"Die Innerzeitigkeit und die Genesis des vulgären Zeitbegriffes,"* II, 6, sec. 81, *Sein und Zeit* (Tübingen: Max Niemeyer Verlag, 1967), pp. 420-428.

coming apocalypse; to the image, in Shelley's "The Triumph of Life," of temporal reversal in the enfolded episode enfolded by what it enfolds, earlier in time becoming later in reading, a figure for time as repetition; to the image, in Robert Browning's "The Englishman in Italy" or in Arnold's "Empedocles on Etna," of the attempt to escape time through temporal movement imaged as the spiral or direct ascent of a mountain; to the geographical figure for the complex temporal relation among the nuns' salvation, the poet's salvation, and the invoked dayspring of the conversion of the English in Hopkins' "The Wreck of the Deutschland" (while the nuns were drowning off the Kentish knock the poet was "Away in the loveable west, / On a pastoral forehead of Wales" [lines 185-186]); to the complex inhabitation (as by ghosts) or inscription (as by a kind of writing) of the landscape and of inanimate objects by past time in Hardy's poetry; to time as a labyrinth without ascertainable center, the "labyrinth of the wind," in Yeats's "Nineteen Hundred and Nineteen"; to the freezing of time into the non-present present of poetic language in an incomplete movement and in an incomplete grammatical phrase in William Carlos Williams' "Young Sycamore"; to the *mise en abyme* of an ever unsatisfied search for a solid foundation, a "cure of the ground," in Stevens' "The Rock" ("And in the lowest deep a lower deep still opens").

Various as these images are, they are all versions of a never completed movement toward total possession of time, a movement that comes forward toward the future in order to go back to the past and appropriate it, or a movement back into the past in order to go forward to a fully appropriated present and future. All these images are in one way or another a search for a ground within, beneath, above, before, or after time, something that will support time, encompass it, still its movement, as when Stevens says of his "green," his "fluent mundo," that when they get it right at the Sorbonne one day that world "will have stopped revolving except in crystal."[5] This book presupposes that such a search for grounding or such a testing of the ground is a fundamental feature of literature, as of human existence. Literature is therefore inalienably ethical, philosophical, metaphysical, even religious. Of course its revelations about the ground may be negative ones, and its metaphysical and ethical implications lie more in the nature and function of its language as such than in any overt thematic statements, important as the latter may be.

This book itself, in its form, corresponds to these issues or itself exemplifies them. My first chapter moves back from Stevens to Arnold to Wordsworth in order then to move from chapter to chapter through history from Wordsworth to Stevens again, moving back in order to move forward in an attempt to appropriate the whole, identified above. My enterprise too is a search to locate a ground beyond language for the linguistic patterns present in my poems. Who would not wish to escape the prison house of language and stand where one could see it from the outside?

The structure of this book, finally, also exemplifies that strange propensity to a reversal of early and late that is a feature of all these spatial images for time. This preface, as I have said, comes first but was written last. It is placed at the beginning for the reader of the book, at its end for the author. The reading of the book, the traversal of the never quite complete circling it makes, will bring the reader back to where he or she is at the beginning. At the beginning, nevertheless, the reader is not quite able to know where he or she is, or it would not be necessary to read the book to get there with a new awareness. For this book too,

[5] Wallace Stevens, "Notes Toward a Supreme Fiction," "It Must Give Pleasure," sec. x, lines 16, 20-21, *The Collected Poems* (New York: Alfred A. Knopf, Inc., 1954), pp. 406-407. See Martin Heidegger, *Der Satz vom Grund* (Pfullingen: Verlag Günther Neske, 1957) for an identification of the modern epoch of technology and of the scientific institutionalizing of knowledge with a certain accentuation of the principle of sufficient reason (*der Satz vom Grund*).

"origin is the goal [*Ursprung ist das Ziel*],"[6] or rather, the goal is that which is simultaneously origin, end, underlying base, and pervasive measure. Is it necessary to add that the goal is never reached—not here and not now, at any rate? The origin remains always something evermore about to be. As Stevens says, "It can never be satisfied, the mind, never."[7]

Insofar as this book is devoted to a testing of the grounds for or of my poems, it may be said to be neither a work of pure literary theory nor a work of pure praxis, a series of explications. It is something between those two or preparatory to them, a clearing of the ground and an attempt to sink foundations. It is criticism in the fundamental sense of critique, or of critical philosophy, a testing of the medium from which the bridge between theory and practice is made. Or rather, I claim that all my poems contain, in one way or another, a critical element in this sense. If so, an adequate interpretation of them will single out for special attention, patiently repeating the work of criticism already present in the poems themselves, that self-testing—as of a man jumping up and down on a plank over an abyss—which I call the linguistic moment in poetry. If criticism as critique is between theory and practice, it is also neither to be identified with hermeneutics, or the search for intentional meaning, on the one side, nor with poetics, or the theory of how texts have meaning, on the other side, though it is closely related to the latter. Critique, however, is a testing of the grounding of language in this or that particular text, not in the abstract or in abstraction from any particular case.

I shall return in the chapter below on Stevens' "The

---

[6] Cited from Karl Krauss, *Worte in Versen*, I, by Walter Benjamin in the fourteenth of the "Theses on the Philosophy of History," *Illuminations*, trans. Harry Zohn (New York: Schocken Books, 1969), p. 261; German: *Illuminationen* (Frankfurt am Main: Suhrkamp Verlag, 1969), p. 276.

[7] Wallace Stevens, "The Well Dressed Man with a Beard," line 17, *The Collected Poems*, p. 257.

Rock" to the image of an attempt to test the ground or to cure it as a figure for the work of poetry and of critique, but all my chapters are an attempt to follow out again the ground-testing performed in a different way in each case by my examples of poetry from Wordsworth to Stevens. The only practical way to test the medium of poetry is through examination of specimens of poetry, not through theoretical speculation. My attempt, following my great exemplar, Matthew Arnold, is in each case "to see the object as in itself it really is."[8] I shall attempt to test out what the language of my poems really is, what it really says, and what it can therefore be trusted to do, what function it can be expected to fulfill for us today.

Since the "object" in this case is made of language, a slow, careful, painstaking study of that language is indispensable. This may still go by the august name of philology, or slow reading, as Nietzsche calls it in that passage from the preface to *Daybreak* quoted above as an epigraph. "For philology," says Nietzsche, "is that venerable art which demands of its votaries one thing above all: to go aside, to take time, to become still, to become slow [*beseite gehn, sich Zeit lassen, still werden, langsam werden*]—it is a goldsmith's art and connoisseurship of the *word* [*Kennerschaft des 'Wortes'*] which has nothing but delicate, continuous work to do and achieves nothing if it does not achieve it *lento*. . . . This art does not so easily get everything done, it teaches to read *well*, that is to say, to read slowly, deeply, looking cautiously before and aft, with reservations, with doors left open, with delicate eyes and fingers [*sie lehrt 'gut' lesen, das heißt langsam, tief, rück- und vorsichtig, mit Hintergedanken, mit offengelassenen Tören, mit zarten Fingern und Augen lesen*]" (Eng. 3; Ger. I, 1016).

This book has been written in an attempt to be true to

---

[8] Matthew Arnold, "The Function of Criticism at the Present Time," *Lectures and Essays in Criticism, The Complete Prose Works*, ed. R. H. Super, III (Ann Arbor: The University of Michigan Press, 1962), p. 258.

this difficult art of philology, of good reading, of slow reading as Nietzsche defines it. Slow reading means slow writing, as Nietzsche also affirms: "in the end one also writes slowly [*endlich schreibt man auch langsam*]" (Eng. 5, slightly altered; Ger. I, 1016). Some splinters, fragments, or offshoots written originally for this book, sections on the image of the centerless labyrinth in Nietzsche and in Freud, interrogations of poems by Stevens and Hardy—"A Primitive Like an Orb," "The Red Fern," "The Torn Letter," and "In Front of the Landscape"—have had to be omitted for lack of space. Polemical sections about the present situation in criticism originally written for this preface have been omitted in order not to distract attention from the main business of the readings of the poems. All of these have been or will be published elsewhere. So part of this book remains still outside the book. Parts of various chapters, as indicated in my acknowledgments, have been previously published in earlier forms. All of these sections have been revised to bring them into conformity with my present understanding. In some cases—for example, in the chapter on Williams, which conflates, contests, much alters and expands two earlier essays—the alterations represent substantial changes in what I am saying. Such changing never comes to an end. This by no means indicates that I do not think I am right in the interpretations here. I believe all right-thinking readers will come to agree with what I say if they go on thinking about my poems long enough. I do mean, however, that there is always more to say about a given poem, as one moves along the line, track, or bridge of critical interpretation, or as "in the lowest deep a lower deep still opens." Each new reading builds on the old, even one's own old readings. "It can never be satisfied, the mind, never." The word *finis* can never be written to the work of interpretation. If a preface comes at both the beginning and the end of a book, enveloping the text within, it is also at the same time a portal opening out toward an undefined future of still more revisions and alterations, by hindsight and foresight, according to that figure Emerson, in "Sea-shore," has the sea propose of itself: "Then I unbar the doors: my paths lead out . . ."[9]

It may be asked, finally, whether I consider these readings exemplary, and if so, exemplifications of what? Of a certain mode of interpretation? Of a certain theory of criticism? Of a way of reading the total work of each of my poets, given in a chosen sample? Of a certain notion of historical development? No, I do not think either the readings as such or the criticism as critique here attempted can ever be exemplary in the sense of being a valid synecdoche of similarity, a genuine sample of some homogeneous whole, in any of the ways mentioned. Each poem is *sui generis*, a species with one member. The intersection of a theory of criticism with an actual poem to be criticized is always unique and always bends the presupposed theory. Nor can a series of such readings ever in other than a deluded and deluding way be organized as the support of a coherent historical story with beginning, middle, and end, a plot of history, though the history of criticism may be the history of a series of yieldings to that delusion. The work of both reading and critique has to be performed anew on each occasion. The results have validity, if they have it at all, only for that occasion.

BETHANY, CONNECTICUT
JUNE 15, 1983

[9] Ralph Waldo Emerson, "Seashore," line 39, *Poems, The Complete Works*, Concord Edition, IX (Boston and New York: Houghton, Mifflin and Company, 1904), p. 243.

THE LINGUISTIC MOMENT

From Stevens to Arnold
to Wordsworth

In an essay describing the changes in Occidental thought associated with the names of Marx, Freud, and Nietzsche, Michel Foucault has said: "Interpretation finally became an infinite task. ·... From the nineteenth century on, signs enchained themselves in an inexhaustible network, itself also infinite, not because they rest on a resemblance without edges, but because there is an irreducible gulf and opening." Foucault relates this opening of an abyss of interpretation to the "rejection of beginning" in Freud, Marx, and Nietzsche. For all three, it is impossible to go back in the activity of interpretation to an unequivocal starting place serving as the foundation of everything that follows. Whenever the interpreter reaches something apparently original, a genetic source behind which it seems impossible to go, he finds himself encountering something that is itself already an interpretation. The apparent source refers to something still further back, and that to something behind it, ad infinitum. "There is nothing absolutely primary to interpret, because at bottom all is already interpretation, each sign is in itself not the thing which offers itself to interpretation, but the interpretation of other signs."[1]

Belief in the interpretative power of origins or in the interpretative power of what is merely further back in history nevertheless still has great force today. One form of this belief is that familiar scheme of literary history whereby the earlier is assumed to be the simpler, so that the complex

[1] Michel Foucault, *"Nietzsche, Freud, Marx," Nietzsche* (Paris: Les Éditions de Minuit, 1967), pp. 187, 189.

later can be explained as a diversification of the simple earlier. This chapter will test that hypothesis by investigating assumptions about the grounding and function of poetry in Wallace Stevens, in Matthew Arnold, and in William Wordsworth. Each is taken by synecdoche as exemplary for his period. This chapter makes a swing backward from modern to Victorian to Romantic, which will be followed by a slower moving forward in time back toward the present in the circular trajectory this book follows.

Nobody doubts that Wallace Stevens is complex, nor that one form in his work of that abyss of interpretation of which Foucault writes is the way many of his poems are poems about poetry. They contain within themselves discussions of what they are and of what they mean. They enact or embody in themselves that function of poetry about which they explicitly talk. This self-labelling opens an abyss of interpretation not so much through the slipping away of an apparently solid origin as through the effacement of extra-linguistic reference initiated by the apparent act of self-reference. The language of the poem both performs its function and defines that function, in a self-mirroring that seems to make the poem a self-sufficient entity. This entity already contains signs and other signs interpreting those signs, both the textual origin and the commentary on that origin, so that the critic's work is already done for him, just as a manhole cover with the words *Manhole Cover* cast in its metal (I have seen such a one in London) does not seem to need our labelling to have a name. The manhole cover seems to be saying: "You do not need to name me. I have named myself." Words in such a poem about poetry perform a double function. They are both text and commentary. The words are both the manhole cover and the words *Manhole Cover*. The poem constantly pulls the rug out from under itself, so to speak, blows its cover. It constantly deprives itself of that origin or ground with which it seems at the same time to provide itself.

A poem like "The Man with the Blue Guitar," moreover,

does not express and exemplify a single theory of poetry. For Stevens, the theory of poetry is the life of poetry, and nothing is more problematic than the theory of poetry. Stevens' poetry is not merely poetry about poetry. It is a poetry that is the battleground among conflicting theories of poetry. The poet tries first one way and then another way in an endlessly renewed, endlessly frustrated, attempt to "get it right," to formulate once and for all an unequivocal definition of what poetry is and to provide an illustration of this definition.

The various theories of poetry that generate in their conflict the vitality of Stevens' poetic language are not modern inventions. They are not tied to a particular time in history. Nor is it an accident that just those theories are present and that the poet cannot choose among them. The conflict among three theories of poetry is as old as our Western tradition. It goes back to Plato and Aristotle, and behind them to their precursors. It may be followed through all the languages and cultures that inherit the Greek tradition. The conflict among these three theories of poetry is woven into the fabric of our Western languages. It is present in the fundamental metaphors and concepts of our speech. To use any version or dialect of that speech is to be caught in an interplay among terms that makes it impossible to adopt one theory of poetry without being led, willy-nilly, to encounter the ambiguous inherence within it of the other two. The three theories are not alternatives among which one may choose. Their contradictory inherence in one another generates the meditative search for "what will suffice" in Stevens' poetry.[2]

One theory of poetry operative in Stevens' work is the idea that poetry is imitation, *mimesis*, analogy, copy. Truth is measured by the equivalence between the structure of

[2] Wallace Stevens, "Of Modern Poetry," *The Collected Poems* (New York: Alfred A. Knopf, Inc., 1954), p. 239. Further citations from Stevens' collected poems in this chapter will be identified as CPSt, followed by the page number.

words and the structure of nonlinguistic reality. Poetry is a mirroring or matching at a distance. The structure of the poem should correspond to the structure of reality. Things as they are on the blue guitar must reflect things as they are in nature. This Aristotelian concept of poetry as imitation has had great force through all the centuries since Aristotle, for example, in nineteenth- and twentieth-century theories of realism in narrative fiction. It is by no means absent in a "sophisticated modern poet" like Stevens.

Already in Aristotle, however, the notion that poetry is imitation was inextricably involved with the notion that poetry is also unveiling, uncovering, revelation, *aletheia*. Poetry is not a mirror but a lamp. The words of poetry are that within which the truth comes to light. This theory assumes that reality, things as they are, is initially hidden. Language is what discovers things, that is to say, reveals them as what they are, in their being. Martin Heidegger's *Der Ursprung des Kunstwerkes*[3] is a distinguished twentieth-century essay exploring the idea that art is *aletheia*, but a key passage in Aristotle's *Poetics* already turns on the conflict between poetry as imitation and poetry as revelation. "Poetry in general," says Aristotle, "seems to have sprung from two causes, each of them lying deep in our nature. First, the instinct of imitation is implanted in man from childhood, one difference between him and other animals being that he is the most imitative of living creatures, and through imitation learns his earliest lessons; and no less universal is the pleasure felt in things imitated. . . . The cause of this again is, that to learn gives the liveliest pleasure, not only to philosophers but to men in general. . . ."[4]

[3] In *Holzwege* (Frankfurt am Main: Klostermann, 1950), also in a somewhat revised edition as *Der Ursprung des Kunstwerkes*, Universal-Bibliothek Nr. 8446/47 (Stuttgart: Reclam, 1960). For an English translation see "The Origin of the Work of Art," *Poetry, Language, Thought*, trans. A. Hofstadter (New York, Evanston, San Francisco, London: Harper & Row, Publishers, 1971), pp. 17-87.

[4] S. H. Butcher, *Aristotle's Theory of Poetry and Fine Art*, with a Critical

Imitation, argues Aristotle, is natural to man, part of man's nature, therefore part of nature, not opposed to it as the lie to the truth. Imitation is not only natural to man. It is also natural for him to take pleasure in it. He takes pleasure in it because he learns by it. He learns by it the nature of things as they are. In the case of that species of *mimesis* called poetry, imitation in words brings things as they are into visibility. In poetry the *logos*, as being or ground, comes into the open by way of the *logos* as words. The *logos*, as the hidden one, is revealed and expressed in the *logos* as the many, in differentiated form, in dramatic action or as trope. The Greek word *logos*, it will be remembered, means mind, intelligence, message, idea, word, ground, measure, order, ratio, proportion, being. Stevens shows great fertility in translating the play of thought in this word into English terms, as in "The Idea of Order at Key West," or in "The Man With the Blue Guitar," or in "A Primitive Like an Orb."

Poetry, according to this second theory, is an act. It is the act of the mind seeking a revelation through the words and in the words. Poetry is a revelation in the visible and reasonable of that which as the base of reason cannot be faced or said directly.

This means that the poetry of imitation, of the *logos* captured in language, is at the same time the annihilation of the *logos* as the hidden one. Being vanishes, dispersed into its representation. This annihilation cannot be shown directly, though it is the source of all poetry, for the moment of the origin of language cannot be shown in language. It is illogical, incompatible with the *logos*. This annihilation, in the root sense of a transformation into nothing at the moment of greatest illumination, is a crucial instant in Stevens' experience of the power of the poetic word. For him the "nothing that is" always stands between the poet and

---

Text and Translation of *The Poetics* (New York: Dover Publications Inc., 1951), p. 15.

the subject of his poetry. Both imagination and reality are liable at any moment to turn into this nothing, what Stevens calls "the dominant blank, the unapproachable" (CPSt, 477). "Reality is a vacuum" in one of the *Adagia*.[5] In stanza 12 of "The Man with the Blue Guitar," the poet in his strumming picks up "That which momentously declares / Itself not to be I and yet / Must be. It could be nothing else" (CPSt, 171). In "The Snow Man," Stevens speaks of "Nothing that is not there and the nothing that is" (CPSt, 10). It seems that what is most logical, the *logos* itself, "being," in Stevens' traditional name for it, turns into the illogical and into non-being when the poet tries to face it directly.

Aristotle's example of something that should not be shown directly on the stage because it is irrational is Oedipus' ignorance of the circumstances of the murder of Laius, his predecessor and unknown father: "Within the action there must be nothing irrational. If the irrational [*alogon*] cannot be excluded, it should be outside the scope of the tragedy. Such is the irrational element in the Oedipus [sic, but the play not the person is meant] of Sophocles" (Butcher trans., p. 57). For Stevens too, poetry has something to do with murder, even with parricide. In stanza 26 of "The Man with the Blue Guitar" he speaks of "the murderous alphabet" (CPSt, 179).

In stanza 19 what it means to say the alphabet is murderous is made explicit in a definition of poetry as a mortal combat between son and father:

> That I may reduce the monster to
> Myself, and then may be myself
>
> In face of the monster, be more than part
> Of it, more than the monstrous player of
>
> One of its monstrous lutes, not be
> Alone, but reduce the monster and be,

[5] Wallace Stevens, *Opus Posthumous* (New York: Alfred A. Knopf, Inc., 1957), p. 168. Henceforth cited as OPSt, followed by the page number.

Two things, the two together as one,
And play of the monster and of myself,

Or better not of myself at all,
But of that as its intelligence,

Being the lion in the lute
Before the lion locked in stone.
                    (CPSt, 175)

For Stevens too, imitation is natural to man. The imagination is then part of nature, "one of the forces of nature," as Stevens says in the *Adagia* (OPSt, 170). In imitation, nature is assimilated into language, which means that language is part of nature, too. In poetry the *logos*, "being," comes to be in language. Poetry is the "intelligence" of nature, the knowledge of it, the inherent reason in it, that is, its *logos*. Stevens is not satisfied to produce poetry that is adjacent to nature or merely part of it. He must "reduce the monster," engulf him, appropriate the monster entirely to himself. When the two have become one, then poetry will not be *about* nature but will be the "intelligence" of nature speaking directly. Only then can the poet be himself in the face of the monster. Poetry is the destruction of things as they are when they are played on the blue guitar. It is the transference of things as they are into language, that is, into what they are not, into their metaphors. In poetry the red of reality is transformed into the blue of imagination. Poetry is the defeat of the lion in the stone by the lion in the lute.

In one of his letters Stevens provides a commentary on stanza 19 of "The Man with the Blue Guitar": "Monster = nature, which I desire to reduce: master, subjugate, acquire complete control over and use freely for my own purpose, as poet. I want, as poet, to be that in nature which constitutes nature's very self. I want to be nature in the form of a man, with all the resources of nature = I want to be the lion in the lute; and then, when I am, I want to face

9

my parent and be his true part. I want to face nature the way two lions face one another—the lion in the lute facing the lion locked in stone. I want, as a man of imagination, to write poetry with all the power of a monster equal in strength to the monster about whom I write. I want man's imagination to be completely adequate in the face of reality."[6] The Oedipal drama, the son's battle to the death with his father, muted in stanza 19 itself, emerges openly in the commentary in the letter. The poet must face his "parent" nature and appropriate his sexual power, "be his true part." Only in this way can man's imagination be completely adequate in the face of reality.

There is still a third theory of poetry present in Stevens' poems. This is the notion that poetry is creation, not discovery. In this theory there is nothing outside the text. All meaning comes into existence with language and in the interplay of language. Meaning exists only in the poem. "The Man with the Blue Guitar" is poetry about poetry. It is metapoetry, a poetry of grammar, in which what counts is the play of words among themselves. Words are repeated, grammatical forms change and alter, and the same word is verb, adjective, noun, in turn. Words become themselves the subject of the discourse, as when, naming the way the blue of imagination is heated to incandescence by its marriage with reality, Stevens speaks of "the amorist Adjective aflame" (CPSt, 172).[7] "The Man with the Blue Guitar" is poetry about poetry in the sense that the poem itself is the action about which it talks. The pervasive metaphor of a man playing the guitar names the action of the poem as it progresses from stanza to stanza. The subject of the poem is the poem itself as an activity. The words about guitars and tunes are the materials of a poem that accomplishes

---

[6] *The Letters of Wallace Stevens* (New York: Alfred A. Knopf, Inc., 1966), p. 790.

[7] See the essay by Mac Hammond, "On the Grammar of Wallace Stevens," *The Act of the Mind: Essays on the Poetry of Wallace Stevens*, ed. R. H. Pearce and J. H. Miller (Baltimore: The Johns Hopkins Press, 1965), pp. 179-184.

what the metaphor only talks about. Language is always referential. There must be real guitars in order for there to be a word *guitar*. Nevertheless, the word *guitar* in this poem, in its interplay with all the other words, effaces in its poetic operation any real guitar. As the word *guitar* is absorbed into its interaction with other words and comes to draw its meaning from that interaction, any referential base tends gradually to disappear and to be abolished. Even the guitar of Picasso, which seems as if it might be referred to by the central image, is finally irrelevant. This may explain why Stevens in a letter told Poggioli, gently but firmly, that he did not want Picasso's *Man With a Guitar* on the cover of Poggioli's translation into Italian of a group of Stevens' poems. Contemplation of Picasso's painting is no more, and no less, help in understanding "The Man with the Blue Guitar" than a visit to Dorsetshire is help in understanding Hardy's *The Return of the Native*. The action of the poem is inside the poem.

An interplay between metaphor and reality, in which the two change places constantly, is characteristic of the structure of thought in this third theory of poetry. This structure is like that hermetic egg, mentioned by Yeats, which turns inside out constantly without breaking its shell. Plato, for example, must use the metaphor of "inscription" to describe the good kind of writing in the soul, though writing is for him secondary and derived.[8] Yeats in the "Supernatural Songs" must use sexual metaphors to describe the intradivine life, though sexuality in these poems is the sign of man's distance from divinity: "Godhead on Godhead in sexual spasm begot / Godhead."[9] "Things below are copies," but that which is copied can come into language only by

---

[8] See Jacques Derrida, *"La Pharmacie de Platon," La dissémination* (Paris: Les Éditions du Seuil, 1972), pp. 71-197. For a discussion of the play in Aristotle's thought between imitation as copy and imitation as revelation, see the second and third sections of J. Derrida, *"La mythologie blanche," Marges* (Paris: Les Éditions de Minuit, 1972), pp. 274-302.

[9] "Ribh in Ecstasy," *The Collected Poems of W. B. Yeats* (New York: The Macmillan Company, 1958), p. 284.

11

way of the transfers of metaphor. In that sense, things above are copies of what is below. Aristotle describes metaphor, "the application of an alien name by transference [*epiphora*]," as the fundamental instrument of poetry: "But the greatest thing by far is to have a command of metaphor" (Butcher trans., pp. 77, 87). The remarks on metaphor in Stevens' *Adagia* and in the essays of *The Necessary Angel*, as well as in the poems themselves, show that he remains true to this traditional notion. The difficulty, however, in Stevens' case at least, is to decide, in the labyrinth of interchanges, which is the metaphor, which the literal origin. In "The Man with the Blue Guitar" the referential level, words describing a man with a guitar, or perhaps a painting of one, turns out to be the derived, metaphorical level. The words and images of the poem name the activity of the poem itself and do so with the help of the man playing the guitar. The language of the poem is made up of an interplay between language about reality and language about the mind in which the two shift back and forth, or in which a single word names both simultaneously. An example is all the terms for air, weather, or atmosphere. These name not only the external weather but *air* as melody or behavior. Words describing the world must be used to describe the mind, for there are no literal words for subjective events, but the things of the external world accede to language only through words, products of the imagination, concoctions of the mind. "Things are as I think they are / And say they are on the blue guitar" (CPSt, 180), according to this third of the three theories of poetry woven inextricably together in the text of "The Man with the Blue Guitar."

My explanation of Stevens by way of the presence in his work of three traditional theories of poetry is, the reader will have noticed, an example of that interpretation by way of origins which I began by challenging, with the help of Foucault. Multiple origins are still origins and imply a causal accounting, however contradictory. The power of Stevens' poetry, the power, in fact, of the work of any great writer, cannot be explained by its sources, even sources that enter so intrinsically into the writing as these three traditional theories enter into Steven's poetry. The authentic voice of Stevens as a poet is not touched by such explanations. That voice is something unpredictable, savage, violent, without ascertainable cause or explanation, irrational, as he said genuine poetry must be. It is both a voice and a way of writing. It is something continuous, murmuring or muttering, sometimes a singsong rhyme or a stammering alliteration. Continuously present in his work, it is nevertheless a principle of discontinuity. It forbids explication by sources. It breaks into the formal order of both thought and shapely poetry. This voice appears intermittently and faintly even in Stevens' earliest journals and poems, for example, those gathered in *Souvenirs and Prophecies*.[10] This note becomes Stevens' characteristic signature in the major poetry from *Harmonium* on, as in "Bantams in Pine-Woods": "Chieftain Iffucan of Azcan in caftan / Of tan with henna hackles, halt!" (CPSt, 75), or in "The Man with the Blue Guitar": "To strike his living hi and ho, / To tick it, tock it, turn it true, / To bang it from a savage blue, / Jangling the metal of the strings . . ." (CPSt, 166), or in "Montrachet-le-Jardin": "O bright, O bright, / The chick, the chidder-barn and grassy chives / And great moon, cricket-impresario, / And, hoy, the impopulous purple-plated past, / Hoy, hoy, the blue bulls kneeling down to rest. / Chome! clicks the clock . . ." (CPSt, 260), or in "The Owl in the Sarcophagus": "She that in the syllable between life / And death cries quickly, in a flash of voice, / Keep you, keep you, I am gone, oh keep you as / My memory, is the mother of us all" (CPSt, 432).

The intrusion of this doubling voice is figured in Stevens, among other ways, by the constant presence, just below the level of rational thinking, of the guitarist with his interminable strumming ("Nothing about him ever stayed the

---

[10] New York: Alfred A. Knopf, Inc. 1977.

same, / Except this hidalgo and his eye and tune" [CPSt, 483]), or it is figured in that other sail of Ulysses, doubling the first one, and "alive with an enigma's flittering" (OPSt, 105). The presence of this "enigma"—in the words and yet not directly named by the words—forbids any understanding of Stevens' poetry by way of origins in his family, in his reading, in the repertoire of theories of poetry in "the Western tradition," in the landscapes of Pennsylvania, New Jersey, and Connecticut, or even in some intrinsic irrational property of language. The flitterings of this groundless enigma in Stevens are sounded in that austere and impersonal "Chome!" and in its variants, which pervade his poetry. Without this, Stevens would not be the great poet he is.

To identify what this disrupting element in Stevens' poetry is, if it is neither imitation, nor "being," nor merely the play of language, would require a full reading of his work. One poem, at least, will be read in more detail in a later chapter of this book. Even the fullest reading, it may be, would yield no more than hints of what cannot be named or identified in so many words, even figurative ones. If the theory of poetry is the life of poetry, it is also the cause that "poetry should resist the intelligence almost successfully" (OPSt, 171). It may be that the time when the poem ceases to resist the intelligence and can be "seen through" theoretically is the moment when the poem fails. It then no longer bears a relation, even figurative, to that "Chome!"—the essential poem at the center of things that may be neither named, nor seen, nor possessed theoretically. The linguistic moment in Stevens is paradoxically not the time of the triumph of logic or theory over the evasive paramour all poets court, but the instant when the language of poetry most "fails," becomes most opague and irrational, the click of the "Chome!" when language almost emerges as surd, not sign, becomes almost a material substance, almost sounds or marks on a page, almost blanched, drenched, drained of meaning.

14

Almost, but not quite. *Chômer* in French means to suspend work during holidays or to leave something unproductive. The "Chome!" of the clock stops the flow of time for a moment, like a catch of the breath. This suspension of the forward-moving working of language toward the production of meaning, in a prolonged, hovering instant of self-reflection, corresponds to what I have said in the preface to this book about the working against work or x1hout work of the linguistic moment in poetry. It corresponds also to what Friedrich Hölderlin calls the anti-rhythmic interruption of the caesura, to be discussed in the next section of this first chapter.

> [I]n fact such a person stands firmly and knows what he is about while the poems stagger weakly & are at their wits end.
> Matthew Arnold, in a letter to his sister[11]

THE MOMENT in the poems of Wallace Stevens when language becomes problematic introduces an oscillation among alternative theories of poetry that cannot be stilled in a decisive choice for one of them. Perhaps a move back to the mid-nineteenth century will discover a solid ground against which the waverings of Wallace Stevens can be plotted. The stern face of Matthew Arnold, mutton-chop whiskers and all, is often conjured up as an antidote to the dissipations of modernism. Arnold is seen as a way back to "sincerity" from the dangerous license of "authenticity."[12] Arnold proposes a giving up of the latter in its Romantic form of "fulness without respect of the means," the temptation "to hoist up the mainsail to the wind and let her

---

[11] *Unpublished Letters of Matthew Arnold.* ed. A. Whitridge (New Haven: Yale University Press, 1923), p. 18.

[12] See Lionel Trilling, *Sincerity and Authenticity* (Cambridge, Mass.: Harvard University Press, 1972).

drive,"[13] in order to get the former in the shape of a "joy whose grounds are true."[14] Arnold is commanded by a divine voice to leave Marguerite: "A God, a God their severance ruled!" (line 22, "To Marguerite—Continued"; PA, 125). It may be that by obeying that rule of severance he may get another, more firmly grounded love and more firmly grounded self. What these might be is explained at the end of "The Buried Life":

> Only—but this is rare—
> When a belovèd hand is laid in ours,
> When, jaded with the rush and glare
> Of the interminable hours,
> Our eyes can in another's eyes read clear,
> When our world-deafened ear
> Is by the tones of a loved voice caressed—
> A bolt is shot back somewhere in our breast,
> And a lost pulse of feeling stirs again
> The eye sinks inward, and the heart lies plain,
> And what we mean, we say, and what we would, we
>   know.
> A man becomes aware of his life's flow,
> And hears its winding murmur; and he sees
> The meadows where it glides, the sun, the breeze.
>   (lines 77-90; PA 275)

When much is resigned, much is given: "And then he thinks he knows / The hills where his life rose, / And the sea where it goes" (lines 96-98; PA, 275). Arnold is remarkable in his firm grasp of the interconnectedness of all these values—selfhood, love, origin, end, underlying ground.

---

[13] *The Letters of Matthew Arnold to Arthur Hugh Clough*, ed. H. F. Lowry (London and New York: Oxford University Press, 1932), pp. 97, 110.

[14] "Obermann Once More," line 238, *The Poems of Matthew Arnold*, ed. Kenneth Allott (London: Longmans, Green & Co. Ltd., 1965), p. 529. Henceforth cited as PA followed by the page number. For *Empedocles on Etna*, citations will first be identified by act and line numbers, scene number in the case of Act I, then by the page number in *Poems*.

To have one is to have all the others. To lack one is to lose the others. The phrase, "the buried life," names them all at once in their systematic interconnection.

Along with the rest goes possession of a true and proper language. In our ordinary state of worldly alienation from the buried life our speech is empty and ungrounded, like our action: "And long we try in vain to speak and act / Our hidden self, and what we say and do / Is eloquent, is well— but 'tis not true!" (lines 64-66; PA, 274). When we possess the buried life even for a moment we get, along with all the rest, a proper language: "What we mean, we say." Resignation gives up false signs and regains a new kind of language, resigning all anew in words that work, that say what they mean. Such words "work" in the way, for example, that the tones of a loved voice have power to open the locked door leading to the buried life. Such a voice makes something happen, whatever it says.

This seems clear enough. Arnold makes an unequivocal distinction between two kinds of language, the grounded and the ungrounded. He makes an unequivocal choice for the one over the other. The matter appears slightly more complicated, however, when one asks in which kind of language "The Buried Life" is written. Which kind of speech or act, speech-act, is it, the grounded or the ungrounded? In particular, what is the exact status of the image of the buried stream that organizes the poem throughout? Is it proper language or improper, grounded or ungrounded? Is it sincere and true, or is it a piece of untrue eloquence, merely "authentic" at best?

This question is the central one in any interpretation of Arnold. The best answer to it is reached by considering that turning point in Arnold's career as a writer, the repudiation of *Empedocles on Etna* in the "Preface" to the *Poems* of 1853. The same question must be asked twice again. What kind of speech-act, if any, is *Empedocles on Etna*; what, if anything, does it make happen? What kind of speech-

17

act, if any, is the repudiation of *Empedocles on Etna* in the "Preface"?

A long history could be written of the fate of Empedocles in the nineteenth and twentieth centuries. It would be, on the whole, the sad story of attempted suicides that did not, for one reason or another, quite come off. Joseph Conrad has the Assistant Commissioner say of Mr. Verloc, the reactionary anarchist of *The Secret Agent*, after he has inadvertently caused his half-witted nephew, Stevie, to blow himself up: "his state of dismay suggested to me an impulsive man who, after committing suicide with the notion that it would end all his troubles, had discovered that it did nothing of the kind."[15] Those modern poets and philosophers who have tried to kill off Empedocles again in order to be the survivors of his death have not even been able to succeed unequivocally in the first stage of their projects. There seems to have been some fatality in the material of Empedocles' legendary life and death that has made them bunglers every one. This story of a story that could not get on with itself might begin with the three versions of Hölderlin's incomplete drama *Der Tod des Empedokles*, with their "commentary," Hölderlin's essay, the *Grund zum Empedokles*. The story would continue with Arnold's play, which was completed but then rejected, for reasons I shall try to identify. The next stage might be those fragmentary notes Friedrich Nietzsche left for a play about Empedocles he never wrote, just as his incomplete *Die Philosophie im tragischen Zeitalter der Griechen* stops short of the projected section on Empedocles.[16] Finally there would be much to

---

[15] Joseph Conrad, *The Secret Agent* (Garden City, N.Y.: Doubleday, Page, 1925), p. 220.

[16] For the former see Friedrich Nietzsche, *Nachgelassene Fragmente, Herbst 1869 bis Herbst 1872*, III, pt. 3, *Werke*, ed. Giorgio Colli and Mazzino Montinari (Berlin, New York: Walter de Gruyter, 1978), pp. 243-247, 281-283. For the latter, see Friedrich Nietzsche, *Werke in Drei Bänden*, ed. Karl Schlechta, III (Munich: Carl Hanser Verlag, 1966), pp. 349-413; for an English translation see Friedrich Nietzsche, *Philosophy in the Tragic Age*

say about Sigmund Freud's admiration for Empedocles. Freud identified his own work as a twentieth-century scientific version of Empedocles' ancient insight into the fact that existence has a double motivating energy: the life force and the death wish.[17] Freud's personal relation to death was complicated. He kept expecting his death to occur on certain anniversaries. Like a millennial sect continually disappointed that the end of the world does not occur on the day prophesied, he kept postponing the promised day. It was a strange kind of unsuccessful suicide. It might be possible to claim that Freud, unlike Hölderlin, Arnold, or Nietzsche, dominated the Empedocles material. *Jenseits der Lustprinzip*, it might be said, is the oblique masterwork on this topic, though it nowhere mentions Empedocles. It is a masterwork, a work of mastery, not because it successfully kills Empedocles, but because it shows the impossibility of dying. All this would be too long a story to tell here. It would involve the strange fact that the story of Empedocles' suicide, in all these cases, is a cover for a story of unsuccessful love that is not told or is told only obscurely.

I shall concentrate here on one exemplary moment in that cover story, the moment of Matthew Arnold's repudiation of his *Empedocles on Etna* in the "Preface" of 1853. The reasons for that repudiation seem straightforward. All imitation, says Arnold, citing Aristotle, gives pleasure, but it is not enough that a poem should merely give pleasure. It must also infuse joy, a joy whose grounds are true. True "joy," for Arnold, is the sign of a connection with the deep,

of the Greeks, trans. Marianne Cowan (Chicago: Henry Regnery Company, 1962).

[17] For Freud's comments on Empedocles, see "Analysis Terminable and Interminable" (1937), *Collected Papers*, ed. James Strachey, v (New York: Basic Books, Inc., 1959), pp. 348-350, and for a discussion of the "influence" of Empedocles on Freud, see Sarah Kofman, *"Freud et Empédocle," Quatre romans analytiques* (Paris: Éditions Galilée, 1974), pp. 33-66. Empedocles is also one of the underlying antecedents for the opposition between the pleasure principle and the death wish in *Beyond the Pleasure Principle* (1920).

buried life. Proper poetry, for Arnold, is performative. It makes something happen by opening a channel to the lost sources of joy and by allowing that joy to flow into the reader from the places where it has lain buried. The logic of Arnold's argument is clear on this point. The specific metaphysical overtones of the word *joy* in his work (as in that of his precursor, Wordsworth) must be remembered, and a full performative force must be felt in the words *inspirit, rejoice, convey,* and *infuse.* As Arnold makes explicit, the word also indicates his allegiance to Schiller's reinterpretation or misreading of the Kantian concept of the aesthetic:

> We all naturally take pleasure, says Aristotle, in any imitation or representation whatever: this is the basis of our love of poetry; and we take pleasure in them, he adds, because all knowledge is naturally agreeable to us . . . .
>
> Any accurate representation may therefore be expected to be interesting; but, if the representation be a poetical one, more than this is demanded. It is demanded, not only that it shall interest, but also that it shall inspirit and rejoice the reader; that it shall convey a charm, and infuse delight. . . . [I]t is not enough that the Poet should add to the knowledge of men, it is required of him also that he should add to their happiness. "All art," says Schiller, "is dedicated to Joy, and there is no higher and no more serious problem, than how to make men happy. The right art is that alone, which creates the highest enjoyment."[18]

"It is demanded"; "it is required." The "it is" here does not name the fact that the general reading public insist on being rejoiced by poetry. "It" "is" an absolute demand on the poet by the universal nature of things, a primordial

[18] I cite the annotated edition of the "Preface" of 1853 in *The Poems of Matthew Arnold,* ed. cit., pp. 591, 592. Further citations from the "Preface" will be identified by PA, followed by the page number in this edition.

establishment, presupposition, or call, like the *es gibt* of Heidegger. "It is" and therefore "it is demanded."

The repudiation of *Empedocles on Etna* appears to follow inevitably from this presupposition or from the implacable conditions of this contractual note: payable on demand. Arnold's poem does not respond to the demand, fulfill the requirement, or pay off the debt. It is therefore spurious, like paper money with nothing behind it, no ground in true gold. Or it is like a counterfeit coin, lacking the true inscription or the true effigy. Such a poem must therefore be called in. It must be cancelled or destroyed—at the very least, marked *void* so that no one will take it for the real thing. The melancholy eloquence of Arnold's rejection of *Empedocles* is an anathema. An anathema is a special kind of speech-act, one of exclusion or annihilation. An anathema is another and peculiar way of doing things with words. It is the reverse of a creative *Fiat*. It says, "Let it not be," or "Let it be as if it were not."

Arnold's "Preface" repudiates *Empedocles*, it will be noted, precisely because the poem is not a speech-act. Neither its hero nor the play itself does anything, and a good play should be the representation of an action. Has not Aristotle said so? In *Empedocles*, the hero endures, the text represents, a situation in which there is nothing done and nothing to be done. *Empedocles* is a closet drama. It is enclosed on all sides, impossible to enact in the theatre because there is no action. The play represents only a lot of talk and passive suffering. It cannot cause in the viewer the change Aristotle calls *catharsis*. Therefore it must be cancelled:

> What then are the situations [asks Arnold], from the representation of which, though accurate, no poetical enjoyment can be derived? They are those in which the suffering finds no vent in action; in which a continuous state of mental distress is prolonged, unrelieved by incident, hope, or resistance; in which there is everything to be endured, nothing to be done. In such situations

there is inevitably something morbid, in the description of them something monotonous. When they occur in actual life, they are painful, not tragic; the representation of them in poetry is painful also.

To this class of situations, poetically faulty as it appears to me, that of Empedocles, as I have endeavoured to represent him, belongs; and I have therefore excluded the poem from the present collection. (PA, 592)

This seems clear enough, as clear as it can be, theoretically perspicuous. There is only one problem with it. Empedocles does in fact do something in Arnold's play. He commits suicide. This act, moreover, is by no means presented as one of passive endurance or of resignation. Empedocles' suicide is an active intervention. It is something positive. Empedocles leaps into the crater while a tiny strand of joy still connects him to the joyful life of the four elements in nature, just when he is about to become "nothing but a devouring flame of thought" (II, 329; PA, 188). Empedocles chooses the joyful flame of nature over the sterile flame of thought. Arnold's commentary, in the Yale manuscript, on the meaning of Empedocles' suicide emphasizes the positive, active aspect of it: "Before he becomes the victim of depression and overtension of mind, to the utter deadness of joy, grandeur, spirit, and animated life, he desires to die; to be reunited with the universe, before by exaggerating his human side he has become utterly estranged from it" (PA, 148). The danger confronting Empedocles is a fate like that of the Hunter Gracchus in Franz Kafka's story. Once Empedocles becomes nothing but a devouring flame of thought, he will be so alien to the universe that it will be impossible for him to die. He will be thrown from reincarnation to reincarnation and "be astray forever" (II, 390; PA, 191). Empedocles chooses real death over this false death in life. His final speech expresses exultant triumph:

And therefore, O ye elements! I know—
Ye know it too—it hath been granted me
Not to die wholly, not to be all enslaved.
I feel it in this hour. The numbing cloud
Mounts off my soul; I feel it, I breathe free.

Is it but for a moment?
—Ah, boil up, ye vapours!
Leap and roar, thou sea of fire!
My soul glows to meet you.
Ere it flag, ere the mists
Of despondency and gloom
Rush over it again,
Receive me, save me!
     [He plunges into the crater.]
      (ii, 404-416; PA, 191-192)

After Empedocles' suicide, the final song of Callicles celebrates Apollo Musagetes. The god of light and poetry
leading the nine Muses on Mount Helicon is an image of
the reconciliation of man, nature, the gods, and the various
forms of art. Callicles is throughout *Empedocles on Etna* the
singer of this ideal harmony, while Empedocles represents
the dangers of what Arnold in the "Preface" calls "the dialogue of the mind with itself" (PA, 591). The latter inhibits
that harmony by introducing something that cannot be assimilated into the economy of existence. Empedocles' act
of suicide rescues his last bit of joy before he becomes pure
mind and therefore wholly detached from nature. It also
makes him, as he was supposed to become in Hölderlin's
unfinished *The Death of Empedocles*, the tragic hero as poet.
Empedocles is the singer who goes out into the empty space
between man, nature, and the gods, opening again a channel for their intercommunication. This opening occurs by
way of language. It is a speech-act, almost as grand or
grandiose a one as can be imagined. If it is not as sublime
as the all-creating *Fiat lux* of God, it is the next thing to it

since it repairs through language a discord in the encompassing harmony of creation.

Why then does Arnold repudiate his poem? The linguistic moment in Arnold's work, dominant in it from one end to the other, is the moment when the notion that poetry may perform an act becomes problematic. The most acute version of this is the apparent contradiction between *Empedocles on Etna* and the later preface attempting to cancel it.

In order better to understand the contradiction, it will be helpful to juxtapose Arnold to Franz Kafka, in one temporal direction, and to Friedrich Hölderlin, in the other. I have written elsewhere in more detail about Kafka's *Von den Gleichnissen* ("On Parables"), but I add here a final twist.[19] Kafka's "On Parables" turns on the question of whether following the sacred parables—for example, when they tell man to "cross over"—occurs in parable or in reality: "concerning this a man once said: Why such reluctance? If you only followed the parables you yourselves would become parables and with that rid of all your daily cares."[20] Is what the man once said literal or parabolic? This question is raised in the little alternating dialogue that ends Kafka's "On Parables":

> Another said: I bet that is also a parable.
> The first said: You have won.
> The second said: But unfortunately only in parable.
> The first said: No, in reality: in parable you have lost.
>
> (*Ibid.*)

"On Parables" is a characteristic example of the specifically Kafkaesque double bind. Either way, for Kafka, you have had it. You lose by winning and lose by losing too. If

[19] See "Parable and Performative in the Gospels and in Modern Literature," *Humanizing America's Iconic Book*, ed. Gene M. Tucker and Douglas A. Knight (Chico, California: Scholars Press, 1982), pp. 57-71.

[20] Franz Kafka, *Parables and Paradoxes*, in German and English (New York: Schocken Books, 1971), p. 11.

you take the parable literally, then you must understand it as naming some literal crossing over from one place to another in reality, in which case you remain in reality, "the only life we have," so following the parable does not make anything happen. If you take the parable parabolically, that means seeing it as merely figurative. In that case neither the parable itself nor following the parable makes anything happen, and so you have lost in parable. Winning in parable could only occur if the crossing over promised in the parable were to occur in reality. Either way you lose, since to win in reality is to lose in parable, and the one thing needful is to win in parable, to find a joy whose grounds are true.

Another turn is added, however, by the fact that "Another" says, "I bet [*Ich wette*] that is also a parable." A bet is a specific kind of performative language. It neither is based on knowledge nor leads to knowledge, but is based on uncertainty. It leads to winning or losing, which can occur only when you have hazarded your gage, entered the game. A bet does not name anything but makes something happen. Kafka's analysis of parables turns on a distinction between constative and performative language. Constative language names something. Performative language makes something happen. Do the parables give knowledge or do they perform something, and does this occur, whichever is the case, when the parables are taken literally or when they are taken parabolically? The opposition between knowledge and action, constative and performative language, on the one hand, and the opposition between literal and parabolic language, on the other, are not the same opposition, and yet they are not entirely different either. Each opposition contaminates the other, crosses over the frontier into the region of the other, preventing clear understanding or a clearheaded option, just as the interpretation of the parables cannot be sharply distinguished from the knowledge they give or the action they instigate. "A man" interprets the parables by saying they must not be interpreted but acted on. What he says im-

25

mediately becomes literature in its turn and subject to the uncertainties of interpretation. Is what the man says literal or parabolic? You cannot know. You can only bet that it is one or the other and see what happens. Kafka's little text is not a parable but a commentary "On Parables," and yet it is clearly in itself a parable about which the same questions must be raised as it raises about the sage's "crossover."

Interpretation, "literary criticism," is not the detached statement of a knowledge objectively obtained. It is the desperation of a bet, an ungrounded doing things with words: "I bet this is a lyric poem," or "I bet this is an elegy," or "I bet that is a parable," followed by the exegesis that is the consequence of the bet. The interpretation following the leap into generic classification is still not rational or perspicuous knowledge. The exegete remains lost in the tangles of the ambiguous result of his initial use of performative language and in its obscure relation to the clear distinction between literal and figurative or parabolic language. They must be different and yet they cannot be clearly distinguished. The realm of criticism remains a matter of winning or losing, and not a matter of knowing or not knowing. It remains, moreover, a realm in which you can never know for sure whether you have won or lost, since winning in reality means losing in parable, and presumably vice versa, whereas really winning in parable is the only thing that would satisfy or give certainty.

Matthew Arnold walked into this double double bind, the double bind of the interpreter of parables doubling the double bind of the parables themselves, when he wrote *Empedocles on Etna* and then withdrew it. Arnold, too, would be satisfied only with a joy whose grounds are true. He wants poetry to be a speech-act infusing such joy. This means both that its language must correspond literally to something real and that the action it induces in the soul of the reader or beholder must be real. Instead of that, Arnold's poetry has wandered into the realm of parable. In that realm material figures arbitrarily name impalpable abstractions—for example, the concept of the buried life, called in *Empedocles* "our only true, deep-buried selves, / Being one with which we are one with the whole world" (II, 371-372; PA, 190).

Characteristic of Arnold's poetic diction is an arbitrary linking of abstract concept with natural image, as when he speaks of "the icebergs of the past" (PA, 531). The multitude of incompatible meanings that are ascribed to certain natural images in his poetry betrays the contingent nature of the connection between image and meaning. The most striking of these images is the motif of water—river, stream, or sea. Water threads its way through all of Arnold's poetry. Sometimes water is an image of temporality, "the river of Time" ("The Future," line 3; PA, 263), sometimes, of the deep buried life. In "Dover Beach" the reader is told that whereas for Sophocles the sound of the sea stood for "the turbid ebb and flow / Of human misery," we moderns "find also in the sound a thought," but for us it is the "melancholy, long, withdrawing roar" of "the Sea of Faith" (lines 17-18, 19, 25, 21; PA, 241-242). In "To Marguerite—Continued" an entirely different allegorical meaning is ascribed to the sea. There, each person—the poet and Marguerite for example—is a separate island "in the sea of life enisled" (line 1; PA, 124), divided by the implacable voice of a god. By the end of the poem, the sea is not so much "life" as the principle of separation, or perhaps life itself has become that estrangement. The poet and Marguerite become islands forever separated by "the unplumbed, salt, estranging sea" (line 24; PA, 125). The reader of Arnold's poems is pretty sure to find water in any one of them, but he would err if he expected the water to have a constant parabolic meaning or to have come from the same reservoir.

Much has been made of the coherence of Arnold's poetic landscape.[21] The countertruth should also be recognized.

[21] See Alan H. Roper, "The Moral Landscape of Arnold's Poetry," *PMLA* LXXVII (1962), 289-296; A. Dwight Culler, *Imaginative Reason: The Poetry*

The same topographical features occur throughout Arnold's poetry and prose, and they make a coherent landscape, but a given topographical feature may have a wild diversity of incompatible meanings in different poems and prose passages. Far from being a preordained correspondence that would make the poetry using such correspondences the means of reaching a joy whose grounds are true, the connection of figure and meaning is freely made up out of the possibilities of language by the poet. Each such correspondence is an arbitrary and groundless positing, thrown out toward a ground that may or may not be there, not a grounded knowledge of what is beyond nature by means of nature.

Empedocles on Etna and the "Preface" of 1853, taken together, are the drama of Arnold's recognition of this fact. They are evidence that he understood the situation he was in and that he found that situation and the kind of poetry he was consequently forced to write intolerable. They were the intolerable as such, "a continuous state of mental distress . . . in which there is everything to be endured, nothing to be done." Nevertheless, there was no escape from it, not even by that peculiar speech-act whereby a man attempts to disaffirm something he has earlier affirmed. Negation is another speech-act of the same sort as the one negated and so performs again another version of the performative that is being negated.

The reader of Arnold's "Preface" of 1853 will remember his violent and disdainful rejection of the notion that the proper goal of poetry is to project an allegory of the poet's mental state. This view was expressed, probably by David Masson, in a review of Alexander Smith's *A Life Drama*: "But the modern critic not only permits a false practice; he absolutely prescribes false aims. 'A true allegory of the

of Matthew Arnold (New Haven and London: Yale University Press, 1966), esp. pp. 1-17; J. H. Miller, "Matthew Arnold," *The Disappearance of God* (Cambridge, Mass.: The Belknap Press of Harvard University Press, 1963), pp. 212-269.

state of one's own mind in a representative history,' the poet is told, 'is perhaps the highest thing that one can attempt in the way of poetry.'[22] And accordingly he attempts it. An allegory of the state of one's own mind, the highest problem of an art which imitates actions! No assuredly, it is not, it never can be so; no great poetical work has ever been produced with such an aim" (PA, 598-599).

There is much that is odd about these sentences in their context. No one can doubt that *Empedocles on Etna* is an allegory of the state of Arnold's mind at the time he wrote it, in the late 1840s, after the debacle of his love for "Marguerite." The violence of his repudiation of such poetry is strengthened by his self-hate for not being able to write any other sort. In the first paragraph of the "Preface" Arnold defends (or at any rate defines the interest of) his *Empedocles*, if not for being an allegory of the poet's own mind, then for being an allegory of the modern state of mind generally. The play appears to be about "one of the last of the Greek religious philosophers." In fact it is a parable of the modern mind. That mind, like Empedocles' mind, is characterized by the fact that it is trapped permanently within itself. Everything it encounters is transformed into a parable of its own state: "Into the feelings of a man so situated [as Empedocles] there entered much that we are accustomed to consider as exclusively modern; how much, the fragments of Empedocles himself which remain to us are sufficient at least to indicate. ... [T]he calm, the cheerfulness, the disinterested objectivity have disappeared: the dialogue of the mind with itself has commenced; modern problems have presented themselves; we hear already the doubts, we witness the discouragement, of Hamlet and of Faust" (PA, 591). The text of the Empedoclean fragments is already modern in being cut off

[22] The passage Arnold cites here appeared in an unsigned review in the *North British Review* XIX (August 1853), 338. Arnold thought the review was by J. M. Ludlow but, as R. H. Super has demonstrated, it was probably by David Masson. See Allott's note, p. 598.

29

from the objective world. It expresses the dialogue of the mind with itself. Arnold takes this material and makes of it another text, a truly modern one, worthy to follow *Hamlet* and *Faust*. It is modern because it expresses the predicament of Arnold himself, another modern man who is trapped inside the dialogue of the mind with itself. Whatever matter Arnold turns to turns into a "true allegory of the state of one's own mind in a representative history," that is, into that form of poetry he most detests. He detests it because it does not make anything happen. It does not infuse joy. It remains caught in a sterile self-enclosed circling in which the self talks to itself.

Arnold proposes in the "Preface" his opposing concept of a proper poetry. Such a poetry makes something happen because it is the objective, cheerful, disinterested representation of an objective action. In the process of defining this poetry, however, something exceedingly peculiar happens. Arnold begins by citing Aristotle on the primacy of plot. He understands Aristotle to be saying plot is primary because it is the dynamic movement of the action in a play that not only represents something happening, but makes something happen. A good play effects the catharsis of pity and fear in the feelings of the spectators. This concept of drama is the basis of Arnold's rejection of *Empedocles on Etna. Empedocles* is a drama with no action, a drama in which everything is to be endured, nothing to be done. This, as I have said, leaves unexplained Arnold's failure to recognize that his Empedocles does after all perform a decisive act. Even if that problem is suspended for the moment, Arnold shows a curious inability to think of action as truly action. The dynamic movement through time of the actions appropriate for Greek tragedy turns, in Arnold's language for it, into the static and marmoreal. "Action" becomes "situation." Arnold's anxiety to describe Greek tragedy as objective, in opposition to the subjective dialogue of the mind with itself in modern literature, leads him to turn literature into something motionless and visual. In Arnold's language, action vanishes from Greek tragedy almost as soon as it is posited there. In spite of himself and apparently without even being aware of it, Arnold is soon back in a description of drama as an inactive situation in which, once more, everything is to be endured, nothing to be done:

> ... the action itself, the situation of Orestes, or Merope, or Alcamaeon, was to stand the central point of interest, unforgotten, absorbing, principal .... The terrible old mythic story on which the drama was founded stood, before he entered the theatre, traced in its bare outlines upon the spectator's mind; it stood in his memory, as a group of statuary, faintly seen, at the end of a long and dark vista: then came the poet, embodying outlines, developing situations, not a word wasted, not a sentiment capriciously thrown in: stroke upon stroke, the drama proceeded: the light deepened upon the group; more and more it revealed itself to the riveted gaze of the spectator: until at last, when the final words were spoken, it stood before him in broad sunlight, a model of immortal beauty. (PA, 596)

In spite of his overt obeisance to Aristotle, Arnold proposes here the anti-Aristotelian notion that the action of tragedy is to expose an eternally poised inaction. Those who have read Arnold's imitation classic drama, *Merope: A Tragedy*, will know the disastrous icy effect of Arnold's inadvertent transformation of time into space, action into situation. In this admirably eloquent passage Arnold seems momentarily to have forgotten the message of Lessing's *Laoköon*. *Empedocles on Etna* is far better than the execrable *Merope*. Something happens in it, and it happens in the words or through the words, but that happening is precisely what Arnold does not want to let or to make happen.

The figure of the motionless statue in the sunlight, in the passage just quoted, brings to the surface deep fissures among three theories of poetry operative in Arnold's thinking: the Romantic aestheticism Arnold represents in spite

31

of himself, the Aristotelian notion of tragic action to which Arnold wants to remain faithful, and a post-Romantic mode of performative poetry toward which he moves without wishing to do so. Arnold's description of the proper operation of tragedy in the "Preface" would seem to affirm the first of these theories of poetry. It matches Hegel's definition of the beautiful as *das sinnliche "Scheinen" der Idee*, the sensible shining forth of the idea.[23] It matches also Martin Heidegger's definition, in *Der Ursprung des Kunstwerkes*, of art as *aletheia*, revelation. For Hegel, for Arnold, for Heidegger, the work of art brings out into the sunlight something that had a prior hidden existence. Art does not create or imitate, but expose. It calls something pre-existing to appear. This idea of poetry, however, is contaminated by the other two, by the Aristotelian notion in the attempt to reaffirm the idea of tragic action from the *Poetics*, by the performative notion in what Empedocles actually does in Arnold's play.

Arnold's Empedocles is the creator of an alternative fire. This fire is not the sun, but that mock sun symbolized in Arnold's play by the "sea of fire" (II, 411; PA, 192), the molten lava in the volcano, and by the defiant Titan Typho, imprisoned under the volcano for defying Zeus. When Callicles sings the story of Typho, "the rebel o'erthrown, / Through whose heart Etna drives her roots of stone / To imbed them in the sea" (II, 42-44; PA, 178), Empedocles' response is a characteristic reading of the poet's objective mythical song as an allegory of his own mind in a representative history. He demystifies the myth and then turns it into an abstract parable, a parable without grounds other than the speaker's say-so. This allegorizing transformation is Arnold's version of the linguistic moment. It is the fundamental action of *Empedocles on Etna* and of Arnold's work generally. It justifies his justification of that work in a letter

[23] G.W.F. Hegel, *Vorlesungen über die Ästhetik*, I, *Werke in zwanzig Bänden*, XIII (Frankfurt am Main: Suhrkamp Verlag, 1970), p. 151.

to his mother as representing "the main movement of mind of the last quarter of a century":[24]

> He fables yet speaks truth!
> ....
> Those rumblings are not Typho's groans, I know!
> Those angry smoke-bursts
> Are not the passionate breath
> Of the mountain-crushed, tortured, intractable Titan
>   king—
> But over all the world
> What suffering is there not seen
> Of plainness oppressed by cunning,
> As the well-counselled Zeus oppressed
> That self-helping son of earth!
>   (II, 89, 95-103; PA, 180, 181)

There is a double movement of allegorization here. This movement is unravelled even as it is woven. The rumblings of Mt. Etna have been mythologized by naive traditional poets like Callicles as the groans of the imprisoned Titan. That myth is first demythologized ("He fables") and then is seen as a "true" allegory of the subjective sufferings of those "self-helping" men, such as Empedocles, who defy the gods and defy nature. In order to make the second of these linguistic moves, Empedocles must perform the first, the cancellation of the objective ground of the figure. The rumblings of the volcano are not really the groans of Typho. That is merely a fable. The fable, nevertheless, speaks the truth parabolically about a certain objective experience. The correspondence between the fable and the truth it tells is arbitrary and contingent, not preordained. It is the truth of allegory, in which anything objective or traditional may be made to stand for more or less anything subjective and modern. The allegorical figuration makes the subjective

---

[24] Matthew Arnold, *Letters: 1848–1888*, ed. George W. E. Russell, II (New York: Macmillan and Co., 1895), p. 10.

truth stand there in the sunlight for all to see, but it does so only by uprooting itself from its traditional base of belief in the myth as literally true.

This double movement of cancellation and reaffirmation in Empedocles' speech about Typho (cancellation as objective truth, reaffirmation as allegory) characterizes the linguistic action of *Empedocles on Etna* as a whole. The long didactic speech of Empedocles to Pausanias in Act I, which so many readers have found so tedious, appears to counsel Stoic resignation. The doctrine is in fact the opposite of Stoic. Stoicism, as propounded by Epictetus or by Marcus Aurelius, advises a yielding of selfish demands on existence to the all-powerful soul of the world, the Stoic *pneuma* of which the individual soul is part. Being one with the *pneuma*, the self is one with the whole world. Empedocles, on the other hand, tells Pausanias that man and nature, subject and object, have nothing whatsoever in common:

> We mortals are no kings
> For each of whom to sway
> A new-made world up-springs,
> Meant merely for his play;
> No, we are strangers here; the world is from of old.
> (I, ii, 177-181; PA, 164)

The resignation Empedocles counsels in Act I is a yielding to a vast impersonal material process of which man is willy-nilly a part: "The world's course proves the terms / On which man wins content" (I, ii, 222-223; PA, 166). Empedocles repeatedly denies that there are any gods. Nor is there any supernatural world beyond this one in which man may hope to escape the incompatability between his needs and the world's course here. "Here," in this world, there is a total dissociation between mind and the material process of nature, but no "there" exists to which man might cross over.

In the light of what Empedocles says in Act I, his suicide in Act II in order to preserve the last strand of connection between his mind and the four elements can be nothing but an allegory. No man's mind has ever had any kinship whatsoever with nature. Empedocles' suicide is therefore only a verbal action. It does not occur in reality but only in parable. It makes nothing happen except in words. To bet that it is a parable is to win in reality but to lose in parable, since it is *really* nothing but an allegory of Arnold's mind or of the modern mind in a representative history. To win in parable Empedocles' suicide would have to enact a genuine movement of transcendence. It would have to go over to another world and re-establish that harmony between man, nature, and the gods Callicles hymns in his final song. Since that going over and that harmony occur only in parable, they do not occur at all in reality. Arnold was therefore right to reject the play as lacking in action. It is indeed prolonged unrelieved suffering in which everything is to be endured, nothing to be done.

The final reversal, however, lies in the fact that this cancellation in the "Preface" completes the action of the play and makes it a true performative, a way of doing something with words. The play and the preface together do make something happen and make it go on happening, both in the overall movement of the play (which is one large linguistic moment) and over and over again in its small-scale deliteralization of referential language into allegory.

How this is so, a retrospective comparison with Hölderlin's *The Death of Empedocles* will make clear, as clear as a statue standing in the sunlight. Hölderlin supposedly wrote the *Grund zum Empedokles* between the second and third versions of his unfinished play on Empedocles. In this essay Hölderlin, like Arnold later (though there was not, so far as I know, any direct "influence" of the one on the other), also proposes a concept of poetry as an allegory of the poet's mind in a representative history. "The tragic poet," says Hölderlin, "because he expresses the deepest innerness, carries over his personality, his subjectivity, as well as the object present to him into a foreign personality, into a for-

35

eign objectivity." The poet is in one subject-object relation-ship, a real one. In order to express the deepest inwardness of this subjectivity in its relation to what it beholds, he must go over into another subject-object relation, one that is "more foreign [*fremder*]." The word *fremder* must be given its full strength here. The alien material has nothing to do with the poet's own situation. It can be made analogous to that situation only by an act of linguistic violence. It is, says Hölderlin, "a bolder, more foreign parable and example [*ein kühneres, fremderes Gleichnis und Beispiel*]."[25] The story the poet goes over into has the arbitrary strangeness of parable, but his deepest innerness can apparently only be expressed in this way. It cannot be expressed literally or even in a closely analogous allegory. Something bolder and more foreign is necessary.

As Andrzej Warminski has brilliantly shown, this oppo-sition between literal and figurative expression is essential within the linguistic and dramatic texture of the *Gleichnis*, too—that is, in the unfinished plays on Empedocles Höl-derlin wrote. An example is the presumably last, unfinished scene of the so-called third version of *The Death of Emped-ocles*, the dialogue of Empedocles and the Egyptian seer Manes. The play as a whole is a figure for the deepest inner life of the poet, but within the parable, figure and ground divide again. There is, so to speak, a figurative figurative and a figurative literal, as there is in Arnold's play. Manes asks Empedocles whether he is literally the new Savior (*der neue Retter*), the mediator who will go out between man and the gods, take Zeus's lightning on his own head, and in his self-sacrifice initiate a new epoch of harmonious interpen-etration of man, nature, and gods. "*Bist du der Mann? der-selbe? bist du diß?*" asks Manes, "Are you that man? the very same? Are you this?" Empedocles answers that in his youth

[25] Friedrich Hölderlin, *Sämtliche Werke und Briefe*, II (Munich: Carl Han-ser Verlag, 1970), pp. 115-116, 115, my trans.

life's enigma (*des Lebens Rätsel*) was solved in word and in figure (*im Wort, im Bilde*), but his suicide will take him over into a realm in which it will be solved in fact. He will enjoy in reality and "no longer in image" (*nicht im Bilde mehr*) what he has had so far only in parable.[26] He will become a parable in parable, not in reality, and so win in parable as well as in reality. He will do this in the only way that is possible: by crossing over the boundary separating the two realms. He will bring them together, erase the frontier, and make the distinction between parable and reality, figurative and literal, no longer possible.

The fundamental question remains unanswered. Does this action *of* the play (not *in* the play) occur in reality or in parable? The answer of course is that it does not occur at all in either mode. Hölderlin was unable or unwilling to complete any of the three versions of his play. Why this was so is impossible to say except speculatively, by a hypothetical movement back into the deepest inner life of the poet. That inwardness, according to the basic presupposition of this linguistic transaction, cannot be spoken of accurately in literal terms. To say Hölderlin reached some irresolvable impasse in the writing of the play, or that he was interrupted, distracted, became bored with it, or went mad would all be equally illicit forms of the attempt to speak literally of what can only be spoken of in some bolder or more foreign parable. All the reader can say is that the poet again and again, three different times with three radically different texts, brought the hero of his *Gleichnis* up to the point of the self-sacrifice that was to have put him literally into the realm of parable, but could not accomplish that crossing over. Hölderlin's willingness to take parable literally seems to have been even less efficacious than Ar-

[26] Friedrich Hölderlin, *Poems and Fragments*, bilingual ed., trans. Michael Hamburger (Cambridge: Cambridge University Press, 1980), pp. 354, 355; 356, 357; 358, 359.

nold's repudiation of the language of poetry for being merely parabolic.

In a remarkable passage in an essay entitled "Comments on *Oedipus*"[27] Hölderlin proposes a theory of caesura that would, if applied to *The Death of Empedocles*, make the suspension of action in his unfinished play the evidence of its power, authenticity, and efficacy:

> The tragic *transport [Transport]* is, in itself, empty and the most unconnected [*der ungebundenste*].
>
> Thereby in the rhythmic succession of representation [*der Vorstellungen*] in which the *transport* is portrayed, *that which in prosody is called the caesura [Zäsur]*, the pure word [*das reine Wort*], the antirhythmic interruption, becomes necessary, in order to embrace the onrushing alternation of representations, at its peak, in such a way that it is no longer the alternation of representations, but rather the representation itself which appears [*sondern die Vorstellung selber erscheint*].[28]

What Hölderlin here calls *caesura* is a version of what I am calling the linguistic moment. The context of Hölderlin's remarks is of course once more Aristotle's *Poetics*. Rhythm, in the sense of harmonious arrangement of parts, is for Aristotle one of the basic features of *mimesis*. Rhythm is necessary to that organic wholeness of beginning, middle, and end required in any good narrative. Poetry may have sprung from the rhythmic motions of the body in dance. The origins of the word *mimesis* (akin of course to *mime*) may suggest this, and it is attested to in the presence in

[27] The "Comments" have received much comment. See, for example, Philippe Lacoue-Labarthe, "*La césure du spéculatif*," in Friedrich Hölderlin, *L'Antigone de Sophocle*, bilingual ed., trans. Philippe Lacoue-Labarthe (Paris: Christian Bourgois Éditeur, 1978), pp. 183-223, and Andrzej Warminski's brilliant essay on Hölderlin, forthcoming in *Glyph* and in his book, *Readings in Interpretation: On Hölderlin, Hegel, Heidegger* (University of Minnesota Press).

[28] Hölderlin, *Werke*, ed. cit., ii, p. 390, my trans.

Greek tragedy of the stately movement of the chorus in strophe and antistrophe. The opening of the *Poetics* includes "the music of the flute and of the lyre" and "dancing" as modes of imitation (*mimesis*), along with the various forms of poetry, "for even dancing imitates character, emotion, and action, by rhythmical movement [*schematizomenon rhythmon*]." Later on, in chapter 4 of the *Poetics*, the instinct for rhythm is included with the instinct for imitation as one of the origins of poetry. "Imitation [*mimeisthai*], then, is one instinct of our nature. Next, there is the instinct for 'harmony' and rhythm [*rhythmon*], meters being manifestly sections of rhythm. Persons, therefore, starting with this natural gift developed by degrees their special aptitudes, till their rude improvisations gave birth to Poetry."[29]

The pleasure of rhythm is then one of the two fundamental sources of pleasure in poetry. The other is the pleasure of learning from imitation. Rhythm is also necessary to that movement of the tragic action which effects the transport of pity and fear and a consequent catharsis. *Transport*: the word means elevation, ecstasy, being carried beyond or out of oneself. It also means going over from here to there. The word is a literal translation of one Greek word for figure or *Gleichnis: metaphora*. Hölderlin is playing on these multiple and to some degree conflicting meanings of the word *transport*. An entire drama, in Aristotle's conception of tragedy, *Oedipus the King*, for example, is a going over from here to there. It effects a transport that transforms, metaphorically transposes, pity and fear into the pleasure appropriate to an imitation. Catharsis and metaphor come, strangely, to the same thing. Each is a figure for the other. Both work by that rhythmic movement of transportation or transformation essential to a successful imitation. The paradox is that transport in the sense of ecstasy is a vertical movement interrupting the forward rhythmical movement of the action. Transport in one sense

[29] Butcher, trans., ed. cit., pp. 6, 7; 8, 9; 14-17.

contradicts transport in the other sense. Transport, as ecstasy, vertical going over, transcendence or transascend-
ence, is caesura, the breaking of the rhythm. It is a movement of poise or pause suspending the action in a prolonged
arhythmical hovering separating the first part of the action
from the last part, the beginning from the end.

Hölderlin says the antirhythmic suspension of the caesura "protects" the beginning from the end or the end from
the beginning. This is an odd notion. It is as if, for Hölderlin, the end would destroy the beginning, the beginning
the end, if the interruption of the caesura did not keep
them apart. In *Oedipus the King* the caesura is Oedipus'
dialogue with Tiresias, model for Empedocles' dialogue
with Manes in Hölderlin's play. I have written elsewhere
of the problematics of beginnings and endings in Aristotle's
theory and in the practice of narrative generally.[30] The
difficulties of getting started may spread out over a whole
play or novel. On the other hand, the whole narrative may
be as Aristotle says is the case in the lost *Lynceus* of Theo-
dectes, the prolonged ending of a story that began and
continued before the beginning of the text. If a narrative
may be all beginning that does not begin or all ending that
does not end, what Hölderlin calls caesura and what I am
calling the linguistic moment suggests that it may also become all middle, without beginning or ending. If the middle, by whatever name it may be called—recognition, climax, reversal, caesura, or transport—is antirhythmic
suspension guarding beginning from ending so they will
not collapse into one another, that suspension may become
total and permanent. It may spread out to define all the
text as one prolonged middle, unrelieved suffering without
action. Transport may become poised elevation rather than
transportation. The text may become all caesura, or it may,
as in the case of Hölderlin's *Empedokles*, be unable to go

---

[30] See "The Problematic of Ending of Narrative," *Nineteenth-Century Fiction* xxxiii, 1 (June 1978), 3-7, and *Ariadne's Thread* (forthcoming).

beyond the caesura to the ending. The caesura may cause the action to break off abruptly and remain hovering in the air, unable to complete itself.

This danger follows from the proper emptiness of the caesura. The caesura lacks connection to anything before, after, or outside itself. It is *der Ungebundenste*, the most unconnected. The danger is that once the suspension of caesura occurs it will be impossible to get back to the forward moving action of the play. The caesura is analogous to that non-correspondence of parable of which Hegel speaks in his comments on the sublime and parable in the *Ästhetik*.[31] All lines of connection are broken, all bridges destroyed, all roads closed. Another way to put this, another way in fact Hölderlin puts it, is to say that the relation of poetic language to something outside language represented by language is broken in the transport of the caesura. What then appears is the pure word, *das reine Wort*, the word as such, not the representation of something, but representation (*die Vorstellung*) in itself. This the reader has already encountered in the undecidable oscillations of literal and figurative locutions in Kafka's "On Parables" and in Arnold's procedure of allegory in his *Empedocles on Etna*. Such a suspension of reference is the linguistic moment in poetry. It is the moment when language itself is foregrounded and becomes problematic. Another name for this pure, suspended word without ascertainable referent is *catachresis*, that form of language whose status as either literal or figurative cannot be known for sure.

[31] Hegel, *Ästhetik*, ed. cit., I, p. 486, and G.W.F. Hegel, *Aesthetics: Lectures on Fine Art*, trans. T. M. Knox, I (New York: Oxford University Press, 1975), p. 378: "What has emerged from sublimity as distinct from strictly unconscious symbolizing consists on the one hand in the separation [*in dem Trennen*] between the meaning, explicitly known in its inwardness, and the concrete appearance divided therefrom; on the other hand in the directly or indirectly emphasized non-correspondence of the two [*Sichnichtentsprechen beider*] wherein the meaning, as the universal, towers above individual reality and its particularity."

If Arnold's *Empedocles on Etna* is, in spite of the poet's wishes, an allegory of the poet's mind in a representative history, Kafka's "On Parables" and Hölderlin's unfinished play with its adjacent essays can be taken to function as implicit parabolic interpretations of Arnold's play and of its retrospective cancellation, the "Preface" of 1853. My own commentary has also necessarily been parabolic or allegorical. As Kafka's "On Parables" indicates, there is no way to talk about parables except parabolically, that is, in language that itself enters into the oscillations of winning and losing in parable and in reality.

The relation between these elements in Arnold is the chiasmus of their relation in Hölderlin. The same elements are present in a crisscross form. The madness of literalism in the claim of Hölderlin's Empedocles that he is the man, that he wins in parable by dwelling literally within the parable, is reversed in Arnold's rejection of his Empedocles for committing suicide only figuratively, therefore committing no real action whatever and in no way helping the reader find his way back to a joy whose grounds are true.

The crisscross arrangement of these materials comes in the end, it may be, to the same thing. Arnold's attempt in the "Preface" to repudiate his play, to delete or erase it, makes the play as a whole, along with the "Preface," one long permanently suspended caesura or transport, a middle without beginning or end. Matthew Arnold's literal act of repudiating his play, at a certain historical moment, in 1853, is a genuine performative. It is a way of doing things with words. It "really" makes something happen, though this something is not what the poet intends. Far from erasing the play, the "Preface" reaffirms or rewrites it. It rewrites it as caesura, as transport or suspension, as the prolonged suffering of a text in which nothing happens. In doing this, the poet enters into his parable "in reality," and so wins in parable, not just in reality. He wins not by finding a way to a joy whose grounds are true, but by writing, in spite of himself, a literature of caesura or catachresis. It is a literature whose "authenticity" lies in the fact that its linguistic action demonstrates the eternal lack of those grounds. It is, for example, impossible to know whether the word *grounds* in Arnold's phrase is to be read literally or to be read figuratively.

This impossibility is the linguistic moment in Arnold. Far from being a single moment of suspension or turning—for example, the turning from poetry to prose in the early 1850s, at the time of the "Preface"—the linguistic moment, as a full exegesis would show, is repeated over and over from one end of Arnold's work to the other. It is repeated in all his writing, in poetry or in prose. It exists in the prose not only in his literary criticism, but also in the social criticism. It exists perhaps most strikingly in the linguistic sophistication of Arnold's three books on religion, books whose importance is even yet not fully recognized: *Literature and Dogma, God and the Bible*, and *St. Paul and Protestantism*. Far from being an unequivocal spokesman for "sincerity," Arnold is as problematic and as equivocal, in his own way, as is Wallace Stevens. Arnold by no means provides a firm ground against which Stevens' waverings or those of "modernism" in general may be accurately measured.

IT MIGHT SEEM that the pattern of irreconcilable self-contradiction I have found so far in Stevens and in a different way in Arnold would not be found in Wordsworth. Conflict there may be in Wordsworth, but this conflict has been seen by many critics as a middle stage in a three-stage dialectic leading from an early harmony with nature to an antithetical period of self-consciousness and alienation. This second stage is the discovery of the dangerous autonomy of the imagination. The final stage is the rejection of that detachment and a consequent return at a higher level to a calm reconciliation with nature, for "Nature never did betray / The heart that loved her."[32] Wordsworth's thought

[32] William Wordsworth, "Tintern Abbey," lines 122-123, *The Poetical*

43

in fact is not dialectical. The early stages of his experience are not transcended in the climax of his poems. They are held suspended in a vibration among alternative ways of thinking that is impossible to fix in a single unequivocal formulation. This oscillation makes Wordsworth as good an example as Stevens or Arnold of the co-presence of irreconcilable movements of thought in poetry that is the subject of this introductory chapter. Movement back in time, in this case at least, by no means leads to simplicity or to the solid ground of a definite origin.

"Resolution and Independence" (1807), to take one example of a poem often said to have this dialectical structure, turns—any critic would be likely to agree—on a conflict between various forms of continuity and various forms of division. The poem seems to affirm an initial and final communion among the various elements that enter into it. The poet apparently draws his ultimate consolation from his regained participation in this continuity. He is at one stage deprived by thought of this participation. When he rejoins the "jocund din" of nature, he is cured of his melancholy. He moves from "Dim sadness—and blind thoughts, I knew not, nor could name" (line 28),[33] to the religious calm of the conclusion:

> "God," said I, "be my help and stay secure;
> I'll think of the Leech-gatherer on the lonely moor!"
> (lines 139-140)

Pre-eminent among the forms of continuity affirmed by the poem is the continuity of nature with itself. Each separable thing is in harmony with all the others. On this beautiful morning nature is a universal symphony that fills space with its resonances:

Works, ed. E. de Selincourt, 2d ed. II (Oxford: Oxford University Press, 1954), p. 262. Further citations from Wordsworth in this chapter will be taken from this edition.

[33] "Resolution and Independence" is in II, pp. 235-240 of *Works*, ed. cit.

The birds are singing in the distant woods;
Over his own sweet voice the Stock-dove broods;
The Jay makes answer as the Magpie chatters;
And all the air is filled with pleasant noise of waters.

(lines 4-7)

In this harmony the poet at first shares, "as happy as a boy" (line 18). After his encounter with the old leech-gatherer the poet recovers the sharing. The other elements that make up the poem seem to share in this second happiness too. The poet participates in the leech-gatherer's life. The leech-gatherer's language appears at first sequential and divided: "His words came feebly, from a feeble chest, / But each in solemn order followed each" (lines 92-93). Ultimately, his speech is assimilated to the noise of waters, in echo of Revelation 1:15: "But now his voice to me was like a stream / Scarce heard; nor word from word could I divide" (lines 107-108). The leech-gatherer himself participates in the life of nature by way of the things to which he is compared—stone, sea-beast, cloud. This continuity assimilates even life and death: "Such seemed this Man, not all alive nor dead" (line 64). The natural scene, moreover, seems to be spokesman for a supernature with which it is entirely pervaded. The old leech-gatherer may be a supernatural visitant, perhaps sign of a "peculiar grace, / A leading from above, a something given" (lines 50-51). He is "like a man from some far region sent / To give me human strength, by apt admonishment" (lines 111-112). Natural language and theological language, finally, may be intertwined, as they are throughout the poem, without fear of incongruity. The poet, his counterpart the old leech-gatherer, the previous poets on whom Wordsworth models himself (in this poem so full of literary echoes), nature, the supernatural, language, even life and death—all are in the end seen as continuous, overlapping, unified.

The difficulty with this reading of "Resolution and Independence," as of such a reading of any of Wordsworth's major poems, begins when the interpreter tries to identify which of the elements entering into this harmonious whole is the central or originating one making the reconciliation possible. Which is the element on which the others depend or from which they derive? The idea of a systematic whole tends to presuppose some center, origin, or head determining the rest of the elements entering into the system. In Wordsworth's case, is nature this center or origin? Is it the spirit behind nature? Is it consciousness? Is it language?

The search for an answer to this question discloses a pervasive uncertainty in the language of the poem. This uncertainty would allow the reader to make a claim for any one of these elements as the source from which the others are derived. In each case, the texts cited to support this claim at the same time would undermine the claim by containing some linguistic detail authorizing an alternative reading. The notion that the leech-gatherer is a supernatural visitant sent to admonish the poet, for example, is undermined by the word *whether* in the first such passage and, in the second passage, by the fact that an alternative possibility is suggested, though not named, and by the fact that both these incompatible possibilities are presented as similes. They are *as ifs.* "Now," says Wordsworth, "whether it were by peculiar grace, / A leading from above, a something given, / Yet it befell that . . ." (lines 50-52). It may be or it may not be, but whether it is or is not, the poet will not say for sure. In the second such passage, the leech-gatherer is "*like* a man from some far region sent," but he is also "*like* one whom I had met with in a dream" (lines 111, 110, my italics). The latter possibility would give him a far different source, perhaps a purely subjective one, depending on one's interpretation of dreams. For Wordsworth, dreams are uncertain in origin and meaning, as in that crux for the reading of Wordsworth, the dream of the Arab in Book v of *The Prelude*, discussed in detail in chapter 2 here. In any case, the old man is only *like* someone met in a dream or *like* someone sent from a far region, not identical to either.

All of these indeterminacies come together in the admirable lines describing the poet's first encounter with the leech-gatherer: "Beside a pool bare to the eye of heaven / I saw a Man before me unawares" (lines 54-55). This may be read as giving priority to the supernatural, to God's eye that sees everything with clairvoyant insight. Or "heaven" may mean simply the natural heaven, the sky with its eye, the sun, day's eye, which looks down on the pool and is reflected in it, as the "uncertain heaven" is reflected in the "bosom" of the "steady lake" in "The Boy of Winander." Or the personification here may be taken as calling attention to the fact that the life of both nature and supernature are projected into them from human consciousness, their source and model. "By our own spirits are we deified" (line 47), the poet has said a moment before. This is a genuinely shocking affirmation of the autonomy and originating power of human consciousness. We make ourselves into gods, just as Satan promised we would if we ate of the apple of knowledge. On the other hand, even this line could be taken to say no more than that the deity works through the human spirit rather than through nature. In any case, personification of nature as a speaking human face, with its mixture of Biblical echoes and echoes of more naturalistic or classical personifications, pervades *The Prelude* and Wordsworth's shorter poems. All such locutions, like "bare to the eye of heaven," are figures, not literal speech. They are examples of those fundamental prosopopoeias whereby we personify nature and supernature. Neither God nor nature may in any literal sense be said to have an "eye."

The source of the irresolvable ambiguities of Wordsworth's verse is the originally figurative nature of language, though the normal concept of source is in this case suspended. The "linguistic moment" or the momentum of language in his poetry is this pervasive shimmering play of figure. In "Resolution and Independence" there is no original and originating ground of the poet's joy on the basis of which the others may be described in figure, or of which the others may be named as figurative representatives. Each element, rather, must be described in terms drawn from the others, in a chain of displacements that has nowhere a fixed center or literal source. The supernatural must be described in language transposed from nature or from the human body. Nature must be named in terms transcribed from the human realm. Consciousness has no literal language of its own, but must be named in terms drawn from the physical world, and so on, in a ceaseless round. In an analogous shift, the poet, in order to talk about himself, must transport himself, according to his common practice, into an alter ego—here, the old leech-gatherer. In another analogous structure, the poem, in its covert relation to its precursors—the Bible, Chaucer, Spenser, Milton, Chatterton, Burns—is the carrying over or distortion of language borrowed from them and put in another place. The reader's interpretation of Wordsworth, finally, must proceed by a sideways movement from poem to poem in which the reader needs "The Boy of Winander" or "The Ruined Cottage" to read "Resolution and Independence," needs the Lucy poems and "The Danish Boy: A Fragment" to read "The Boy of Winander," and so on, in an unfixable sequence of deferred readings. In "Resolution and Independence," as in Wordsworth's poetry generally, nothing is what it is, but exists as the displaced version of something else. *Displaced* and *version* must be given their full force here: put out of place, put in an improper place, and turned into something else, "troped," in a movement of usurpation the peculiarity of which is that there is no legitimate king whose place may be taken. *Displaced version* is a way of saying *metaphor*. Consciousness is the deferred version of nature or its metaphor; nature is the delegate of the supernatural, its metaphor; the supernatural is the projection of the human spirit, its metaphor, in an endless wandering like that of the old leech-gatherer, or like that of the poet, or like that of all those other wanderers in Wordsworth. Margaret in "The Ruined Cottage" wanders into despondency, madness, and death through her fidelity to one dear particular place and to the hope that is rooted there. In an analogous way (but these analogies, in my own discourse, are another example of what I am describing), the joy of the young poet in "Resolution and Independence" leads to melancholy and madness. These are its deferred counterparts, not its opposite. If the child is father to the man, the man is the child in another guise, and madness is another form of joy, not its total absence:

We Poets in our youth begin in gladness;
But thereof come in the end despondency and madness.
(lines 48-49)

Lewis Carroll in his parody of "Resolution and Independence" brilliantly catches the movement of wandering in the poem and its dependence on linguistic equivocations. Such equivocations betray the penchant of language toward figure. This figurative quality is not so much a bias or wandering from the literal toward the figurative as an unstable basis on initial figurative bifurcations. The poet does not lose his way. He never had a *way* in the first place, in the sense of a straightforward journey of thought to take from beginning to middle to end. The irresolutions of "Resolution and Independence" are splendidly mimed by Carroll in the way the White Knight's song has a series of alternative titles. Each title is displaced from the others in a play on words that brings into the open the fissures between what a thing is, what it is called, what it is named, what the name is called, and so on, in a potentially unending series of quandaries, conundrums, or forks in the linguistic path. The passage in *Through the Looking-Glass* is an admirable example of parody as acute literary criticism:

"You are sad," the Knight said in an anxious tone: "let me sing you a song to comfort you."

49

"Is it very long?" Alice asked, for she had heard a good deal of poetry that day.

"It's long," said the Knight, "but it's very, *very* beautiful. Everybody that hears me sing it—either it brings the *tears* into their eyes, or else—"

"Or else what," said Alice, for the Knight had made a sudden pause.

"Or else it doesn't, you know. The name of the song is called '*Haddocks' Eyes.*' "

"Oh, that's the name of the song, is it?" Alice said, trying to feel interested.

"No, you don't understand," the Knight said, looking a little vexed. "That's what the name is called. The name really *is* '*The Aged Aged Man.*' "

"Then I ought to have said 'That's what the *song* is called'?" Alice corrected herself.

"No, you oughtn't: that's quite another thing! The *song* is called '*Ways and Means*': but that's only what it's *called*, you know!"

"Well, what *is* the song, then?" said Alice, who was by this time completely bewildered.

"I was coming to that," the Knight said. "The song really *is* '*A-sitting On A Gate*': and the tune's my own invention."[34]

If "Haddocks' Eyes" makes fun of Wordsworth's attention to small, insignificant, "unpoetic," even ugly things, "The Aged Aged Man" not only names a characteristic hero of his poetry, but also mimes Wordsworth's tendency toward hyperbole as a means of reaching the sublime or of transcending those small insignificant things by using them as stepping stones. Hyperbole takes the poet across the border between life and death, the threshold from the ordinary to the extraordinary. This was not just an aged man.

[34] Lewis Carroll, *Through the Looking-Glass, Alice in Wonderland*, ed. Donald J. Gray (New York: W. W. Norton & Company, Inc., 1971), pp. 186-187.

He was *really* old, "aged aged," so old he had gone over the border between life and death. "Ways and Means" somewhat cruelly calls attention to what is calculating, economic, even parsimonious about Wordsworth. He always wants to get much out of little and is cunning in figuring (pun intended) ways and means to do it. "A-sitting On A Gate," finally, expresses Wordsworth's penchant for fence-sitting, or rather gate-sitting, that hovering between alternatives I have been identifying in "Resolution and Independence." It is a poise that both indicates the gateways that will take you from here to there, from this place to that place, or from one field of thought to another and, at the same time, refuses to go resolutely into one field or the other. Wordsworth keeps his independence by refraining from choice. It is appropriate in the White Knight's bewildering series of sidesteps from false title to false title that the tune in fact should *not* be the Knight's own invention, but be stolen from a poem beginning "I give thee all—I can no more" and *called* "My Heart and Lute," by Thomas Moore. Carroll has not willfully imposed a wavering on Wordsworth's poem that is not really there. He has identified the essential movement in place of "Resolution and Independence" and the dependence of that movement on the figurative nature of language.

Wordsworth's recognition of this movement is expressed in the admirable passage in the "Preface" of 1815 where he discusses the lines in "Resolution and Independence" comparing the old man to a stone, a sea-beast, and a cloud. In this extraordinary paragraph the essence of the poetic imagination is said to lie in the exercise by the mind of a sovereign power over what is outside it, whether that outside is called nature or the supernatural. The imagination manifests itself in the poet's gift of linguistic displacement or usurpation, that is, in his ability to call things what they are not, and thereby to move something else into the places properly occupied by those things. Poetry is the effect of a conferring, divesting, and transforming energy. For

51

Wordsworth, too, things as they are, are changed on the blue guitar of poetry. The instrument of this change is language, or, more exactly, figures of speech, verbal transfers:

> In these images [says Wordsworth of stanza nine of "Resolution and Independence"], the conferring, the abstracting, and the modifying powers of the Imagination, immediately and mediately acting, are all brought into conjunction. The stone is endowed with something of the power of life to approximate it to the sea-beast; and the sea-beast stripped of some of its vital qualities to assimilate it to the stone; which intermediate image is thus treated for the purpose of bringing the original image, that of the stone, to a nearer resemblance to the figure and condition of the aged Man; who is divested of so much of the indications of life and motion as to bring him to the point where the two objects unite and coalesce in just comparison. After what has been said, the image of the cloud need not be commented upon.[35]

It need not be commented on because the reader by this time knows that it will be one more link in a virtually endless series of figural substitutions, mergers of the unlike into likeness. These make the life of Wordsworth's poetry. Far from being resolvable into any fixed formulation, Wordsworth's poetry oscillates in meaning like a Gestaltist diagram. Such a diagram, however, oscillates back and forth between only two alternative ways of being seen, duck or rabbit. The peculiarity of Wordsworth's poetry, and the limitations of any visual metaphor that might be used to describe it, lies in the fact that a poem like "Resolution and Independence" alternates between at least four irreconcilable ways of being read, depending upon whether nature, the supernatural, consciousness, or language is taken as the central feature around which the others organize them-

[35] *Works*, ed. cit., *II*, p. 438.

selves in a systematic pattern. Each of these "centers" when it is interrogated turns out to be no center at all, but only a figurative replacement or stand-in for one or more of the others. To enter a poem by Wordsworth is to open the gate into a place of ceaseless labyrinthine wandering, just as is the case, in a different way, with the poetry of Stevens and even with that of Arnold. For all three poets the result is the endless failure of any movement of interpretation to "get it right" and so put a stop to the movement.

The movement will continue unless some arbitrary and illicit "governor" is imposed, a choice made among alternatives for which the text itself provides no grounds. A critic independent of one or another of those presuppositions which make life and letters so much simpler, if such a critic is even possible, is left uncomfortably irresolute, uneasily a-sitting on a gate. It might be argued that such a poise is sterile, against life, or that the fact that the meaning of poems is indeterminate is one of those de-idealizing truths it might be better not to know. A strong critic, it might be said, will willfully affirm some meaning or other, take possession of the poem, put it aside, and put himself in its place, usurp it for some pragmatic purpose and so make the reading of poems an ethical rather than an epistemological act. But I should not call that interpretation, rather, precisely, usurpation. Such univocal readings imposed "pragmatically" are, moreover, not freely invented but are arrived at by accentuating one of the possible meanings of the poem, muting the others, though never wholly silencing them. Such a critic is still subject to the text, allowing himself to be programmed by it. Nor am I persuaded that good can come of such playing with the truth about poems as that involved in the imposition of univocal meaning, for however highminded and ethical or pragmatic a purpose. As Joe says to Pip in *Great Expectations*: "There's one thing you may be sure of, Pip, . . . namely, that lies is lies. Howsoever they come, they didn't ought to come, and they come from the father of lies, and work round to the same. Don't you tell no more of 'em, Pip" (chap. 9). Of course it is also the case that Pip builds his whole life, for better or worse, on that form of lying which is the excess or margin of imagination over things as they are. The first step is to see this activity, as it manifests itself in poems or in the criticism of poems, for what it is, before going on to the pragmatic or ethical stage of taking possession of the poem or making use of it for life. Epistemology should take precedence over ethics, and if it is the case, as Blake and Hazlitt "cheerfully assure us," "that the grandest poetry is immoral,"[36] then any ethical values based on poetry are likely to be odd ones, to say the least.

THIS CHAPTER has presented three examples in support of the hypothesis that any cultural expression in our tradition, such as a literary text, is undecidable in meaning, though the choices the text offers (among which the reader cannot except arbitrarily decide) may be precisely defined. This plurality, in my examples at least, does not result from any confusion on the part of the author, his inability to get his thoughts straight or to say what he means. Nor does it result from some remediable error or willful overcomplication of things on the part of the interpreter, though a new definition of the proper relation between reader and text would emerge from what I have found in my examples. A good reader, my examples suggest, would do well to suspend the search for grounds in a poem for a single, definitive, univocal, determinate meaning. The plurality of meanings in a literary work, the presence of what Gerard Manley Hopkins calls an "underthought" inextricably interwoven with each "overthought," arises as an intrinsic necessity of language. This is the case insofar as the work depends, as all texts in our language do, on conceptual terms, metaphors, and narrative patterns drawn from the finite reservoir of

---

[36] Harold Bloom, *Agon: Towards a Theory of Revisionism* (New York, Oxford: Oxford University Press, 1982), p. 18.

such elements in our Western family of languages. Anti-Platonism was already present within the dialogues of Plato, not added later by Plato's antagonists. What necessity it is in our Western languages that keeps any user of them from ever "getting it right" is being interrogated in one way or another by many critics, philosophers, and linguists today. This book is an exploration of those moments in poems from Wordsworth to Stevens in which the intrinsic equivocations of ordinary language interfere with the expression of a univocal meaning.

My three examples suggest a notion of history—literary, cultural, or of history as such—different from the familiar paradigm of a series of self-enclosed "epochs," each with its own intrinsic set of forms, its own "world picture." Not that there is not such a thing as history, in the sense of intrinsic differences between epoch and epoch, country and country, individual and individual, text and text. Each text, person, country, and epoch are indeed different from one another, and these differences are in part determined by the different context in each case. In the case of literary works that context includes nonlinguistic factors, socioeconomic ones, modes of production, distribution, and so on. Nevertheless, these contextual factors can do no more than enhance the selection of some possibilities of language rather than others, and those possibilities have remained more or less the same for twenty-five hundred years. Language is an airy and spacious prison (and the prisoners may bend the bars outward a little), but it remains a prison all the same. The writings of the Romantics and Post-Romantics are the latest comers in a long line of repetitions with a difference of concepts, figures of speech, and myths going back to Plato and the Bible, and behind them to their antecedents. These elements contain within themselves the genetic possibility of all the poems of Wordsworth, Arnold, Stevens, and the rest, even of poets as yet unborn, in virtually inexhaustible though not unbounded permutation. To try to take possession of language for some use or pragmatic purpose, ethically laudable though that may be, is to be taken possession of by it.

I conclude this chapter with an admirable passage from Pater's *Plato and Platonism*. This will bring me back full circle to my initial citation of Foucault's expression of the modern rejection of origins. The passage from Pater, with its picture of time coulisses receding back indefinitely into the mists of prehistory, carries to a hyperbolic extreme my procedure of chronological reversal. This reversal is directed against the genetic concept of literary history. Rather than going from Wordsworth to Hopkins to Stevens, so suggesting some development in the theories of poetic language in Romantic and Post-Romantic poetry, I have wished to indicate, in going at first backwards from Stevens to Hopkins to Wordsworth, that in the search for explanatory origins by way of such a movement against the current of time, the literary archaeologist never finds the presumed simplicity of beginnings. However far back he goes, he finds only the complexity and self-contradiction of something already derived. Whatever he reaches shows already the presence within itself of incompatible genetic strains. These are signs of some primal catastrophe or bifurcation, or of the laying down of incongruous lines. These lines can never be followed back to a point. In the beginning was already the division.

The passage from Pater is a definitive qualification, before the fact, of Whitehead's celebrated dictum that all Western history is a footnote to Plato:

> Plato's achievement may well seem an absolutely fresh thing in the morning of the mind's history. Yet in truth the world Plato had entered into was already almost weary of philosophical debate, bewildered by the oppositions of sects, the claims of rival schools. Language and the processes of thought were already become sophisticated, the very air he breathed sickly with off-cast speculative atoms. . . .

Some of the results of patient earlier thinkers, even then dead and gone, are of the structure of his philosophy. They are everywhere in it, not as the stray carved corner of some older edifice, to be found here or there amid the new, but rather like minute relics of earlier organic life in the very stone he builds with. The central and most intimate principles of his teaching challenge us to go back beyond them, not merely to his own immediate, somewhat enigmatic master—to Socrates, who survives chiefly in his pages—but to various precedent schools of speculative thought, in Greece, in Ionia, in Italy; beyond these into that age of poetry, in which the first efforts of philosophic apprehension had hardly understood themselves; beyond that unconscious philosophy, again, to certain constitutional tendencies, persuasions, forecasts of the intellect itself, such as had given birth, it would seem, to thoughts akin to Plato's in the older civilizations of India and of Egypt, as they still exercise their authority over ourselves.[37]

In Pater's exemplary rejection of origin and of originality, each text is seen as referring to some still earlier text, that to still another, and so on. All those texts are multiple in themselves. None is single or singular. Each is like a thousand borrowed atoms dancing in the air or like stone made of minute, once-living fragments agglomerated. Moreover, *influence* is not a matter of conscious borrowing, but something that, like a disease, in fact like *influenza*, insinuates itself into the air the poet breathes, as in the splendid phrase, quintessentially Paterian, describing the air of Plato's Athens as miasmal, "sickly with offcast speculative atoms," *sophisticated* in the sense of contaminated. Each poet's precursors are present, whether or not he knows it or wishes it, in the intimate texture of his material, in the

[37] Walter Pater, *Plato and Platonism* (London: Macmillan and Co., Limited, 1910), pp. 6, 7.

words he must use to speak or write at all, there in language like tiny fossils in the builder's stone. If each modern poet is another footnote to Plato, Plato was himself already a footnote to still earlier footnotes, in an endless chain of footnotes to footnotes, with nowhere a primary text as such.

Wordsworth

> If any man speak in an unknown tongue, let
> it be by two, or at the most by three, and that
> by course; and let one interpret.
>
> (1 Corinthians 14.27)

In the first chapter here, as the first swing of the circular temporal trajectory of this book, I have moved backward, against the stream of time, from Stevens to Arnold to Wordsworth and, with some help from Pater, even back to Plato and before. My movement was like Empedocles climbing to the sources of Etna's brooks and then beyond, above, or like Wordsworth magisterially commanding the river: "Flow backward, Duddon," or even like Stevens, in "The River of Rivers in Connecticut," encountering "an unnamed flowing," "a curriculum," "the river that flows nowhere, like a sea," one (perhaps false) name for which is time.[1] Having reached back to Wordsworth and beyond, my chapters will now be allowed to flow forward with the stream of time from Wordsworth to Stevens again, in a series of stages named for various poets—Shelley, Browning, Hopkins, Hardy, Yeats, and Williams. I have moved backward in order to come forward. Mine has been a circular movement in place, which gives one spatial figure for human temporality, the temporality of individual or collective history. In history too the child is father to the man. That gnomic formula may be read in either temporal direction, from late to early or from early to late.

---

[1] Wallace Stevens, *The Collected Poems* (New York: Alfred A. Knopf, Inc., 1954) p. 333.

I BEGIN the forward movement with an investigation of poetic form in Wordsworth. To raise, in connection with "Composed upon Westminster Bridge," or with any other poem by Wordsworth, the question of form is to encounter immediately an intricate web of issues branching out to weave into itself everything that is problematical in the work of this poet.

The word or the concept of *form* is heavy with a weight of metaphysical presuppositions. These may be traced back from modern contexts through the various meanings of the Latin *forma* and its sister words to the Greek concepts of form, whether as *morphe*, or as *eidos, logos, paradeigma, arche, aitia, tupos*, or *schema*, in their proliferating interconnections. The "originating" texts are the discussions of form or *idea* in the dialogues of Plato and the analysis of formal cause as one of the four causes in Aristotle's *Physics* and *Metaphysics*,[2] but Plato and Aristotle are of course already interpreting terms and models of thought inherited from earlier Greek philosophers, by no means, as Pater reminds us, noncontradictory ones. The air Plato and Aristotle breathed was "sickly with offcast speculative atoms," as Pater says, and these motes were the germs of many diseases, not just one, the legion of not wholly compatible speculative systems making up Western metaphysics.

To follow in detail the ramifications of the notion of form in our tradition would be to construct one version of the history of the aftercourse of those speculative systems. Complex as is the history of the concept of form, a single paradoxical structure persists through all its permutations. The notion of form has always presupposed a bifurcation between shape and substance, origin and result, cause and effect, model and copy, mold and molded. In one way or another it has been assumed that the meaning or design

[2] See the discussion of the three beds in Book x of the *Republic* and the sections on the four causes in Aristotle, *Physics* B, *Metaphysics* A, 3-7. 983a-988b, and *Metaphysics* D, 1-2.1013a-b.

of that which is formed pre-exists it, stands outside it, sustains it, and validates it. The authenticity of the formed lies in the adequacy of its correspondence to its formal cause, to its source or origin. The formed must copy its form. One mode or another of the aesthetics of imitation is therefore implicit in the word *form*.

The paradox lies in the fact that the English word *form*, like the Greek *tupos*, is used to name both the model and its copy. This paradox is not accidental. It brings into the open an intrinsic undecidability in the concept of form. The Indo-European root of the modern English word *form* and its analogues in other languages is apparently *mer-bh-* or *mer-gwh-*, "to gleam, sparkle."[3] This root names the manifestation of a thing, its outer appearance or coming into sight. With this root meaning may be associated all those meanings of *form*, or of the Latin *forma* and the Greek *morphe*, as outward appearance, external aspect, shape, contour, structure, design, pattern, or beauty. On the other hand, the word *form* is the English equivalent for the range of meanings covered by the Greek *arche, eidos*, or *logos*, that is, principle, essence, underlying cause, source, origin, beginning. For Plato any material bed presupposed the eternal form or idea of bed in the mind of the One, and the painting of a bed is the copy of a copy. For Aristotle the formal cause enters necessarily into the constitution of a thing and is presupposed by it. *Form* means both the structuring power and that which is structured, both what can be seen and the shaping force pushing what can be seen into the open. The word contains in itself the philosophical or aesthetic problem that it must be used to solve. The difficulty is that any expression of a solution will always turn out to be a restatement of the problem, for example, in that formulation of Hegel's, already cited here, defining

---

[3] William Morris, ed., *The American Heritage Dictionary of the English Language* (Boston: American Heritage Publishing Co., Inc., and Houghton Mifflin Company, 1969), p. 1529.

beauty as *das sinnliche "Scheinen" der Idee*. The problem is inscribed in the metaphorical texture of our languages, locked within their key words.

The so-called "deconstruction of metaphysics" has always been a part of metaphysics, a shadow within its light, off-spring of one of those speculative atoms dancing in the sun. An example is the self-subversion of "Platonism" in the *Sophist*. This dismantling has taken special forms re-cently. One way to define this turn in the road is to say that there has been an attempt to escape from the doubleness of the concept of form by rejecting the dichotomy of form and substance, of model and copy. In place of the twofold use of the word *form*, some recent thinkers have proposed the notion that there is no center of meaning or informing power preceding a given structure of signs. Meaning is generated by the interplay of elements rather than by the copying of some pre-existing signification.[4] Form itself con-stitutes meaning, in both senses of *constitutes*. The form-making act is the creator rather than the copier of meaning. Meaning arises from the internal relationships of signs to one another. In poetry these include echoing repetitions or rhythm, syntax, rhyme, alliteration, and figurative lan-guage. Meaning in poetry, versions of such a structuralist, or, with some differences, post-structuralist, theory would argue, arises from all the forms of similarity in difference within the text,[5] rather than from the correspondence of

[4] Cf. Jacques Derrida, *"La structure, le signe et le jeu dans le discours des sciences humaines,"* *L'écriture et la différence* (Paris: Les Éditions du Seuil, 1967), pp. 409-428; trans. as "Structure, Sign, and Play in the Discourse of the Human Sciences," *Writing and Difference*, trans. Alan Bass (Chicago: The University of Chicago Press, 1978), pp. 278-293.

[5] For theories of poetry based on this concept see Roman Jakobson, "Concluding Statement: Linguistics and Poetics," *Style in Language*, ed. Thomas A. Seboek (Cambridge, Mass.: The M.I.T. Press, 1960), pp. 350-377, and Gerard Manley Hopkins, "On the Origin of Beauty: A Platonic Dialogue" and "Poetry and Verse," *The Journals and Papers of Gerard Manley Hopkins*, ed. Humphry House and Graham Storey (London: Oxford University Press, 1959), pp. 86-114, 289-290.

signs to some already existing pattern of meaning. The meaning of a structure of words transcends the physical energy that is differentiated in that structure, or that went into its production. There is an incompatibility between any form and its preformal sources, the incompatibility between meaning and the meaningless.

The conflict between these two concepts of form is central in Wordsworth's poetry. Much of what is sometimes considered the special contribution of late twentieth-century thought in this area is anticipated either explicitly or in practice by Wordsworth. Once more the child is father to the man. To put this another way, Wordsworth played an important role in the eighteenth- and early nineteenth-century form of the deconstruction of metaphysics, which Geoffrey Hartman calls the humanizing or demystifying of romance.[6] One way to identify this strain in Wordsworth's poetry is to investigate not only the use of poetic form in his verse but also the ways in which the problem of form enters into his work as one of its essential themes.

If Wordsworth adjured the critic to "Scorn not the Sonnet" and wrote so many poems in this form, binding himself to its laws of rhyme and rhythm, and to its brief compass, this was not because of an admiration for the miniature as such. As the metaphors employed in the two sonnets on sonnets suggest, Wordsworth saw the small size and rigid laws of the sonnet as paradoxically allowing for one kind of largeness or another. In "Nuns fret not at their convent's narrow room"[7] the sonnet is compared to the nun's small room, to the hermit's cell, and to the student's "citadel."

[6] See especially "False Themes and Gentle Minds" and "Romantic Poetry and the Genius Loci," *Beyond Formalism: Literary Essays 1958–1970* (New Haven and London: Yale University Press, 1970), pp. 283-297, 311-336.

[7] E. de Selincourt and Helen Darbishire, eds., *The Poetical Works of William Wordsworth*, 2d ed., III (Oxford: Oxford University Press, 1954), pp. 1-2. Further citations in this chapter from all poems and essays by Wordsworth except *The Prelude* will be from this edition and will be identified by volume and page numbers.

All these are enclosures making possible an expansiveness
of meditation or speculation, a concern with first and last
things. The sonnet, in the two suggestive metaphors that
follow, is said to be like a spinning wheel or like a weaver's
loom. The sonnet is a forming matrix that allows the tan-
gled fibers of language to be spun into thread and then
woven into the texture of a poetic text. Without this patterning there can be no cloth. The following metaphor of
the bee that gives up the open spaces within which he may
freely "soar" in order to "murmur by the hour in foxglove
bells" anticipates the various musical tropes in "Scorn not
the Sonnet." Melody depends on limitation, and the sonnet,
in spite of the fact that it is a "scanty plot of ground," is no
prison. Its exigencies are freely accepted. They are accepted as an escape from the paradoxical "weight of too
much liberty."

To understand what might be meant by "too much liberty," it is helpful to remember the paralysis that seizes the
poet at the beginning of *The Prelude*. He has been freed
from the stifling enclosure of the city and is now able to
give his whole life to the writing of poetry, but the breath
of inspiration soon fails him:

> . . . my soul
> Once more made trial of her strength, nor lacked
> Æolian visitations; but the harp
> Was soon defrauded, and the banded host
> Of harmony dispersed in straggling sounds,
> And lastly utter silence![8]

Wordsworth, it will be recalled, was never able to complete the large poem, *The Recluse*, the major work to which
The Prelude was only a prelude. *The Prelude* is, like À *la*

[8] Ernest de Selincourt, ed., *The Prelude or Growth of a Poet's Mind*, 2d ed.
rev. by Helen Darbishire (Oxford: Oxford University Press, 1959), 1850
text, Book I, lines 94-99. Further citations from *The Prelude* in this chapter
will be from this edition, identified as Pre, followed by book and line
numbers. Citations will be from the 1850 text unless otherwise noted.

recherche du temps perdu, a paradoxical work, which has as its subject an attempt to account for the fact that the narrator has been unable to write the great work that turns out to be in the act of being written as he describes his failure to write it. Wordsworth's use of the sonnet and his theory of its use must be understood in the context of this theme of poetic impotence, an impotence born of the poet's largeness of ambition and self-imposed inclusiveness of scope. In an apologetic letter to Walter Savage Landor of April 20, 1822, Wordsworth explained that the sonnet was a form in which he had written because he had wanted the courage to write larger works. He now looks back on the habit of writing sonnets as something about which he should feel guilty, as though it were like a fondness for checkers or crossword puzzles: "... since that time, from want of resolution to take up anything of length, I have filled up many a moment in writing Sonnets, which, if I had never fallen into the practice, might easily have been better employed."[9]

The second sonnet on sonnets, "Scorn not the Sonnet,"[10] proceeds from Shakespeare to Petrarch, Tasso, Camöens, Dante, Spenser, and Milton in its litany of the great poets who have employed the form. The sonnet is called successively a key, a lute, a pipe, a gay myrtle leaf, a glow-worm lamp, and a trumpet. A miniature system of thought underlies the interconnection among these metaphors. In each case the image is of something small and enclosed that is nevertheless articulated. Since it has a design, it can serve as the means by which inarticulate energies are at once controlled and released. They are given expression by being circumscribed and modulated. The sonnet is the "key" with which "Shakespeare unlocked his heart." The delicately fashioned notches, grooves, and teeth of this key opened what would else have remained locked and gave Shakespeare a power of self-expression otherwise impossible. For

[9] Cited in III, 417.
[10] III, 20-21.

Petrarch the sonnet was a "small lute," for Tasso a "pipe." In both cases the notion is that the small "scale" of the sonnet, its limitation to a certain range of notes and melodies, gives it a special power of easing Petrarch's wound and of soothing in Camöens an exile's grief. The metaphors used for Dante and Spenser introduce the Hegelian idea of radiance. The neat pattern of the "gay myrtle leaf," reticulated like a key, "glittered," "Amid the cypress with which Dante crowned / His visionary brow." Within Dante's work as a whole the sonnet was light against darkness, but light patterned, articulated. This theme is missing from the image of the "glow-worm lamp" that cheered mild Spenser, but the image of small scope that is a projective source of light in the darkness remains.

These metaphors suggest that the miniature scale of the sonnet allows it to release powerful energies by turning them into harmony. This notion is especially clear in the final image of the sonnet as a trumpet through which Milton "blew / Soul-animating strains—alas, too few!" Milton's creative spirit had to be controlled, channeled, tuned, limited by the resonances already built into the trumpet. Like any wind instrument, a trumpet will sound only certain notes. This limitation allows it to transform the undifferentiated breath of the trumpeter into distinct tones that may then be combined into melodies. Only this articulation of the inarticulate strength of Milton's spirit gives other men access to it. The spiral tubes of the trumpet pass breath across to breath, spirit to spirit. Milton's sonnets thereby become "soul-animating," a source of inspiration for their readers, according to a traditional metaphor defining spiritual energy, whether individual or universal, as wind or breath. Wordsworth finds this figurative equation already inscribed in our languages, for example, in the words *anima* and *psyche*. The metaphor is pervasive in his verse—for example, the imagery of wind that opens *The Prelude* ("O there is blessing in this gentle breeze") and persists throughout that poem as one of its structuring images. Without differentiation, without the division of a diffuse and inarticulate power into definite pattern, there can be no transmission of the spirit.

This idea or image is given fuller expression in the dream of the Arab with his stone and shell in Book v of *The Prelude*. There the sound the dreaming poet hears when he puts the shell to his ear, spiral against spiral, is at once a melody and at the same time the inarticulate sound of the sea. It is a roar or "Blouaugh!" like the bellow of William Carlos Williams' sea elephant, or like the unmelodious song of wind and water from which the singer by the seashore determines her harmonies in Wallace Stevens' "The Idea of Order at Key West": "It may be that in all her phrases stirred / The grinding water and the gasping wind."[11] The sound of the sea and the wind is at once a song and not a song. The paradox here, again a traditional one, is based on the opposition between the original and originating Word, source of all language, which is yet no word because it holds all words undistinguished within it, and on the other hand the tune played on the lute, pipe, trumpet, or sonnet. This tune both reveals and hides the Word. The forms of articulated speech or melody make the unworded blast of the original Word available by turning it into definite tones or speech. At the same time they limit it, transform it, obscure it, veil it over, traduce it by translating it, not least by making it impossible to decide whether the source is in fact a spiritual Word or whether it is a mere physical rushing noise of wind or water.

This paradoxical relation of the sonnet to its origin does not fail to introduce paradox into the melody itself, the tune Wordsworth plays on this small pipe, for example, in "Composed upon Westminster Bridge" (iii, 38). Though the harmony is controlled, the linguistic "tones" finite in

[11] William Carlos Williams, *The Collected Earlier Poems* (Norfolk, Conn.: New Directions, 1951), p. 73, and Wallace Stevens, *The Collected Poems*, ed. cit., p. 129.

number, the compass small, the relation among the parts seems impossible to fix. This poem, like "Resolution and Independence," cannot be reduced to a formal pattern of elements that may be comprehended as an unambiguous meaning by the reasoning mind. It seems as if the vertical incommensurability between the spiritual or material energy that is the nonoriginating "source" of the finite elements of language, and those elements themselves, enters somehow into the horizontal relations among the words. This incompatibility, it may be, makes it impossible to resolve the horizontal relations unambiguously, as well as impossible to decide on the nature of the source. An encounter with the blankness of an irresolution is an essential component of any thoughtful reading of Wordsworth's shorter poems. This irresolution is constituted by the *suspens vibratoire*, in Mallarmé's phrase,[12] of enigmatic juxtapositions among the words of the poem.

In "Composed upon Westminster Bridge" this characteristic indeterminateness of Wordsworth's lyric poems arises partly from the use of negatives, partly from a pattern of metaphors that lies like an almost invisible garment of light over the realistic texture of the poem. These linguistic elements are two versions of the condensation or displacement essential to all poetic language. They put the straightforward literal meaning of the poem "beside itself." Such language says two things at once. In this double saying the poem establishes vibrations of meaning that resonate outward in diffusive circles of sense. If the source of the sonnet is a boundless breath, it moves through the limitations imposed by its form back to another openness. It goes from the unarticulated to the articulate and back to an unsayable. The latter is achieved, strangely enough, through those devices of differentiation that are basic to poetry. It seems as if the melodies played on the small lute of the sonnet,

---

[12] Stéphane Mallarmé, *Oeuvres complètes*, éd. de la Pléiade (Paris: Éditions Gallimard, 1945), p. 386.

in their attempt to be true to the all-inclusive word or breath
that is their origin, must displace referential language in
such a way that another form of indetermination is introduced within the small confines of the poem itself. This
new uncertainty arises from the suggestiveness of lateral
relationships between one element of the poem and another. The pressure of the word or breath, the *inflatus*
behind the loud prophetic blast, pushes each word aside
from its representational meaning and forces it to become
figurative, to say more or other than it says. Language is
formed in such a way that it is impossible to speak of anything without speaking of it *as* something else. Language
is irreducibly metaphorical. To speak of something is to
assimilate it into an already existing system of language.
Within that system each thing is put beside itself and spoken
of in terms of something else.[13]

The language of "Composed upon Westminster Bridge"
has an undeniably mimetic dimension. This dimension is
not to be dismissed or transcended by further interpretation. The sonnet is exactly dated: "September 3, 1802."
Though it was, so it seems, composed on July 31, 1802,
and perhaps revised in September,[14] nevertheless, the date,
the title, and the use of the present tense mean that at least
within the fiction of the poem the reader is invited to think
of it not as emotion recollected in tranquillity but as present
speech of the poet on a particular day as he crosses a real
bridge in the early morning and looks at the silent city.
What he sees and feels are reported in straightforward
referential language. "Ships, towers, domes, theatres, and
temples" are named, as well as the river, houses, fields, sky,
sun, and the fact that there is no smoke in the air. The

[13] See Heidegger's discussion of *Logos* and the *as* structure of language
in *Sein und Zeit* (Tübingen: Max Niemeyer Verlag, 1967), pp. 32-34, 148-
160.
[14] See De Selincourt's discussion of this in III, 431: "It is possible that
the sonnet was inspired and drafted on July 31, 1802, and rewritten on
Sept. 3, when W. was again in London."

mimetic aspect of the language of the poem corresponds closely to the circumstantial vividness of the corresponding passage in Dorothy Wordsworth's journal for 1802: "It was a beautiful morning. The city, St. Paul's, with the river, and a multitude of little boats, made a most beautiful sight as we crossed Westminster Bridge. The houses were not overhung by their cloud of smoke, and they were spread out endlessly, yet the sun shone so brightly, with such a fierce light, that there was something like the purity of one of nature's own grand spectacles."[15]

The poet's subjective reaction, in the sonnet, is reported in language just as mimetic as that describing the outer scene: "Ne'er saw I, never felt, a calm so deep!" This line, in its matching of an outer calm ("Ne'er saw I") and an inner calm ("never felt"), might in fact be taken as the climax of the poem. Such a reading would see Wordsworth as an epistemological poet, a poet concerned with the relation between subject and object.[16] Inner calm matches outer calm. The poet "feels" the deep calm within the city as if it were a calm deep within himself. The word *deep* refers both to the depths of the scene and to the depths of the poet's mind and heart. In this sympathy subject and object are reconciled, made one. Such a reading interprets the poem according to assumed correspondences between its language and some extra-linguistic reality. Such realities, whether mental or physical, are presumed to have existed outside that language and not to depend on it for their existence. By investigating, however, relations not between language and things named by the poem but between words "deep" within the poem, it is possible to identify a nonmimetic meaning present side by side with this mimetic one.

Negatives, it has often been observed, have a paradoxical

[15] Cited in III, 431.

[16] For this way of reading Wordsworth see Earl R. Wasserman, "The English Romantics: The Grounds of Knowledge," *Studies in Romanticism* IV (Autumn 1964), 17-34.

power in poetry. According to Freud, there are no negatives as such in dreams, since whatever we dream has a positive emblematic existence, which is to say, it exists as both yes and no, as image. In a related way, the introduction of negatives in poetry adds more than it takes away. It creates a shadowy existence for what is denied. If I say, "I shall not compare thee to a summer's day, a rose, a running brook," I have in spite of myself made those comparisons, and the day, the rose, and the brook have positive existence in my speech. The syntactical armature of "Composed upon Westminster Bridge" is made up of the negatives in lines 1, 9, and 11: not, never, Ne'er, and never. To these may be added the implicit negatives, reinforced by the explicit ones, in lines 2-3, 12, and 14. To say, "Earth has not anything to show more fair," is to invite the reader to think of scenes that might be claimed to be fairer, or that others have said to be fairer, or that the poet himself at other times has described as fairer. To say "Dull would he be of soul who could pass by / A sight so touching in its majesty" is to suppose that there are in fact such dullards, souls who would be unmoved by the beauty of the city, just as a primrose, to Peter Bell, was only a primrose. The next negative ("Never did sun more beautifully steep / In his first splendour, valley, rock, or hill") brings into the open the alternative candidate for "fair," namely rural nature.

This comparison between nature and the city, introduced by way of the negatives, is fundamental to the poem. "Ne'er saw I, never felt, a calm so deep!" invites the reader to think of all those other contexts, scattered through Wordsworth's poetry and almost always involving pastoral rather than urban landscapes, in which the poet responds to what he sees with a combination of deep excitement and calm, calm hovering on the edge of ecstasy. This combination is characteristic of the Wordsworthian "gentle shock of mild surprise." In that gentle shock the outer scene enters deeply into the soul of the beholder, as when the Boy of Winander "hung / Listening" and the silence "carried far into his heart the voice / Of mountain torrents; or the visible scene / Would enter unawares into his mind" (Pre, v, 381-385). To say "The river glideth at his own sweet will" or "And all that mighty heart is lying still!" is to ask the reader to think of situations in which the river might in one way or another be coerced, or to think of what it might mean to say that the mighty heart of the city is beating rather than lying still. The negatives and quasi-negatives throughout the poem have a strange power to create as a shimmering mirage lying over their explicit assertions the presence of what they deny.

Not less important than the negatives in rippling the representative surface of "Composed upon Westminster Bridge" are the figures of speech used unobtrusively throughout. Like the negatives, the figures make the mimetic language move aside from itself and create, through what Wordsworth in the "Preface" of 1815 calls the "daring" of the imagination, a second realm. As I have suggested in the first chapter here, this new place exists only in the words for it, as a product of linguistic displacements. The new place is superimposed or stamped on the first as a shadow generated by what Wordsworth describes as "the conferring, the abstracting, and the modifying powers of the Imagination." By such powers "the Imagination also shapes and *creates*." Rarely has the sovereignty of the mind over things been more extravagantly asserted than by Wordsworth, both in theory and in practice. This sovereignty, as his discussion in the "Preface" of examples from Virgil, Milton, and his own verse demonstrates, is a linguistic force. It acts through figures of speech to create verbal fictions. Within these fictions "images" are "endowed by the mind with properties that do not inhere in them, upon an incitement from properties and qualities the existence of which is inherent and obvious."[17] The transformation exists not literally but in image.

[17] These citations are all from the "Preface" of 1815, ii, 437-438.

The pervasive figure in "Composed upon Westminster Bridge" is the personification of the city as a sleeping human figure who wears only the transparent garment of the morning, as opposed to the usual clothing of smoke.[18] This figure, who seems by implication to be female, lies "Open unto the fields, and to the sky," as in Tennyson's "Now sleeps the crimson petal, now the white," the Earth lies "all Danaë to the stars." The point of radical ambiguity arises in the contrast between the penultimate line, "Dear God! the very houses seem asleep," and the last line; "And all that mighty heart is lying still!" The former line suggests that the lady is asleep. The latter would seem to mean that the city is like a corpse. It is like a corpse because there are no human consciousnesses present within it. Only if all human minds are absent can the city be like that other scene, the rural one, brought into the poem by way of negative: "Never did sun more beautifully steep / In his first splendour, valley, rock or hill." The contours of valley, rock, or hill obscurely correspond to the contours of a human body and reinforce the personification of the city by the implied congruence of the rural and urban scenes. Only if there are no human minds present to hide the city from the sun, as the manmade smoke usually covers the buildings, the ships, and the river, and only if there are no human beings present to turn the river willfully to their own uses, can the city be like a fair woman, sleeping or dead, or can the river glide at his own sweet will. The openness to the radiant presence signified by the sunlight is possible only if the city is like a corpse, its heart stilled.

[18] Wordsworth intended the beautiful oxymoron of a garment that yet leaves its wearer "bare," as is indicated in the letters cited by De Selincourt in a note (III, 431): "John Kenyon wrote to W. (Aug. 22, 1836) that his wife had made the criticism, 'If the beauty of the morning be worn "like a garment"—how bare? If "like a garment"mean anything (and it is somewhat vague at best) there is a contradiction in thought, and if it mean nothing there is a contradiction in words.' W. replied: 'The contradiction is in the *words* only—bare, as not being covered with smoke or vapour;—clothed, as being attired in the beams of the morning.' "

But what of the poet? He is there all along, wide awake and watching. He claims to participate in a deep calm that is possible only if all waking human minds are absent and all the mighty heart of the city is lying still. The poet shares in a calm that can only exist if he is absent. He is both there and not there, as if he were his own ghost.

To follow the implications of the negatives and of the figurative language in "Composed upon Westminster Bridge" leads the interpreter away from an unambiguous mimetic reading toward the recognition that the poem expresses an oscillation between consciousness and nature, life and death, presence and absence, motion and stillness. This recognition is the characteristic endpoint of any careful reading of Wordsworth's best poems. Another example would be the enigmatic interplay between the first and last stanzas of "A Slumber Did My Spirit Seal." In the second stanza the awakened poet discovers that Lucy can be a "thing" beyond the touch of earthly years only by indeed becoming a thing, "Rolled round in earth's diurnal course, / With rocks, and stones, and trees" (II, 216). She can fulfill the promise of her seeming immortal vitality only by dying. Just as the scene witnessed by the poet in "Composed upon Westminster Bridge" is both "still" and at the same time gliding with the river, so Lucy, now that she has died, has "no motion" and yet moves ceaselessly with the rotation of the earth. In both poems the poet is the survivor of a death that is by implication his own death. The death that he anticipates or takes into himself or projects outward on nature is the force behind the imagination's transformation of the literal scene. This transformation turns what is "really there" into emblem, that is, into a corpse: "And all that mighty heart is lying still!"[19]

The doubleness generated by the opening out of time

[19] For "A Slumber Did My Spirit Seal," see my "On Edge: The Crossways of Contemporary Criticism," *Bulletin of the American Academy of Arts and Sciences* XXXII, 4 (January 1979), 20-31.

and death through the activity of the imagination may be seen in the twofold implications of the river's gliding. The flowing of the river is the free movement of nature when man is not there, when consciousness is absent or dead. This gliding never dies and thereby combines permanence and change, like the woods and waterfalls of the Alps in Book VI of the *Prelude*: "The immeasurable height / Of woods decaying, never to be decayed, / The stationary blasts of waterfalls" (Pre, VI, 624-626). At the same time the gliding river is transformed by the metaphorical displacements of the poem into a sign of the reaching toward death of a human mind that has accepted death or that has survived the death of another. Such a mind dwells free of illusion in the space of the imagination, that is, in the space between life and death. This region is characterized by a paradoxical movement in stillness expressed here in the immobile motion of the scene. The memorializing of the dead by the poet or by his personae, so ubiquitous a theme in Wordsworth's poetry—for example, in "The Thorn," in "Michael," in the Matthew poems, in "The Ruined Cottage," and in "The Boy of Winander"[20]—is present here in the

[20] It may be noted here that the analogies in structure and theme between any one poem by Wordsworth and other poems, often a large number of other poems, do not provide an escape from the ambiguity or shifting of meaning I am describing in "Composed upon Westminster Bridge." It is not possible to set Wordsworth's poems side by side to extract some common or central meaning present in them all. Each new poem turns out, when it is scrutinized, to be another expression of the same alternations between one meaning and another that it may have been called upon to control in the first poem examined. No poem is the archetype that may be used to interpret all the others. Whatever poem is chosen as the focus of attention reveals itself to be just as problematical as the others. Moreover, the relation between one poem by Wordsworth and another is itself problematical, another form of the same oscillation of meaning encountered within each single poem. To what degree, for example, is it legitimate to read all the so-called "Lucy poems" as a group and to propose an interpretation of any one of them based on a global interpretation of them all? The insoluble problem of the relations among Wordsworth's shorter poems is mirrored in *The Prelude* in the pregnant

way the speaker of the sonnet has outlived the death of the human consciousness ascribed to the city. The poem might be defined as the epitaph for a dead city. Here too the death of another puts the poet beyond ordinary life, and here too the proleptic awareness of his own death places him in a precarious situation of sudden insight. This insight Wordsworth often expresses in a metaphor of abrupt pause or "hanging," as in "The Boy of Winander": "in that silence while he hung / Listening." This poise, when it appears in Wordsworth, indicates that the poet has entered into full awareness of the powers and dangers of the human imagination. It involves always the co-presence of motion and stillness as essential components of human time.

In Book v of *The Prelude* the poet laments that the "Mind," though "gifted with such powers to send abroad / Her spirit," has only books, those "frail" "shrines," to "stamp her image on" (Pre, v, 45-49). In fact the daring of the imagination in its transactions with the external world, as in "Composed upon Westminster Bridge," is just such a stamping. It creates out of the dislocations of literal language a rural scene and figure, sleeping or dead, where there was only London on a September morning. In this verbalized transformation the poet stamps his image on nature, inscribes himself on

---

ambiguities generated throughout by enigmatic juxtapositions of episode with episode. What meaning lies in the blanks between unit and unit in *The Prelude*? Why, for example, is "The Boy of Winander" put in the book about books, sandwiched between an attack on modern educationists and the episode of the drowned man in Esthwaite's Lake? The displacements, exclusions, and extensions performed by the various versions of *The Prelude* make these questions more difficult. According to what principle did Wordsworth decide to move a given episode to a different place? Answers to this and to other such questions may certainly be proposed, but such answers never satisfy the mind's need for certainty. The answers represent one form of that extrapolation or reading between the lines that is a necessary danger to be embraced by the man rash enough to undertake the interpretation of Wordsworth. The critic of Wordsworth must, like the Boy of Winander, hang listening in the silence, the blank between the poet's words, and his commentary must consequently dare to "speak silence."

it, makes nature into emblem. In so doing he brings death, imagination, and human time into being, in the signs for them. This act is identical with the composition of the poem. It may be called the linguistic moment in Wordsworth. The power to make signs creates the realm of the imagination. In that realm things are not what or where they are. They dwell in a continual flickering displacement, the displacement described in the splendid metaphor of the aurora borealis used in Book v of *The Prelude* to define the strange space of those verbal fictions "forged" by the imagination: "Space like a heaven filled up with northern lights, / Here, nowhere, there, and everywhere at once" (Pre, v, 532-533).

The auroral alternation between one interpretation and another so characteristic of the final insight the reader reaches by working his or her way into one of Wordsworth's poems, even into so apparently innocent and straightforward a poem as "Composed upon Westminster Bridge," is in that poem exemplified in the vibration between the two meanings of the gliding river. On the one hand, as I have said, the line may be taken literally, as an expression of the poet's recognition of the natural time of everlasting stillness and motion. On the other hand, all the images of the poem may be taken as emblems of the poet's own consciousness as an inhabitant of that place beyond death and yet moving ever toward it. The poise of this motionless motion characterizes the space constructed by the imagination's daring in Wordsworth's poems. Between mimesis and emblem, between imitative form and creative form, the images of the poem hang balanced.

To return, then, to the question of poetic form. Most concepts of form in poetry presuppose covertly or overtly the existence of a center outside the play of elements in the poem. This center is at once the origin of meaning and at the same time the control over meaning. It keeps the meaning from having an indefinitely expanding resonance of implication initiated by the give and take of words within the poem. In our tradition this center has taken the names

77

of *source, end, consciousness, God, the Word,* and so on. The metaphor of wind articulated into melody by the trumpet and other similar metaphors in the sonnets discussed here would seem to confirm Wordsworth's allegiance to one form of that concept of a centered structure. Nevertheless, Wordsworth's poetry pervasively puts this concept into question, as my examples show. If the "source" is an undifferentiated wind, then it is without meaning in itself. The wind or breath is only the possibility of meaning, not a forming matrix. It is not a simple or single origin, but a cacophony. It is no Word, but rather the murmur or roar that is the unformed possibility of all words. Meaning comes into existence only in the modulation of this primal multiplicity into distinct sounds. This form-giving activity, as "Composed upon Westminster Bridge" demonstrates in the uncertainty of its negatives and metaphors, creates a form controlled by no still center outside itself. In a poem with such a form, meaning arises from an act which makes that meaning impossible to fix definitely. Moreover, it is a form in which the issue of form is one of the thematic elements entering into what is formed. The poem raises questions about its own mode of existence.

A FULLER INVESTIGATION of this torsion of Wordsworth's poetry back on itself may be made by way of a discussion of the admirable dream of the Arab in Book v, lines 1-165, of *The Prelude*. Critics from De Quincey on have recognized the special importance and difficulty of this passage, as well as its great power.[21]

[21] See Thomas De Quincey, "The Lake Poets: William Wordsworth," *Collected Writings*, ed. David Masson, ii (London: A. & C. Black, 1896), pp. 268-269; W. H. Auden, *The Enchafèd Flood* (New York: Vintage, 1950); Jane Worthington Smyser, "Wordsworth's Dream of Poetry and Sciences," *PMLA* LXXI, 1 (March 1956), 269-275; W. G. Stobie, "A Reading of *The Prelude*, Book v," *Modern Language Quarterly* XXIV, 4 (December 1963), 365-373; David Perkins, *Wordsworth and the Poetry of Sincerity* (Cambridge, Mass.: The Belknap Press of Harvard University Press, 1964), pp. 103-

Wordsworth has often been enlisted into the ranks of those who see poetry as primarily oral. This view looks upon written language as a copy of living speech. Some passages by Wordsworth seem to affirm this view, but in fact Wordsworth's thinking on this matter is more complicated. If he sometimes seems to see authentic poetry as existing only in a "spontaneous" "pouring forth" of the poet's "soul" "in measured strains" (Pre, I, 48, 52), on the other hand he is a poet "not used to make / A present joy the matter of a song" (Pre, I, 46-47). His poetry was in fact written down, though he much disliked the physical act of writing it or copying it later. The distinction between immediate experience and the poetry that arises later on when that experience is recollected in tranquillity implies enough distance from immediate experience to allow it to be recorded in a secondary present. In fact, Wordsworth says this even of the experience of spontaneous oral poetic creation described at the opening of *The Prelude* (Pre, I, 50). This

---

106; Geoffrey Hartman, *Wordsworth's Poetry 1787–1814* (New Haven: Yale University Press, 1964), pp. 226-231; Evelyn Shakir, "Books, Death, and Immortality: A Study of Book v of *The Prelude*," *Studies in Romanticism* VIII, 3 (Spring 1969), 156-167; Harold Bloom, *The Visionary Company*, rev. and enl. ed. (Ithaca & London: Cornell University Press, 1971), pp. 150-151; Richard J. Onorato, *The Character of the Poet: Wordworth in The Prelude* (Princeton: Princeton University Press, 1971), pp. 369, 372-377; Joel Morkan, "Structure and Meaning in *The Prelude*, Book v," *PMLA* LXXXVII, 2 (March 1972), 246-253; Frank D. McConnell, *The Confessional Imagination: A Reading of Wordsworth's Prelude* (Baltimore: The Johns Hopkins University Press, 1974), pp. 129-135; Melvyn New, "Wordsworth's Shell of Poetry," *Philological Quarterly* LIII, 2 (Spring 1974), 275-281; Timothy Bahti, "Figures of Interpretation, The Interpretation of Figures: A Reading of Wordsworth's 'Dream of the Arab,' " *Studies in Romanticism* XVIII, 4 (Winter 1979), 601-627; Cynthia Chase, "The Accidents of Disfiguration: Limits to Literal and Rhetorical Reading in Book v of *The Prelude*," *Studies in Romanticism* XVIII, 4 (Winter 1979), 547-565; Michael Ragussis, "Wordsworth: The Arab Dream: The Language Behind Nature and Art," *The Subterfuge of Art: Language and the Romantic Tradition* (Baltimore and London: The Johns Hopkins University Press, 1978), pp. 17-34. The latest, so far, in this long line is Andrzej Warminski's brilliant "Missed Crossing: Wordsworth's Apocalypses," forthcoming in *MLN*.

puts the written text at a double remove from the experience that it describes. The spontaneous overflow of powerful feelings when the original emotion is recollected is in its turn recorded on the page. This is a representation of a representation. The writing down of a poetic text is a making present for the reader of what was itself the making present of an experience once present but no longer so. On the other hand, both in theory and in practice, the recollection in tranquillity for Wordsworth brings something new into existence, something not present in the original experience. If this is so, might it not also be the case with the act of writing down the experience as re-experienced? The issue here is not the opposition between primary oral speech and secondary written language, but a more fundamental question that lies behind this opposition. Does expression in either oral or written form bring new meaning into the world or does it only copy a pre-existing meaning?

Wordsworth's concern for this question is indicated by his fascination with all kinds of written language. This includes not only the "Books" that are the overt title and subject of Book v of *The Prelude*, but also many other forms of inscription—epitaphs, monuments, memorial plaques, signs, and so on. One of Wordsworth's earliest poems is called "Lines left upon a Seat in a Yew-Tree, which stands near the Lake of Esthwaite, on a desolate part of the Shore, commanding a beautiful prospect." The "Essays upon Epitaphs" investigate that kind of poetry which is inscribed on stone to mark a grave. One section of the collected poems is called "Epitaphs and Elegiac Pieces." Another is called "Inscriptions."[22] The latter group contains short poems

[22] Geoffrey Hartmann has discussed the traditions that lie behind Wordsworth's poems in this mode and their significance in Wordsworth's work: "Wordsworth, Inscriptions, and Romantic Nature Poetry" *Beyond Formalism*, ed. cit., pp. 206-230. See also Ernest Bernhardt-Kabisch, "Wordsworth: The Monumental Poet," *Philological Quarterly* XLIV, 4 (October 1965), 503-518, and Eugenio Donato's admirable essay, "The Ruins

with titles like the following: "Written with a Pencil upon a Stone in the Wall of the House (an Out-house), on the Island at Grasmere," "Written with a Slate Pencil on a Stone, on the Side of the Mountain of Black Comb," "Written with a Slate Pencil upon a Stone, the largest of a Heap lying near a deserted Quarry, upon one of the Islands at Rydal." These titles, almost longer than the poems they name, are striking in the extreme circumstantiality of detail with which they identify the act whereby the poem was given physical existence. The exact place, the stone, the act of writing, the tool used for the inscription—all are described with precision. This precision suggests that the most important aspect of these particular poems may be the act of writing them. In that act a mute stone becomes the bearer of marks speaking a silent message to any passerby. Such poems are by their titles so wedded to the stone on which they were written that one wonders if they can survive being copied in the book in which we read them today. Their "primary" existence was not as living speech but as marks made with a slate pencil on a particular place.

Stones play an important role in Wordsworth's poetry— for example, the rocks and stones to which Lucy is assimilated after her death in "A Slumber Did My Spirit Seal," or the comparison of the old leech-gatherer to a huge stone "Couched on the bald top of an eminence" in "Resolution and Independence," or the moving line of "Michael," "And never lifted up a single stone," or the "old grey stone," "a rude mass / Of native rock," which used to stand in the square of the village where Wordsworth grew up (Pre, II, 38; 33-34). Charles Du Bos, commenting with great insight on a passage from "The Thorn" and on another from Book XIV of *The Prelude*,[23] has observed that stones for Words-

---

of Memory: Archeological Fragments and Textual Artifacts," *MLN* XCIII, 4 (May 1978), 575-596.

[23] The texts in question are the following:

> It is a mass of knotted joints,
> A wretched thing forlorn.

worth are often seen as vital, alive with an obscure organic existence that may assimilate them to trees. Such a living stone, says Du Bos, is Wordsworth's best symbol for his inmost being.[24] Not only was Wordsworth fascinated by stones in themselves.[25] He also was impelled, when he found on an island or on a mountain top a stone he especially admired, to scratch a poem on it. Such inscriptions are evidence that Wordsworth, far from believing that poetry exists primarily as spoken language, sometimes felt that a poem best exists when it has been inscribed permanently on the perdurable substance of a rock. The implications of this strange strand in Wordsworth's conception of poetry are brought more clearly into the open in the dream of the Arab in *The Prelude*. Here the role of written language both as an indispensable metaphor for what it seems to derive from and as an originating act in itself becomes the overt subject of Wordsworth's verse.

It stands erect, and like a stone
With lichens is it overgrown.
("The Thorn," lines 8-11, II,
241)

. . . but for thee, dear Friend!
My soul, too reckless of mild grace, had stood
In her original self too confident,
Retained too long a countenance severe;
A rock with torrents roaring, with the clouds
Familiar, and a favourite of the stars:
But thou didst plant its crevices with flowers,
Hang it with shrubs that twinkle in the breeze,
And teach the little birds to build their nests
And warble in its chambers.
(Pre, xiv, 247-256)

[24] Charles Du Bos, *Du Spirituel dans l'ordre littéraire* (Paris: Corti, 1967), pp. 144, 147.

[25] Evidence for this is given in the lines from a poem included in a letter to John Kenyon of 1831 (*The Letters of William and Dorothy Wordsworth: The Later Years, 1831–40*, II, ed. Ernest de Selincourt [Oxford: Oxford University Press, 1939], p. 572): "from the builder's hand this Stone / . . . Was rescued by the Bard." This poem is discussed later in this chapter.

The opening lines of Book v of *The Prelude* establish the theme that is to be investigated in the dream that follows. The theme is established in terms of a metaphor of the book. This is latent throughout but becomes explicit in the closing lines of the introductory section, lines 45-49. In these lines the fragility of books is lamented. The human mind has power to project itself outside itself. It has power to articulate itself in verbal or symbolic structures, poetry or geometry. These productions of "Bard or Sage" constitute "adamantine holds of truth / By reason built, or passion" (Pre, v, 39-40). The "sadness" is that these rocklike grips on truth must be embodied in material that, far from being adamantine, may be easily destroyed by fire or flood—the paper, ink, glue, cardboard, or leather of which books are made:

> Oh! why hath not the Mind
> Some element to stamp her image on
> In nature somewhat nearer to her own?
> Why, gifted with such powers to send abroad
> Her spirit, must it lodge in shrines so frail?
> (Pre, v, 45-49)

The system of thought leading up to these lines is peculiar, as is so often the case with Wordsworth. Peculiar also is the relation of the introductory section to the narrative of the dream that follows it. That narrative is at once an extension of the introduction, a commentary on it, and a reversal of its apparent premises. Its elements, literal and metaphorical, are rearranged to generate unforeseen permutations of meaning. The book is part of a double metaphor in which the secondary is used as the figurative expression of the primary, of that from which it is derived or on which it is modeled. This reversal may be traced back at least to Plato. It appears to be one of those patterns of thought inherent in the metaphorical tissue of our languages.

The relation between the "soul divine," as Wordsworth

calls it in the 1805 text (Pre, v, 16), and nature is like the relation between the human soul and its body. Just as the human body, especially the face, is the "image" of the soul that is diffused throughout that body and animates it, so nature is the body of the "sovereign Intellect" that lies behind and within nature. This intellect uses nature as its means of self-expression and as its means of communicating to man. The personification of nature as a human body and in particular as an expressive and speaking face runs throughout *The Prelude* and Wordsworth's works generally. It is present, for example, in the sonnet written on Westminster Bridge and in the grand climactic passage on the Simplon Pass in Book VI of *The Prelude*. There the intermingled elements of the Alpine scene "Were all like workings of one mind, the features / Of the same face" (Pre, VI, 636-637). Names belonging to a part of the creation, man, are used to describe the working of the creator in his relation to the creation as a whole:

> Hitherto,
> In progress through this Verse, my mind hath looked
> Upon the speaking face of earth and heaven
> As her prime teacher, intercourse with man
> Established by the sovereign Intellect,
> Who through that bodily image hath diffused,
> As might appear to the eye of fleeting time,
> A deathless spirit.
> (Pre, v, 11-18)

The difference, doubtless, between the combination of spirit and body in a man and the combination of intellect and physical nature in the creation is that the human mind is limited. Its perspective is that of "fleeting time." The human body, moreover, is mortal. The divine intellect, on the other hand, is "sovereign." It has a regal power of origination, establishment, and government. It cannot die, or at any rate it "appears" to be "a deathless spirit." The element on which it stamps itself or that it makes use of as

the medium of its speech is also indestructible. If apocalyptic fire and earthquake were to come to burn the earth
and dry up the ocean, even then the sovereign Intellect
and the earth that is its speaking face would remain. Nature
would still be the living countenance and the book of God:

> Yet would the living Presence still subsist
> Victorious, and composure would ensue,
> And kindlings like the morning—presage sure
> Of day returning and of life revived.
>
> (Pre, v, 34-37)

Only in a line added in the 1850 version, "As might
appear to the eye of fleeting time," is any doubt cast on the
adequacy of Wordsworth's formulation. The apparently in-
nocuous words "as might appear" raise the shade of a suspicion that the vision of earth as a "speaking face" expressing the thoughts of a "sovereign Intellect" may be an
appearance. It may be a prosopopoeia projected on nature
by the "eye of fleeting time." The personification of nature
may be generated by the temporal transience of the human
perspective on nature. The human mind dwells and moves
within time. Its power of seeing is created by time's movement. This movement is determined by man's mortality.
Could it be that the interpretation of nature as a speaking
face is generated by the movement of a finite consciousness
within time toward death? The romantic poets, says Georges
Poulet, responded to an acute experience of the transience
of human time by developing a human equivalent of the
divine *totum simul*. This equivalent was found in certain
privileged moments that seemed to escape from time's remorseless flowing. These moments created what Poulet calls
une éternité à leur usage propre, an eternity for their private
use.[26] An eternity for the poet's private use will have a
different structure from the *nunc stans* attributed to the
eternity of God. The temporal experience described by

[26] See *Mesure de l'instant* (Paris: Plon, 1968), pp. 163-164.

Wordsworth in the dream of the Arab is one example of an eternity paradoxically generated from the *nunc fluens* of human time as it flows toward its last end.

The paradox of the human soul and its body as the metaphor for that on which it is modeled, the relation of the immortal intellect to nature, is made more problematical by the introduction, at first surreptitiously, of a second metaphor, that of the book. If nature is the bodily image of a deathless spirit, the things man has wrought for commerce of his nature with itself are not vocal or bodily expressions, but books. The articulation of the deathless spirit behind nature into the signs on the speaking face of earth is like the articulation of man's spirit in the words stamped on the printed page. The book replaces the human body as the incarnation of the otherwise undifferentiated power of the human spirit. Body and book are the same, and vocal and written speech are seen as performing a similar differentiating function. In both there is the same structure of spiritual energy, modulating instrument, and expressive signs (musical notes or words) that is present in Wordsworth's sonnets on sonnets. The traditional metaphor describing the body as the garment of the soul—rags the soul will no more need in heaven—is here transferred to the books men write. Wordsworth says it causes "tremblings of the heart" "to think that our immortal being / No more shall need such garments" (Pre, v, 22-24). Wordsworth always found it difficult and frightening to imagine any state of disembodiment, even that of heavenly beatitude. He here expresses a similar trembling before the thought of a condition in which man would no longer need books. The speaking face of nature is necessary for the "intercourse" of the sovereign intellect with man. The deathless spirit behind nature would be invisible or inaudible if it were not for its articulation in natural types and symbols. In an analogous way man must have books in order to maintain "commerce of [his] nature with herself" (Pre, v, 19), in a kind of continuous internal dialogue.

Wordsworth's phrasing recalls the use by Plato in the *Philebus* of the image of the book to describe that inner conversation that takes place for a man when there are no other men with whom to talk.[27] The mind of man in order to communicate with itself must separate itself from itself, project itself into the external and mediate form of books. The mind must divide its oneness into the multiplicity of signs stamped on the printed page, add to its natural power the supplementary power of the written word. In heaven we shall need neither book nor body, those garments of the soul, but as long as we are children of the earth we cannot go naked.

The peculiarity of this situation merits meditation. The sovereign intellect, however regal its power, cannot communicate directly to man, but must go outside itself into nature. It must use the things of nature as mediate signs by means of which it can speak to man. In the "same way" (But what is the ground of this "sameness"? Which is the original on which the other is modeled?), the mind of man cannot communicate with itself, either collectively or individually, without a rupture of its unity, simplicity, and self-enclosed perfection. Man cannot hear God's voice directly but must read what God has to say as he has printed it on nature. Man too, in order to speak even to himself, must divide himself from himself, project himself outside himself, exile himself into his printed image or double. If he remains unbroken, he is naked, forlorn. He becomes whole or sole only when he has been rent. He must be divided into immortal being and those strange garments woven of geometrical or poetic texts. Man's naked spirit must clothe itself in the leaves of a book. The lover in Shakespeare's Sonnet LXIV, cited by Wordsworth here, is tormented by the thought that his beloved must die. He

---

[27] See Plato, *Philebus*, 28e: "*Socrates*: It seems to me that at such times our soul is like a book," trans. R. Hackforth, *The Collected Dialogues*, ed. Edith Hamilton and Huntington Cairns, Bollingen Series LXXI (Princeton: Princeton University Press, 1973), p. 1118.

suffers that thought as if it were of his own death. The anticipation of the loss of his book is to a man, says Wordsworth, a similar foretaste of death. In this death he foresees a loss that would leave him his own survivor, alive still but denuded, unable to speak to himself or to others, "Abject, depressed, forlorn, disconsolate" (Pre, v, 28). To " 'weep to have' what he may lose" (Pre, v, 26) brings death into his mind as a present reality. Though physical nature would, so the poet says, survive any catastrophe and still be available as the book of God, the lament of this poem is not only that books are destructible but that they must inevitably be destroyed. When this happens man will be left bare of those holds on truth he has made for commerce of his nature with itself:

> And yet we feel—we cannot choose but feel—
> That they must perish.
> (Pre, v, 21-22)

The dream of the Arab is a further transposition of what has already been transposed from the mind/body relation to the mind/book relation. The dream is in fact a complex system of displacements, displacements within displacements, displacements added in chain fashion to previous displacements, displacements interwoven with other displacements. This movement of dislocation is the structuring principle of the text as well as its theme. By threading her or his way through the labyrinth of these permutations, the reader can interpret the extraordinary climax of the passage. This is the waking poet's reaffirmation of the Arab's madness, his sober daylight assertion that, in view of the coming end of the world, "by signs in earth / Or heaven made manifest" (Pre, v, 158-159), the proper thing to do, in order to protect and preserve the great books of the world, is to bury them. What can this mean?

The dream as a whole is a displacement in the sense that it is a response to the poet's waking anxiety about the fragility of books. Like all dreams it is a reworking of elements drawn from waking experience. If it demands interpretation, it is itself an interpretation. In this case the relation between dream and waking is so immediate and so explicit that the dream may almost be called a daydream. It is a so-called hypnagogic dream. If an ordinary dream is the rising up of buried images and memories during deep sleep, this is that sort of dream which provides an immediate reworking by a man who has just fallen asleep of what he has been perceiving and thinking. The poet has been reading *Don Quixote* in a rocky cave by the wide sea and meditating once again on the sad destructibility of books, though what they enshrine, poetry and geometric truth, would seem exempt from "internal injury." Quixote, poetry, geometry, rock, cave, shore, sea, sultry air—all return in the dream, but transformed. The poet returns to them once again when the dream is over. The sequence from waking to dream to waking again establishes a chain of sideways substitutions in which each scene is an interpretation of the others or is interpreted by them.

Thomas De Quincey, in reminiscences written some twenty years after he had seen parts of *The Prelude* in manuscript form, emphasized this aspect of the sequence. "The form of the dream," he said, ". . . is not arbitrary; but, with exquisite skill in the art of composition, is made to arise out of the situation in which the poet had previously found himself, and is faintly prefigured in the elements of that situation."[28] The dream refashions the elements that have been present to the poet just before he falls asleep, so that, for example, the end of the world in the dream is to come by flood rather than by fire and earthquake, just as in the poet's waking reverie. His waking thoughts at the end fashion the dream into the fancy that there might really be such a man, "A gentle dweller in the desert, crazed / By love and feeling, and internal thought / Protracted among endless solitudes" (Pre, v, 145-147). This man's mad quest takes

[28] *Collected Writings*, ed. cit., II, p. 268.

the form of wishing to preserve books from the end of the world rather than to care, as most men would, for wife, child, or "virgin loves" (Pre, v, 154). The shift from loved ones to books—parallel in phrasing to Christ's injunction to leave "house or parents, or brethren, or wife, or children, for the kingdom of God's sake" (Luke 18.29), though Wordsworth adds "virgin loves"—is of course another displacement, based upon other metaphorical ratios. As most men are to their beloveds, so the semi-Quixote of Wordsworth's waking fancy is to books. As the Christian must choose Christ over family, so this madman chooses books over family, as though salvation abode within them. The poet transfers the madness once more when he takes upon himself the "Maniac's anxiousness" and his "errand":

> Oftimes at least
> Me hath such strong entrancement overcome,
> When I have held a volume in my hand . . .
> (Pre, v, 161-163)

The dream itself is structured around a sequence of metaphorical condensations or metonymic displacements in which one thing is two things at once, or in which one thing stands for another that was contiguous to it.[29] The essential "daring" of the imagination in great poetry is defined in Wordsworth's "Preface" of 1815, as I have already said in chapter 1, as the "operations of the mind upon [absent external] objects" (II, 436). These operations produce a linguistic transfer whereby one thing or group of things is given the name of another. The imagination is the power of the mind over the external world, the power of the mind to "endow" the "images" of things "with properties that do not inhere in them," to "assimilate" things to one another (metaphor) or to "approximate" them to one another (me-

---

[29] For a discussion of the relations between metaphor and metonymy, see Gérard Genette, "*Métonymie chez Proust,*" *Figures III* (Paris: Éditions du Seuil, 1972), pp. 41-63.

tonymy) (II, 437-438). So Milton, describing Satan as like a far-off fleet, "dares to represent it as *hanging in the clouds*" (II, 437). Rarely has "the mind in its activity, for its own gratification" (II, 436), renaming things at will and so re-making them, been so blithely celebrated in its dominion over things as they are, as in the "Preface" of 1815. In the dream of the Arab this dominion is affirmed not as figures of speech but as the paradoxical reality beheld by the dreamer. This is appropriate for a dream, since dreams enact as vivid images what poetic language performs in overt tropes. In any case, this dream exists only in the words on the page. Even the appearances in a "real" dream are signs, emblems, not perceptions (if such things exist). In his dream the poet sees a stone and shell that are also books and an Arab who is at the same time Don Quixote. "I won-dered not," he says, "although I plainly saw / The one to be a stone, the other a shell; / Nor doubted once but that they both were books" (Pre, v, 111-113) and of the Arab: "He, to my fancy, had become the knight / Whose tale Cer-vantes tells; yet not the knight, / But was an Arab of the desert too; / Of these was neither, and was both at once" (Pre, v, 122-125). Of these was neither, and was both at once—in dream as in the language of poetry, nothing is its solid self. It is neither what it is nor the thing whose name or whose image displaces it, but is both at once. It is nothing but the interchange between the two—stone or shell for books, Arab for Quixote.

This pattern of replacement operates, then, not only in the relation of the dream to what precedes and follows it but also within the dream itself. It may also be detected in the relation of the dream to its sources. Wordsworth's dreamer has been reading *Don Quixote* before he falls asleep. His dream is in one of its aspects a commentary on Cer-vantes' book. Just as Don Quixote was crazed by reading romances, and just as his madness took the form of seeing giants in place of windmills, an army in a herd of sheep (it was a power of transfer engendered by reading too many fictions; Quixote saw each thing in its metaphor), so the dream of Wordsworth's speaker has been generated by reading and by his Quixotic anxiety about the fragility of books. He too sees things as what they are not. Cervantes' novel is supposed, within its own fiction, to have been written by an Arab. It is also supposed to be reproduced from an incomplete manuscript, its lacunae testifying to the fact that it has survived a catastrophe, perhaps like the one which awaits those books the Arab hurries to bury in Wordsworth's dream. An episode of book burning in *Don Quixote* demonstrates that Cervantes, like Wordsworth, was concerned not only for the power to induce madness possessed by books, but also for their impermanence. Multiple resonances associate the passage in Wordsworth with the book that is overtly mentioned as one of its sources.

There are other sources for the dream. Apparently Wordsworth himself did not dream it. It is not so much a real dream as the deliberate invention of a dream sequence.[30] In the 1805 version of *The Prelude* the dreamer is not the poet but the "Philosophic Friend," perhaps Michel Beaupuy, perhaps Coleridge, to whom he says he had expressed his anxiety about the vulnerability of books. As Jane Worthington Smyser has demonstrated,[31] the dream was probably not dreamed by the "Friend" either, but was borrowed from one of the three famous dreams of Descartes described in Baillet's *Life of Descartes* (1691). Descartes, like Wordsworth's dreamer, also dreamed of two books, a dictionary gathering all the sciences and a *Corpus Poetarum*. The two together contained all human knowledge and wisdom. Descartes also dreamed of a mysterious stranger with whom he discussed the books. Descartes, like Wordsworth's dreamer, interpreted the elements in the

[30] Freud has discussed the special problems involved in analyzing such a fictional dream in "Delusions and Dreams in Jensen's *Gradiva*" (1907), trans. James Strachey, in *Complete Psychological Works*, st. ed., IX (London: The Hogarth Press and the Institute of Psycho-Analysis, 1959), pp. 7-95.

[31] See her essay cited in note 21 above.

dream while he was dreaming it—in particular, the two books. Descartes resolved when he woke up to undertake a religious pilgrimage, just as the awakened poet in *The Prelude* says that when he contemplates the signs of the approaching apocalyptic deluge he shares "that maniac's fond anxiety" and feels that he too could "go / Upon like errand" (Pre, v, 160-161). From Descartes to the philosophic friend to Wordsworth the dream has migrated, undergoing accretions and mutations in each metempsychosis. In this chain of interpretations and reinterpretations, Descartes' dream, like any other dream, is not an origin but is itself already interpretation. It is a series of enigmatic signs for a hidden meaning that always remains prior to its manifest expression.[32]

From all these forms of displacement it may be concluded that the process of substitution is not only the form but also the theme of the dream of the Arab. Its theme, to put this another way, is the book. A book, like a dream, is the replacement of a reality, which always remains at a distance from its image. The theme of the dream is language or the sign-making power. The essence of this power in the dream is the naming of one thing by the name of another which puts in question the possibility of literal naming. All names, it may be, are metaphors, moved aside from any direct

---

[32] For modern discussions of Descartes' dream, see Georges Poulet, "*Le Songe de Descartes*," *Études sur le temps humain* (Paris: Plon, 1953), pp. 16-47, and Jacques Maritain, *Le Songe de Descartes* (Paris: R.-A. Correa, 1932). Behind Descartes' dream, of course, lies the Biblical, medieval, and Renaissance topos of the two books, the book of nature and the book of revealed Scripture. If the Bible is the word of God revealed in a written text, the heavens too declare the glory of God, just as, in a secular displacement of this traditional topos, all human wisdom, for Descartes or for Wordsworth's dreamer, is divided into geometry or the sciences, on the one hand—the codified knowledge of the spaces of the creation—and on the other hand, poetry, human wisdom as incarnated in the written word. See E. R. Curtius' magisterial discussion of the topos of the book, "*Das Buch als Symbol*," *Europäische Literatur und Lateinisches Mittelalter* (Bern: A. Francke, 1948), pp. 304-351.

correspondence to the thing named by their reference to other names that precede and follow them in an endless chain. But why do just these elements enter into the transformations of the dream—Arab and Quixote; stone and shell; book of geometry and book of poetry; desert and deluge?

The stone and the shell have the same relation to one another as do the stone and geometry, or the shell and poetry, or geometry and poetry. The same similarity in difference forming a multiple ratio may be traced in all the relations among these four elements. Binary opposition is as important a structural principle of the dream as is the movement of displacement. The transpositions take place as permutations of balanced opposites that are similar in their difference. Each pair forms a unit in which each member is neither simply itself nor its opposite, and yet is both at once. The shell is like a stone hollowed out, as if it had been carved, fluted, articulated, so that it may speak with voices more than all the winds. Poetry is a transformation of the kind of reason that produces geometry. Passion, the generator of poetry, is, says Wordsworth, "highest reason in a soul sublime" (Pre, v, 41).

The difference between the two forms of wisdom is indicated in the difference between the signs for them. A stone uninscribed, uncarved, unhollowed, is just itself. It does not refer beyond itself in any form of displacement. It is not a sign, or it is a null sign, a sign for the absence of signs, like a blank face or a sheet of paper on which nothing has been written. A stone is self-contained, incapable of any lateral displacement of signification. It commands space by its fixity. It is disturbed neither by spatial nor by temporal distances. The stone knows not time. The stone shares the permanence, composure, and peace of nature. Just this value is ascribed to geometry. The book carried by the Arab is Euclid's *Elements*, a book, said the Arab to the dreamer, "that held acquaintance with the stars, / And wedded soul to soul in purest bond / Of reason, un-

94

disturbed by space or time" (Pre, v, 103-105). In the passage on the consolations of geometry in Book vi of *The Prelude* (Pre, vi, 115-167), Wordsworth remembers how John Newton when he was shipwrecked was comforted by drawing geometric diagrams on the sand with his long staff.[33] Geometry has a mighty charm for the man who has "a mind beset / With images, and haunted by herself" (Pre, vi, 159-160), a mind, that is, like that of the poet as he describes himself, for example, in "Resolution and Independence." The mind alone is as "abject, depressed, forlorn, disconsolate" as a shipwrecked mariner. Geometry provides an escape from this by lifting the mind to recognize the universal laws of nature that are above mortal vicissitudes. Geometry indicates that behind nature is a creator, God, whose being is expressed in the permanence of nature and who is "to the boundaries of space and time, / Of melancholy space and doleful time, / Superior, and incapable of change, / Nor touched by welterings of passion" (Pre, vi, 135-138).[34]

To substitute the shell for the stone, or to turn the stone

[33] This is a place in Wordsworth, among so many others, in which attention is called to the act of inscription, in this case not on stone or on paper, but on those tiny, pulverized stones, the sands which in the dream passage form the environment of the "Arab phantom's" solitude and of his crazy quest. For John Newton, see R. D. Havens, *The Mind of a Poet* (Baltimore: The Johns Hopkins University Press, 1941), pp. 412-413.

[34] Another passage on geometrical diagrams in Book xiii of *The Prelude* indicates the associations Wordsworth habitually makes between geometry and the measurement or representation of the fixed patterns of the starry heavens. This is a passage about the Druid markings on Salisbury Plain. Since these markings involve stones, another connection between stones and geometry is established—that is, the use of stones as elementary marking or measuring devices, as the stones of Stonehenge are arranged in relation to the summer solstice. "[T]he Plain," says Wordsworth, "Was figured o'er with circles, lines, or mounds, / That yet survive, a work, as some divine, / Shaped by the Druids, so to represent / Their knowledge of the heavens, and image forth / The constellations" (Pre, xiii, 337-342). Gene W. Ruoff called my attention to the relevance of this text to Book v.

into a shell by carving it or by hollowing it and so making it a speaking stone, replaces the calm of geometry for that weltering of passion which Wordsworth associates with poetry, as in "Resolution and Independence." A stone inscribed with an epitaph speaks. The poet hears "an Ode, in Passion uttered" (Pre, v, 96) when he puts the Arab's shell to his ear. The passion of poetry arises not from any care that might be assuaged, but from an anxiety about last things. This anxiety finds its emblem in the substitution of the spiral tube of the shell for the uninscribed stone. The shell articulates the uniform sound of the sea, or of "background noise," or of the rush of blood in the listening ear, into differentiated harmony, just as the singer by the sea in Stevens' "The Idea of Order at Key West" modulates the rush of wind and sea sounds into her song, and just as the poet in "Resolution and Independence" speaks for the dizzying roar of waters. The rocky cave in which the waking poet in *The Prelude* sits by the sea is an example of those many nooks or caves in Wordsworth's verse or in Shelley's. Such a cave is a figure for subjectivity looking out on the world. This figure reappears in the dream as the enclosed hollow of the shell. With the shell's fracturing, featuring, or dividing of the single and featureless, come into existence man's anxious consciousness, human temporality, signs or the power of sign making and of sign reading, desire, the anticipation of death, poetry, and the imagination of apocalypse. All these are different forms of one another. All are also names for the act of displacement, substitution, or stepping aside, that splitting apart or distinguishing which marks a thing so that it ceases to be itself and becomes a sign pointing toward something absent. That absent something exists, already and elsewhere, or not yet. It exists, for man, in the signs for it, that is, "It is and it / Is not and, therefore, is."[35]

[35] Wallace Stevens, "A Primitive Like an Orb," *The Collected Poems*, ed. cit., p. 440.

Geoffrey Hartman, in his commentary on the dream of the Arab, identifies as "imagination" the waters of the deep, which are the fulfillment of the prophecy of the shell.[36] This flood is a displacement from the signs of poetry heard in the shell to the signs of nature seen by the dreamer's eye. The flood approaches in a glittering wall over the sand toward the Arab as he hurries to bury the two books. Hartman's identification is correct, but it would be as true to say that the coming flood is death, or that it is the movement of human time, as that it is imagination. All three are names for that human dimension which is opened by the marks on a rock or by the spiral flutings of a shell. Such markings turn things into what they are not, that is, into signs for something absent. If the dream is an example of poetry, in which everything is and is not some other thing, it also contains its own explication. It turns back on itself by presenting in the shell a symbol of its process. The radiant shell, "of a surpassing brightness," "so beautiful in shape / In colour so resplendent" (Pre, v, 80, 90-91), objectifies the process of the birth of poetry.

The sound the dreamer hears in the shell is "a loud prophetic blast," like a single note from a trumpet. At the same time it is "articulate sounds," a "harmony," a voice that speaks "in an unknown tongue" the dreamer can nevertheless "understand" (Pre, v, 93-95).[37] This language

---

[36] See Geoffrey H. Hartman, *Wordsworth's Poetry 1787–1814*, pp. 229-231.

[37] Behind these lines lies St. Paul's meditation on language and on speaking in tongues, glossolalia, in 1 Corinthians 14. Among the key terms in Paul's discourse are "prophesy," "unknown tongue," "interpretation," and "understanding," all of which reappear in Wordsworth. Even the trumpet appears in the passage. "Now, brethren," says Paul, "if I come unto you speaking with tongues, what shall I profit you, except I shall speak to you either by revelation, or by knowledge, or by prophesying, or by doctrine? And even things without life giving sound, whether pipe or harp, except they give a distinction in the sounds, how shall it be known what is piped or harped? For if the trumpet give an uncertain sound, who shall prepare himself to the battle? So likewise ye, except ye utter by the tongue words

is analogous to the inscriptions apparently written by God on nature. The latter, too, are in no human tongue and yet may be deciphered. The sound the dreamer hears in the shell seems to enact the birth of language from the grinding water and gasping wind, but it is in fact his own blood beating in his ear that he hears. He projects this noise into the shell. He then hears it echo back seemingly as the sound of wind and wave wrought objectively into the shell and able to be played back to the man who listens. This natural sound is then interpreted in its turn as harmonious language, as the voice not of the wind but of "a god, yea many gods" (Pre, v, 106). This voice is not single but a multitudinous murmur of "voices more than all the winds" (Pre, v, 107). The originating sound from which all words derive is not a single word but a multiplicity of possible words all overlapping or sounded at once. This cacophony must be simplified, filtered, or strained in order to become articulate sounds, but those sounds are still marked by the disharmony of their source. The original voice is already doubled, divided against itself, equivocal not univocal, "voices" not a voice.

Such multiform voices, when they have been interpreted into "an Ode, in passion uttered" (Pre, v, 96), can have only one message: "Destruction to the children of the earth / By deluge, now at hand" (Pre, v, 97-98). This apocalyptic news is the fundamental theme of poetry. The stone knows no time; geometry is a godlike natural science, free of time and space; Lucy knows not time when she has become a corpse "Rolled round in earth's diurnal course, / With rocks, and stones, and trees,"[38] but the shell brings human time into existence in the signs of it. With human time comes the proleptic awareness of death, as something "now at

---

easy to be understood, how shall it be known what is spoken? for ye shall speak into the air. There are, it may be, so many kinds of voices in the world, and none of them is without signification" (1 Corinthians 14.6-10).

[38] "A Slumber Did My Spirit Seal," lines 7-8, ii, 216.

hand." In this multiple process of interpretation, a subjective sound is interpreted as outer, and that sound is in turn interpreted as manifold signs. These signs are poetry. They speak with the voices of the many gods who seem to lie within and behind nature. Such signs have a paradoxical function. On the one hand they have "power / To exhilarate the spirit, and to sooth, / Through every clime, the heart of human kind" (Pre, v, 107-109). On the other hand, this soothing is performed by unveiling the future and telling man the end of the world is at hand. Poetry both soothes and is apocalyptic.

The dream as a whole is structured around interpretative dislocations from benign to ominous. The real sea, which was before the dreamer when he was awake, is transformed into the final flood. The book he was reading becomes a stone and a shell and then the two books of the dream, that is, physical objects inscribed with signs bringing awareness of the imminence of death into existence. As the dreamer listens to the shell, imagination is born of the differentiations making language of inarticulate sounds. The interpretation of nature generated by these signs is then projected outward on the world as an objective and pre-existing reality. Since signs produce consciousness, which produces the sense of time, which produces the ever present awareness of the imminence of death, it is no accident that the message the poet hears in the shell is a forewarning of the end of the world.

In this process it may be seen that the stamping of the mind's image on a book is the same operation as the stamping of that image on physical nature. If the differentiations of traced word or of articulated voice bring into existence the human mind and its basic thoughts, powers, or dimensions—death, time, and the imagination—the same operation is performed in the reading of nature as signs of some sovereign intellect. When the poet sees nature as types and symbols, or personifies it as a speaking face, he treats it in the same way that he treats the paper or stone on which he writes a poem or an epitaph. The two acts of "stamping" are almost identical. The answer to the question, "why hath not the Mind / Some element to stamp her image on / In nature somewhat nearer to her own?" is that nature is man's book, too. There can be no sign without a physical embodiment, but as long as the physical world exists, even if all printed books have been destroyed, man will still have rocks, sand, and winds to stamp his image on.

An important passage in Book One of *The Excursion* (lines 108-279, v, 11-17) also combines in a characteristically problematical way the motifs of the printed book, the book of nature, the book of Scripture, the lineaments of a speaking face, and the projection into nature of the presence of an immortal mind, or the interpretation of nature as the abiding place of such a mind. Describing the childhood of the Wanderer, that extraordinary potential poet, Wordsworth says that the Wanderer was taught by his pious parents "a reverence for God's word" (line 115). The Bible, books of "the life and death of martyrs" in the times of the Scottish Covenant, and "a straggling volume, torn and incomplete," a romance illustrated with coarse woodcuts, made up all his store of books (lines 170ff.). He had, however, "small need of books" (line 163), not only because oral traditional tales abounded in his remote mountain area, but also because nature was a book to him. In one passage, a text offering in its sequence of "or . . . or . . . or" a series of contradictory possibilities for the source of the feeling that nature is the residence of a living mind, the Wanderer is shown tracing the lineaments of that mind in the rocks of wild caves:

> —in the after-day
> Of boyhood, many an hour in caves forlorn,
> And 'mid the hollow depths of naked crags
> He sate, and even in their fixed lineaments,
> Or from the power of a peculiar eye,
> Or by creative feeling overborne,
> Or by predominance of thought oppressed,

> Even in their fixed and steady lineaments
> He traced an ebbing and a flowing mind,
> Expression ever varying!
> > (lines 153-162)

Though this passage will not commit itself definitely, the doubt is not whether the source of the experience is subjective, but whether it comes from the senses, from feeling, or from thought. Some lines further on, in a passage that brings all these motifs together, the boy herdsman reads in nature the same message he had encountered already in the Bible. The book of Scripture and the book of nature are inscribed with the same promise; nature too is seen as if it were a written text. I find the phrase in this passage about the "volume that displays / The mystery" fundamentally ambiguous. The "volume" may be the Bible, and this would be supported by the lines in "The Ruined Cottage" (that is, the earlier version of Book One of *The Excursion*) which assert that the Wanderer, as a child, "had learned to read / His bible in a school that stood alone" (lines 55-56, v, 380). On the other hand the book of Scripture may already be in this phrase the vehicle of a metaphor describing that nature which the Wanderer already knows deeply as a book. As is so often the case with such texts in Wordsworth, only the interpreter's tact can decide between meanings that remain in themselves "undecidable." If the second reading is taken, then the passage says that all nature is a volume that the Wanderer can read as a written promise of immortality, but in the mountains this promise is also deeply *felt*. The ambiguity of the term *immortality* is suggested not only by the complexity of the uses of the word in other contexts in Wordsworth, but also by the final lines of the passage. There the boy's spirit is once more described as "shaping" the universe he sees:

> A Herdsman on the lonely mountain-tops,
> Such intercourse was his, and in this sort
> Was his existence oftentimes *possessed*.
> O then how beautiful, how bright, appeared

The written promise! Early had he learned
To reverence the volume that displays
The mystery, the life which cannot die;
But in the mountains did he *feel* his faith.
All things, responsive to the writing, there
Breathed immortality, revolving life,
And greatness still revolving; infinite:
There littleness was not; the least of things
Seemed infinite; and there his spirit shaped
Her prospects, nor did he believe,—he *saw*.
(lines 219-232)

In the dream of the Arab, to return to that, the shift
from what the poet hears in the shell to what he sees, the
coming deluge, fulfils the verbalized prophecy in the visible
emblems of nature. This is a displacement from language
to natural signs, but the two kinds of signs are the same.
The fulfillment of the prophecy is reinforced by another
lateral dislocation of the kind so frequent in this text, the
reappearance of the "surpassing brightness" of the shell in
the "bed of glittering light" (Pre, v, 80, 129) as the deluge
hurries over the sand. The shell embodies the coming apocalypse not only in the sounds heard within it but also in its
external looks. Both are examples of the stamping of the
mind's image on physical elements. The sound in the shell
is interpreted as a prophetic ode, just as the sea before the
waking poet is turned into the glittering wall of water he
sees in his dream. This shining wall is the emblem of the
opening out of consciousness in a moving stasis. This movement in place is the approach of that "something evermore
about to be" (Pre, vi, 608) which constitutes, for Wordsworth, human temporality. The coming of the waters, always approaching but never here, is a static movement of
poised violence. It is an emblem of the gap or interruption,
the distance between one sign and another, between signs
and what they signify, between now and the future, between life and death, in the ecstasies of finite human time.
The terror of a temporal predicament that one approaches

by fleeing from it, and in which one awakes from one terror to find oneself confronting the same elements still, in forms whose peacefulness only makes them more ominous, is admirably expressed in the final lines of Wordsworth's dream:

> I called after him aloud:
> He heeded not; but, with his twofold charge
> Still in his grasp, before me, full in view,
> Went hurrying o'er the illimitable waste,
> With the fleet waters of a drowning world
> In chase of him; whereat I waked in terror,
> And saw the sea before me, and the book,
> In which I had been reading, at my side.
>   (Pre, v, 133-140)

There is more to be said about the assembly of elements that enters into the end of the poet's dream. First, it may be asked, what, exactly, is a book of poetry or of fiction for Wordsworth? Death, time, imagination, the book, inscriptions or other stamped images—all are intertwined aspects of the originating act that brings fictions into the world by changing things into what they are not. Wordsworth later in Book v celebrates those storytellers who have charmed children, lovers, and all men and women through the ages. They are "dreamers" "forgers of daring tales," cruelly named "imposters" by the "ape / Philosophy" (Pre, v, 523-526). Such forgers create by the daring of the imagination's impostures that realm of literature in which each thing is remade into some other thing. In that remaking, a new space is created made of signs that are at once null and at the same time universal. This space of the imagination is "here, nowhere, there, and everywhere at once" (Pre, v, 533). The real sea the dreamer faces before and after he falls asleep becomes in his dream an apocalyptic sign, just as the Alpine scene in the passage of the crossing of the Simplon becomes "like workings of one mind, the features / Of the same face, blossoms upon one tree" (Pre, vi, 636-637). In the latter transformation, too—the change of woods, waterfalls, winds,

103

and rocks into mind, face, and blossom—the physical world becomes a book, a collection of signs, "Characters of the great Apocalypse, / The types and symbols of Eternity / Of first, and last, and midst, and without end" (Pre, vi, 638-640). Such eternities exist in the signs for them. They are eternities generated paradoxically out of finitude. Eternity is a self-sustaining temporal structure built by language over the abyss of death.

The projection of the basic patterns structuring human existence on the external world is made more explicit in several passages in Book vii of *The Prelude*. There the poet considers whether the "presence" may be objective, but concludes that it exists "as things that are, are not, / As the mind answers to them, or the heart / Is prompt, or slow, to feel" (Pre, vii, 669-671). A little before, after giving an example of his power to experience the external world as vision, as allegory, as "second-sight procession," Wordsworth affirms once more the mind's sovereign constructive power over things as they are: "Though reared upon the base of outward things, / Structures like these the excited spirit mainly / Builds for herself" (Pre, vii, 633, 650-652).[39] A book—a "Shakespeare," a "Milton," a "Wordsworth," as we call such volumes by a familiar metonymy—is the fragile record or reshaping on paper of the outline of one of those structures such chosen spirits have mainly built for themselves.

But why should those books be buried? The end of the poet's dream of the Arab presents one example of such a structure. It is a model of human temporality as it is interpreted by the excited spirit from the appearances of things. In the dream, human time is not only a hurrying away from death, which is a moving toward it, but also the representation of this structure in words. The book enters into the "building" itself as part of it. The representation is an inextricable part of what it represents, and the referent could not exist without the referrer, which is another

[39] See also Pre (1805), ii, 410-413, and Pre (1805), iii, 122-127.

way of saying that structures like these the excited spirit mainly builds for herself and builds of the building blocks of words or other signs. The "linguistic moment" here is the appearance of books as an integral part of the apocalyptic dream. The Arab hurries toward a burying of the books, which will confess to their death, but at the same time preserve them. This double movement is toward something always approaching, always "at hand," but never quite here.

In order for there to be poetry there must be distance between one sign and another, but what language says, in a characteristic turning back on itself, is this distance. The distance is both spatial and temporal. It is the expression of a temporal distance by way of spatial emblems. The distance between here and there figures the temporal distance between now and the coming apocalypse—always on the way but never yet here. Signs, language, the book, are essential instruments of the opening out of this gap. The death that gets spoken or written down in literature is not death itself. Death is as mute, signless, and senseless as a stone. The death that can be spoken is death as the finitude of human consciousness, death as a feature of linguistic structures, as what underlies, undermines, and determines human consciousness, human time, and manmade structures of signs—all three. Death is the gap between here and now and what the here and now point toward, between signifier and signified. This gap makes signs possible or, in the simultaneous emergence of all these elements, is generated by signs. Any printed poem means death, the imminent approach of death, but it is also dead. It is the corpse of its meaning, the spirit turned letter, mute marks on paper. The poem on the page is a dead body. It is, in the phrase Wordsworth borrows from an "ancient Philosopher" to describe a corpse in the "Essays upon Epitaphs," "the shell of the flown bird."[40] Like any dead body, a book

[40] William Wordsworth, "Essays upon Epitaphs," *Prose Works*, ed. W.J.B. Owen and Jane Worthington Smyser, II (Oxford: Clarendon Press, 1974),

must be given decent burial, which is why it is appropriate the Arab should bury the books. When a book has been buried it will become manifestly what it already is, a funerary inscription, both coffin or shrine for relics and the memorial inscription engraved on the monument above that coffin: "Poor earthly casket or immortal verse, / Shakespeare, or Milton, labourers divine!" (Pre, v, 164-165).

Any genuine poem—Shakespeare's sonnets, Milton's *Paradise Lost*, Wordsworth's *The Prelude*—tells man of death. It reminds him of his imminent danger of death. It is a prelude to death, but the book—poor earthly casket of immortal verse, traces of a vanished spirituality—also protects man from death by giving him a way to stamp his image on matter. All poems are in one way or another epitaphs. An epitaph may be inscribed on a rock. In its graven muteness it is an expression of man's finitude, of his share in physical nature, of his mortality. This mortality is man's identification at death with the indestructibility of nature, so paradoxically it is a kind of immortality. At the same time, the epitaph brings into existence in the carvings on the rock the human space of signs—here, nowhere, there, and everywhere at once. A structure of signs is at

---

p. 52. Gene Ruoff has suggested to me that the shell may be an appropriate emblem for poetry because, though it is stonelike in its hardness, it has been made by a living creature. A seashell is in fact the husk of a departed creature, which is Wordsworth's definition of a corpse. Like a book of poems, a shell is at once its maker's home, his most permanent creation, the indication of his immortality, and at the same time his casket or tomb. The association of body, stone, and tomb is at least as old as Plato, as a passage in the *Gorgias* will indicate:

Socrates: Then those who are in need of nothing are not rightly called happy.

Callicles: No, in that case stones and corpses would be supremely happy.

Socrates: Well, life as you describe it is a strange affair. I should not be surprised, you know, if Euripides was right when he said, "Who knows, if life be death, and death be life?" And perhaps we are actually dead, for I once heard one of our wise men say that we are now dead, and that our body [*soma*] is a tomb [*sema*] ... (*Gorgias* 492e-493a, trans. W. D. Woodhead, *The Collected Dialogues*, ed. cit., pp. 274-275).

once dead, the shell of the flown bird, and at the same time it is a survivor of that death. As such, it is able, as a stone or corpse never can be, to be revivified perpetually as long as there are men or women to read the inscription, to hear the voice from the inscribed stone, or the Ode, in passion uttered, from the shell. In this sense, poetry, unlike the poets who write it down, is immortal. This immortality is not the same as the immortality of matter, though it is carried by it. Each immortality is the counterpart of the other, its differential form, not its opposite.

The immortality of verse is its revelation of mortality. The Quixotic madness of the Arab in hurrying to bury the revelation as if it were a dead body is an exposure of that meaning, but it is exposed only so long as the burying remains something evermore about to be, a not-quite-yet, never a has-been. This never completed burial will be both a preservation and a renunciation, like that of Prospero when he buries his broken staff and drowns his book.[41] The burying will only reaffirm what happens when the mind inscribes itself in a book, recording in language one of those structures it builds mainly for itself. In such recording the mind confines itself to a poor earthly casket where it becomes, to adapt a striking phrase used in passing as a simile in Book VIII of *The Prelude*, "exposed, and lifeless as a written book" (Pre, VIII, 576). The same metaphor had already been used in Book III, where the poet speaks of all the books he did not read at Cambridge as "those long vistas, sacred catacombs, / Where mighty *minds* lie visibly entombed" (Pre, III, 341-342). In both cases the paradox is of a hiding away that is at the same time a making visible, an exposure, even an indecent exposure, apocalyptic in the etymological sense of revelation, unveiling, as if a corpse

[41] I owe this analogy to C. M. Hancher, Jr. The idea that burying the books is a means of preserving them was long ago expressed by De Quincey: "[H]is mission is to secure the two great interests of poetry and mathematics from sharing in the watery ruin" (*Collected Writings*, ed. cit., II, p. 269).

were to be left in the open, as in the *Antigone,* or put in a glass-covered coffin, as in Goethe's *Die Wahlverwandt-schaften,* or made by death helplessly open to the sky, as Lucy is in "A Slumber Did my Spirit Seal" when she joins the diurnal round of rocks and stones and trees.

The book both buries the mind and exposes it by a divine labor giving the mind immortality. For Wordsworth, the mind comes into existence, that is, moves out into the open, in its externalization in language. The book of earth, engraved with its "Characters of the great Apocalypse" (Pre, vi, 638), signs in earth and heaven made manifest, Shakespeare's, Milton's books, the book we hold in our hands when we read *The Prelude,* the pages of a critic's commentary, such as the one here—all are versions of the same book, its translation from place to place and from text to text. These books are all books of the dead, that is, books of those who have survived death in the replicas of life, as in the Egyptian prototype, *The Book of the Dead.*

Shakespeare, for example, needs no monument and no epitaph because his poetry is already his tombstone. Each poem as he writes it is another nail in his coffin. Each new poem commits his spirit once more to the realm of the dead letter. At the same time Shakespeare's work ensures his immortality. It gives him entrance into that library-mausoleum which will preserve his mind as long as there are books and men and women to read them. Each poem is implicitly posthumous and presupposes the vanishing of its author. The poet in writing his poems prefigures his death and writes his own epitaph. This is just what Milton said in the poem on Shakespeare that Wordsworth quotes the "Essays upon Epitaphs." The same poem was in his mind when he wrote the concluding lines of the dream of the Arab. These lines define Shakespeare's books and Milton's as "earthly caskets" of their "immortal verse" and affirm the poet's sympathy for the Arab's project of burying the books:

. . . yea, will I say,
Contemplating in soberness the approach
Of an event so dire, by signs in earth
Or heaven made manifest, that I could share
That maniac's fond anxiety, and go
Upon like errand. Oftentimes at least
Me hath such strong entrancement overcome,
When I have held a volume in my hand,
Poor earthly casket of immortal verse,
Shakespeare, or Milton, labourers divine!
(Pre, v, 156-165)

Wordsworth's dream of the Arab is a commentary on the lines by Milton alluded to here. It is an extension and permutation of the idea that the poet creates his own tombstone in writing his verse. This idea is affirmed in a poem by Milton that provides for Shakespeare the epitaph, the witness to his name, which the poem says Shakespeare does not need. Wordsworth's lines in turn are an epitaph upon an epitaph upon an epitaph, each text playing simultaneously the role of corpse and of epitaph upon a prior life of which it is the relic, the worthless shell, the dead body, so calling forth another epitaph in its turn. A modern commentary on Wordsworth's poem, such as the one here, enters into this chain of interpretations that both kill and give life to the texts of the past. Any explication buries the poem it unfolds under a new epitaph, folds it back up again, implicitly recognizing that the poem needs no epitaph but speaks for itself, with a voice that is both dead and alive. Each poem is a voice from the tomb that goes on though its speaker has long since died. It goes on speaking only if the later reader, poet, or critic gives it voice, keeps its fame and memory alive:

What needs my *Shakespear* for his honour'd Bones,
The labour of an age in piled Stones,
Or that his hallow'd reliques should be hid
Under a Star-ypointing *Pyramid*?

109

> Dear son of memory, great heir of Fame,
> What need'st thou such weak witness of thy name?
> Thou in our wonder and astonishment
> Hast built thy self a live-long Monument.
> ....
> And so Sepulcher'd in such pomp dost lie,
> That Kings for such a Tomb would wish to die.[42]

The Arab in his care for books displaces the care usually taken by father, husband, or lover for their beloved wives, children, or virgin loves. He will survive the books after he has buried them in the same way that the characters in so many of Wordsworth's poems have survived the deaths of those they love. They have survived by entering proleptically into the space beyond death that is literature. The proper way, for Wordsworth, of "taking in charge" what one most loves is to bury it. Having buried it, one must write its epitaph, outlive it by memorializing it in verse. The Arab lives on in Wordsworth's dream, beyond the apocalypse that threatens to engulf him, when that dream has been written down. The new poet's relation to the already existing poems—Wordsworth's relation to Milton or to Shakespeare, Milton's to Shakespeare, ours to all three—is the same as the relation of the poet to the Boy of Winander, or of Michael to his son, or of the heroine of "The Ruined Cottage" to her husband, or of Matthew to his daughter, or of the poet to Lucy. Wordsworth's poetry is an epitaph for the work of all the dead poets. That work is both prolonged in his own work and buried by it, as that earlier poetry was both his inspiration and at the same time the prophecy of his own death in poetry. In the same way the death of the Boy of Winander allows Wordsworth to experience his own death by anticipation and to write as his own survivor a poem that is his own epitaph. Only in

---

[42] "On *Shakespear*. 1630," lines 1-8, 15-16, *The Poetical Works of John Milton*, ed. Helen Darbishire (London: Oxford University Press, 1960), p. 418.

this way, by being both dead loved one and survivor of that death, can he hope to short-circuit the perpetually self-renewing structure of epitaph beyond epitaph beyond epitaph. Of course, even such a double poem calls forth more poems, more commentary, in defiance of its attempt to close the cycle by providing its own commentary, writing its own epitaph. The relation between survivor and the dead, so frequent a subject in Wordsworth's poetry, is the emblem of the relation between Wordsworth's poems and those previous poems, frail printed pages one may hold in one's hand or bury. The verse of Shakespeare or Milton prefigured Wordsworth's verse in the same way that the death of Lucy or of the Boy of Winander prefigured Wordsworth's death.

In a profoundly revealing act that recapitulates the sequence I have followed in the dream of the Arab and in other poems by Wordsworth, the poet took that stone which he had preserved from the builders (see note 25), set it up in a newly purchased field next to his garden at Rydal Mount, and composed for it an inscription. This epitaph for a dead stone calls attention to the stone as the material embodiment of the poem. It also uses the stone for its only appropriate purpose, that is, as the bearer of an epitaph that is in fact the poet's own epitaph composed for himself. The poem uses for the stone the "rest in peace" usually addressed to the corpse beneath the tombstone. The verses written for the stone are at once the anticipation of the poet's death and at the same time the affirmation of that immortality which all authentic poetry, for Wordsworth, attains.

> Under the shade of some Pollard Oaks, and on a green Terrace in that field, we have lived no small part of the long bright days of the summer gone by; and in a hazel nook of this favourite piece of ground is a Stone, for which I wrote one day the following serious Inscription, you will forgive its Egotism.

> In these fair Vales, hath many a tree
> At Wordsworth's suit been spared,
> And from the builder's hand this Stone,
> For some rude beauty of its own,
> Was rescued by the Bard;
> Long may it rest in peace! and here
> Perchance the tender-hearted
> Will heave a gentle sigh for him
> As One of the Departed.[43]

In the shift from *it* to *him* the poet himself becomes the stone on which his own epitaph is carved. When *it* becomes *him*, the poet becomes the stone or the stone the poet. The power and form of poetry, for Wordsworth, is indicated by this act of carving one's own epitaph on stone. Such an inscribing is both death-dealing and life-giving. It makes the poet himself into both immortal verse and memorial relic, as dead as any stone. That final displacement ensures, in a strange way, that the Bard will not become in fact "One of the Departed," but will appropriate the permanence and quasi-immortality of the stone. On the other hand, by confiding himself to the inscribed stone, by transferring himself into the space of literature, that is, into one of those structures the excited spirit builds mainly for itself, the poet has already departed. He gives himself that death he fears, in the most hyperbolic use of those conferring, abstracting, and modifying powers of the poet celebrated in the "Preface" of 1815. Those powers can assimilate a living man to a stone. The most extravagant and yet most appropriate use of these powers is for the poet to direct them against himself. The linguistic moment in Wordsworth is this transfer of the poet himself into language. In the constant displacement between the spiritual life this marking creates and its inertness as body, between shell in stone and stone in shell, the dream of the Arab, like all Wordsworth's best

---

[43] *The Letters of William and Dorothy Wordsworth*, ed. cit., ii, pp. 571-572.

poems, oscillates. This indetermination generates the power Wordsworth's poetry has to tease its reader out of thought and out of words. From this oscillation springs also the poem's power to move the reader-critic to add one more link in the chain of epitaphs.

CHAPTER THREE

Shelley

"The Triumph of Life" is so difficult a poem, conceptually, in its play of figures, and in its formal organization, that the reader needs all the help he can get in trying to understand it.[1] One form of help comes by seeing the poem, as many previous readers have seen it, as an interpretation

[1] Among studies of the poem Donald H. Reiman's *Shelley's "The Triumph of Life": A Critical Study, Illinois Studies in Language and Literature*, 55 (Urbana: University of Illinois Press, 1965) is the most important not only for the critical study it contains but for establishing the definitive text of the poem all future students of the poem must use. His bibliography lists all important studies of the poem prior to 1965. Valuable studies of "The Triumph of Life," or of Shelley's skepticism, or of Shelley generally, include: G. M. Matthews, "On Shelley's 'The Triumph of Life,' " *Studia Neophilologica* xxxiv, 1 (1962), 104-134; C. E. Pulos, *The Deep Truth: A Study of Shelley's Skepticism* (Lincoln: The University of Nebraska Press, 1954); Harold Bloom, "The Triumph of Life," *Shelley's Mythmaking* (New Haven: Yale University Press, 1959), pp. 220-275; Donald H. Reiman, "Shelley's 'The Triumph of Life': The Biographical Problem," *PMLA* lxxviii (December 1963), 536-550; Jerome J. McGann, "The Secrets of an Elder Day: Shelley after 'Hellas,' " *Keats' Shelley Journal* xv (Winter 1966), 25-41, and *ibid.*, "Shelley's Veils: A Thousand Images of Loveliness," *Romantic & Victorian*, ed. W. Paul Elledge and Richard L. Hoffman (Cranbury, New Jersey: Fairleigh Dickinson University Press, 1971), pp. 198-218; Meyer H. Abrams, *Natural Supernaturalism* (New York: W. W. Norton & Company, Inc., 1971), pp. 441-442; Earl R. Wasserman, *Shelley: A Critical Reading* (Baltimore: The Johns Hopkins Press, 1971), esp. chap. 1; John A. Hodgson, "The World's Mysterious Doom: Shelley's *The Triumph of Life*," *ELH* xlii, 4 (Winter 1975), 595-622; Edward Duffy, *Rousseau in England: The Context for Shelley's Critique of the Enlightenment* (Berkeley: University of California Press, 1979); Paul de Man, "Shelley Disfigured," *Deconstruction and Criticism* (New York: The Seabury Press, 1979), pp. 39-73; Lloyd Abbey, *Destroyer and Preserver: Shelley's Poetic Skepticism* (Lincoln: University of Nebraska Press, 1980); Lisa M. Steinman, "From 'Alastor' to 'The Triumph of Life': Shelley on the Nature and Source of Linguistic Pleasure," *Romanticism Past and Present* vii, 1 (Winter 1983), 23-36.

of the work of Wordsworth, the first poet in my sequence of eight. In my attempt to identify the particular form the linguistic moment takes in this poem, however, I shall focus on the relation of Shelley's work to that of Rousseau. Rousseau is after all an actual personage in "The Triumph of Life," which Wordsworth is not, though of course it has been possible to see that as a covering of the real influence. In the other direction, help may be gained by identifying the way Thomas Hardy, one of the poets discussed later in this book, read Shelley. If Shelley was a brilliant reader of Rousseau and Wordsworth, as one can tell from his poems more than from explicit comments he made, Shelley in his turn was read, often more subtly than one might expect, by Browning, by Hardy, and by Yeats, among my eight poets.

Hardy's work, as is well known, is so inhabited by echoes of Shelley's work that it might almost be defined as from beginning to end a large-scale interpretation of Shelley, one of the best and strongest we have. It might perhaps at first appear to be ascribing to Shelley more idealism than he had and then asserting as its own a dark vision of the triumph of life that was already Shelley's. That Hardy knew what Shelley was saying, however, is suggested by the ironic appositeness of the explicit citations from Shelley in his work. When the context of the fragment from Shelley is superimposed on the context into which it is grafted in Hardy, it tends to undermine the idealistic mystification of the character to whom it is applied. The character's mistaken belief is defined as a linguistic error. An example is the passage from *The Revolt of Islam* applied to Henchard in *The Mayor of Casterbridge*. The passage from Shelley works with the narrator's own dismantling of Henchard's self-interpretation to affirm that what seems to Henchard to be an externally existing malign transcendent force is only, in Shelley's phrase, a "shade from his own soul upthrown." It is an error in interpretation, a mistaken reading of inner for outer, just as in "The Triumph of Life" some of the

115

victims of "Life" "mournfully within the gloom / Of their own shadow walked, and called it death . . ." (lines 58-59).[2]

Hardy's dialogue with Shelley is reflected in the ascription to the characters in the novels of an attitude that corresponds to a common misreading of Shelley as an idealist, perhaps an error Hardy had encountered in others or had initially made himself, while the narrator of the novels reads Shelley correctly as already, even in early works like *The Revolt of Islam*, a Romantic skeptic who saw man as the dupe of self-generated signs, not as the victim of gods either dark or bright. The dialogue between Hardy and Shelley is repeated by a conflict within Hardy's own writing between mystified and demystified ways of interpreting life. That dialogue in turn is analogous (the exact force of the word *analogous* here would need to be interrogated) to the dialogues within Shelley's own work, for example, that between "Rousseau" and the primary "I" in "The Triumph of Life." The dialogue re-forms itself, once more, in the conflicts among warring interpretations of Shelley or of Hardy, for example, in the disagreement between Harold Bloom and Meyer Abrams about the meaning of "The Triumph of Life."[3]

[2] I have throughout this chapter cited the text of "The Triumph of Life" from Donald H. Reiman's *Shelley's "The Triumph of Life": A Critical Study*. Other poems by Shelley are cited from *Shelley's Poetical Works*, ed. Thomas Hutchinson, corrected by G. M. Matthews (London, Oxford, New York: Oxford University Press, 1970).

[3] "Many readers," writes Bloom, "want to believe that the poem would have ended in some affirmation, had it been completed, but there is little in the poem to encourage such speculations. . . . What Yeats called the *antithetical* quest, undertaken against the natural man and his human affections, which Shelley had begun to pursue in *Alastor*, here attains its shattering climax. The best (and most restrained) statement of a more hopeful reading of the poem can be found in M. H. Abrams' *Natural Supernaturalism*" (*Romantic Poetry and Prose*, ed. Harold Bloom and Lionel Trilling, *The Oxford Anthology of English Literature* [New York: Oxford University Press, 1973], p. 478). Abrams' statement (*Natural Supernaturalism*, pp. 441-442), even if it were given in full here, would hardly appear to constitute a *reading*. It is more a characteristically humane and

Dialogue, war, palimpsest, grafting, apocalyptic or ana-calyptic unveiling, layer on layer, inhabitation by ghostly guests or echoes—these are figures for that presence of the work of one poet within the work of another. This presence is most visible in actual citation. It may perhaps be most comprehensively figured in the reversible relation of par-asite and host.[4] Is the later text parasitical on the earlier one, or is it the other way around? Does *The Mayor of Cas-terbridge* feed parasitically on *The Revolt of Islam*, or does it serve as the host maintaining in a borrowed life the citation from *The Revolt of Islam*? The relation seems to work both ways at once.

---

generous, but in this case at least, interpretatively unfounded, hope, like that of Hardy's darkling thrush ("Some blessed Hope, whereof he knew / And I was unaware."). In fact, the next section of *Natural Supernaturalism*, following the paragraphs on "The Triumph of Life," begins: "As for hope . . ." The statement by Abrams in the headnote to "The Triumph of Life" in the *Norton Anthology*, though in good part word for word the same as that in *Natural Supernaturalism*, is longer and fuller: ". . . although we lack Shelley's answer to the question posed at the end of the fragment—'then, what is Life?'—there is no definitive evidence that he planned to depart from the precedent of all his other long poems, in which he allowed some scope of possibility for redeeming life by the cardinal Shelleyan virtues; and above all by . . . love . . . . *The Triumph of Life* does not sound like the voice of a defeated poet at the end of his tether, but of a poet who, just attaining the height of his powers, was making a masterful new beginning, when fate slit the thin spun life" (*The Norton Anthology of English Literature*, rev.ed., ed. M. H. Abrams *et al.*, II [New York: W. W. Norton & Company, Inc., 1968], p. 472). The last word here has a strangely ironic clang if one thinks of how Shelley defines "life," including his own, or at any rate that of the speaker of the poem, in "The Triumph of Life." I said Abrams here is characteristically humane and generous. The sentences are also characteristic of Abrams in their reductive rhetoric ("defeated poet at the end of his tether") addressed against the view opposing his own. The putting in question of transcendent grounds for human values is not necessarily "nihilistic" or "defeatist." It may be a form of exuberant cre-ative joy, as it is in fact for Shelley.

[4] For this figure in Shelley, see my "The Critic as Host," in *Deconstruction and Criticism*, pp. 215-253. For the word *anacalyptic*, see Michael Ferber, "Coleridge's 'Anacalyptic' Blake: An Exegesis," *Modern Philology* LXXVI, 2 (November 1978), 189-193.

The context in *The Mayor of Casterbridge* in which *The Revolt of Islam* is cited has to do with love, with narcissism, and, obliquely, with incest, as all of Hardy's work, in its long dialogue with Shelley, has to do. Another example of this would be *The Well-Beloved*, perhaps of all Hardy's novels the one most directly grappling with Shelley, from its epigraph, again from *The Revolt of Islam*, on to the two endings in the two versions of the novel.[5] In *The Mayor of Casterbridge*, Henchard, just before he wanders off into the countryside to die, the volcanic energy of his demand on life burned out at last, stands at the door of Elizabeth-Jane's wedding party watching the daughter who is no true daughter of his. He watches her dance not with her bridegroom, Farfrae, but with Newson, her real father. The latter has displaced Henchard in her filial affection. It is at this moment that Henchard stands "like a dark ruin, 'obscured by the shade from his own soul upthrown.' "[6]

The rest of the passage in Shelley suggests that it is not only Henchard's assumption that he has been the victim of a malign external force that is a projection. The whole pattern of his loving, forming and re-forming itself anew throughout his life with different women, and with men too—with Susan, with Farfrae, with Elizabeth-Jane—in a constantly self-destroying compulsion, has been a form of narcissism. It has been a love for his own face in the mirror. He has made an impossible attempt to love himself as other and to engender himself, or to engender another on the basis of a relation to himself. "What is that Power?" asks the heroine of *The Revolt of Islam*. (*Laon and Cythna*, the first version of *The Revolt of Islam*, reads more directly, "What then is God?") The answer is that the evil of Christianity is a narcissistic reflection, one's own face in the glass:

[5] See my "*The Well-Beloved*: The Compulsion to Stop Repeating," in *Fiction and Repetition* (Cambridge, Mass.: Harvard University Press, 1982), pp. 147-175.

[6] I have discussed this episode and its relation to Shelley in *Thomas Hardy: Distance and Desire* (Cambridge, Mass.: The Belknap Press of Harvard University Press, 1970), pp. 148-150.

Some moon-struck sophist stood
Watching the shade from his own soul upthrown
Fill Heaven and darken Earth, and in such mood
The Form he saw and worshipped was his own,
His likeness in the world's vast mirror shown.
(lines 3244-3248)

Belief in a God of wrath is for Shelley a form of self-worship. It is self-destructive self-love. Can the metaphorical equation be reversed to define erotic love as a self-destroying form of theological projection? Just this is done in one of the most powerfully negative passages in "The Triumph of Life." Just as the epigraph for Hardy's *The Well-Beloved* ("one shape of many names") takes a passage that in Shelley describes the evil power, "God," and transfers it to name that phantom beloved projected by the hero into the various women he desires, so in "The Triumph of Life" the systematic description of human life, in religion, in politics, and in social intercourse, as universally the projection of "shadows" (the word is a key one in the poem) is given one of its darkest expressions in its application to sexual love. The "maidens & youths" dancing wildly in the train of the triumphal car of Life are like moths attracted to a fire, except that each member of each pair of lovers is both moth and flame. Their mutual incandescence is generated by proximity. The lovers do not need to touch to be ignited. Each needs only to enter, like a meteor, into the atmosphere of the beloved. Moreover, this burning is invisible. It is a kind of dark light:

[The lovers] now recede, and now
Bending within each other's atmosphere

Kindle invisibly; and as they glow
Like moths by light attracted & repelled,
Oft to new bright destruction come & go.
(lines 150-154)

If proximity brings a dark erotic glow, touching is mutual destruction, like that of particle and anti-particle in twen-

119

tieth-century physics, or, in Shelley's own images, like two
clouds colliding and destroying one another in a valley
thunderstorm, or like the impact of wave and shore that
leaves behind only foam as remnant: "nor other trace I find
/ But as of foam after the Ocean's wrath / Is spent upon
the desert shore" (lines 162-164).

The pattern applied here to erotic love is the pattern of
"The Triumph of Life" as a whole. It is repeated over and
over with different materials throughout the poem and
throughout the sad history it describes. In each repetition
two elements confront one another. The pair seem to be
opposites, as of male and female, darkness and light, dream
and waking, vision and reality, passive and active, figurative
and literal language, sight and sound, and so on. In fact,
the members of each pair are differentiated versions of one
another, like Narcissus in love with his twin sister, or with
his own image in the pool. When the two meet they annihilate one another. On the rhetorical level this may be
called "self-deconstruction." It is the creation of a linguistic
aporia that both affirms and denies at the same time and
so is impossible to formulate in a single determinate meaning.

As soon as something can be seen and therefore named,
it must be seen and named according to antitheses. These
appear to be true oppositions naming ontological differences and generating the progressions of dialectical thought
or dialectical progressions in history. To be seen at all, to
be distinguishable as an "idea," in the etymological sense
of a perceptible pattern, a thing must combine light and
shadow. The "shape all light" who appears to Rousseau in
the penultimate vision of the poem is a nonsensical oxymoron. A "shape all light" has no shape and is therefore
invisible. The necessity of combining light and shadow in
anything visible is matched by the necessity of speaking of
anything that appears under the sun and on the stage of
history according to binary oppositions.

These oppositions cannot be made the basis for progressive movement, either in thought or in "real history." Each pair is made only of different modes of the same thing. They collapse into that same thing. "Action" and "suffering," for example, seem to be opposites. In fact action is suffering, suffering action. Both are equally victims of Life the conqueror. On the other hand (in another version of this thinking and naming according to an either/ or), those who refuse either to act or to suffer, either the action which is suffering or the suffering which is action, disappear into the undifferentiated light that is the source of both. In either case they vanish.

Thinking and naming by oppositions makes a non-advancing repetitive series, like the chain of scenes in the "The Triumph of Life," or like the long woeful pageant of history as the poem presents it, or like certain passages in the poem where the language of the speaker breaks down into a stuttering series of pairs that seem to be governed more by sound similarities than by rigor of thought. Such a chain seems capable of continuing indefinitely in a sequence of locutions taking the form "*A* or *B*." This form of speech or writing is like a linguistic tic in which the poet has become trapped. It can be broken only by an abrupt hiatus in the poem. The series is not getting anywhere, and yet it could continue indefinitely.

The most striking example of this comes early in the poem, in a long sentence in the past tense describing the captives of Life. The sentence finally ends with two periods of ellipsis. Then the language begins again in the present tense. It is as though the poet had drawn himself up, paused, broken the sterile repeating pattern, and then started over again. He starts again to give the most extreme version of the opposites that are no opposites and destroy one another in their confrontation: the vision of erotic love as like two clouds meeting in tumult. A long citation is necessary to demonstrate the self-perpetuating movement of Shelley's language here:

                    . . . where'er

The chariot rolled a captive multitude
    Was driven; all those who had grown old in power
Or misery,—all who have their age subdued,

    By action or by suffering, and whose hour
Was drained to its last sand in weal or woe,
    So that the trunk survived both fruit & flower;

All those whose fame or infamy must grow
    Till the great winter lay the form & name
Of their own earth with them forever low,

    All but the sacred few who could not tame
Their spirits to the Conqueror, but as soon
    As they had touched the world with living flame

Fled back like eagles to their native noon,
    Or those who put aside the diadem
Of earthly thrones or gems, till the last one

    Were there;—for they of Athens & Jerusalem
Were neither mid the mighty captives seen
    Nor mid the ribald crowd that followed them

Or fled before . . .
    (lines 118-137)

This extraordinary passage, the reader can see, is the prisoner of its binary oppositions. Each pair vanishes as it is formulated, only to be replaced by a new one, which vanishes once more before the levelling power of Life. Power or misery, action or suffering, weal or woe, fruit & flower (*or* and *and* coming here oddly to the same thing, since the *or* is not a true dialectical antithesis), fame or infamy, form & name, the sacred few or those who resigned thrones or gems; the captives or the crowd who followed them or fled before—the passage generates itself as a continual chain of melting antitheses. What, for example, is the difference between a thing's form and its name? This is one of the chief issues of the poem. Does naming give form, or does form precede name, or is form another kind of name, the seeing of the undifferentiated as a sign—seeing, for example, the nameless light as a "shape all light," hence as a person, then as an allegorical sign? In the end the grand opposition between those who succumb to Life and those who do not comes to the same thing in the vanishing of distinctions into that undifferentiated light of a noon which is both life and death and which obliterates both forms and names at once.

It is impossible to tell, for example, whether or not Rousseau is a victim of Life. On the one hand, he has not, like those "of Athens & Jerusalem," returned like an eagle to his native noon. He has succumbed to corruption, a corruption that he blames on the bad quality of the food or fuel this world has supplied: ". . . if the spark with which Heaven lit my spirit / Earth had with purer nutriment supplied / Corruption would not now thus much inherit / Of what was once Rousseau—nor this disguise / Stained that within which still disdains to wear it" (lines 201-205). The corruption caused by bad ignition or bad digestion, so to speak, has created a mask that is the form in which Rousseau's divine spark must appear on earth. He appears as shadow or as sign rather than as unstained light. This exemplifies the general law of invisible light and visible shadowy mask of that light that governs Life for Shelley.

On the other hand, Rousseau's spark, stained in its earthly appearance though it has been, has had an incendiary power. It has had a profound effect on history and on culture by determining the thought patterns and the patterns of political domination in those who have read him. "If I have been extinguished," says Rousseau, "yet there rise / A thousand beacons from the spark I bore" (lines 206-207). Rousseau's writings have had political and personal power, even power to create suffering, just because of Rousseau's contamination by Life. Because of that contamination his "works" are not abstract but a form of action, an embodied deed:

123

"I / have suffered what I wrote, or viler pain!— / And so my words were seeds of misery— / Even as the deeds of others" (lines 278-281).

Nevertheless this determination of thought, institutions, and distribution of power is, as the rest of the poem makes clear, not made by the light itself but by the fictional figures that light takes when it manifests itself on earth. Rousseau's effect on history is the evidence that he has succumbed to Life.

On the other hand, again, Rousseau distinguishes himself from those common anarchs, demagogues, and sages, "Voltaire, / Frederic, & Kant, Catherine, & Leopold" (lines 235-236). The latter have been defeated by Life the conqueror, but Rousseau—at least so he says—has been defeated by himself, by the incompatibility between his desires and any finite object for those desires: "I was overcome / By my own heart alone, which neither age / Nor tears nor infamy nor now the tomb / Could temper to its object" (lines 240-243).

On the other hand, once more and finally, Rousseau describes himself as having plunged into the "thickest billows of the living storm" of Life and as having "bared [his] bosom to the clime / Of that cold light, whose airs too soon deform" (lines 466-468). He was, it seems, after all a victim of Life, like the others.

Back and forth Rousseau oscillates in his self-interpretation between saying he has succumbed to Life and saying he has not. This oscillation, I am suggesting, derives from an irreducible ambiguity in the concept of Life. Life, for Shelley, is both the opposite of the light of "Heaven" and, at the same time, not its opposite but another form of it. Turning toward the sun and turning toward the cold light of Life come to the same thing in the end. Either way you will have had it. You will have had it according to distinctions that are not real differences, but different forms of the same. The general formula for this "same" is that whatever exists must exist in the form of antithetical oppositions that are not true opposites and therefore cannot be constructively synthesized. One comprehensive formulation of this universal law is made by the poet after his vision of Napoleon: "And much I grieved to think how power & will / In opposition rule our mortal day— / And why God made irreconcilable / Good & the means of good" (lines 228-231). Those who have the will to do good do not have the power. Those with the power, like Napoleon, do not by any means use it for good, though power and will are not really opposites. Will is always a will to power, though it is efficacious only if it is a will to destructive and self-destructive power, as in the case of Napoleon.

This uncertainty—distinguishing power from will, for example, but not allowing them to be seen as true antitheses—determines that when any two "opposites" (which are not true opposites but the same in the other) meet, their annihilation, each of the other, leaves a residue. Something too little or too much on one side or on the other makes the pair an imperfect fit, and so their vanishing leaves a trace. This remnant is the true triumph of Life, not the annihilation that puts the lovers beyond their suffering, snaps "the fiery band which held / Their natures" (lines 157-158). The remnant is Aphrodite's foam, the trace on the shore, a genetic pattern, sperm, or seed that starts the process all over again in another generation and with new elements. These once more seem opposites but are mirror images. They interact once more in a dance of love leading to mutual annihilation. This act or passion once more does not quite come out right and so once more leaves a new remainder, more foam on the shore generating a new cycle, and so on, ad infinitum, wave after wave.

The extraordinary pace and verve of "The Triumph of Life" is the rapid formation and destruction of ever new versions of this pattern. The process moves so fast in the poem that the pattern itself becomes visible. It emerges as something that transcends any particular elements that may enter into it. The pattern has the power to annihilate them all but not the power to annihilate itself. This pattern is what Shelley calls "Life." The darkest aspect of the triumph of Life is that Life cannot die. "Let them pass," cries the poet, after his vision of all "The Wise, / The great, the unforgotten: they who wore / Mitres & helms & crowns, or wreathes of light, / Signs of thought's empire over thought" (lines 208-211)—Napoleon, Voltaire, Frederic, and Kant, Catherine, and Leopold. The poet wishes these great hierarchs to vanish because they are evidence that history is not progressive. It can only appear to be progressive if all predecessors are wholly forgotten:

> "the world & its mysterious doom
>
> Is not so much more glorious than it was
>   That I desire to worship those who drew
> New figures on its false & fragile glass
>
> "As the old faded."
> (lines 244-248)

To which Rousseau, playing Virgil to Shelley's Dante in this new dream vision—repetition, with a difference, of Dante's vision in *The Divine Comedy*—answers, in a formulation crucial for understanding the form of the poem and its vision of human history:

> —"Figures ever new
> Rise on the bubble, paint them how you may,
>   We have but thrown, as those before us threw,
>
> "Our shadows on it as it past away."
> (lines 248-251)

Figures is a key word here, in its multiple meanings, along with *shadows*. The "world" is the phenomenal field of sensation and perception within which each individual lives and sees, actor and spectator at once in the *theatrum mundis*. This world is a "false & fragile glass." It is a colorless screen, without character. It is false to boot. The "world" is an illusion or fabrication. This illusion, moreover, is constantly passing away, so fragile is it, to be replaced by a new bubble.

The falseness of the bubble derives from the fact that it is a projection blown outward by men and women in their collective living together. It is thrown out as a neutral glass or screen which seems to be the given condition of their world, something already there, objectively. On this screen they "paint" the shadowy figures of their successive ideologies. Background and figure are equally "false & fragile." Each ideology is subjective in origin. Each therefore constantly changes. It dies and is born anew in a different form. However carefully these figures are constructed ("paint them how you may"), they have no possibility of permanence. There are three reasons for this. Each ideology contains the seeds of its own self-destruction in its internal contradictions. As a result, each rapidly consumes itself. All are in any case subjective projections, shadows, not something made of "real" materials. The screen on which they are projected is evanescent too. Even if they had more substantiality and staying power than they do, each would vanish in the perpetual passing away of the screen.

Shelley's figure in "The Triumph of Life" of the bubble or glass painted over with shadowy figures is quite different from the apparently similar and better known image at the end of "Adonais":

> Life, like a dome of many-coloured glass,
> Stains the white radiance of Eternity,
> Until Death tramples it to fragments . . .
> (lines 462-464)

The version of this figure in "The Triumph of Life" also defines "Life" as a dome of many-colored glass. The bubble in "The Triumph," however, is a collective entity, constantly self-renewing, not able to be shattered by the death of one man, whereas in "Adonais" an individual death—for example, the death of John Keats—tramples the dome of many-colored glass to fragments. In "The Triumph"

127

death is part of life and the two together, the one entity made of both, cannot die. There is no immediate reference to the "white radiance of Eternity" in "The Triumph." The image of a luminous and undifferentiated Eternity does appear elsewhere in "The Triumph," in the figure of the sun, which opens the poem, in the description of the "sacred few" who did not tame their spirits to the Conqueror Life, but "Fled back like eagles to their native noon" (line 131), and in the attack on Popes Gregory and John and their ilk, on Roman Catholicism generally as a world power. The popes are defined as shadows eclipsing and quenching the "true sun" of God. The role of the figure of the sun in "The Triumph of Life" remains to be interrogated in detail, but it may be said now that one effect of the poem is to deconstruct the notion affirmed in "Adonais," the notion that eternity lies behind the glass, while at the same time reaffirming it. This alternation is the "life" or poetic vitality of "The Triumph of Life." The "sacred few," "they of Athens & Jerusalem," are no doubt Socrates and Jesus. Socrates and Jesus are figures who exist in literature. They exist as personages in texts composed by others, not even in texts composed by themselves. The idea that they come from some transcendent light and return unstained to it is an affirmation of the texts that create their images, the Platonic dialogues, the New Testament Gospels. These texts are examples of those figures projected on the false and fragile glass. Like all human fabrications they are without certain authenticity. The idea that light is a figure for a transcendent source is, moreover, explicitly dismantled throughout the main action of "The Triumph of Life," even though it is also intermittently reasserted.

Each successive thinker, politician, king, poet, or philosopher, including Plato and the Gospel-makers, projects illusory shadows, generated within himself, on that illusory screen, the world, in a constant series, that has no teleology. No one of them makes the "world" "much more glorious than it was." What is "mysterious" about the "doom" of the "world" is that it does not seem in any way to be oriented toward a goal. It is a random series of false projections on a false screen. These projections seem almost instantly to die of their internal conflicts, to be replaced by the next figures painted on the bubble by the next man who wields thought's empire over thought.

The projected shadows on the screen are figures in the triple sense of being at once legible signs, projections like those shadows in Plato's cave, and metaphorical substitutions. These figures generate a rhetorical play of tropes ungoverned by a literal base. They make a chain of dislocations without identifiable beginning, end, or base. The triumph of life is therefore for Shelley the triumph of language, the prolonged inescapable persistence of what I call the linguistic moment.

"The Triumph of Life" ends with a question by the poet and Rousseau's fragmentary answer to the question. This question the poem has both repeatedly asked and definitively answered, in spite of the incompletion of the poem. To the poet's question, "Then what is life?" Rousseau answers with a sentence broken off in the middle. The broken sentence, the one Shelley did not live to complete, is perhaps the best answer of all. It is a sentence whose ending no reader can ever know, not by the most extravagant effort of extrapolation, emendation, or reconstruction: "Happy those for whom the fold / Of" (lines 547-548). What the reader has, however, he can interpret. He is given the word *fold*, put emphatically at the end of a line. The word hovers between its alternative contradictory meanings. It can mean a safe enclosure, on the one hand, as in *sheepfold*, and it can mean division, seam, line of juncture, on the other, as in the *fold* or *folding* of a book. The reader is also given an implied opposition between happiness and unhappiness. Whatever Shelley was going to say, it would have separated the sheep from the goats in this fold, the happy from the unhappy. The reader knows, finally, that the poem ends with one half of a locution that is a fold in itself: "the fold

/ Of [something or other]," "the A of B." This syntactical pattern, folding one thing back on another thing and superimposing them, is one form of a figure juxtaposing in one way or another two things, opposing them, apposing them, placing one inside the other, as within a fold or envelope, or one around the other as a fence or frame, or dividing one from the other, as by a fold or fissure, in any case doubling one thing against another but separating them at the same time. This figure organizes "The Triumph of Life" from beginning to end, both in its fine detail, and in its large-scale repetitive form.

The elements of that pattern are a placing of one thing against another thing, which composes a self-destroying figurative substitution of A for B and of B for A. This interchange is incarnated in the body and spirit of one man after another in world history: lovers, poets, philosophers, emperors, kings, politicians, popes. These were thinkers all, thinkers whose thoughts had power, a power born of their incarnation. It was an affective power. Action is generated by passion, passion by action, in one important version of the folding that runs through the poem. This embodied figurative exchange projects itself from one man or woman after another on the false and fragile glass of the world, in shadows that are figures of what already are figures. The outward flow of projection doubles the inward play of substitution. That activity of projection exhausts itself through its own internal contradictions and in the effects of its external expressions as erotic love, as social institution, as political state, or as religious or philosophical system. The gamut of self-consuming human forms leaves in each case the remnant that initiates a new sequence, now C folded on D, replacing and repeating with a difference A on B, or perhaps now C on B, in a displacement of B from secondary to primary. This new folding creates a new projective power that destroys once more both itself and those whom it enslaves or enchants.

Affirmation of the fact that life is repetition is given early in the poem, in the poet's sense of *déjà vu* just before his vision of the triumphal car. That his situation and the scene—mountain slope, flowing stream, and waking visionary—is repeated later on for Rousseau (lines 308-320) tells the reader that this repetition occurs not only within a single life but from life to life. It recurs in a perpetual transmigration bringing the same situation and the same pattern of elements back with a difference, again and again, for the same person and for different persons. The separateness of the self, along with the uniqueness of each moment of time and of each experience within that moment, is challenged by this experience of what is seen as having always already been seen before:

> . . . I knew
>
> That I had felt the freshness of that dawn,
> Bathed in the same cold dew my brow & hair
> And sate as thus upon that slope of lawn
>
> Under the self same bough, & heard as there
> The birds, the fountains & the Ocean hold
> Sweet talk in music through the enamoured air.
> (lines 33-39)

Of what are all these repeated projections figures? What, for Shelley, is the base, the origin, or the goal that controls this internal and external play of substitutions? This question arises inevitably in the reader's mind as he works his way into the poem and through it. It is one meaning of the repeated question, "Then, what is Life?" It is present in the recurrent question in the poem about the origin and end of the series that makes up the poem. "Whence camest thou & whither goest thou?" the poet asks Rousseau, "How did thy course begin . . . & why?" (lines 296-297). Later Rousseau asks almost the same question of the luminous figure he encounters, that figure usually thought to personify Wordsworthian Nature. He substitutes *where* for the poet's *whither*: "If, as it doth seem, / Thou comest from the realm without a name, / Into this valley of perpetual dream, / Shew whence I came, and where I am, and why— / Pass not away upon the passing stream" (lines 395-399).

The "realm" without a name" would seem to be that transcendent region, source, end, and ground of all in the phenomenal world of "Life," in which Shelley as an idealist is supposed to have believed. If this realm cannot be named directly, if it has no literal name, it can perhaps be named in figure. It is given once in the poem the traditional figurative name, *God*, but the pervasive figure for it is the sun, or, more generally, light. The sun seems to be the prime representative of the fathering power governing the whole sequence of "Life" forms, while remaining safely outside their play. Or perhaps the sun *is* that power. No conceptual and figurative motif could be more traditional, nor more traditional the equivocation as to whether the sun is the power or a sign for it.

What then are Shelley's figures, figures of? What is their base or common measure? The answers to these questions can be given only by interrogating the play of light and shadow that is the structural form organizing "The Triumph of Life" from its beginning to its broken ending. It is clear what the two possible answers are. One would take literally Shelley's belief in a transcendent realm without a name, beyond the interchanges and substitutions of names. This would make Shelley an idealist. The other answer would see the words *sun*, *light*, and *God* as names like the others, subject as much as their opposites, *shadow*, *star*, or *Life*, to the play of substitutions. The "realm without a name" would then be, for Shelley, not a pre-existing, pre-linguistic ground that controls the whole series, but a phantasmal effect of the interplay of its elements. This would make Shelley a skeptic, or even a nihilist. This opposition is the traditional one in the criticism of Shelley.

The question might be posed in terms of that figure of parasite and host already introduced above. Is there somewhere a presiding host, "patron of origins," in Wallace Stevens' phrase? This would be a nameless and invisible king whose visible vicar is, in Stevens' phrase again, that "furiously burning father-fire,"[7] the sun. Such a host would be a supervising master of the revels or lord of the tourneys, overseer of the polemical combat of terms and elements, which he watches occurring far below his dais. These terms and elements would be secondary, subsidiary. They would be representative at best, parasitical guests at a feast in which they eat and are eaten by their mirroring counterparts. On the other hand, there may be no such host above the battle, the game, the feast. Only the terms and elements may exist, in a constantly moving interchange in which "host" or "patron" is a position, a function in a system of displacements. In such a system each element exists only in terms of its difference from its counterpart. In this brotherbattle any element may change roles with its "opposite," since the role depends on its placing and not on anything intrinsic to the element itself. There would be in such a system no host without parasite or guest, but host and guest might change places, host becoming guest and guest, host, as their common etymology suggests.

Only a closer interrogation of the text of "The Triumph of Life" will make possible a critical discrimination between these possibilities and a decision between them, putting each in the right fold. Or will it? That remains to be seen.

"The Triumph of Life" begins with a splendidly exuberant and rapid-paced description of a sunrise in the Apennines. The first line of the poem contains a fold, the doubling of an *as*. The problematic status of this *as* raises at the beginning the question that remains open through the long chain of similar doublings that makes up the poem. The word *similar* here is another form of the *as*. It raises the same questions. What is the exact force of the *as* in the

[7] "Patron of origins" is from line 88 of "A Primitive Like an Orb," *The Collected Poems of Wallace Stevens* (New York: Alfred A. Knopf, Inc., 1954), p. 443. "Furiously burning father-fire" is from line 12 of "The Red Fern," *ibid.*, p. 365.

opening sentence of the poem? What is the nature of the analogy between this doubling and the other similar analogies throughout the poem? Is the sun really a spirit or is this only a poetic fancy, a way of speaking born of those dark thoughts the poet has had by starlight? What justifies seeing the sun as a superhuman person and on the basis of this initial personification spinning out all the other personifications that make up the verbal fabric of the poem? "The Triumph of Life" all hangs on the fold of the *as*:

> Swift as a spirit hastening to his task
>   Of glory & of good, the Sun sprang forth
> Rejoicing in his splendour, & the mask
>
>   Of darkness fell from the awakened Earth.
>   (lines 1-4)

The opening simile becomes immediately a metaphorical personification without the qualification of the *as*. The sun springs and rejoices. It is spoken of, apparently literally, as a "he." The figure personifying the sun (if it is a "figure" in the usual sense) is continued through the first twenty lines of the poem in a series of further figures personifying the various aspects of nature that are "awakened" by the sun. The figurative structure here is complex. It is more the superimposition of several different simultaneously developing figures than the deployment of a single *as* structure. The sun is like a king rejoicing in his own splendor, sufficient unto himself. At the same time, the sun is like a spirit. This suggests something more or less than human, not quite a human being as such. A spirit is disembodied and aerial, perhaps like Ariel. Moreover, this "spirit" is not so much sovereign as, like Ariel, or like the spirit in *Comus*, subject to a higher master who has laid on him a task. The sun is both a king and a dauphin, both the light and a vicar of a higher Light, the Light of the World. In the theological metaphor that becomes explicit as the passage develops, the sun is both a father and a son, both God and Christ.

If the earth is subject to the sun, the sun is slave in his turn, in a concatenation characteristic of this poem. The sun plays the same role in relation to a higher power as the earth plays in relation to it.

If the sun is both a personified sovereign and the mediator of a higher power, his relation to earth is multiple in a different way. It must be described in an overlapping of different incompatible metaphors. When the mask of darkness is withdrawn it reveals a person or persons, an "awakened Earth." The relation between this personified earth and the sun is described in a quadruple metaphor. It is simultaneously like the relation between God and worshipper, like that between despotic ruler and the people, like that between father and child, and like that between lover and beloved.

The snow-covered mountains are "smokeless altars," the ocean's early morning activity is an "Orison," the birdsong is a "matin lay," the exhaling of scent by the flowers in the warmth of dawn is the swinging of little burning censers, and all nature is a vast cathedral of worshippers engaged in a sacramental activity adoring the sun.

At the same time the sun is a father, but also a taskmaster, something of a tyrant, as W. B. Yeats said.[8] The work he imposes on his subjects is something that he has first taken upon himself from some higher power, as Christ took upon himself the world's burdens but then imposes on all men the task of becoming God-worthy or God-like through the imitation of Christ. The sun is both Father and Son, both tyrant and slave:

> And in succession due, did Continent,
>
> Isle, Ocean, & all things that in them wear
> The form & character of mortal mould
> Rise as the Sun their father rose, to bear

---

[8] W. B. Yeats, "The Philosophy of Shelley's Poetry," *Essays and Introductions* (London: Macmillan & Co., Ltd., 1961), pp. 93-94: "in *The Triumph of Life* . . . [the sun's] power is the being and the source of all tyrannies."

> Their portion of the toil which he of old
>> Took as his own & then imposed on them . . .
>>> (lines 15-20)

If two complex metaphors, a family one and a political one, overlap here, similar overlapping of erotic and religious imagery has occurred a moment earlier in the poem. The reader might think that the figure of love could be reconciled with the figure of the father's relation to his child. The explicitly erotic overtones of Shelley's language here forbid that, or at the best (or worst) would force the reader to add incestuous desire, on both sides, to the relation of father and son. There has always been a troubling implication of homosexuality and of incest in the figuring of God or Christ as a lover, the soul as the beloved. The generations and the sexes are disturbingly mixed or crossed in the family metaphors of Christianity. It is easier, however, to see Shelley's figure here as a straightforward image of heterosexual longing:

> All flowers in field or forest which unclose

>> Their trembling eyelids to the kiss of day,
> Swinging their censers in the element,
>> With orient incense lit by the new ray

> Burned slow & inconsumably, & sent
>> Their odorous sighs up to the smiling air . . .
>>> (lines 9-14)

The inconsumable burning here is both that of religious worship and that of awakened erotic desire. The admirably swift moving forward together of four different figures for the intercourse of sun, earth, and all things in the earth is like a complex wave, with waves within the wave, each interfering with the others and reinforcing them by turns, each with a different period, but all together always making for the shore. There the wave of forward verbal motion will break, as it does repeatedly in this poem, to leave a trace behind, a mark on the sand that is not quite wholly erased in the dispersal of the elements that make up the wave. This figure of the wave appears not only in the description of self-destructive erotic love already discussed, but also, later in the poem, in the splendid passage describing the effect on Rousseau's mind and imagination of drinking the cup of forgetful Nepenthe offered by the glowing queenly vision of embodied Nature. She offers the cup in response to his question about his origin, present position, and reason for being where he is. Far from getting an answer, Rousseau forgets even the question. A new vision replaces the old. The chariot of Life replaces the figure of Nature with a new scene blotting out the previous one:

"I rose; and, bending at her sweet command,
　　Touched with faint lips the cup she raised,
And suddenly my brain became as sand

　"Where the first wave had more than half erased
The track of deer on desert Labrador,
　　Whilst the fierce wolf from which they fled amazed

"Leaves his stamp visibly upon the shore
　　Until the second bursts—so on my sight
Burst a new Vision never seen before.—"
　　　　　　　　　　(lines 403-411)

In the case of the first vision of all, that of the sunrise which opens the poem, the remnant left by the breaking of the wave is the poet himself. He abruptly obtrudes at the beginning of a line as the thing left over that does not fit: "But I . . ." The poet's falling asleep, which reverses the movement of the sun's rising, initiates the next wave and the next vision:

But I, whom thoughts which must remain untold

　Had kept as wakeful as the stars that gem
The cone of night, now they were laid asleep,
　　Stretched my faint limbs beneath the hoary stem

137

Which an old chestnut flung athwart the steep
Of a green Apennine . . .
(lines 21-26)

The unassimilated survival of the poet, the *I* of the poem, casts back to raise questions dismantling the power and the homogeneous meaning of the opening wave. What is the basis of the personifications in this inaugural sequence? Is it something objectively there in nature or something projected on nature by the poet? Could their source be no more than that *I* which remains left over as a *but* that cannot be incorporated into that of which it is nevertheless the ground? The poem's radical theory of subjectivity as the source of the "shadows" making up the phenomenal world would confirm this.

What exactly, however, is the *I* of the poet? Is it a subjectivity in the sense of a person or a self? Little in the poem supports this assumption. The speaker of the poem tells the reader nothing about his inner life. He rather describes the visions of which that subjectivity is the neutral witness, as if he were a spectator in a theatre. Are those visions his selfhood? His selfhood would then be nothing but a series of constantly changing projected visions. It would be nothing but that plus the "Power" which both motivates and witnesses these, just as the sun is not a swift spirit but is seen as a spirit by way of arbitrary linguistic substitutions. The latter are spontaneously generated out of the nocturnal, starlit thoughts of the spectator *I*. The only direct reference to the poet's intimate presence of himself to himself is an odd refusal to speak of it: "But I, whom thoughts which must remain untold / Had kept as wakeful as the stars that gem / The cone of night . . ." Why must they remain untold? Is there some intrinsic incompatibility between thoughts of wakeful self-presence in the nighttime and any telling? Perhaps the latter will necessarily distort those "thoughts," make them figurative fictions. Much elsewhere in the poem would suggest that this is the case. It is, on the other hand, that there just is not time now, or that this is not the time, since the thoughts of the previous night form the wave previous to the wave with which the poet begins? The law of the poem is that each wave in its self-destruction leaves behind the materials out of which the next wave is to be made by a crisscross substitution of its elements. The scene that opens the poem is therefore dependent for its materials on the "thoughts which must remain untold," that is, on the thoughts of the previous night. What were those thoughts? The reader would like to know, and he would like to know why the poet cannot tell them.[9]

The question about the basis, guarantee, or source of the opening personifications is connected systematically to a series of related questions. What is the literal subject of which the other terms in the opening sequence are figures? Which of the four figures—erotic, familial, political, theological—is the dominant one that governs the others, making them secondary figures of it? Or is it possible to make a hierarchy of the figures in this or in any other way? From what place is the poet or the *I* of the poem speaking? The poem is in the past tense and speaks of a series of visions and of visions within visions that have already long ago— or at any rate, some time ago—occurred when the poem opens. "The Triumph of Life," in its unfinished state at least, never brings the retrospective narrative back up to the now from which the poet speaks. Is that now within life or perhaps beyond life in death? What would it mean, in the poem, to see life from the perspective of death? Is the question about whether the poet speaks from life or from death the same as the question of whether he speaks from within the waking daytime world of sunlight, the nat-

[9] Little is gained by superimposing biographical information on the poem at this point and asserting that the thoughts which must remain untold have to do with the poet's love for his friend's wife, Jane Williams. The poem says nothing about Jane Williams and nothing in the poem justifies bringing her in.

ural Italian scene of the opening, or from within the world of night, darkness, stars, and the imagination from which he briefly emerges, only to go to sleep? That sleep is of course not the same state as the wakeful darkness that has preceded the opening. What would it mean to speak of the sun's world from the perspective of starlight, that light which the sun extinguishes in order to make itself visible?

The answer to the first of these questions—the question of which is the literal base of which the figures are figures— would appear to be easy. The literal subject of the opening is the sunrise. The literal words here are *Sun, mountain snows, Ocean, birds, flowers, field, forest,* and so on. The rest of the terms in this beginning—religious, political, familial, and erotic—are figures for this literal referent. The matter turns out to be not quite so simple, however, when it is questioned a little further. Why are the words *Sun, Earth,* and *Ocean* capitalized, as are *Continent* and *Isle* later in the passage? Presumably to personify them, though no doubt capitalized nouns were more common in Shelley's time than in ours. The personifications have contaminated even the most literal words in the passage, if only in the apparently innocent matter of orthography. Once this process has begun, it spreads out, so that even objects which are not actively personified, the flowers, for example, are seen as persons. When the poet says "Isle," not "isle," the reader understands that as a personification.

As the poet says, "All things that in them wear / The form & character of mortal mould / Rise as the Sun their father rose." To appear at all, all things must appear as the sun appears, swinging up from occultation in the invisible place below the horizon, springing forth and dropping the "mask of darkness." This act of unveiling recurs as a basic trope throughout the poem. Perhaps it is the most fundamental trope or turning. The unveiling is also simultaneously a reveiling. One mask is dropped to reveal another mask behind it. Not only the sun but all things manifest themselves, the poet says, not as literal objects, but as al-

ready personified, as turned into persons with a "character." *Persona*—Shelley's word *mask* translates the Latin word.
Like father, like son. To wear the form and character of
mortal mould is to have the human form. According to
one of the puns in the complex system of double meanings
in the word *character*, to have mortal mould is to have features, a visible character, like a human face or mask, and
at the same time it is to be inscribed with *characters* in the
sense of legible signs. To appear is to appear as language.
To be a visible object on the earth and under the sun is to
be already like a person in the double sense of being mortal,
doomed to *moulder*, and of being at the same time *moulded*
in the human form. This means wearing the mask of human language, being inscribed with its characters. The things
of the opening sequence all wear, in order to be visible at
all, the mark of the quadruple personification in terms of
which the poet necessarily sees and names them. Otherwise
they would be invisible and without names, like the sun
when it is below the horizon.

The trajectory of the sun, its rising and setting, its alter-
nate visibility and invisibility, has been since before Aristotle
a paradigm, perhaps the most basic paradigm, both for
truth, *aletheia* in its veiling and unveiling, and for metaphor
in its covert dependence on catachresis, the figurative naming of that which has no literal name. Aristotle's example
of the latter is the sun. Since it may not be seen when it is
below the horizon, its name is not a fully proper one. Literal
naming depends on a matching of name and sensation.
Since the complete trajectory of the sun cannot be seen,
there is no proper name for the sun in the totality of its
diurnal movement. The word *sun* is in part only a transfer
to the nameless and invisible of a term which, in this new
application, is neither literal, since it does not correspond
to anything visible, nor figurative, since it does not substitute for a proper term, and the definition of a figurative
term is that it must substitute for a literal term. Since the
sun governs the visibility of all things under the sun, all

words are heliotropes, metaphors of the sun, rising as the sun their father rises. All the photological or heliocentric terminology of traditional poetic and philosophical language from Aristotle, Plato, and before, down to Shelley and Wallace Stevens, rests uneasily on the shaky ground of the originating catachresis, which names the sun.[10]

The paradox that governs the opening sequence of "The Triumph of Life" also determines the other scenes or "waves" of the poem. This paradox emerges as the true subject of the poem. The paradox is the following: When the sun rises and the mask of darkness falls from the awakened earth to bring things into visibility, they do not appear as what they are. They are instantly masked with the personifications whose source is the person of the poet. Catachresis and prosopopoeia are intimately connected, though they do not by any means wholly overlap. The connection appears in common examples of catachresis: leg of a table, face of a mountain. The poet, however, is no person in the usual sense. He is a power of imagination, a power to have the thoughts of darkness, that is a power to make tropes, to see and name one thing as another—the sun as a spirit, flowers as censers, and so on. Throughout the poem, imagination is defined as the projection on the world of "shadows," which have a subjective source but which reflect backward, in an instant metalepsis, to affirm the selfhood of the anonymous energy of troping, which is their source. At the same time this energy consumes its source, as in the final terrifying vision of "Life." "Life" is Shelley's name for this crisscross process of personification:

> "From every firmest limb & fairest face
> The strength & freshness fell like dust, & left
> The action & the shape without the grace
>
> "Of life . . ."

(lines 520-523)

[10] On this topic see Jacques Derrida, "*La mythologie blanche*," *Marges de la philosophie* (Paris: Les Éditions de Minuit, 1972), pp. 292-307.

The air in this last scene is filled with grotesque huma-
noid figures. These are embodied "personifications." They
are the form taken by the shadows that emanate from all
men and women collectively—kings, despots, poets, priests,
lovers, and the rest—in a vision of the human power of
projecting *simulacra* of thoughts and passions that Shelley
borrowed from Book IV of the *De rerum natura* of Lucretius.
The process of this emanation, the constant activity of unmasking and remasking that is Life, at the same time bit
by bit hideously deforms those from whom the shadows
emanate and leaves them bereft of life, as Rousseau is turned
into an old root:

> ". . . each one
> Of that great crowd sent forth incessantly
>   These shadows, numerous as the dead leaves blown
>
> "In Autumn evening from a poplar tree—
>   Each like himself & like each other were,
> At first, but soon distorted, seemed to be
>
> "Obscure clouds moulded by the casual air;
> And of this stuff the car's creative ray
>   Wrought all the busy phantoms that were there
>
> "As the sun shapes the clouds—thus, on the way
>   Mask after mask fell from the countenance
> And form of all, and long before the day
>
> "Was old, the joy which waked like Heaven's glance
> The sleepers in the oblivious valley, died,
>   And some grew weary of the ghastly dance
>
> "And fell, as I have fallen by the way side,
>   Those soonest from whose forms most shadows past
> And least of strength & beauty did abide."—
>   (lines 526-543)

The same elements appear here, in the last scene of the
poem, as are used in the opening scene: the sun, the mask,
and so on. There seem to be in this poem only a limited

repertoire of available figures. The poem is like an Indian *raga* in which only certain notes may appear, but are given in many permutations and combinations according to certain definite rules. The same elements reappear, but they have different structural functions. Strength and beauty are now not intrinsic to the men and women who possess them, but are "masks" that drop one by one, in layers, *persona* after *persona*, from each countenance, as "shadows" are projected. This unmasking leaves ultimately only a joyless residue. The mask in the first scene, on the contrary, was the mask of darkness that was drawn away by the sun to reveal the strength and beauty of all created and personified things of earth—mountains, flowers, and so on. In fact they were personified by a force emanating from the darkness, the fictional *I* of the poet. The sun in the last scene is now not the apparent original of which the other things are the delegated representatives. The sun now is the power of Life or a figure for the power of Life. The uncanny Life-light shapes the shadows, "*as* the sun shapes the clouds" (my italics). The sun is a figure now for a collective human emotional energy. This subjective power takes the shadows emanating from each individual and shapes them into the personified phantoms, all those illusions which throng and clog the air. These destroy in their coming to life the human energy and beauty that was their source. In the system of sun, mask; light, shadow; sleep, waking that makes up the poem there is no original, no literal element. There is only a nameless power of substitution, which reveals itself in effects that are always figurative. In this constant shifting only the vacant schema remains fixed. No term, not even the sun, has a fixed place that is outside the system. All terms are exchangeable for others, in a constant dislocation, since the place the reader and the speaker are in is the darkness—place of displacement, place of thoughts that must remain untold or told only cryptically, in masks and veiled expressions.

Answers to the other questions posed earlier follow necessarily from the answer to the first one. If there is no literal term in the first scene, then the four interwoven figures there cannot be arranged in any hierarchical structure of ascending order. No one of the figures commands the others. Each trope is an alternative personification, each as unjustified as the others. They are unjustified in the sense of not being based on any extralinguistic base. Each is therefore on the same plane as the others. They exist side by side, reinforcing one another, interfering with one another—one momentarily dominating and then becoming subsidiary in the verbal weaving of the text—like threads stranded together to form a rope.

If there is no literal base and therefore no hierarchy of figures, this is because the placement of the speaker-poet is not out in the light, face to face with the sun, but within the darkness of the human mind and the darkness of human language. The poet, that is, is also within life. This means he is within the darkness of death or of death-in-life. This is another example of a pair of opposites that are not opposites but different names for one another. The poet speaks from that nameless realm that is darkness and light, action and passion, life and death, at once. He speaks from no identifiable place or time, except that, since the poem is in the past tense, it can be said that he always speaks from some time after the scenes presented in the poem occur. He speaks retrospectively, transforming memory into language. This language, necessarily, belongs to night or to starlight: "But I . . . had kept as wakeful as the stars."

Is this *I* the ground, a perdurable self that outlives life, death, and all the permutations of life? Is the *I* able always, as an indestructible survivor, to speak from outside time and outside place of what he has witnessed? I do not think so. The *I* is the remnant as a power of personification that sees nature, for example, as a beautiful woman, mother, sister, spouse. That power has no basis except in language. The *I* is the great shifter, a name for the linguistic energy of substitution. The *I* has no propriety, but applies promiscuously here, there, everywhere at once. The *I* of the poem projects pronouns and the attributes of pronouns on the sun and on the other things of inanimate nature. These in turn generate as the remainder of their mutual destruction the figure of a person, the "But I." This figure reflects backward to create in the reader a feeling that the speaker of the poem is an *I* in the sense of a personality, a self. The ground of the *as* personifying the sun and the things it shines on can only be the person of the poet, but the poet is no person. He is only a power of naming in figures and personifications. Outer personification is the ground of inner, and vice versa, in a constant reversal. Whichever one looks at needs the other as its source, as if it were the empty focus of an ellipsis, with the paternal and substantial sun always at the other focus. The interaction of the two foci creates the trajectory or narrative line of the poem, like the movement of a planet in elliptical orbit around the sun. Each scene of the poem goes in and out like a Gestaltist diagram. First the sun, then the poet, is foregrounded. First the light, then the darkness. Each seems in turn to be the figure of which the other is the literal ground.

The law of the poem, I have said, is that when any given case of this interaction of light and dark has reached its climax and vanishes, the next scene is constructed of the remnants of this catastrophe. It is constructed with the same elements in reversed positions, as antistrophe. A striking example of this is the relation between the first and second scenes of the poem. In the first, the mask of darkness falls from the awakened earth as the sun rises. In the second, the *I* of the poet, the leftover, who has been wakeful while the sun slept, now goes to sleep or, more precisely, into a waking dream, as everything else wakes up. His visionary trance is a veil, now not of darkness but of light. This veil of light is drawn over nature, but the natural scene may be seen through it. Light is now placed in the same position and fulfills the same function as darkness did in the first scene:

> ... before me fled
> The night; behind me rose the day; the Deep
>
> Was at my feet, & Heaven above my head
> When a strange trance over my fancy grew
> Which was not slumber, for the shade it spread
>
> Was so transparent that the scene came through
> As clear as when a veil of light is drawn
> O'er evening hills they glimmer ...
>
> (lines 26-33)

The poet's "waking dream" is his vision of the triumphal car of Life, driven by a "Janus-visaged Shadow" (line 94), and surrounded by all the swarm of people who have been the victims of Life, in "one mighty torrent" (line 53). The climax of this vision, spread like a veil of light over the Apennine scene the poet still at first half sees through the vision, is the shift to the present tense for the scene of erotic self-destruction already cited. The remainder in this case takes the form of the "old men, and women foully disarrayed," exhausted by love. They destroy themselves in the attempt to recover what they have lost through its own fulfillment. They fall to the dust to die and to be veiled by corruption (lines 170-175). The scene of the grotesque impotent desire of the aged is a little cycle within the larger cycle of the poet's waking vision. The remnant that ends that larger cycle performs the same function here as the words "But I" did at the end of the first scene. This remnant is the word *Life* uttered by the old root Rousseau in answer to the poet's half-uttered questions: "And what is this? / Whose shape is that within the car? & why?" and to the question he does not speak out loud, "is all here amiss?" (lines 177-179). The word *Life* is the turning point to a new vision, Rousseau's speech in answer to the poet. This retrospective episode is a vision within a vision, or a vision beside a vision. It comes later in the sequence of the poem, but earlier in chronology. Each of these scenes at once

147

reverses the one before, exists inside it, and surrounds it as its explanatory enfolding container. Each next vision follows later in the time of reading, but contains elements prior to the now of the previous scene, as Rousseau's recollected vision precedes any experience the poet has had. The next scene is adjacent to the one before, inside it, outside it, prior to it as its source, and later than it as its consequence, all at once. The apparently heliocentric system of the "first" scene, with the sun as God or as the vicar of God, still exists in the "second" scene. Now, however, there is a new arrangement of light and shadow that makes Life the source of a feigned or cold light. Of that false light the sunlight of "truth" is a false projection. The new vision dismantles the old.

What the poet sees in his waking dream is presented as a parody of Plato's parable of the cave. All men and women, young and old, "numerous as gnats upon the evening gleam" (line 46) or as "the million leaves of summer's bier" (line 51), live according to a "serious folly" that is described, in the passage echoing the one in "The Revolt of Islam" cited by Hardy, as the pursuit or shunning of shadows cast by the sun's action on clouds or on other things that may intervene between the sun and the ground:

> . . . others mournfully within the gloom
>
> Of their own shadow walked, and called it death . . .
>   And some fled from it as it were a ghost,
> Half fainting in the affliction of vain breath.
>
>   But more with motions which each other crost
> Pursued or shunned the shadows the clouds threw
>   Or birds within the noonday either lost,
>
> Upon that path where flowers never grew . . .
>   (lines 58-65)

This undoubtedly recalls Plato, but the scheme of equivalences is different in several ways. There is nothing in

Shelley's scene comparable to Plato's cave. All takes place in the broad out-of-doors. This means that there is no possibility of making a movement into the light of reality by turning round and going out of the cave. Though the victims of Shelley's shadow world could turn to see the clouds and the birds that were casting the shadows beguiling them, and though they could try to look the sun in the eye, this turning would leave them still in the same place, not liberated from the cave into the light of day. Though both Plato's and Shelley's scenes are parabolic, the referents of the parabolic elements are not quite the same for both. In Plato's case the interior of the cave is human life generally, while the sunlight world outside the cave is the realm of ideas—the realities of which the things of this lower world are shadowy copies. In Shelley's parable the single realm he presents is inside the poet's waking dream. The sun is not the real sun of the opening scene. It is, rather, part of an emblematic scene representing all human life as the production and then the pursuit or shunning of shadows. Even the real sun of the opening was of course already veiled by the personifications in terms of which the wakeful poet must see it and name it.

The human act of projecting shadows in Shelley is different, finally, from its seeming source in Plato. Among the most important of the shadows pursued and shunned by Shelley's victims of Life, it appears, are those projected by the victims themselves. Plato, in the parable of the cave in Book VII the *Republic*, makes little of the fact that among the shadows the prisoners in the cave see are their own images. Though the fact is mentioned in passing, the emphasis is on the contrast between the shadows of things on the wall of the cave and the real things out in the sunlight. Even though idealist affirmations are present in Shelley's poem, as in an apparently unequivocal use of the term *God* to name the light of the world, this idealism is constantly twisted to become a figure for that cold light of Life that tropes all things, making man himself and all he can see

149

self-projected shadowy figures. There is for Shelley no possibility of the Platonic turning from shadows to realities,
only the constant substitution of one shadow for another.
Since the shadows on the road in "The Triumph of Life"
are within life, the light that casts these shadows is no natural or supernatural sun. It is that icy cold glare thrown
out by the chariot of Life. This light in fact is a form of
darkness. It is darkness as division or doubling, shadow on
shadow. The source of the light from the chariot is a "Janus-
visaged Shadow." The light of the chariot of Life both
"quenches" the sun (line 102) and at the same time is what
the word *sun* stands for. The word *sun*, for Shelley, as the
reader has seen, can only have a figurative referent. The
sun is one name for the shape-changing, shadow-casting
light of Life.

The chain pattern of "The Triumph of Life" as a whole
is not so much an alternation of light and shadow as it is
the replacement of one light source by another light source
that puts out the previous one. The previous one soon can
no longer be remembered, or is only indistinctly remembered as though it were being seen through an almost opaque
screen. One name for Life would therefore be the impossibility of remembering. "The Triumph of Life" reverses
the pattern of Platonic reminiscence, as it is apparently (but
not in fact, as Shelley knew) present in Wordsworth's "Intimations" ode. Shelley's poem presents the mirror image
or, perhaps it would be better to say, something like a
photographic negative, of the Platonic system of light and
dark. Shelley's light is not a Platonic principle of seeing, of
remembering, of unveiling, and of revelation, as when the
prisoners in the cave come dazzled out into the sunlight,
but just the reverse, a principle of covering over and of
oblivion. Light for Shelley is the condition of human seeing
and naming, which means it is the principle of substitution
and forgetting. Each thing is seen as another thing and so
forgotten. Each new light at once veils the old and affirms
itself as a new source of illumination. This light is always

a screen. It covers over as it illuminates, since it is a power of figuration that makes things be what they are not.

As the poet in the opening scene of the poem will not tell the thoughts of the starlit night, and as the sun puts out the stars, so his personifications put out the sun, as does the waking vision that draws a "veil of light" over the Apennine scene. In the same way the "Shape" of Life in the chariot puts out the sun with his cold glare. Shelley's waking vision is in turn replaced by Rousseau's narrative of his own life, with its climactic vision of the shape all light, the beautiful female figure who offers the glass of Nepenthe, drug of forgetfulness. This new shape obliterates the sun and then is once more obliterated in her turn by the last vision of all in the poem as we have it. This is Rousseau's confrontation of the chariot of Life and of the play of shadows projected by all the human victims of Life. The last scene is the ultimate version of the potentially endless turning that makes the chain of scenes in the poem, each scene erasing the previous one, until the break in the fold of the last fragmentary sentence ends all we have.

"The Triumph of Life" enacts a process of life as continuous forgetting. Each scene does indeed deconstruct the previous one, but not in the sense of giving the reader mastery over it. Rather, each new scene gives the elements of the poem another twist, making him forget what had come before, masking it. The reader never learns what are those thoughts that must remain untold and that precede the poem. The poem's ending was cut off by death and must remain forever blank. The reader cannot even clearly hold in his mind all at once the intricate sequence of permutations making up the poem as we have it. However many times he has read the poem, he partly forgets where he has come from and where he is going when he concentrates on any part of it.

This experience of amnesia is repeated again and again throughout the poem, but two passages, that describing the new moon embracing the old and that describing the shape

151

all light, give perhaps the fullest means of understanding it.

The logic of the first of these passages comes to seem more odd the more the reader attempts to untwist its figures and give the passage a single unequivocal meaning:

> And a cold glare, intenser than the noon
>   But icy cold, obscured with   light [sic]
> The Sun as he the stars. Like the young moon
>
>   When on the sunlit limits of the night
> Her white shell trembles amid crimson air
>   And whilst the sleeping tempest gathers might
>
> Doth, as a herald of its coming, bear
>   The ghost of her dead Mother, whose dim form
> Bends in dark ether from her infant's chair,
>
>   So came a chariot on the silent storm
> Of its own rushing splendour, and a Shape
>   So sate within as one whom years deform
>
> Beneath a dusky hood & double cape
>   Crouching within the shadow of a tomb,
> And o'er what seemed the head, a cloud like crape,
>
>   Was bent a dun & faint etherial gloom
> Tempering the light . . .
>   (lines 77-93)

What, exactly, is Shelley saying here, or what is his poetic persona saying? The passage seems at first straightforward enough. As the sun obscured the stars in the opening scene, so now the cold glare of Life, intenser than the noon, obscures the sun. The three lights, in chain sequence, seem to be essentially different from one another as sources of illumination. There are, it appears, at least three different kinds of light. The figure of the moon, however, does strange things to this theoretically plausible differentiation of each source of light from the others. The problem begins, as

152

always in such cases, with the shift from seeing to saying or to writing, even if this shift involves, as in this instance, no more than seeing something visible, the new moon, as a figure of speech for something else. The moon of course shines with light reflected from the sun. This fact is especially evident at that liminal moment when the new moon appears at dusk in a crimson air still half illuminated by a sun that has just set. The moon is the presence of the sun when it has disappeared below the horizon. This means that the moon is the sun's presence as non-presence, as trope, though, as the opening scene makes clear, even in broad daylight, even at high noon, the sun can only appear tropologically, veiled in a personification. If the sun seems at first the source of moonlight, it is in fact, as the reader knows, in any of its appearances, only another version of that universal light that appears always as figure, or as a figure, as a veil of light, or as light veiled in a figure, as a shape all light. This is the case whether the light in question is starlight, sunlight, or moonlight.

Moreover, the figure of the new moon with the old moon in its arms reverses metaleptically the temporal sequence of cause and effect. The figure makes the later the bearer or cause of the earlier, as the vehicle of a metaphor bears its tenor. The new moon carries the ghost of her dead mother. The child becomes the mother of her mother, but mother of a mother who persists as a ghost, as the dim white form of the full moon circled with a faint rim of bright new light. For the relation of sun to moon, apparently primary light to secondary reflected light, is substituted the relation of moon to moon. That it is an act of substitution is indicated by the fact that Shelley says "*like* the new moon" (my italics). The result of this figurative substitution is a reversal of normal causal and temporal sequence. Whatever source of light is present at this moment before the spectator (in this case the cold glare of the chariot of Life) becomes apparently the generative source of what preceded it. This is so in the sense that whatever remains of the past exists now only as the dead ghost of itself carried by the present figure of light, as the new moon carries the ghost of her dead mother. This relation is generalized later in the poem as the paradoxical relation of remembering and forgetting that any present scene has to the previous ones that exist as ghosts or figures within it. They are present as non-presences. This reversal of causal and temporal sequence is, for Shelley, as for his remembered precursors, the presage of a storm. This storm is consistently defined in "The Triumph of Life" as a deafening cacophonous co-presence, in illogical mixture, of warring elements appealing to all the senses at once. These elements refuse to be sorted out or to sort themselves out in logical or causal sequence. The new moon as the mother of her mother is the sign of this reversal and confusion of the order of generation.

The relation of the new moon to the old defines not only the connection of one scene to the next contiguous one in this poem. It also defines the mode of presence within the poem of all those precursor texts that are there as ghostly echoes or figures—passages from *Ezekiel, Revelation*, Dante, Milton, Rousseau, Wordsworth, Coleridge, Blake. Each of these becomes the caused of what it causes when it is simultaneously remembered and forgotten in the poem, at once resurrected and killed. Each previous passage exists as a white ghost of allusion within the new poem, as each earlier example had itself once been both mother and child, carrying its own precursors, remembering them and forgetting them at once, bringing them to life and obliterating them, as the chariot of *Revelation* unveils and at the same time obscures the chariot of *Ezekiel*. One version of this kind of chain is the image of the moon here. It comes from Coleridge's "Dejection: An Ode," which takes it from "Sir Patrick Spens." Coleridge's borrowing is already inserted by him in a context that has to do with the storm of synesthesia and with the dependence of the past on a present that may or may not have power to make that past live again. It may or may not have that power because whatever life that past has is the phantasmal life given to it by the shaping spirit of imagination in the present.

In "The Triumph of Life" the image from Coleridge is transformed again to become a figure of dark light or of darkness visible. This figure is applied not only to the relation of the glare of the chariot of Life to the sunlight it both displaces and encloses, but also, within the cold glare itself, to the relation between the head of Life and the ghastly halo that surrounds it. The head is a "cloud like crape." Around the head is "a dun & faint etherial gloom / Tempering the light," as the new moon surrounds the white shell of the old. The head of Life is a reversed parody of the new moon, its negative image: gloom as a halo around a black cloud. The differentiation that is necessary to make a visible figure out of undifferentiated light exists within any scene of light, whether of sunlight or of dark light (but they are "the same"), as well as in the relation between any one scene and its predecessor. This is another version of the cleft, or fold, the divisions, and divisions within divisions, that organize this poem throughout. The chariot of Life, appropriately, is guided by a "Janus-visaged Shadow," actually with four faces, a doubling redoubled. Without some form of doubling, nothing would be visible, but this making visible is at the same time a blinding, since it veils the pure light as such. As the poet says, "All the four faces of that charioteer / Had their eyes banded" (lines 99-100). The relation of seeing and blinded vision matches the relation of remembering and forgetting in the poem. What is remembered is remembered as image or ghost, just as what can be seen is always only a veiled figure for the light.

Rousseau's recollected vision of the shape all light walking on the waters of the forest stream both restates the complex figuration of the image of the new moon bearing the old, and at the same time undoes it. The new vision unties the lines that bound the previous one together and allowed it to function as a way of understanding the relation

155

of one scene to another in the pageant of political, personal, or literary history, however alogical the model for that understanding was. The passage in question is initiated by the poet's command to Rousseau: "Speak." It runs from line 300 to line 432. This episode is surely the most beautiful and powerful in a poem of great beauty and power throughout. The episode constitutes a reading both of Wordsworth and of Rousseau.

This reading has sometimes been misunderstood by critics in the same way as Hardy's reading of Shelley has been misunderstood. Shelley did not read Wordsworth and Rousseau in a characteristic nineteenth-century or even twentieth-century way, as straightforward transcendentalists, as writers who believed in a harmony between nature, self, language, and in a "visionary gleam" from beyond nature but mediated by nature. Shelley, the poem indicates, penetrated into the actual skepticism of Wordsworth and Rousseau concerning those harmonies and liaisons, just as Hardy's poems and novels are evidence that Hardy was a far better reader of Shelley than late-Victorian critics like Edward Dowden. It is probably best to assume that a great poet is a better reader than most critics, better certainly than the standard misreading of his own age. Whatever powerful motives a strong poet may have for misinterpreting his predecessors, these misreadings do not necessarily repeat the most banal errors of interpretation current in his time. His blindness may be the distortion of a more genuine insight.

Rousseau's answer to the poet's "Speak," the reader will remember, is ostensibly in response to those basic questions of the poem: "Whence camest thou & whither goest thou? / How did thy course begin, . . . & why?" (lines 296-297). Rousseau answers that he "seems" "partly" to know where he has come from and how he got where he is, but has no idea where he is going or why. His narrative demonstrates that the force of the "partly I seem to know" is such as to remove any possibility of ever reaching, by a recollected moving backward against the stream of time, any but a figurative or illusory origin. First the shape all light appears, "as if she were the Dawn" (line 353). She is accompanied by the rainbow of Iris, an echo no doubt of the rainbow in the epigraph to Wordsworth's "Intimations" ode, as well as of other rainbows in other texts back to the one in *Exodus*. The shape all light manifests herself in a natural scene that, in another echo of Wordsworth, still "seem[s] to keep" in "broad day, a gentle trace / Of light diviner than the common Sun / Sheds on the common Earth" (lines 336-339). A similar natural scene had been presented earlier in the poem (lines 66-72) as an escape from submission to Life that is ignored by all Life's shadow-chasing captives, but this later scene shows how illusory this promise of release is. When the shape all light is replaced by the chariot of Life, the light of the chariot is accompanied by a new rainbow, "the vermilion / And green & azure plumes of Iris" (lines 439-440) built by this new light. The shape all light is now in her turn an indistinct figure moving along the stream. She becomes herself no more than a trace, seen "More dimly than a day appearing dream, / The ghost of a forgotten form of sleep, / A light from Heaven whose half extinguished beam / Through the sick day in which we wake to weep / Glimmers, forever sought, forever lost" (lines 427-431). The *than* here makes the dream, the ghost, and the light from heaven merely tropes. They are figurative names given to the half-recollected previous scene of light from the point of view of the present one. Those figures, it will be remembered, are originated by the witnessing self. That self projects the masks of various personifications that give a new shape to the light in scene after scene. The self itself, however, the reader will also remember, is another mask, an effect of the impersonal energy of troping that governs all these changes, both inside and outside the encompassing and encompassed consciousness of the poet. Inside, that power appears as the seeming self. Outside, it appears as the ubiquitous light, or rather, since the light as such is invisible, it appears in whatever projected shape the light happens to take at the moment. The process is a narcissistic reflection of shape by shape, inner mask meeting outer mask as its mirror image or sister echo.

In an analogous way, elements in the outer world of perception in this poem seem always to found themselves on a prior element that not only came first but operates as their transcendent ground. The "Wordsworthian" visionary gleam is a projection backward of an origin that can never be experienced by the present because it is not there and was never there. The "gentle trace / Of light diviner than the common Sun / Sheds on the common Earth" is just that, a trace, something in the present taken as the sign of something absent. It is a fiction generated by that working of signs which sustains meaning. This was the case for Wordsworth too, as I have shown in the previous chapter. For Shelley as for Wordsworth, the visionary gleam is an element in those "structures the excited spirit builds mainly for itself." Wherever the excited spectator is *now*, what he sees casts magically backward to create the apparition of a transcendent light *then* as its source, but this is merely a seeming. The shape all light "seems" to come from "the realm without a name," and the glare of the chariot of Life makes the dim ghost of the shape all light "seem" as if she had been a light from Heaven. The rapid substitution, in the text, of one version after another of this structure, with exactly the same elements—double light source, one extinguishing the other, personification, rainbow, synesthesia, and so on—brings into the open, for a moment, before the juxtaposition fades from memory (for it cannot be held for long in the mind), the fact that the whole system is a reversal of cause and effect. The apparently originary gleam is an effect of "present" light as trace or sign, as trope, as heliotrope with no *helos* in the sense of central and abiding light source. The trace creates the illusion of that to which it seems to refer. Shelley's light is phototropic, not heli-

otropic—phototropic in the sense of being the endless turning and substitution of one shape of light for another.

The beautiful female form walking the waters like Venus,
appears, the poet says, "as on the summer evening breeze
/ Up from the lake a shape of golden dew / Between two
rocks, athwart the rising moon, / Moves up the east, where
eagle never flew" (lines 378-381). The odd final phrase here
about the eagle, along with the image of the rising moon
and the mention of the east, means that this ghostly figure
is not "oriented" by the sun but is a substitute for it. It rises
in the east, like the sun, and it is contiguous to the rising
moon, the figure in the poem for the borrowed or secondary quality of any light that can be seen. This shape of
golden dew flies where eagle never flew because it is not
drawn by the sun. The traditional image of the eagle who
ascends into the eye of the sun, its "native noon," appears
earlier in the poem as a figure for the sacred few who could
not tame their spirits to the conqueror, Life.

Any lingering conviction that the visionary gleam is the
glimpse of a transcendent source is further undone by the
poet's insistence that any light in the "present" is above all
a power of forgetting. It is a power obliterating the past
and substituting for it a fictional past whose truth value can
never be tested. The motif of forgetting also undoes whatever generative continuity seems implicit in the image of
the new moon with the old moon, her mother, in her arms.
Rousseau tells the poet that he remembers waking up in
April in a scene that is one of the archetypal Shelleyan or
Romantic landscapes: a mountain with a cavern from which
flows a stream down through a flowery forest. The scene
is archetypal in the sense that it recurs and in the special
sense that it always has something to do with the unsuccessful search for an archetype, the original form of which
it is the repetition. In fact Rousseau's waking repeats the
first scene of the poet's waking. As the reader may remember (in defiance of Shelley's theory of forgetting), the first
scene was presented as itself a repetition, something already

seen and felt: "and I knew / That I had felt the freshness of that dawn . . ." The poem, however, forgets, or at any rate does not explicitly note this repetition in Rousseau's experience of something experienced earlier by the poet as already a repetition. Or rather, since Rousseau's experience of waking, in historical time if not in its presentation in the poem, precedes the poet's experience of waking, the poem forgets to note that the poet's sense of *déjà vu* in the opening scene may have been a dimly remembered repetition of something that had happened to someone else, a strange species of metempsychosis. The writing and then the reading of the poem demonstrates that impossibility of remembering that the poem affirms.

I said above that Rousseau wakes in the springtime scene. In fact, he says, "I found myself asleep." No doubt this literally means, "I woke up," but it is an odd way to put it. What follows confirms the fact that, for Shelley or for the Rousseau of this poem, to be awake is to be asleep. It is to be asleep in the sense of forgetting all those things one usually assumes the waking mind remembers. To find oneself in the sense of becoming conscious of oneself and conscious of what is there immediately before one is to be asleep. To find oneself is to find oneself asleep. This is so in a double sense. The presence of the natural scene makes the spectator first forget all the past and become totally absorbed by the present. It then makes him even forget himself. His mind becomes a *tabula rasa* from which every thought has been erased. This is in fact what the historical Rousseau said of the relation between the self and nature, and of course it has many analogies in eighteenth-century English and French empiricism. Juliet Flower MacCannell has demonstrated this for Rousseau in a brilliant essay, and Paul de Man has argued the same thing as one facet of a more comprehensive reading of Rousseau.[11] Contrary to

[11] See Juliet Flower MacCannell, "Nature and Self-Love: A Reinterpretation of Rousseau's 'Passion primitive,' " *PMLA* XCII, 5 (October 1977), 890-902, and Paul de Man, "Part II, Rousseau," *Allegories of Reading* (New Haven and London: Yale University Press, 1979), pp. 133-301.

what is often said about Rousseau's theory of the relation of the self to nature, Rousseau saw nature as no ground for the self but rather as a danger to it in its multitudinous appeal to the senses. The self responds to this danger by an elaborate effort of metaphorical construction and substitution. Using these instruments the self creates a fictive world that is against nature, "unnatural," a falsification of nature and a shield against its dangerous power. This effort, far from securing the self as a stable entity not in need of nature for its support, makes the self a principle of instability and insubstantiality. The self is itself a trope, and it turns everything it encounters into more tropes.

Shelley wrote the word *Julie* in the margin of the manuscript of "The Triumph of Life."[12] The section of the poem on Rousseau is in part an admirable interpretation of Rousseau's *Julie, ou la Nouvelle Héloïse*. "The Triumph of Life" is evidence that Shelley was a superb reader of Rousseau. He was a superb reader on just those points having to do with the nature of the self and with the relation of the self to nature. Shelley differs from Rousseau not in the elements that enter into his analysis of the relation between the self and nature, but in his greater emphasis on the fragility of the constructed self and on the fragility of the projected personifications of nature. He also puts even more emphasis on the suffering those ungrounded fabrications cause. Shelley's vision is even darker and more shadowed. For all its rapid pace and linguistic exuberance, "The Triumph of Life" is surely one of the darkest and most shadowed of all major poems in English. Nevertheless, the conceptual and rhetorical systems of Rousseau and Shelley are similar. They are analogical, for example, in the way both see a negative power in a natural spectacle that has been metaphorically transformed by a self seen as

[12] Or at any rate Donald Reiman thinks he reads the word there. See his *Shelley's "The Triumph of Life": A Critical Study*, p. 211: "the word GM [G. M. Matthews] reads as 'Jane' I believe to be 'Julie' . . ." And see Reiman's extensive discussion of the presence of Rousseau in "The Triumph of Life" (*ibid.*, pp. 39-85).

161

itself an impersonal power to make such transformations—turning one thing into another thing. This negative energy projected on nature is expressed for both Rouseau and Shelley as its ability to make the spectator forget everything but itself. The self forgets everything, inside the self and outside, including the self itself. "The spectacle," writes Saint Preux to Julie of his Alpine experience, "has I know not what of the magical about it, something surnatural which ravishes the spirit and the senses; one forgets all, one forgets oneself, one no longer knows where one is."[13] *Surnatural* here, as the context makes clear, does not mean supernatural, in the sense of coming from a transcendent realm. It names that second nature imposed over nature by the figurative energy of the imagination, as the poets of a later generation were to speak of "surrealism."

A similar energy, an energy both creative and destructive, has confected the April scene in which Shelley's Rousseau finds himself asleep. The first effect, for Shelley as for the Rousseau of *La Nouvelle Héloïse*, of finding oneself asleep in nature is the obliteration of all memory of the past. The stream "fill[s] the grove / With sound which all who hear must needs forget / All pleasure & all pain, all hate & love, / Which they had known before that hour of rest" (lines 317-320). Pleasure and pain, hate and love, are additional examples of those nondialectical binary oppositions into which experience and the naming of experience divide as soon as there is naming and experience at all. They are also the passive and active names for the primary feelings that are for Shelley here, as for Rousseau, the chief motive power behind the projection of thoughts. Such thoughts make those figures on the bubble of life described

---

[13] The passage is from the twenty-third letter of the first part of *La Nouvelle Héloïse* (J.-J. Rousseau, *Oeuvres complètes*, ed. B. Gagnebin and M. Raymond, II [Paris: Bibliothèque de la Pléiade, 1964], p. 79): "*le spectacle a je ne sais quoi de magique, de surnaturel qui ravit l'esprit et les sens; on oublie tout, on s'oublie soi-même, on ne sait plus où l'on est.*" See MacCannell, "Nature and Self-Love," pp. 895-896 for a commentary on this letter.

162

earlier in the poem. Since pleasure and pain, hate and love make those figures, they make also the pageant of human life and of human history. The confrontation of nature leads to the forgetting of the thoughts born of all anterior passions and to the forgetting also of the ills to which those passions led. The sense-impressions of nature are indeed a kind of morphine, inducing sleep. "I found myself asleep" is to be taken literally and does not mean "I woke up." "Thou wouldst forget," says Rousseau of the sounds filling the April scene, "thus vainly to deplore / Ills, which if ills, can find no cure from thee, / The thought of which no other sleep will quell / Nor other music blot from memory— / So sweet & deep is the oblivious spell" (lines 327-331).

The effect of nature is to blot all memory of the past. One implication of this is that seeking origins or causal sequences is a quest doomed to failure. There is no way in which an answer to the poet's question about origin can be given except fictively, as an illusory projection backward from the present. Rousseau says he has no certain knowledge of what his life was like before he found himself asleep: "Whether my life had been before that sleep / The Heaven which I imagine, or a Hell / Like this harsh world in which I wake to weep, / I know not" (lines 332-335). He does not know whether he remembers or forgets. This is immediately followed by the passage, already cited, describing the way the scene "seems" to keep the gentle trace of light diviner than the common sun sheds on the common earth. Any notion of an anterior heaven as source is an imagination, a seeming. It may be a valid notion. It may not. Whether or not it is valid is forever undecidable.

A generative link between past and present was affirmed, in however complex a way, by the image of the new moon carrying the old in her arms. The breaking of this link in Rousseau's narrative is accomplished by two striking images, one personal, one political. These are images for the pains of memory nature makes us forget. The power of nature transfigured by the imagination is such that it would

163

make a mother forget, even in her dreams, the child who has just died. It would even make a king just deposed forget to envy his deposer: "A sleeping mother then would dream not of / The only child who died upon her breast / At eventide, a king would mourn no more / The crown of which his brow was dispossest / When the sun lingered o'er the Ocean floor / To gild his rival's new prosperity" (lines 321-326). The human situation, these images suggest, is to be cut off toward the future, without progeny, like a mother whose only child has died or like a king who has been deprived of the power to establish a dynastic succession. These images, in another case of metalepsis, stand for that process of constant forgetting which forbids any access to the past as a possible origin of the present. Detachment from the future goes along with detachment from the past. Each is a figure for the other. Such radical forgetting forbids any establishment of an authenticity for the present based on its succession from the past. In place of such images of continuity as the relation of mother to child, or of new moon to old, or of king to king in regular succession, the poem puts a picture of human life as a discontinuous series of presents. Each of these violently cuts itself off from the past. It obliterates that past from memory, and at the same time, by that self-destructive violence, forbids the present to have any future, any progeny. Each present moment consumes itself through the efforts of its own creative energy. The power of the light of the present natural scene in which Rousseau finds himself is like a dreamless sleep in the darkness which consigns all that happened during the previous day to oblivion. It obliterates even what happened at the end of that day when the sun was just sinking into the ocean, even the death of a child, the loss of a crown.

The paradox of Rousseau's narration, it will be seen, is that he remembers and is able to tell in detail what at the same time he says he has forgotten, both through the effect of the natural scene and through the effect of the Nepenthe. He not only remembers he has forgotten, he even remembers what it is he has forgotten. The effect of the natural scene and of the lady who personifies it is to make Rousseau forget the past. Their effect is even to make him forget himself and all the thoughts of that self in the present. His mind loses all power of thinking and becomes a vessel empty of thoughts, an extinguished fire, a blank slate washed clean of any writing: "And still her feet, no less than the sweet tune / To which they moved, seemed as they moved, to blot / The thoughts of him who gazed on them, & soon / All that was seemed as if it had been not, / As if the gazer's mind was strewn beneath / Her feet like embers & she, thought by thought, / Trampled its fires into the dust of death" (lines 382-388).[14] In this utmost violence of object on subject, the reversible relation of night and day is reversed again. The lady is said now to be not like night obliterating day but like day obliterating night. The spectator is blinded by light. The lady's feet extinguish Rousseau's thought "As Day upon the threshold of the east / Treads out the lamps of night, until the breath / Of darkness reillumines even the least / Of heaven's living eyes— like day she came, / Making the night a dream" (lines 389-393).

In the "light" of these lines the full functioning of the image of the effect of the Nepenthe on Rousseau as like a wave washing out marks on sand may be identified. Shelley has twice used the word *blot* to describe the "disremembering, dismembering"[15] effect first of the April scene itself, then of the feet of the shape all light moving on the waters:

---

[14] See Paul de Man's discussion of this image in "Shelley Disfigured," *Deconstruction and Criticism*, pp. 50-66. My chapter here on "The Triumph of Life" was written before de Man's admirable study, though of course his was published earlier. Our conversations about the poem before either essay was written nevertheless deeply influenced my thinking about it.

[15] Gerard Manley Hopkins, "Spelt from Sibyl's Leaves," line 7, *Poems*, 4th ed., ed. W. H. Gardner and N. H. MacKenzie (London, Oxford, New York: Oxford University Press, 1970), p. 97.

165

"blot from memory"; "seemed as they moved to blot / The thoughts of him who gazed on them." This figure describes the mind as a slate or writing tablet and light as something that effaces what had been written on that tablet. When Rousseau touches his lips to the cup of Nepenthe, his brain becomes as sand. This sand is not only something diffuse, heavy, and shapeless. It is also a flat surface on which marks may be made. The wave that more than half erases the deer's track must stand for the light and its power of obliteration, though the light, or rather the play of light and shadows that makes visible shapes of light, is also the power that writes on the sand. The light writes, and erases at once. The instrument of oblivion is not the vanishing of signs but the imposition of new signs over the old ones in palimpsest. Shelley's scene of writing anticipates Freud's scene of writing in "The Magic Writing-Block," though apparently without Freud's structure of layers and of ineffaceable memory traces.[16] That Shelley too sees forgetting as never total is suggested by the qualification in "more than half erased," as well as by the fact that Rousseau remembers what he says he forgot and by the fact that the poem itself, "The Triumph of Life," remains as the traces of the thoughts it records. At least it remains as long as a copy of the poem survives.

For Shelley, as for Freud, thinking and perception are forms of writing. This means that the problems of life are always also problems of language. As a consequence, the linguistic moment, for Shelley, is not an intermittent fea-

[16] See Sigmund Freud, *"Notiz über den 'Wunderblock' "* (1925), *Gesammelten Werke*, xiv (London: Imago Publishing Co., Ltd., 1948), pp. 3-8, trans. James Strachey, "A Note upon the 'Mystic Writing-Pad,' " *The Complete Psychological Works*, std. ed., xix (London: The Hogarth Press, 1953–66), pp. 225-232. For a commentary on Freud's essay, see Jacques Derrida, *"Freud et la scène de l'écriture," L'écriture et la différence* (Paris: Éditions du Seuil, 1967), pp. 293-340, trans. Alan Bass, "Freud and the Scene of Writing," *Writing and Difference* (Chicago: The University of Chicago Press, 1978), pp. 196-231.

ture in an interchange between mind and world involving primarily perception, thinking, and feeling, and language only secondarily. The linguistic moment in Shelley too, as in Wordsworth or in Arnold in different ways, has such momentum that it spreads out to occupy the whole poem or rolls up that whole so that there is no thinking, feeling, or perceiving that is not at the same time a process of inscription. This constant writing is performed by a light that is both inner and outer at once. To put this in another way, the light obliterates the membrane between inner and outer. The light is an energy constantly making marks or "figures" on the screen as it abolishes that screen. The screen is there and not there, inner and outer at once, at the borderline between mind and "Life." As the light writes, it obliterates the figures that were there before. The light is a beam that writes and erases at once, as the stamp of the wolf's footprint replaces the deer's track when the wolf chases the deer, or as each successive ocean wave washes out the marks that were made on the sand by the previous wave, or as each successive vision, in Shelley's poem, makes a visible shape of light that in its visibility consigns the previous scene to oblivion, or at least to a vague half-visi-bility, as the shape all light is still barely visible in the glare of Life, like the ghost of a forgotten form of sleep, or as the deer's track is only half erased, or as Rousseau in fact remembers what he says he has forgotten, or at any rate can narrate it, tracing in that narration more figures on the bubble of Life, figures that repeat earlier figures, or as this sentence, in its shifting serial syntax, mimes the Shel-leyan sequence that is not incoherent but cannot be held all in the mind at once and destroys its integrity in its own inexhaustible power of continuation.

If the "shape all light" is a visible oxymoron, since a shape all light has no shape, she is not a personification of nature, Wordsworthian or simply "Romantic," but just what she is said to be—light, that medium of seeing which pervades this poem as what is common to all of its scenes. Light is what generates spectacle, the theatrically visible, and also what generates concept, theory, or idea. Theatre and theory have of course the same Greek root (*theoria*, what can be seen), and *idea* in Greek means perceptible image, again what can be seen. The light can only be seen in theatrical personifications. It is never seen as itself. It must always be seen in image or in figure. To be seen it must be turned away from itself, masked. It is always seen veiled but revealed in its veiling, forgotten and remembered at once. The shape all light is the manifestation in Shelley's poem of the incompatibility between pure seeing or pure theory, and that instant interpretation of the light that names it, gives it a shape, makes it a sign, a figure, or an allegorical person.

The constant substitution of one such figure for another will indicate the meaning of that sense-confusing (in both senses of the word *sense*) synesthesia which is so conspicuous a feature of the poem. Synesthesia appears especially in the penultimate scene of the shape all light and in the last scene of the shadow-making glare of Life. Light, sound, smell, and feeling are all interchanged in these scenes. Music is the primary trope for this synesthesia. The mixture of appeals to the various senses makes a medley like the "many sounds woven into one / Oblivious melody, confusing sense" (lines 340-341) in the first of these scenes, or like the "savage music, stunning music" of Rousseau's "Vision" of the chariot of Life in the second (lines 434-435). That music is not Apollonian, in spite of its association with the sun, but Dionysiac, irrational. Shelley's light, even his sunlight, is always the dark light of Life. The savage music of nature deprives its auditors of clear-headed reason, like that music, echo of Shelley's, in Yeats's "News for the Delphic Oracle": "Down the mountain walls / From where Pan's cavern is / Intolerable music falls."[17] Rousseau's vision turns

[17] Lines 30-32, W. B. Yeats, *The Variorium Edition of the Poems*, ed. Peter Allt and Russell K. Alspach (New York: Macmillan Publishing Co., Inc., 1977), p. 612.

into audition, which destroys the integrity of clear seeing. For Shelley, whatever is seen, heard, smelled, or felt with one sense turns into something perceived by a different sense. The constant exchange of one sense for another is like stunning music that tramples out thought and memory as well as even the power of distinct perception itself.

Shelley's insistence on images of feet treading or trampling indicates the physical violence of this blotting from memory. As de Man has seen, the motif of treading joins the image of music to indicate that the instrument of oblivion is not undifferentiated sense experience, the appeal to all the senses of the natural scene, but the metrical, rhythmical ordering of sense data. As a mere sound becomes music when it is joined to other sounds at regular intervals and rhythmically ordered, so sounds become words and words become poetry when they are differentiated, modulated, and then divided into "feet." The patterning that makes order and beauty in music or poetry at the same time gives them a power to "stun" their auditors, to obliterate the past and even to blot out clarity of mind in the present. For Shelley, as I have indicated, there is no pure perception as such. Whatever is seen, heard, or felt is seen, heard, or felt as already turned into signs. For this reason, the linguistic moment for him is not intermittent but perpetual. This transformation of perception into interpretation, the projection and reading of signs, at once makes things intelligible and at the same time deprives them of intelligibility or deprives the victim of the power to read them. It is not so much signs as such that have this stunning power as the rhythmic patterning of these signs, the repeatable metrical or syntactical paradigms into which they are ordered and which is the condition of their beauty and of their intelligibility. An example would be the arrangement and rearrangement of the same figurative and conceptual elements that make up the sequence of scenes in "The Triumph of Life." The identification of this recurrent pattern is both the means by which the reader comprehends

169

the poem, and at the same time it is a musical ordering
that numbs his mind and deprives him of the power to
remember the specificity of previous scenes or even to see
clearly what is going on in the present one just before his
eyes. The effect of the poem on its reader re-enacts the
effect of the savage music on Rousseau. The reader of the
poem experiences again what Rousseau experienced when
his brain became as sand.

The exchanges of figuration that take place under the
aegis of the shape all light are, it can be "seen," by no means
viewed as a benign process by Shelley. This is indicated in
the way all light displaces the sun. When the sun rises on
the April morning in which Rousseau finds himself asleep,
it is seen, as it was for the poet in the opening scene, as a
radiant male figure narcissistically admiring himself reflected in his creation. As Rousseau says, the "Sun's image
radiantly intense / Burned on the waters of the well that
glowed / Like gold, and threaded all the forest maze / With
winding paths of emerald fire" (lines 345-348). The sun
reflects himself to himself in masculine splendor (lines 349-
350), but the female figure of the shape all light, mother,
sister, mistress, muse, "[stands] / Amid the sun, as he amid
the blaze / Of his own glory" (lines 348-350). She interferes
with the self-enclosed circuit of the sun and image of the
sun, displacing it, blotting it out, unmanning the sun. Sexual differentiation blocks the perfection of male self-ad-
miration and induces a wandering into figurative substitutions with no identifiable beginning, end, or answer to
the question, "Why?" The shape all light stands amid the
sun *as* the sun stands in his own glory. In that *as*, the turning
begins again, and the light henceforth can never return to
itself. The diverted play of reflection forbids the light to
return to the *heliologos*, its seeming paternal source, just as
Narcissus, in one version of his story, can never join himself
to himself by way of that twin sister he has loved, and just
as Shelley's heroes in his various quest-poems can never
satisfy a desire for unity with a counterpart of the other
sex. That desire is consistently dramatized by Shelley, from

"Laon and Cythna" on, as incestuous love. Sexual desire appears in "The Triumph of Life" not only in the early sequence about erotic love but also in the relation of Rousseau to the lady all light who offers him Nepenthe, so making him forget nature, which had made him forget himself, and so making him one more of light's victims. The female light as shape-changer stands between a man and the masculine sun, unmanning that sun by making it appear no more than one of the changing shapes of light. This revelation renders powerless the man who seeks through the mediation of the female shape all light to take possession of the sun's power or of the power behind the sun.

This subversive feminine shifting of the light is figured in the identification of the lady with that star which in the morning is called Lucifer, in the evening Venus. The passage is of great beauty:

> "—so on my sight
> Burst a new Vision never seen before.—
>
> "And the fair shape waned in the coming light
>   As veil by veil the silent splendour drops
>   From Lucifer, amid the chrysolite
>
> "Of sunrise ere it strike the mountain tops—
>   And as the presence of that fairest planet
> Although unseen is felt by one who hopes
>
> "That his day's path may end as he began it
> In that star's smile, whose light is like the scent
>   Of a jonquil when evening breezes fan it,
>
> "Or the soft note in which his dear lament
>   The Brescian shepherd breathes, or the caress
> That turned his weary slumber to content,—
>
> "So knew I in that light's severe excess
> The presence of that shape which on the stream
>   Moved . . ."
>
> (lines 410-426)

171

The process dramatized here is only by a chiasmic reversal called a removing of veils, a revelation or "apocalypse" in the literal sense. What is revealed is invisibility. It is as if the light itself were a veil, a cover for the black light of Lucifer. As the sun rises, veil after veil of the silent splendor of the morning star drops not to reveal the star in all its naked glory but to darken it completely. To present the ubiquitous light in the allegorical figure of the lady and then to identify her with starlight distinguishes this light from sunlight or from any of sunlight's derivatives—for example, the secondary light of the moon. This presentation also identifies the light of the shape all light with the internal, sign-making, poetry-writing light of the human imagination. Starlight was, at the beginning of the poem, the reader will remember, used as a figure for the poet's nighttime thoughts that must remain untold. Since the star in question is in the morning named Lucifer, the light must be diabolical, subversive, Satanic, a counterlight challenging the apparent originality of the sun. The name *Lucifer* means of course light-bearer, just as the word *metaphor* means, etymologically, bear across. Both words contain the same root, *fer* or *phor*—"carry." To call the shape all light Lucifer is to name her the principle of figurative transfer. She is the one who presides over that slipping of the universal principle of light from shape to shape in a constant substitution of one figure for another. "The Triumph of Life" enacts this process from beginning to broken "end."

The feminine principle of slippage has power even over the sun. It has power to force the spectator to see the sun itself as only another shape of light. In the passage using the figure of the morning and evening star, the sun itself has become merely a figure. It is an image for the light of the chariot of Life. That light displaces the shape all light, "as" the sun puts out the morning star. The light is borne here, there, elsewhere, by whatever shape happens for the moment to carry it as temporary "Lucifer." Lucifer proper, the morning star, becomes in the evening Venus, star of love. This is a further example of metaphorical slipping and of its connection with a naming that is never really "proper" but always in one way or another figurative.

That the star of diabolical shape-changing is also the star of love identifies the drama of figuration with a drama of sexual desire. The early passage about the dancing lovers has already shown this to be the case. To love is to become subject to the shifting of light and so to become a victim of Life and a captive of his triumphal car. This casts an ironic light on the claim sometimes made by critics that Love, for Shelley, is a transcendental principle free of the play of substitutions and governing it. One passage (lines 471-480) describes the generation of legions of shadows by the victims of Life as a wonder worthy of Dante's rhyme. This passage might seem to authorize a universalizing of Love. It affirms that Dante showed "how all things are transfigured, except Love," and it projects the sphere of Venus as a serene realm "whose light is melody to lovers," far above the wrathful sea of Life. In the perspective of the identification of Lucifer and Venus with one another and with the shape all light made a little earlier in the poem, however, to say all things are transfigured, except Love, is to say no more than that the light persists through all its changes of figure. This includes those transfigurations motivated by erotic love and by its special power to cast shadows in the light. This is dramatized again in the final vision of the multitude of self-consuming shadows projected by the victims of Life. This process is a wonder worthy of Dante's rhyme because it is the same wonder as the one he dramatized, in Shelley's skeptical reinterpretation of what Dante meant by showing how all things are transfigured, except Love.

The passage about the double-named star makes explicit the identification of synesthesia with metaphorical substitution. The star that is both Lucifer and Venus is like a flower's scent, or like a song, or like a love caress, because it is the emblem of that principle of interfiguration among

173

all things that may be seen, smelled, heard, or felt. These make a potentially endless chain: or . . . or . . . or. A final form of this interchange is that from one sex to another. In the passage describing the displacement of the female shape by the Vision of Life, Life is also apparently a woman. She is now figured as female sun or star. This is indicated by the pronoun *her* in line 438. The four-faced charioteer must be the locus of another interchange of the sexes, like that between Lucifer and Venus. The reader is at first inclined to assume that Life, as a conquering general celebrating his triumph in battle, must be unequivocally masculine, like the sun. This warrior must be also female, however, even in his/her first appearance to the poet, if the implications of the image of the moon are accepted. The charioteer is the mother moon held in the arms of her more luminous daughter, the halo around her head.

When the light of Lucifer-Venus is put out, or almost put out, by the sun that is no sun but another shape of light here troped as the sun, Rousseau, as he says, soon plunges into the "thickest billows of the living storm" and bares his bosom to the clime of Life's cold light (lines 466-468). This gesture of plunging leads to the end of the poem as we have it. It will lead also to the last move in my zigzag course threading through "The Triumph of Life." I have moved back and forth across the surface of this text like an ant exploring the patterns of a quilt, tracing its warp and woof in mingled multicolored yarn. My last step returns to the issue of comprehension. Does the poem provide answers to the questions it so insistently asks about the origin, end, and why of Life? Does the poet find answers to these questions? Does Rousseau? Can I as critic formulate answers that the reader of this essay can comprehend rationally and take away as a total interpretation of the poem?

I do not think a positive answer can be given to any of these questions. The final impasse both of the poem and of the vision of life the poem proposes is that neither of these can be understood by either of the two strategies of comprehension the poem itself proposes. One of these is the spectator's detachment that sees all comprehensively and with cool rationality from the outside. "The onlookers see most of the game." The other is that actor's involvement which plunges into the storm and understands it from within, as experience proved on the pulses. Neither strategy of understanding works, for reasons that the poem specifies. The alternatives surface most explicitly in Rousseau's ironic invitation to the poet in answer to his questions about the whence, the whereto, and the why:

"But follow thou, & from spectator turn
    Actor or victim in this wretchedness,

"And what thou wouldst be taught I then may learn
    From thee.—"

                  (lines 305-308)

What happens if this strategy is followed Rousseau's own example shows. It leads to obliteration, oblivion, the undoing of memory. One's brain becomes as sand. All hope of finding origin, end, or ground is lost. Neither involvement nor detachment finds an answer to the questions posed by the poem, though life forces each man and woman to try one or the other strategy, or both. The uninvolved spectator sees nothing but a confused spectacle, and so sees nothing. Life can only be explored from within. The involved actor, however, is always a victim of the light's perpetually renewed power of disremembering, and so he too sees nothing but a confused spectacle. He has no hope even of knowing what came just before or will come just after, so blinded is his vision. Much less can he hope to know the source, the goal, or the cause of the whole chain of visions that imprisons him. Thinking according to polar oppositions here breaks down once more. To be an actor is to be a victim, the victim is an actor, as the poem abundantly shows. It shows this both for the main protagonists, the poet and Rousseau, and in its historical portraits—for example, that of Napoleon. A spectator is already willy-nilly an actor, since even the most passive and detached seeing is always an activity of interpretation. Interpretation plunges the spectator into the thickest billows of the living storm and so obliterates for him the beginning and end of that storm.

This situation applies equally to human life as it is dramatized within Shelley's poem and to the situation of the reader or critic who would seek to understand the poem totally, to encompass and command it. A complete comprehension of either a single work by a writer or of his work as a whole would see all around that work and recapitulate it from some *point de départ*, perhaps in the author's *cogito* or act of self-consciousness, to some endpoint toward which that work moves in obedience to its own laws. Such comprehension is forbidden by the fact that to understand the work at all it is necessary to enter into it, to abandon oneself to the itinerary traced out by the text. To do so is to become lost in interminable wanderings within that text. These wanderings are only arbitrarily put in order and concluded by some *finis*. No critical essay does final justice to the poem in question. Each leaves the work of criticism to be done over again. The reader adds himself to the chain made by Shelley, by Rousseau, and by all those precursors fading back like ancestors in a genealogical tree: Milton, Dante, St. John, Ezekiel. The reader's position is no different from theirs and no more capable of achieving mastery over life or over language. To attempt to see the game, the play of language in "The Triumph of Life," the reader must enter into it. He must play the game himself. This means becoming himself a victim of Life and of language. This victimization, for the critic, takes the form of an experience of uncertainty about the meaning of the poem. This uncertainty is constituted by the fact that he cannot decide for sure whether or not the text is readable, in the sense of being open to a univocal reading. He cannot demonstrate whether or not the poem is open to a single definitive interpretation, and so he must continue his exploration of it.

To become a victim of the poem means experiencing the impossibility of ever unravelling all its threads. Instead of that final straightening out he seeks, the reader untwists one part of the poem while in that act he twists up again another part. The chain as a whole remains as knotted as ever. The critic's activity—for example, mine in this essay—is a moving back and forth across the text attempting to untangle it all, but tangling it up again in some other section when the one on which attention is centered is straightened out. This frustrating activity—Penelope performing the day's weaving and the night's unweaving in the same gesture—is, to vary the metaphor, a remembering that is at the same time a forgetting. It never succeeds in holding the whole text in an absolute clarity of understanding all in the mind at once. Since it never succeeds, it may never be completed. Reading too is an experience of an-anamnesis, the reverse of Platonic remembering.

This essay has proceeded through a sequence of sections focusing narrowly on one passage after another of the poem. The essay is at once too short and too long. It is too short because it by no means exhaustively interprets the whole poem. Much that could and should be said is left unsaid. On the other hand, it is too long to be seen through perspicuously (as Aristotle said should happen with a good work) or to be held all in the mind at once. In a critical essay too, the intense concentration on a given passage or topic necessitates the forgetting, or at least the partial forgetting, of what has already been said. The experience of reading the critical essay corresponds to the experience of reading the poem. This is so not because the essay foolishly attempts to be "poetic," but because the critic too is caught in a double bind. If he writes something wholly logical and transparent, a shapely essay, he will falsify the poem. If he does even approximate justice to this admirably intricate poem, he will present again in his own essay the pattern

177

of forgetting and remembering that the poem itself both exemplifies and is "about."

This simultaneous remembering and forgetting is described and enacted within the poem itself. The metaphors of the traces on the sand and of the figures on the bubble that fade as they are drawn are tropes of writing. They are tropes, that is, for the writing of the poem and for its reading. Rousseau answers the poet's questions with more speech, and I in my turn, or any other critic, must do the same. To do this is a way of turning from spectator to actor and so of becoming another victim of Life, that is, of language. My situation as reader of the poem is no different from that of Rousseau as seer, since reading and seeing are the same in the sense that both are acts of deciphering. This deciphering at the same time creates more cryptic signs to be decoded. It covers the signs to be read with more signs. The new signs cause the earlier ones to fade into oblivion, as Lucifer fades in the morning light.

The moment of reading is the moment of forgetting. It is the moment when one turns from spectator to actor and enters into the text in an attempt to answer those questions basic to literary criticism since Aristotle: whence, where, and why. Instead of an answer the reader gets Nepenthe, literature as the drug of forgetfulness. However hard the reader tries to stay awake, his brain becomes as sand. It is washed clean, or almost clean, by a great wave of light. The reader then gets the next vision, the next writing on the screen or shore or bubble of the next shadowy figure, the next sand-script replacing that just effaced. The new writing is inscribed in palimpsest over what has almost been effaced, as each episode replaces the last in "The Triumph of Life," or as this essay is written over the text of the poem and repeats its serial structure. Each new writing both obliterates what came before and unwittingly prolongs it. This act is unwitting because its relation to what it replaces can never be wholly clear, neither to the commentator nor to his readers. It can never give, once and for all, an answer to the whence, the whither, and the why.

At the end of all my commentary, I find myself where I began. As a reader of "The Triumph of Life" I am the next in a chain of repetitions without beginning or end. I find myself again enfolded in a fold, asleep under a caverned mountain beside a brook, watching a sequence of shapes all light, projecting in my turn figures over those shapes, figures that fade even as they are traced, to be replaced by others, in an unending production of signs over signs . . .

CHAPTER FOUR

Browning

Mann ist was er isst. (Man is what he eats.)
Ludwig Feuerbach

If Shelley's "The Triumph of Life" is in part an interpretation of Wordsworth's "Immortality" ode, and if Hardy's work so overlaps Shelley's that it almost seems the prior writing with which Shelley had to struggle in order to become himself, "The Englishman in Italy," as other critics have noted, is in part a rewriting of Shelley's "Lines Written Among the Euganean Hills."[1] In all these relations of priority and posteriority the linguistic moment, the moment when language becomes problematic and assumes a momentum of its own, is occasioned by the later poet's implicit critique of a naive taking for granted of language. This he either ironically or mistakenly ascribes to the earlier poet. I say "either ironically or mistakenly" because the work of the

[1] See Lawrence Poston III, "Browning and the Altered Romantic Landscape," *Nature and the Victorian Imagination*, ed. U. C. Knoepflmacher and G. B. Tennyson (Berkeley, Los Angeles, London: University of California Press, 1977), pp. 434-435. Commentary on "The Englishman in Italy" has been relatively sparse. See the entry on the poem in William Clyde DeVane, *A Browning Handbook*, 2d ed. (New York: Appleton-Century-Crofts, Inc., 1955), pp. 157-159, and see, for example, Barbara Melchiori, *Browning's Poetry of Reticence* (New York: Barnes & Noble, Inc., 1968), pp. 124, 130; Philip Drew, *The Poetry of Browning: A Critical Introduction* (London: Metheun & Co. Ltd., 1970), pp. 77, 118, 269, 285-286; Donald S. Hair, *Browning's Experiments with Genre* (Toronto and Buffalo: University of Toronto Press, 1972), p. 80; William E. Harrold, *The Variance and the Unity* (Athens, Ohio: Ohio University Press, 1973), pp. 67-77; Michael Ross, "Browning's Art of Perspective: 'The Englishman in Italy,' " *English Studies in Canada* VII, 1 (Spring 1981), 54-67. Ross discusses the poem from the point of view of "perspective," that is, of seeing and perception, not, as I do, from the point of view of language and the "linguistic moment."

earlier poet, when it is examined closely, turns out to be as sophisticated in this matter as the work of the later poet. There is not much evidence, not at least among my poets, for any progression in linguistic sophistication.

"The Englishman in Italy" is one of Robert Browning's most splendidly exuberant poems of appropriation through language. By naming, in memory, one by one, a great number of the items in the landscape of the Sorrento plain, along with details of the way of life of the people there, the speaker makes the landscape and the people his own. Through language the Englishman comes to be truly at home in Italy, not just an alien presence there. He comes to be surrounded by the Sorrento plain as by his own proper environment. More particularly, he achieves a kind of intimacy with Fortù, the Italian girl to whom his monologue is spoken. The means of this appropriation is synecdoche, part standing for whole, but always needing yet another part to make again the gesture of reaching out toward the whole. The speaker's memory is total. He can effortlessly call all things back from the past and name them. This procedure is precisely defined in that image which the speaker uses to explain to his auditor what he is going to do: "Let me keep you amused till he [Scirocco] vanish / In black from the skies, / With telling my memories over / As you tell your beads."[2] Each memory is a kind of globular whole, a distinct unit of remembered experience that contains a specific meaning or vitality. This can be recovered in the act of renaming it, "telling it over." The whole lot of them makes a chain that is rounded ultimately into a larger circular whole. Or at any rate the poem moves toward such a rounding off. "The Englishman in Italy" is made of an intricate overlapping of different modes of this pattern.

[2] Lines 7-10. Citations from Browning's poems are made from Robert Browning, The Complete Works, ed. Roma A. King, Jr. et al. (Athens, Ohio: Ohio University Press, 1969ff.). "The Englishman in Italy" is in IV, pp. 173-182 of this edition.

One mode is the rhyme scheme. The poem is made of a strong anapestic rhythm in alternating lines of three and two stresses. The longer lines do not rhyme. The shorter ones rhyme in delayed couplets, so that a given nine-line segment would rhyme as *a b c b d e f e g*:

Time for rain! for your long hot dry Autumn	*a*
Had net-worked with brown	*b*
The white skin of each grape on the bunches,	*c*
Marked like a quail's crown,	*b*
Those creatures you make such account of,	*d*
Whose heads,—speckled white	*e*
Over brown like a great spider's back,	*f*
As I told you last night,—	*e*
Your mother bites off for her supper.	*g*

(lines 13-21)

The effect of this intermittent chiming, abetted by the usual strong end-stop on the second rhyme word while the long lines often have feminine endings, is to turn every fourth line back on the one, two lines before. Each segment of four lines is experienced as a kind of spherical unit with its own completeness, like a bead on a string. Part of the pleasure of the poem is the suspension as the reader waits through two lines to see what word Browning will find as a rhyme this time. He shows great virtuosity in finding decisive chiming words, for example snails/regales, or pomp/stomp. This self-completeness tends to be reinforced by a syntactical, nominal, or thematic unity within each four-line unit, as, for example, the first four lines of the passage just quoted describe the grapes.

The image of the globular unit, introduced in Browning's figure of memories as like beads, is reinforced by the fact that so many of the things itemized in the poem are spherical or at any rate self-enclosed bundles of energy—for example, the quails' heads, the grapes, and the spider in the passage cited above. As the poem continues, among other things of this sort the reader encounters pomegranates, figs, tomatoes, the "curd-white smooth cheese-ball" (line 107), the flask of wine, the "fruit-balls" of the myrtles (line 137), the "hairy gold orbs" of the sorbapple (line 140), and even the "strange lumps" of the "pink and gray jellies, your sea-fruit" (lines 58, 57).

The intervening unrhymed lines, on the other hand, break up the reader's sense that the poem is a series of enclosed units. The unrhymed lines form, so to speak, the string on which the beads are strung. The reader half expects these lines too to be answered by some echoing word, and, since they are not, the fulfillment of his expectation is indefinitely postponed. The string continues, strung with bead after bead of rhyme-words and of self-contained memory units.

These memory units are not wholly self-contained. The constantly self-renewing quality of the poem is supported by many syntactical, rhythmical, and figurative elements in Browning's language. Just when the reader thinks the poem is going to come to an end or at least to the definite conclusion of a unit of meaning, the Englishman takes breath again and continues. His voice is indefatigable in mentioning item after item in the scene, as if each could only be assimilated by being named. No poem of moderate length by Browning gives more admirably that effect of interminability which is a special feature of his verse. It is the interminability of a garrulous murmuring voice that goes on and on talking, caught in the groove of a constantly self-generating rhythmical pattern, almost like a record that "skips."

"The Englishman in Italy" provides indirectly an image for this in the description of Fortú's brother treading the grapes, always receiving more just when he seems to have beaten down the ones he already has:

> In the vat, halfway up in our house-side,
>   Like blood the juice spins,
> While your brother all bare-legged is dancing

> Till breathless he grins
> Dead-beaten in effort on effort
> To keep the grapes under,
> Since still when he seems all but master.
> In pours the fresh plunder . . .
>
> (lines 73-80)

This sentence continues for twenty more lines before it is firmly stopped by a period and a strong masculine monosyllabic rhyme: ropes/popes. Then follows a new sentence introduced by the word *Meantime*. This starts the language going once more, as if new grapes had been thrown in the vat. The sentences mime the thing about which they talk. The effect of tireless continuation is partly achieved by the use of enjambment, as in "speckled white / Over brown" in the passage first quoted above, or by the addition of an unexpected new phrase to a syntactical unit that is already complete, as in the phrase "As I told you last night,—" which makes up line 20. It is partly achieved by the insertion within dashes or parentheses—Browning is a master of the dash—of a unit of meaning that postpones the uttering of the verb or noun that will complete the sense of the main clause, as in: "Whose heads—speckled white / Over brown like a great spider's back / As I told you last night,— / Your mother bites off for her supper." Or the effect of virtual endlessness is achieved by semicolons or colons or by a sequence of conjunctions making a run-on sentence strung on a series of *ands* and *ors*:

> Red-ripe as could be,
> Pomegranates were chapping and splitting
> In halves on the tree:
> And betwixt the loose walls of great flintstone,
> Or in the thick dust
> On the path, or straight out of the rock-side,
> Wherever could thrust
> Some burnt sprig of bold hardy rock-flower

Its yellow face up,
For the prize were great butterflies fighting,
Some five for one cup.
                    (lines 22-32)

The effect of an enchainment threading the beads together is strongly reinforced by Browning's use of figure,
especially of simile. Much of the poem is vigorously literal
in its language. Word after word naming a thing or its
qualities, often in a sequence of monosyllables or disylla-
bles, is uttered as a means of evoking the thing in question
in all its specificity. An example is the line: "Some burnt
sprig of bold hardy rock-flower." Figurative language is
present here only in the rather unostentatious personification, "bold hardy," unless "burnt" is seen as a metaphor.
Figures are nevertheless constantly used in aid of specificity, as when the Englishman says the brown network over
the white skin of each grape marks it "like a quail's crown."
In most ways a grape and a quail's head are dissimilar, but
in one way they are alike, though this likeness is only partial.
Grapes are a brown net over white, while the quail's head
is "speckled white / Over brown like a great spider's back."
The poem, as the reader can see, moves laterally from
likeness to likeness. The quail's head, brought in merely as
an illustrative simile, then becomes a subject of its own,
earning six lines of the poem. The quail's head, in turn, is
said to be "like" a spider's back. The effect of these similes
is not just to create a chain saying "this is like that is like
that," but to suggest that all these items are there side by
side in a kind of spatial array, bound together by a network
of partial similarity, not just of contiguity. This allows the
poet to move sideways or back and forth at will from one
to another.

To the image of the thread must be added the image of
the net. The latter is present not only in the description of
the grapes and the quail's heads, but also, a few lines later,
in the description of "the quick rustle-down of the quail-

nets" as they are dropped in preparation for the storm (lines 33-44). In all three instances the net is cast over a contiguous array of centers of self-enclosed energy or life: the grapes, the quails' heads, the living quails for which the nets are set. In a similar way the crisscrossing threads of various forms of continuous and self-renewing language in Browning's poem are cast as a retiform grid over the individual beads of rhymed units, each a distinct memory called back from the past by the Englishman's words, and all put there side by side in the poem, captured in the net of words.

I have spoken of these globular units as self-contained corpuscles of energy. The evidence for this is the way so many of them in one way or another open themselves out to the world. This may happen as a pushing up of things from their occultation in rock or earth, as the bold, hardy rock-flower "thrusts itself up," or as the "silver-gray fume-weed," the rosemary, the lentisks, and the unnamed third plant, which "shows a branch / Coral-coloured, transparent, with circlets / Of pale seagreen leaves," spring from the mountain rocks later in the poem (lines 157-166), or as the "scorpion with wide angry nippers," at the poem's end, will come out of the garden wall if you tap with a hoe on the plaster (lines 281-285). The coming forth may happen as an explosive bursting open, as the pomegranates "were chapping and splitting," as the figs are split to dry in the sun, as the old bottles filled with gunpowder are "popped" to honor Mary's image at "the Feast / Of the Rosary's Virgin" (lines 250-251), and as the "sea-fruit," in one of the most splendid passages in the poem, open when you touch them:

> No seeing our skiff
> Arrive about noon from Amalfi,
> —Our fisher arrive,
> And pitch down his basket before us,

All trembling alive
With pink and gray jellies, your sea-fruit;
　You touch the strange lumps,
And mouths gape there, eyes open, all manner
　Of horns and of humps,
Which only the fisher looks grave at . . .
(lines 52-61)

The opening of the mouths and eyes of the strange sea-creatures produces a corresponding opening of the spectators' mouths in smiling or in laughter. The opener is opened. The exposure of the world as these things one by one come into the open and appear, first in themselves and then again when they are revealed retrospectively by being named, causes a reciprocal opening of the witness of all this activity. The major expression of this in the poem, as the reader will no doubt already have noticed, is eating. "The Englishman in Italy" is one of the greatest of gustatory poems. The celebration of life on the Sorrento plain is based on the paradox of a harsh, stony, inedible soil and a salt inhospitable sea that bring forth food abundantly for the inhabitants. In England's green and pleasant land, on the contrary, men and women starve because not enough corn is produced and absurd laws forbid its sufficient importation. Item after item in the list, bead after bead strung on the string or caught within the net, names something new to be eaten: the grapes, the quails, the pomegranates, the rock-flower's cup sipped by the butterflies, the split figs, the "pink and grey jellies, your sea-fruit," tomatoes, snails, lasagne, purple gourds, the "curd-white smooth cheese-ball / That peels, flake by flake, / Like an onion, each smoother and whiter" (lines 107-109), the flask of wine, the prickly pear, olives, the vine boughs that are fodder for the mules and cows, the fruit-balls of the myrtles, "black, glossy and luscious" (line 137), the "hairy gold orbs" of the sorbapples, the windfalls from the Scirocco that the hog comes out to share in when the storm is over. Even the orchestra music

187

that follows the Dominican brother's sermon at the Feast of the Virgin is spoken of as "the feast's second course" (line 268), as if to call attention to the gustatory image in that word *Feast*. It would be necessary to cite and discuss more or less the whole poem in order to demonstrate in detail the way Browning, partly by the use of strongly tactile and qualitative words in aid of the images of taste (e.g. "curd-white smooth cheese-balls" or "prickly-pear's red flesh" [lines 107, 113]) conveys to the reader the sense that this is a world to be perceived in its color and shape, to be touched with the fingers, lips, tongue, palate, throat, but most of all to be tasted and so to be assimilated.

The world of the Amalfi coast in all its particularity is appropriated by a foreigner and a spectator. In doing so he ceases to be an outsider. He makes the world that so temptingly opens itself from a hundred centers his own by literally taking it into himself. What the natives of the *Piano di Sorrento* do by right of ownership, the Englishman does in his turn through language. The reader too then repeats the act of assimilation as he responds in imagination to the invitation made overtly to the Englishman's auditor, Fortù, but also made implicitly to the real listener-reader of the poem, you or me, as the last in the series. For analogies in other poetry in English, one thinks of some passages in Keats, in one direction, and of certain poems by William Carlos Williams, in the other—for example, the poem about the plums the poet's wife left in the refrigerator and the poet ate: "This is Just to Say."[3] But Browning exceeds even Keats and Williams for sheer sensuous appeal to the faculty of taste. Here is one of the most extraordinary of such sequences in the poem. I begin my citation thirteen lines into a sentence that begins at line 73:

> For under the hedges of aloe,
>   And where, on its bed
> Of the orchard's black mould, the love-apple

---

[3] William Carlos Williams, *The Collected Earlier Poems* (New York: New Directions, 1951), p. 354.

Lies pulpy and red,
All the young [girls] are kneeling and filling
   Their laps with the snails
Tempted out by this first rainy weather,—
   Your best of regales,
As to-night will be proved to my sorrow,
   When, supping in state,
We shall feast our grape-gleaners (two dozen,
   Three over one plate)
With lasagne so tempting to swallow
   In slippery ropes,
And gourds fried in great purple slices,
   That color of popes.
Meantime, see the grape bunch they've brought you:
   The rain-water slips
O'er the heavy blue bloom on each globe
   Which the wasp to your lips
Still follows the fretful persistence:
   Nay, taste, while awake,
This half of a curd-white smooth cheese-ball
   That peels, flake by flake,
Like an onion, each smoother and whiter;
   Next, sip this weak wine
From the thin green glass flask, with its stopper
   A leaf of the vine;
And end with the prickly-pear's red flesh
   That leaves thro' its juice
The stony black seeds on your pearl-teeth.
                    (lines 85-115)

The appeal to Fortù, as I have said, is indirectly an appeal to the reader to taste, chew and swallow these things in imagination. There is more to say about this, however. If the reader reads these lines out loud, the experience of expressing vocally Browning's savory and almost over-rich language is a linguistic miming of the act of tasting and eating that the lines describe. The lines are full of strong labials, gutterals, heavy vowels, *ahs* and *ohs* and consonantal clusters, for example: "with lasagne so tempting to swallow / In slippery ropes." To put this another way, Browning's act of naming things, mouthing them, or his imaginary Englishman's act of doing so, is a performative action. Things are assimilated by being spoken, almost as if they were being eaten. If for Feuerbach man is what he eats, for Browning man is what he utters. To name something is to appropriate it. It is a way of doing things with words. The act of nomination makes the thing one's own in an almost magical act. It seems to be for this reason that the Englishman makes his inventory of all the things in the Sorrento plain, telling over to Fortù, who is native to the place, what surely she abundantly knows and hardly needs to be told about.

I have spoken so far as if the Englishman's speech-act were exclusively an act of recollection, a bringing back of the past and taking possession of it. As a matter of fact, as the reader has no doubt already observed, "The Englishman in Italy" is by no means simply a poem of memory, whatever the Englishman initially says, unless "memory" is taken, as it is for example in the Scotist terminology Gerard Manley Hopkins adopted, as a term for immediate sensation, addressed to all three dimensions of time. *Memoria*, for Scotus and for Hopkins, perhaps in his own way for Browning too, is the opening out of the senses and of the self to receive things that offer themselves to be appropriated in past, present, and future. In any case, Browning's poem is by no means limited to memories in the strict sense of recollections from the past. The opening sequence about the grapes, the pomegranates, the figs, and the beginning of the grape harvest is in the past tense. It describes something that has just occurred that morning. This quickly becomes first a description in the present tense of what is going on now (the treading of grapes, the gathering of snails), and then a projection into the future, in the future tense—an anticipation of the harvest feast of lasagne and fried gourds. This has not yet happened, but is so sure to happen, because it has always happened that way, that the future feast can be seen and tasted in language as though it were being remembered from the past. Then the poem slips, by way of the word *meantime*, back to the immediate presences in the present, in the exhortations to Fortù to see the grape bunch, taste the cheese-ball, sip the wine, and eat the prickly pear.

The temporal structure of "The Englishman in Italy" is complex. It would require a long analysis to follow it in detail. The law of this structure is a constant, more or less rapid movement back and forth across the face of time: back into a past more distant that the grape harvest, but never further away than the night before, when the Englishman made his climb to the top of Mount Calvano and had his conversation with Fortù about quails. The poem then moves up to the rainy morning just past, finally up to a present that occurs in the very moments in which the Englishman puts it into words, then forward into future events that are sure to happen (the harvest feast, the religious celebration on the morrow), or which sometimes (as in the excursion to the Galli Isles the Englishman proposes to Fortù) are given as hypothetical possibilities: "Fortù, shall we sail there together . . . ?" (line 209). The image of telling "memories" over like beads is fulfilled in a movement to and fro across time that draws the series of globular units ultimately into a ring or circle. This movement goes back into the past in order to come up to the present and into the future, or goes into the future in order more surely to appropriate the past. The Englishman's possession of the landscape and of all its contents is at the same time also a possession of time or, more precisely, of human temporality, both his own private temporality and that of the people of the region. I say "temporality" rather than "time," since it is a matter of a dynamic movement back into the recent past in memory, then forward to the anticipated future, and back again to a present that encompasses both, making of time not a straight line but a circle or a globular whole. Since everything that happens in the *Piano di Sorrento*, in the diurnal round of day and night and in the annual round of the seasons, has happened over and over since time immemorial, memory, anticipation, and present experience come in the end to the same thing. All together make a perpetual present in which whatever happens happens as repetition, that is, as something that has always gone on before and is always going on happening, in a "moment, one and infinite," to use Browning's phrase from "By the Fireside." Both religious ritual, the Feast of the Virgin, and the natural ritual of fishing, planting, and harvest, turning with the weather and with the seasons, belong to this perpetual present. Past, present, and future are drawn together into one and held there, first in reality, and then in their telling over in the performative language of the poet. The taking possession of this unification is a speech-act.

The notion of an infinite moment is overtly dramatized in the poem in another way. I have spoken so far as if the telling over of the memory beads were a lateral nonprogressive movement, all on the same plane, a free sweeping back and forth across time. But the rosary beads are an image of time as a linear series of prayers making ultimately a round that signifies a leap out of time into eternity. This initial figure for the structure of the poem is reinforced later on by the fact that the religious celebration about to occur on the morrow is "the Feast / Of the *Rosary's* Virgin" (lines 250-251, my italics). Twice in the poem the reader is presented with an ascending spiral of spatial movement leading ultimately to an explosive instant of escape from time into total possession of time and space. Along with this goes momentary insight into infinity and eternity.

The first such passage extends from line 133 to line 196. This is the Englishman's description of how he climbed Mount Calvano on muleback, guided by Fortù's brother. In this climb linear sequence became ascending circles until at the summit, in the Englishman's recounting, past tense

becomes present tense by way of an exclamatory ejacula-
tion. In this exclamation, past, present, and future vanish.
All space—above, below, around—are possessed at once in
a moment out of time and transcending space. The vacant
blue sky, "heaven" in one sense, becomes the means of
glimpsing "heaven" in the sense of the "terrible crystal" of
infinity and eternity. Though Browning says there is "no
rampart," the word, along with the gem-imagery implicit
in "terrible crystal," introduces surreptitiously the figure
from *Revelation* of the heavenly Jerusalem, visionary city of
eternal life, substantial and transparent at once:

> Till, round after round,
> He [the mule] climbed to the top of Calvano,
>   And God's own profound
> Was above me, and round me the mountains,
>   And under, the sea,
> And within me my heart to bear witness
>   What was and shall be.
> Oh, heaven and the terrible crystal!
>   No rampart excludes
> Your eye from the life to be lived
>   In the blue solitudes.
>   (lines 170-180)

If the image of the string of beads in linear series is
replaced here by the ascending spiral, the image in turn is
replaced by the figure of globe within globe within globe,
in expanding and contracting rounds. In this passage the
Englishman is finally *in* Italy in the sense of being surrounded by it on all sides, just as in the other direction, his
heart as witness is within his body, and just as, beyond the
encompassing sky, mountains, and sea, all time is simultaneously present from *alpha* to *omega*, what was and shall
be. Beyond that again are heaven and the terrible crystal.
These are in one sense the outside of the outside, but in
another sense, in a reversal characteristic of such imagery,
they are the inside of the inside. The blue solitudes incor-

porate a "life to be lived" that is pierced by the eye. At least to that degree it is entered and possessed in a momentary glimpse of eternal life.

The second such passage comes a few lines later. It is hypothetical and proleptic, but otherwise has a similar structure. "Shall we sail there together," to the "isles of the siren, the Galli," the Englishman asks Fortù, and then he imagines what it would be like to "sail round and round them" (lines 209, 213), landing finally to explore the tower on the largest isle, "the strange square black turret / With never a door" (lines 219-220). This tower recalls that of "Childe Roland to the Dark Tower Came." It has a similar function as a central blind point where another inside-out reversal occurs—the punctual, limited, and enclosed becoming suddenly the means of access to limitless openness, to totality:

> Then, stand there and hear
> The birds' quiet singing, that tells us
>   What life is, so clear?
> —The secret they sang to Ulysses
>   When, ages ago,
> He heard and he knew this life's secret
>   I hear and I know.
>   (lines 222-228)

The question mark at the end of the third of these lines just quoted comes at the end of a long sentence addressed interrogatively to Fortù: "shall we sail there together . . . ?" That future hypothetical present ("that tells us / What life is, so clear") becomes then the re-enactment of a far distant past when Ulysses, strapped to the mast, heard the Siren's song and learned the secret of life. That song is repeated now whenever the birds sing, at least in this place and listened to in the right way. The passage ends in a future present that may or may not occur: "I hear and I know."

Once more the spatial circling in on a point widens to include all time, all space, and even what is beyond all time
and space as their secret, their ground and being. The
Englishman affirms he will learn "what life *is*" (my italics).

These two passages, especially the first, are in part a
rewriting of the climactic passage in Shelley's "Lines Written Among the Euganean Hills."[4] In that poem the speaker
spends all day on a Euganean hilltop watching the sun rise,
move across the sky, and set. The passage in question (lines
285-319) occurs at the stroke of noon. Like the passages in
Browning's poem it broadens out from that point (the poet's
consciousness) and that moment (the sun's apogee) to include all the spatial scene in "interpenetration." Noon "descends," on this autumn day, in a "soft and purple mist"
that "far / From the curved horizon's bound / To the point
of heaven's profound, / Fills the overflowing sky" (lines 285-
293). The speaker's mind and all the objects around overlap
and permeate one another, like perfume pervading air, or,
to use Shelley's own figure, "Like a vaporous amethyst, /
Or an air-dissolvèd star / Mingling light and fragrance"
(lines 288-290). This emphasis on the way objects dissolve
in one another and in a diffused mist, light, and fragrance,
in a synesthetic unity, is quite different from Browning's
affirmation that things may join a unity without ever ceasing to be their own particular selves.

Shelley's infinite moment differs from Browning's in yet
another way. Browning's time out of time is still a dynamic
temporal movement. In the first passage, just after the exclamatory taking-possession of all and even of what is beyond the all ("Oh, heaven and the terrible crystal!"), the
Englishman turns back down to the mountains and sees
them as a perpetual movement in place. They move with

---

[4] I cite the poem from *Shelley's Poetical Works*, ed. Thomas Hutchinson,
corrected by G. M. Matthews (London, Oxford, New York: Oxford University Press, 1970), pp. 554-558.

195

the spectator and move in themselves. They are not a static expanse, but precisely an "infinite movement":

> Oh, those mountains, their infinite movement!
>> Still moving with you;
> For, ever some new head and breast of them
>> Thrusts into view
> To observe the intruder; you see it
>> If quickly you turn
> And, before they escape you, surprise them.
>
> (lines 181-187)

For Shelley, on the other hand, noon is a static moment of poise, surrounded by a fixed spatial array. Everything for him is laid out motionlessly in place. Noon "descends" as if it had been dropped straight down from the zenith. The circumambient atmosphere is "filled" with a soft and purple mist from the horizon to the highest point overhead. The poet himself has been motionless on his hilltop since before the sunrise. Nothing is said about how he got there. If noon descends, the air is windless and the grass blades point straight up. The landscape is made of motionless lines, "trellised lines" of the vine rows (line 300), line of the "olive-sandalled" Apennine in the south (line 306), line of the snow-covered Alps to the north. The mode of connection among these things is that of contiguity. They are all there side by side together. The syntactic signals for that are the word *and* and the semicolon: and this; and then that; and then another thing. The word *and* appears five times in the passage, always at the beginning of a line, and there are eight semicolons. The verbal phrase that completes this long series asserts that all these things, including the poet's own "spirit," "Interpenetrated lie / By the glory of the sky" (lines 313-314). The passage ends with another kind of poise, the poise of a repeated *or*, connecting alternatives among which the poet cannot choose. The glory of the sky may be an objective unifying power appealing to one or another of the senses, "light," "harmony," or "odor,"

196

or it may be a universal ethical power, "love," or it may be a transcendent spiritual power that "falls" from "Heaven" as the dew falls or as the noon descends, or it may be "the mind which feeds this verse," that is, the poet's own mind, which is "peopling the lone universe," giving life and the appearance of harmonious interpenetration to what is in itself without life and without interconnection. Among these possibilities Shelley remains poised, unable to affirm any one of them.

Browning decisively rewrites Shelley, though with many explicit echoes of this passage, for example, in the use of the word *profound* to name the depths of the sky. Time, as I have said, is an essential dimension of Browning's landscape. His is a world of dynamic spatial and temporal movement. The poet moves round and round to reach the mountaintop or the isles of the Galli. The landscape is itself the place of an "infinite movement" that can only be seen if the spectator moves, too. Browning, moreover, claims to be able to penetrate, by his movement through a moving scene, beyond Shelley's indecisive *ors*. He comes (or will come) to know the secret ground of all the phenomenal world: "I hear and I know."

One final positive aspect of "The Englishman in Italy" must be identified. This too has its analogies with Shelley's "Euganean Hills." When Shelley's speaker says he may be "peopling the lone universe" by projecting his mind into it, he describes the act of prosopopoeia, the attribution of human life to what is without life, a speaking for things inanimate or dead. A number of lightly sketched personifications appear in Shelley's lines, as when he speaks of the "infant Frost" treading "with his morning-winged feet," or of the "olive-sandalled Apennine." Browning systematically exploits this figurative power in his poem. This has already been seen in the passage about the "head and breast" of the mountains observing the intruder but trying to avoid being observed in turn. Somewhat earlier in the poem, as the Englishman was climbing round after round to the top of the mountain, the "piles of loose stones" were said to be "like the loose broken teeth / Of some monster which climbed there to die / From the ocean beneath" (lines 153-156). This is a fine grotesque personification recalling similar ones in "Childe Roland to the Dark Tower Came." The latter is also of course a poem of quest and sudden spiritual revelation. Later in "The Englishman in Italy," just after the passage already cited about how one must turn quickly to catch the human-like presence in the mountains, the speaker explains why they are so evasive:

> They grudge you should learn
> How the soft plains they look on, lean over
>   And love (they pretend)
> —Cower beneath them, the flat sea-pine crouches,
>   The wild fruit-trees bend,
> E'en the myrtle-leaves curl, shrink and shut:
>   All is silent and grave:
> 'Tis a sensual and timorous beauty,
>   How fair! but a slave.
>   (lines 188-196)

Here a brief phrase in Shelley's "Euganean Hills" ("And the plains that silent lie / Underneath" [lines 294-295]) is developed by Browning into an admirable extended prosopopoeia. This projects into the landscape an elaborated interpersonal relation of master to slave and of masculine sexual domination over shrinking and feminine beauty. The plains appear to be "silent," as Shelley said they were, but if you look sharply and suddenly, changing your perspective, moving with the mountains and plains instead of looking passively at them, you can glimpse an intense drama of sexual appropriation taking place. This appropriation is matched by the Englishman's own vigorous act of appropriating the landscape. The lines are a splendid example of Browning's extraordinary ability to mime in language a life attributed to things and, through the use of strong, active, muscular verbs, to relive in his own body that external life. He internalizes what is outside through a kind of kinesthetic reproduction. The words encourage the reader to do the same in her or his turn, so that her or his own body subliminally "cowers," "crouches," and "bends," and her or his hands or some other part of the body "curl, shrink and shut" like the myrtle-leaves when she or he reads the lines. Like William Carlos Williams in "Asphodel, That Greeny Flower" or in the poem about the whole field of Queen Anne's Lace,[5] Browning achieves a sexualization of the entire landscape. He shares that sexualization through his own body and passes it on in words to the reader. World, body, and words overlap. If the goal of "The Englishman in Italy" is to take possession of all the Sorrento landscape, personification is one of the indispensable instruments of the poet's act of appropriation. Through personification the Englishman does really come to be *in* Italy in the fullest sense of the word.

There is still more to say of this. The relation of the mountains to the plains as the Englishman sees it duplicates with a difference the relationship of the Englishman to Fortù. To the other dimensions of the act of taking possession must be added the Englishman's effort to make Fortù his own. The relationship of the Englishman to Fortù is problematic. As in the case of Browning's other dramatic monologues, this one is addressed to someone who, by the rules of the genre, does not get a chance to speak in her own voice, though the speaker may respond to something his addressee says. The Englishman, near the end of this poem, cites something Fortù has just said," 'Such trifles!' you say?" (line 286). Her remark is the occasion of his coda about the absurdity of the debate in the English parliament over abolishing the Corn Laws. To argue about whether or not those laws should be suspended is as absurd as to

---

[5] The first is in *Pictures from Brueghel and Other Poems* (New York: New Directions, 1962), pp. 153-182. "Queen-Ann's-Lace" is in *The Collected Earlier Poems*, p. 210. Williams drops the *e* in *Anne*.

argue about whether or not it is "proper" that "Scirocco," the destructive but ultimately fructifying autumn storm, "should vanish / In black from the skies!" (lines 291-292) so the natural round of the seasons can continue. The contrast is between the artificiality of English politics, its detachment from reality, and the harmony between man and nature in the south of Italy. Italy may be a poorer country, Browning is saying, less "civilized" than urban England, but they eat better there, much better. The good eating is the sign of a way of life that is in every way better. This way is built on propriety, on the proper, and on appropriations, making things one's own, of the various sorts I have identified. Even though the Englishman would remain to some degree alien to Italy however long he lived there, paradoxically he has a better chance at possession both of the land and of its people in Italy than he does of the land and people in England, since England is essentially a place of separation. It is impossible to be "in England" in the way one can be "in Italy."

This implication of Browning's poem is "in" the poem for the English reader rather than available to Fortù. This exemplifies another law of the genre of the dramatic monologue. The relation of the speaker to his hearer is an indirect expression of the poet's relation to his readers. By pretending to be an expatriated Englishman speaking to an Italian girl, Browning in a roundabout way expresses his political opinion about the Corn Laws and conveys to his English readers his manifold admiration for southern Italy. Italy is even a good place for the successful accomplishment of the sort of religious quest that is a central theme in Browning's poetry from the beginning to the end. In Italy more than in England one is likely to reach a point where one can exclaim, "Oh, heaven and the terrible crystal!" or say, "I hear and I know."

Nevertheless, the reader wants to know into what fictional relation the poet-reader relationship is displaced. If a dramatic monologue is always indirectly addressed to the reader by the poet, it is another law of the genre that some more or less obscure human story is implicitly revealed by the speaker of a dramatic monologue. The reader of "Andrea del Sarto" learns more than Andrea means to express about his relation to his wife and to his art. The speaker in "My Last Duchess" gives himself away, behind all his punctilious courtesy, as the murderous villain he is. What, exactly, is the relation of the Englishman to Fortù?

The answer to this question is more difficult to give with certainty than in most of Browning's monologues. That Fortù is an Italian girl who is part of the community the Englishman has entered, there can be no doubt. Probably *Fortù* is a nickname for *Fortunata*. The reader knows something of her family. The Englishman speaks of the way Fortù's mother bites off the quails' heads for her supper. Fortù's brother has served as the Englishman's guide on the climb of Calvano. He is in the "now" of the poem the one who is treading out the grapes as they are brought basket after basket by the older girls. The dramatic situation of the poem is clear enough, too. The Englishman and Fortù sit side by side, or rather she sits by his side with her feet on his knees (an odd posture, if you think of it, or think of trying to do it). They sit and watch the progress of the storm and all the manifold activity of the grape harvest while the Englishman tells his memories over to Fortù to keep her amused during the sirocco. Near the end of the poem the storm breaks, the sun comes out, and the Englishman invites Fortù to "Wake up and come out now" (line 245), so they can go down to see the decorations at the church for the coming Feast Day. She apparently refuses, and he asks her at least to go with him to the end of the garden to see the "scorpion with wide angry nippers!" (line 285). It is to this that she says: "Such trifles!" Her exclamation may apply to all he has said, to all the memory beads he has told over for her, one by one.

The Englishman, as the reader can see, has a specific motivation for speech. He is trying to amuse Fortù, to make her laugh, to keep her awake during the storm. This can be extrapolated a little further. It is a feature of all the self-enclosed rounded objects named so lovingly in the poem that they open themselves to the beholder and offer themselves to be appropriated, to be eaten. The pomegranates break open, the figs are split, mouths gape, eyes open in the sea-fruit. This opening occurs again in recollection when the Englishman describes these things in language. Fortù is included among the rest of such things. He wants her, too, to "open [her] eyes," to wake up and keep awake, to offer herself to appropriation like the rest. His speech to her, no one can doubt it, is an indirect form of courtship. If a man can make a girl laugh, he is making some headway with her. Later in the poem he offers her cheese, wine, and fruit, another invitation to intimacy. The means of courtship the Englishman uses, his naming over of those things that are daily before Fortù's eyes, is parallel to the motivation of realistic art as Fra Lippo Lippi justifies it in Browning's poem of that name. We pass things a hundred times a day and do not see them, says Fra Lippo, but when they are reproduced exactly in art we then first see them. We open ourselves to them then because the artist has opened them to us:

> . . . Don't object, "His works
> Are here already; nature is complete:
> Suppose you reproduce her—(which you can't)
> There's no advantage! You must beat her, then."
> For, don't you mark? we're made so that we love
> First when we see them painted, things we have passed
> Perhaps a hundred times nor cared to see;
> And so they are better, painted—better to us,
> Which is the same thing. Art was given for that . . .
> ("Fra Lippo Lippi," lines 296-304)[6]

This is Browning's version of the Romantic notion that art removes the veil of familiarity from the world. Truth

[6] King ed., v, pp. 192-193.

as reproduction leads to truth as revelation, for we see things in their imitations that we have passed in reality over and over without seeing. "The Englishman in Italy" is, in its lovingly exact recapitulation of all there is to be seen, touched, felt, and tasted on the Sorrento plain, a magnificent exemplification of this theory, but if it is really addressed to the English reader who has, most probably, never been to the Amalfi coast at all, this invitation to *see* is repeated within the poem in the Englishman's attempt to get Fortù to open her eyes and wake up to what is extraordinary about the reality around her. That reality she so takes for granted that it seems merely "trifles," but if he names it over for her perhaps she will see it, open herself to it, and thereby to him.

This still leaves open the question of the exact nature of the Englishman's relationship to Fortù. I do not think the poem allows a clear decision about this. There are four possibilities, more or less. Fortù may be a young girl of the community, sister to one of the workmen on the estate. This would leave entirely unanswered the questions of why she is not out there with the other young girls gathering snails and why the Englishman uses such adult language in speaking to her. A second possibility is that she is an older girl on the estate, but if she is that then she should be out with the other older girls bringing the grapes to the vat to be trodden out. Fortù must be especially privileged in some way, "Fortunata" indeed, either by illness or by some other incapacity, or, as is more likely, because she is the daughter of the house. As such, she can be a spectator of the work of the others, even though her brother, as the owner's son, participates in the important business of treading the grapes. This remains speculation. Nothing at all anywhere in the poem is said about Fortù's father, though her mother is mentioned. In any case, the grape harvesters bring Fortù a bunch of grapes as she sits there close beside the Englishman listening to him as he talks on and on (line 101). Her status is clearly a special one.

If Fortù is a grown-up girl and the daughter of the house,

that still leaves open the question of the Englishman's exact relationship to her. The question turns on the value given to the phrase "my beloved one" in the opening line. Is it a conventional term of endearment, *mia cara*, "my dear," so indicating that he is an honored guest on the estate, no more? Or is it to be taken with more force, as indicating that he is her suitor or fiancé, perhaps even that she is his mistress? The poem is intentionally vague on that score. It can be said with certainty that the Englishman's tone with Fortù is caressing and intimate. He can speak freely to her of his inmost thoughts and feelings. Insofar as the poem is to be thought of as spoken to her, it is an invitation to Fortù to stay awake, to laugh, to respond to him, to open herself to him, and to allow herself in one way or another to be possessed like all the other things of the *Piano di Sorrento* he has made his own. The relationship of the Englishman to Fortù, their physical orientation to one another as he talks, as well as their moral relation, may be obliquely and somewhat ominously expressed in that image of the mountains leaning over the soft, silent, shrinking plains they pretend to love but in fact enslave: " 'Tis a sensual and timorous beauty / How fair! but a slave" (pp. 195-196).

To the other forms of appropriation in the poem must be added the appropriation of one person by another in an interpersonal relation that is strongly incarnated, even sexualized. It is a relation of one body to another as well as a moral relation. The Englishman's personification of the mountains and plains expands that interpersonal relation. The relationship of the Englishman to Fortù is enacted within the landscape as a whole as well as in the relation of the Englishman himself to the landscape. He personifies the scene as like another person to whom he may be related in a way analogous to his relationship to Fortù. The uncertainty about the exact nature of this relationship may function implicitly as a trope for some covert ambiguity about the nature of the Englishman's relation to the Sorrento plain, however unambiguously positive and celebratory that relation may appear to be.

Putting that suspicion aside for the moment, it may be said that "The Englishman in Italy" is a poem, like so many others by Browning, in which language is used as an instrument of power. In this admirably masculine poem, language is employed as a means of appropriating space and its contents, time, eternity, and another person, all at once. The Englishman (and indirectly Browning himself) affirms himself, gives himself substance, by appropriating all the landscape, assimilating it to himself, belonging to it and making it belong to him by naming it over, becoming one with it. The Englishman (and the poet) sweeps down on the landscape like the sirocco. Assimilating the landscape in memory, the Englishman also assimilates time by turning it into a dynamically moving circular structure, like a string of beads snapped shut. He also makes Fortù his own. All these speech-acts are used as a means of transcending time, space, objects, and other people in an explosion of time into eternity that may occur and yet occur again, punctuating linear time here and there, as tiny black holes are said to interrupt space in certain theories of contemporary physicists: "Oh, heaven and the terrible crystal"; "I see and I hear."

There seems to be little here of the negative questioning of language I have found in other poems to qualify this wholly positive accomplishment. Far from being problematic, language is here for once taken for granted as effectively referential. It is not just referential, but reaches out strongly to grasp and assimilate the world it names. There does not seem to be any linguistic moment at all, in the sense I have defined it, in "The Englishman in Italy."

And yet—about this there is, to borrow one of Browning's titles, "One Word More" to say. If the reader of "The Englishman in Italy" happens to ask himself in what language the Englishman speaks to Fortù, the difficulty in answering this question works as a loose thread unravelling all the carefully woven fabric of a positive reading of the poem such as the one I have so far made. There is no indication that Fortù knows English. On the evidence of the poem it seems unlikely that she does. If the Englishman speaks to her in English, she will not understand him. If he speaks to her in Italian, his English readers, or a least many of them, will not understand him. The poem must be simultaneously in Italian and in English (an absurdity), or it must be a poem originally in Italian silently translated into English for the convenience of its English readers or so it will fit into a book of English poems. Certain locutions in the poem, for example, the opening "my beloved one," sound awkward in English, as though they were being transposed from idiomatic Italian. There is one place in the poem where the Englishman forgets or does not know either the English or the Italian word for a plant. (Which is it he has forgotten? Is it both?) The lines obliquely call attention to the problem of nomenclature, to the problem of the relation of word and thing, and to the problem of translation:

> And . . . what shows a branch
> Coral-coloured, transparent, with circlets
> Of pale seagreen leaves . . .
> (lines 164-166)

Only one phrase in Italian appears in the whole poem, the subtitle; *Piano di Sorrento*.[7] Otherwise, with the exception of place names and proper names, which belong equally to either language—Calvano, Scirocco, Amalfi, Bellini, Auber—the law of the poem is that everything is in English.

---

[7] I am indebted here to a brilliant paper on Browning's "The Glove" by Alan Bass, written some years ago but not, so far as I know, ever published. Bass's analysis starts with the strange subtitle of "The Glove": *Peter Ronsard loquitur*." If Ronsard is speaking he presumably must be speaking in French, though not a single word of French appears in the poem. Three phrases in Latin do appear. They suffice to raise obliquely the problems of language, of idiom, and of translation that I find in a different way in "The Englishman in Italy."

The Italian language is abolished, as if to ensure that the reader will not notice the problem I am now trying to identify. *Piano di Sorrento* is of course a proper name too, but *piano* is also a common Italian noun. In the body of the poem, for example, at line 11, the English word *plain* is consistently used. For a moment, at the beginning of the poem, the reader is reminded that for Fortù, for all her family, and for all the members of her community, every single thing the Englishman names in English with such bold vigor and precision, appropriating them by naming them, has a different name. For them the Sorrento plain is named with all those Italian words the Englishman's speech effaces. *Piano di Sorrento* is the linguistic moment in Browning's poem. Or perhaps it might be better to say that the linguistic moment in this poem is the fissure between the subtitle and the poem proper. There is a barely perceptible hitch or intake of breath as the reader passes the invisible border from one linguistic country to a different one, like going through the looking glass.

Once the reader notices the problems raised by *Piano di Sorrento*, he may be more likely to notice other peculiarities of the language of the poem. He may see that there is something odd about both *Scirocco* and *Calvano*. The normal spelling of the first in English is of course *sirocco*, and the proper name for that mountain is *Vico Alvano*. Browning climbed this mountain during his second visit to Italy, in 1844.[8] The experiences recorded in the poem presumably occurred during this visit, though whether there was a real Fortù is another (perhaps unanswerable) question. Were the changes in names the result of ignorance on Browning's part, or did he deliberately change the words to make them seem more alien and obliquely to call attention to the problem of translation? If the latter, the functioning of this is different in each case. *Sirocco* (English) may be either *scirocco* or *sirocco* in Italian. Browning spells

[8] See DeVane, *A Browning Handbook*, p. 158.

the word in the Italian way throughout the poem. It counts as another bit of Italian, another linguistic loose end, as though he had said Livorno rather then Leghorn in a text in English. *Calvano* would presumably sound wrong to For-tù's ear, though an English reader is unlikely to know the name is wrong. The English reader is much more likely to find something peculiar about *Scirocco*, to wonder why Browning spells it that way, and to be led by that to begin asking the sorts of questions about the language of the poem I am now raising.

The linguistic anomaly of *Piano di Sorrento*, if the reader happens to notice it, sets up an oscillation in which the reader sees the poem at once as originally in English and as translated from the Italian. The reader sees the poem as spoken and as written at once. A gap is opened up be-tween Browning and the Englishman. The poem is Brown-ing's own appropriation of the Italian countryside, Brown-ing's expression of his doctrine of the infinite moment, and at the same time it is the ascription of this taking possession to an imaginary personage, with however much or little reservation and irony. The reader sees the poem at once as a marvelous piece of verisimilitude and as a complicated artifice obeying all sorts of conventions. In this it is like the sermon for the morrow's Feast mentioned in the poem. That sermon gives the reader obliquely the terms by which to define the poem itself. The sermon is: "the off-hand discourse / Which (all nature, no art) / The Dominican brother, these three weeks, / Was getting by heart" (lines 253-256).

"The Englishman in Italy" also gives the illusion of being "all nature, no art," but if the reader looks at it from a slightly different angle, he can see it is the result of a com-plicated set of conventions. It might be said that this need cause no difficulty. The wise reader takes these conventions for granted and goes past them to the heart of the poem. It is a convention of the dramatic monologue that a poem written down and printed is to be taken as spoken. It is a convention of Browning's dramatic monologues that they all be in English, whatever language their original speakers would have used. It is a convention of the dramatic monologue that a speech which would have been made in colloquial prose is given in a complex metrical and rhymed patterning, just as it is a convention in opera that lovers sing their passion. It is a convention of the dramatic monologue that it be spoken to someone but that this someone not be allowed to speak in return. And so on. My answer is that this is just the point I am making. The poem is "all art no nature," and the poem itself says that this is so. *Piano di Sorrento* is the overt mark of the poem's artifice on the poem, like a pontil mark on a glass. The phrase is the poem's oblique self-description. This explicit presence forbids the reader to take the conventions for granted. *Piano di Sorrento* in its own way is like those odd places where a novel defines itself as a novel, or it is like those manhole covers mentioned in the first chapter here, which have cast in them the words *Manhole Cover*. It is a characteristic of poems, too, that somewhere or other they name themselves. They utter the law of the genre to which they belong. The status of such uttering is peculiar. It is an important version of what I am calling the linguistic moment.[9]

One peculiarity is the difficulty of deciding who speaks (or writes) *Piano di Sorrento*. Another is the impossibility of deciding whether it is part of the poem or outside it as an impersonal label. *Piano di Sorrento*, like stage directions in a play, is the evidence in the printed version of the poem that it is something written down pretending to be the record of living speech. The poem bears the same relation to oral utterance that musical notation does to the sound

[9] For the strange status of locutions in which a work names its own genre see Jacques Derrida, "*La Loi du genre*/The Law of Genre," in French and in English, the trans. by Avital Ronell, with a note by the translator, *Glyph 7* (Baltimore and London: The Johns Hopkins University Press, 1980), pp. 176-232. The English translation is reprinted in *Critical Inquiry* VII, 1 (Autumn 1980), 55-81.

of the music when it is played or when a trained musician reads the score and plays it over in his mind's ear. Relatively few people are adept at doing this with music. Most literate people do it so easily with written language that it is easy to forget the words on the page too are as much conventional notation as a musical score.

Who speaks *Piano di Sorrento*? It would certainly not have been spoken by the Englishman. Though one might be tempted to say it is speech or writing by Robert Browning, the poet, the law of the dramatic monologue is that the poet nowhere speaks in his own voice, except perhaps in the exterior labelling of the title. *Piano di Sorrento* is further inside the poem than the title, neither quite inside nor quite outside, or inside and outside at once, at the liminal border. It marks the threshold across which the reader enters into a linguistic place where Italian is transformed magically into English, speech into writing, past into present, mountains into "heads" and "breasts." If the reader attempts to say aloud the title, the subtitle, and the first lines of the poem, he will not find it easy to decide in what tone to read *Piano di Sorrento*, nor how to convey to a listener what it is doing there, without awkward explanation. "This is where the poem is supposed to be taking place. *Piano* is Italian for 'plain.' The *Piano di Sorrento* is on the Amalfi coast. The Englishman is not just in Italy, but in this particular place in Italy," and so on. It is as if *Piano di Sorrento* were spoken not by Browning but by some murmuring or resonating disembodied voice, the spirit of the place uttering forth its own name, the manhole cover saying "Manhole Cover." It is as if all the things of the plain were obscurely speaking their own names: "I am a pomegranate"; "I am rosemary"; "I am a lentisk"; "I am the Sorrento plain." Indeed I think this seems to occur for most of us as we look out at the world of distinct objects around us. The names of things seem to be part of the things, attached to them not as removable labels but as intrinsic parts of themselves. Each thing, as Gerard Manley Hopkins says, "fling[s] out broad its name," "selves—goes itself; *myself* it speaks and spells."[10]

Speaks itself in what language? In this case, is it in Italian or in English? The *Piano di Sorrento* speaks its name in Italian. For Fortù and for all her family and friends each thing on the plain has as part of itself its proper Italian name. The Englishman or rather the poem itself takes those names away one by one and substitutes for them improper English names. The poem dispossesses thereby both the things and the people who possess them in Italian. Anyone who has lived in a foreign country where she or he only imperfectly knows the language may have had the oddly unsettling experience of realizing that all those familiar things—trees, flowers, birds, and rocks—have different names for the inhabitants from those names she or he would give them. To experience this is to suffer a painful kind of aphasia, like that of Alice in *Through the Looking-Glass*. It is to be returned suddenly in adulthood to the infant state, in the etymological sense of *infans*, "without language." I for one find this condition intolerable. Conrad has dramatized it in the experience of Yanko Goorall in "Amy Foster."

There are two ways out of this situation. One is to learn the native words for things, to ask and ask again, "What is the Italian for 'pomegranate'?" "How do you say 'cheeseball' in Italian, or 'prickly-pear,' or 'lentisk'?" One must go on asking and learning until finally one is *in* Italy in the sense of being surrounded by things that now have for the once alien visitor the same names they have for the natives. One can only really be in a place by being inside its language. The other alternative is to rename things firmly with the names brought in from one's own outlandish language, so appropriating them in that way for oneself. The English in the New World gave the name *robin* to a bird different

[10] "As kingfishers catch fire," lines 4, 7, *Poems*, 4th ed. (London, Oxford, New York: Oxford University Press, 1970), p. 90.

from the English robin. This is the strategy Browning's poem adopts. The result is that all that extraordinary effort of taking possession, assimilation, and appropriation I have described is at the same time an act of disappropriation. The poem takes things one by one away from Fortù and from all her community by renaming them in English. So named they are displaced, alienated from their proper linguistic placing. In the end the Englishman is not in Italy at all. He has transposed the whole *Piano di Sorrento* into English and into England. He has renamed it the Sorrento plain so it may be assimilated through the instrumentality of the poem by the poem's English readers. It is perhaps most in this destructive act of dispossession that the Englishman and the poet are most like the sirocco.

The poem as it stands goes out of its way to obscure this fact, for example, in the way the title asserts that the Englishman is *in* Italy. Two earlier cancelled titles indicate Browning's awareness that the poem is a problematic transaction between two countries and two languages. The poem was first called "England in Italy. Autumn at Sorrento" and then "England in Italy [Piano di Sorrento]."[11] To say the poem puts England in Italy is a manifest absurdity, though one supposes the Englishman might be described as a portable bit of England inserted into Italy. The first title contains no Italian, and the second puts it within brackets. The final title puts not England but the Englishman in Italy. This title shifts the emphasis away from a territorial encroachment to the question of what it means to be inside an alien land, where the names for things are different. The final version also takes the subtitle out of brackets. This puts forward the problem of differing tongues in the open juxtaposition of one phrase in English, one in Italian, both within the same linguistic space.

To say, as I have, that the Englishman has transposed Italy to England, rather than putting himself in Italy, is a way of saying he has transposed Italy into the poem and

[11] See DeVane, *A Browning Handbook*, pp. 158, 157.

has given it a new kind of existence there. The puzzle about which language the poem is in brings to the surface the way all poetry is a transposition of things into a detached linguistic realm. There they go on existing and happening, but only in words. The reader would go to the *Piano di Sorrento* in vain to find the things named in this poem. They exist only in that Sorrento plain the poem itself brings into existence in a strange form of speech-act.

Once the reader sees that this is happening, a different and much more apparently negative reading of the whole poem opens out. This new reading superimposes itself on the positive reading I began by giving. If the poem is an act of dispossession, taking things one by one away from Fortù and giving them a new existence within the artifice of language, the Englishman's claim to have succeeded in making a linear series into an infinite circle leaping out of time and space cannot work. Rather than appropriating the eternal ground beneath or above things through the act of naming things, Browning's speaker takes possession only of the signs for things. This failure of the poem's basic enterprise is betrayed in a number of ways in the poem itself, as well as in that small fissure opened up by the way the subtitle raises the question of language.

For one thing, the actual form of the poem is far from being a straightforward movement through a linear series up to a climax that transcends sequence. This pattern is present in "Childe Roland to the Dark Tower Came," with its climactic blowing of the slug-horn and its climactic ex-clamation, iterating the title, even though Childe Roland's moment of triumph is of course also the moment of his defeat by all those fearsome precursor questers turned fa-thers:

> And yet
> Dauntless the slug-horn to my lips I set,
> And blew. *"Childe Roland to the Dark Tower Came."*
> (lines 202-204)[12]

12 King ed., v, p. 256.

In "The Englishman in Italy," on the contrary, the narration rises up to one climax, the memory of the speaker's climb to the top of Calvano the evening before: "Oh, heaven and the terrible crystal!" The poem then falls back through the recognition of the "infinite movement" of the mountains. Temporality and flux are seen to be part even of the zenith, and even of any conceivable human experience of wholeness. The poem drops through that recognition to focus on the plain. These are seen according to that master-slave relation I have discussed. I have so far read this personification positively. It seems to register a kinship between human life and that infinite vitality which is a center to the vitality of each individual thing. It is just as possible to see such prosopopoeias as evidence of the way the speaker projects himself into the landscape. He falsely sees it as alive, as like a monster or as like the relation between himself and Fortù. Personification is intimately related both to the sublime, about which I shall have something to say later, and to that fundamental act of catachresis whereby man gives to things names that are neither literal nor figurative. Such names are a cover for man's ignorance. They are an assimilation of things to himself in the negative sense of "assimilate." He sees things as like himself and so does not see them. He puts a manhole cover over things. Mountains do not really have "heads," "breasts," or "faces," but we have no better terms for their shapes than those drawn from the human body: "For, ever some new head and breast of them / Thrusts into view / To observe the intruder . . ." (lines 183-185). It is only a step from these conventional catachreses to a full-fledged personification projecting a human drama of pretended love and actual enslavement into the scene. Naming the mountains in this way, the Englishman possesses only himself and reveals only the impossibility of naming adequately the hidden life in nature, if hidden life there is.

Having fallen back from his "O altitudo" to this self-betraying personification of the plains, the speaker reveals the insufficiency of the whole section about the climb up

Calvano by the first word in the transitional phrase to the next section: "*So*, I turned to the sea; and there slumbered / As greenly as ever / Those isles of the siren, your Galli" (lines 197-199, my italics). That did not work, so I shall try this. The poem then continues its linear sequence and tries once more to rise to a time-stopping infinite moment. This time, however, the time out of time is not a memory but a hypothetical imagination of something the Englishman and Fortù might do: "Fortù, shall we sail there together . . . ?" (line 209). If we go there, then I might hear the song the Sirens sang to Ulysses and so learn, as he did, the secret of life. The status of the present tense in the final lines of this section is peculiar:

> —The secret they sang to Ulysses
>   When, ages ago,
> He heard and he knew this life's secret
>   I hear and I know.
>   (lines 225-228)

He does not yet hear and know anything of the sort. The present tense here is proleptic. It exists only as an "if," as a "once was and perhaps may be." The fact that the poet can speak of this non-present insight in such ringing present-tense terms reveals the fact that there is never any present as such in poetry. There is only a simulated presence of things and experiences in language. This linguistic presence presupposes the absence of the things themselves. The whole of "The Englishman in Italy" creates such a non-present present in its temporal comings and goings, back into the past, forward to the future, back again to the "present" of the Englishman's speech to Fortù, and so on, in a continual zigzag. This movement back and forth is admirably named in Mallarmé's "Mimique": "*ici devançant, là remémorant, au futur, au passé, sous une apparence fausse de présent* [here anticipating, there remembering, in the future, in the past, *under a false appearance of the present*]."[13]

[13] Stéphane Mallarmé, *Oeuvres Complètes*, éd. de la Pléiade (Paris: Éditions Gallimard, 1945), p. 310.

Even if the reader were to go to the *Piano di Sorrento*, to the top of Vico Alvano, or out to the Galli, and read Browning's poem out loud there he would not be present to the experience the poem names, nor even present to the places named in the poem. Those experiences and those places exist only in that false appearance of the present and of presence that the words of the poem speak into existence. This, paradoxically, justifies the Englishman's proleptic "I hear and I know," just as it justifies the vivid present-tense description, a little earlier in the poem, of the fisherman returning with sea-fruit ("And mouths gape there, eyes open . . ."), even though that whole passage is presented under the shadow of its initiating negatives: "Nor use seemed in trying / To get out the boats and go fishing . . . / No seeing our skiff / Arrive about noon from Amalfi, / —Our fisher arrive . . ." (lines 48-49, 52-54). Scirocco has come and the fishermen cannot go out, but that does not prevent the Englishman from describing in circumstantial detail what would happen if they did go out. Since everything in the poem, in any case, exists under the aegis of a *not*, this event that did not take place has as much reality as those that *did*. Everything in poetry is not-present, except in words. In poetry as in dreams there are no negatives, since something presented with a qualifying negative has just as much positive existence, no more and no less, as something presented in positive and present-tense terms.

Poets exploit the power of language to create places that can be visited only in the poems, even though these poetic *topoi* transform our sense of the real place if we happen to go there. No reader of "The Englishman in Italy" could go to the *Piano di Sorrento* and not see it differently, just as someone who has read Henry James's *The Wings of the Dove* can never again see Lancaster Gate in London in the same way.[14] As Wallace Stevens, says, apropos of his poem, "De-

[14] This is the countertruth to the one proposed by Michael Riffaterre in "Interpretation and Descriptive Poetry: A Reading of Wordsworth's

scription without Place," "we live in the description of a place and not in the place itself."[15] Browning's poem too is "description without place," utopian. Michael Riffaterre is right. The place the poem names can only be visited in the book of poems by Browning in which it is placed. If the Englishman is not in Italy, he is not in England either. This is because "The Englishman in Italy" can only be found between "The Italian in England" and "The Leader" in Browning's volume of 1845, *Dramatic Romances and Lyrics*, or in whatever other volume it is placed or misplaced. John Locke wittily expresses this point:

> . . . if anyone should ask, in what place are the Verses, which report the story of *Nisus* and *Euralius*, 'twould be very improper to determine this Place, by saying, they were in such a part of the Earth or in Bodly's Library: But the right designation of the place, would be by the parts of Virgil's work; and the proper Answer would be, That these Verses were about the middle of the Ninth Book of his *Aenids*: And that they have always been constantly in the same Place ever since *Virgil* was printed: which is true, though the Book itself had moved a Thousand times, the use of the Idea of Place here, being to know only, in what part of the Book the Story is; that so upon occasion, we may know where to find it, and have recourse to it for our own use.[16]

'Yew-Trees,' " *New Literary History* IV, 2 (Winter 1973), 232; "In fact any name will do as a place name, so long as grammar introduces it as such and it is italicized." This is hardly the case for "The Englishman in Italy," as the reader of the poem can verify by imagining the poem with "The Wye Valley" as subtitle, or even "Lago di Como." Or is Riffaterre right, and does the place name in its grammatical place make the topographical place? That is just the question here.

[15] Wallace Stevens, *Letters*, ed. Holly Stevens (New York: Alfred A. Knopf, Inc., 1966), p. 494. I am indebted here to an unpublished essay by Ian Balfour on Stevens' "Description without Place."

[16] John Locke, *An Essay Concerning Human Understanding*, ed. Peter H. Nidditch (Oxford: The Clarendon Press, 1975), pp. 170-171. Balfour's essay called this admirable passage to my attention.

The propriety of 'The Englishman in Italy," its proper place, is its impropriety, its lack of proper place. It exists in that strange unfixed place located within the covers of all the books in which it is printed. The power of poetry to create such a placeless place, "description without place," is signaled in "The Englishman in Italy" by the positive presence within the poem of things and events that, even within the poem, have only hypothetical or negative status. Even those things which, within the fiction of the poem, belong to the immediate present of the Englishman's perception and speech, have dispossessed the real inhabitants of the *Piano di Sorrento*. The poem transfers all their milieu—grapes, figs, cheese, pomegranates, mountains, plain, and all—into a realm they could not visit by any act of physical dislocation, but only by learning to read English.

It is a characteristic of this realm that since it exists only negatively, hypothetically, or linguistically, it can never be complete, round, or whole. It must remain, after all the poet's or all the Englishman's efforts, paratactic, one item after another. "The Englishman in Italy" rises up to the remembered "Oh" of the top of Calvano, falls back again, tries again with the imagined future of the trip to the Galli, falls back again to the present and to a renewed listing of the things to be seen there as the storm ends, moves forward into the future to imagine the Feast of the Virgin on the morrow and then peters out like a stream dispersing in the sand, or beads dropping from a broken string, into the final "trifling" detail of the scorpion with wide, angry nippers in the garden wall. This is followed, in the poem as we now have it, by the somewhat baffling coda about the Corn Laws, a most uncharacteristic allusion, for Browning, to contemporary politics. The coda was added later, months after the rest of the poem had been completed. As DeVane shows, the coda has received widely divergent interpretations.[17] It is evidence of the difficulty Browning had in

[17] DeVane, *A Browning Handbook*, pp. 158-159.

ending his poem and of his dissatisfaction with the ending about the scorpion. The new ending is just as inconclusive. It is one more item in what is potentially an endless series of items, remembered, anticipated, "present."

It is possible to read "The Englishman in Italy" as a triumphant transcendence of time into the infinite moment by a dynamic movement back and forth across time. The fact that this is the "false appearance" of an infinite present is betrayed by the winning out of linearity over circularity or globular wholeness in the formal structure of the poem. Far from bringing his string of memory beads back around to themselves in analogy to the Rosary, that circular image of eternity, the Englishman's discourse remains one bead after another. It is even beads that slip from any narrative string and follow one another in unconnected contingency: first the scorpion, then the allusion to the Corn Laws, then a final mention of the Scirocco, then silence, the end of the poem, leaving the reader more than a little dissatisfied, if wholeness is what he wants.

One evidence of the inability of the poem to accomplish the goals it sets for itself is the story of the failure of the Englishman's relation to Fortù that can be read between the lines. This forms the dramatic action, such as it is, of the poem. I said earlier that whatever the exact nature of the Englishman's relationship to Fortù it is clear from the caressing tone of the poem that his speech is an attempt to win possession of her, along with everything else he sees, names, touches, tastes. He wants her to laugh, to open her eyes to him and to the reality of the world she is surrounded by but so takes for granted that she apparently does not see anything remarkable about it. It may be the outsider who has the most chance to see the place, whereas the insider is so thoroughly "in" that he no longer notices any-thing. Everything, for the insider, is covered with a veil of familiarity. The speaker's appeal to Fortù is the figurative expression of the poet's appeal to the reader. The poet invites us too to open our eyes and our other senses to the place Browning makes available to us in the poem. We would then no longer be among those who "seeing see not; and hearing they hear not, neither do they understand" (Matthew 13.13). We too are outsiders who may have a better chance to see.

Whatever may be said for the reader's possession of the *Piano di Sorrento* through its representation in words, the parabolic vehicle of that appeal to appropriation, the Englishman's appeal to Fortù, is a resounding failure. During the Englishman's loving enumeration of his memory beads, justified at the beginning as a way of keeping Fortù amused during the storm, Fortù apparently goes fast asleep. She seems to wake up briefly when he feeds her the grapes, the cheese, the wine, the prickly-pear: "Nay, taste, while awake" (line 106). Fortù falls asleep again through the rest of his recitation and has to be wakened again: "All is over. Wake up and come out now . . ." (line 245). She has apparently heard almost nothing he has said. Even when Fortù is awake she seems distinctly unimpressed by his praise of her countryside: " 'Such trifles!' you say?" (line 286). The Englishman, in short, signally fails in his enterprise of waking Fortù to the reality of things around her. This may be taken as a parabolic analogue for the failure of the poem in relation to the reader. It opens to us not the place itself but "description without place," that atopical realm which exists only in words.

"The Englishman in Italy" is a magnificently positive poem dramatizing a taking-possession of a real place through words, and through that act appropriating another person, all time and space, the infinite moment beyond time and space. At the same time it is a poem covertly about the failure of this enterprise. This "underthought" is the result of the subversive spreading out of the linguistic moment in the poem. The poem means these two things simultaneously. They may not be reconciled. Neither may be given priority over the other. Each is inherent as a possibility in the other. Each calls up the other as its shadowy counterpart, without which it cannot be expressed, though each counterpart undermines its mirroring mate. The significance of the poem is the co-presence and interaction of the two possibilities. It is like a Gestaltist drawing that is a single set of elements sketched on paper but that nevertheless alternates back and forth between two ways of being seen. Both are there in the elements, not imposed willfully from outside. The two meanings are imposed willy-nilly on the spectator in an alternation of which he is the helpless witness, or rather, on the reader, since it is in this case not a matter of perception but a matter of the interpretation of words.

A better understanding of these two ways "The Englishman in Italy" forces us to read it may be gained by an analogy with the distinction Hegel makes between sign and symbol.[18] I am not claiming that Browning read Hegel or was influenced by him, even indirectly. There is a resonance, nevertheless, between two theories of language in Hegel and the two theories of language implicit in "The Englishman in Italy." For Hegel a sign has only an arbitrary and contingent relation to what it stands for. His example is a national flag. The French tricolor is not really like France, nor like liberty, equality, and fraternity either. A symbol, on the other hand, though it is not identical to what it stands for, nevertheless is like its referent. The symbol participates in what it symbolizes. It is thrown together with it, as the word indicates. Something red is really like blood. It should be noted that Hegel does not say the word *red* is like blood. The name is a sign. The thing is a symbol. It is all those globular things the Englishman names in "The Englishman in Italy" that are symbols of the perfection of eternity, not the names for them in either Italian or English. In symbol, the sensory itself, the color red, has something in common with the signified, blood.

[18] For a discussion of this see Paul de Man, "Sign and Symbol in Hegel's Aesthetics," *Critical Inquiry* VIII, 4 (Summer 1982), 761-775.

It might be expected that Hegel would validate symbol over sign, the natural over the artificial, participatory similarity over arbitrary and distant notation. Indeed he does so for the most part in the *Ästhetik*. There the symbolic art of the ancients precedes classical art and modern, that is, "Romantic," art, though the term *symbolic* has a universal linguistic meaning for Hegel, as well as an historical one, as Paul de Man has observed.[19] In either of its meanings, historical or linguistic, participatory art is in the *Ästhetik* placed above the art of the arbitrary sign. In the *Ästhetik*, art in general, the beautiful, or the "aesthetic" as such, is defined, in the phrase already cited in chapter 1 here, as "the sensible shining forth of the idea [*das sinnliche "Scheinen" der Idee*]." The symbol embodies, incarnates, the supersensible idea. In Hegel's *Encyklopedie*, on the other hand, the sign is valued over the symbol. Signs are essential to the activity of thought and to its predications. The mind can only take possession of things it has turned into signs.

The distinction, as Paul de Man has brilliantly shown, turns on the opposition between two kinds of memory, *Erinnerung* and *Gedächtnis*. *Erinnerung* is memory as interiorization and as recollection. It is a gathering together into one, like the Englishman's full prior possession, all at once, of the memories he is going to tell over as Fortù tells her beads. *Erinnerung* as "innering" is prior to language and does not depend on it. What is gathered in recollection may be named by words after the fact, as the Englishman tells over for the reader and for Fortù what he already has and knows from within. *Gedächtnis*, on the other hand, is memorization as learning by heart or as appropriation by means of words. The linguistic moment is essential to *Gedächtnis*. *Gedächtnis* depends absolutely on language. Language in this case is seen as an arbitrary system of signs that can be learned as one learns a foreign language. Such

[19] "Reply to Raymond Geuss," *Critical Inquiry* x, 2 (December 1983), 385-386.

language can be written down, preserved, and passed from person to person, as "The Englishman in Italy" can be printed and reprinted. Thought as such is dependent on *Gedächtnis*. In *Gedächtnis* the link between the name and the thing is broken. The thing is turned into its arbitrary name and appropriated as its name. This means its disappropriation as sensible reality. Once the names are established, they may then be manipulated freely in systems of predication—for example, in a poem like "The Englishman in Italy." A poem may be written down, reproduced at will, and reappropriated by any reader who knows the language in which it is written.

Erinnerung is like the full sensory aural experience of a piece of music. *Gedächtnis* is like that piece of music written down in arbitrary notation where it my be "read" by those who have the skill, played over for the mind's ear, but without any actual sounds anywhere. Such music is a silent set of abstract relationships for thinking through. In the same way the competent reader of "The Englishman in Italy" can follow silently through the words on the page, re-creating the poem in his mind without ever uttering a sound and without ever encountering one single object of sense experience. In the poem there are no grapes, no quails, no wine, no cheese, no pomegranates, no soft touch of Fortù's little feet on one's knees, only the signs for these. Composition in both music and poetry, as opposed to evanescent improvisation in either medium, depends on notation, on the possibility of writing down what has been composed in either medium so it can be replayed or reread.

Hegel, in a celebrated dictum, says art is a thing of the past. This may be taken either to mean that true art is a matter of symbol and of memory as *Erinnerung*, or on the other hand that art depends for its existence on the sign and on *Gedächtnis*. That Hegel saw certain forms of genuine art as dependent on signs is confirmed in the section on the sublime in the *Ästhetik*. There the sublime is seen as a valid kind of art. It gives names to the ineffable, to the

223

transcendent, to what is beyond direct comprehension and literal naming. An example would appear to be the Englishman's apprehension of the secret of life or of "heaven and the terrible crystal." Hegel, surprisingly, groups the sublime with parable, fable, apologue, and metamorphosis. All are forms of what Hegel calls "conscious symbolism" and are characterized by the inadequacy of the symbol in relation to what it symbolizes. In this the sublime is like that anthropomorphizing prosopopoeia which falsely gives the mountain a head, a breast, or a face. "What has emerged from sublimity," says Hegel, "as distinct from strictly unconscious symbolizing [symbolizing as intuitive *Erinnerung*], consists on the one hand in the *separation* [*in dem trennen*] between the meaning, explicitly known in its inwardness, and the concrete appearance divided therefrom; on the other hand in the directly or indirectly emphasized *noncorrespondence* of the two [*in dem direkter oder inderekter hervorgehobenen Sichnichtentsprechen beider*], wherein the meaning, as the universal, towers above the individual reality and its particularity."[20]

"The Englishman in Italy" is generated by the overlapping or superimposition, in inextricable co-presence and yet mutual contradiction, of what Hegel calls *Erinnerung* with what Hegel calls *Gedächtnis*. The two modes cross in the failure of naming by means of either mode in the two sublime exclamations that punctuate the poem: "Oh, heaven and the terrible crystal!"; "I see and I hear." These expressions are not symbolic, in the sense of participating by literal

[20] G.W.F. von Hegel, *Aesthetics: Lectures on Fine Art*, trans. T. M. Knox, I (New York: Oxford University Press, 1975), p. 378; *Vorlesungen über die Ästhetik, Werkausgabe*, I (Frankfurt am Main: Suhrkamp, 1970), p. 486. See my discussion of this passage, apropos of parable, in "Parable and Performative in the Gospels and in Modern Literature," *Humanizing America's Iconic Book*, ed. Gene M. Tucker and Douglas A. Knight (Chico, California: Scholars Press, 1982), pp. 58-59, and see the fuller discussion, from a somewhat different perspective, of Hegel's theory of the sublime in Paul de Man, "Hegel on the Sublime," *Displacement: Derrida and After*, ed. Mark Krupnick (Bloomington: Indiana University Press, 1983), pp. 139-153.

resemblance in what they "name." The blue sky is only a catachresis for the Heaven beyond the heavens. Nor are they signs within a system of adequate mnemonic notation developed inside the poem, sign referring to sign in a self-generating whole. Each mode calls on the other, which fails in its turn, and refers the reader back to the first.

The dynamic movement of "The Englishman in Italy" is a recapitulation of the recollected past to come forward through the present to the anticipated future, or it is a moving forward into the future in order to come back to the past, thereby bringing past and future together in a timeless moment drawing the circle tight and breaking through into the infinite moment. This effort is not successful. The circle is never complete. As Matthew Arnold's Empedocles puts it, "Man's measures cannot mete the immeasurable All."[21] There is no possibility of an exhaustive inventory, accounting, or telling over. There is no possibility that the part or a finite collection of parts should adequately stand for the whole. The failure of an inventory to be complete results not so much from the fact that in principle synecdoche cannot lean away from its penchant toward contingent metonymy in the direction of its contrary penchant, metaphorical similarity or symbolism of participation. A successful inventory is impossible because the act of expressing this verbally moves the expression into another realm. As soon as symbol is recorded in ordinary language, English or Italian, it is translated into a realm where all, even symbol, is arbitrary rather than motivated, an artificial notation. All the speaker in Browning's poem can do is make again and again the gesture in which Italian things with Italian names are renamed with English names and so alienated. They are displaced in the act of being appropriated, uprooted, turned from things alive in their proper environment into dried specimens in a *hortus*

[21] *Empedocles on Etna*, i, ii, 341, *Poems*, ed. Kenneth Allott (London: Longmans, Green & Co., Ltd., 1965), p. 170.

siccus, or rather into illustrations of such specimens. The Englishman relates to Fortù everything she already knows and has, but he relates it in such a way that he takes it away from her, as surely as the anthropologist dispossesses the native of the culture he so lovingly describes. He takes it away by telling it over in a language she does not understand. At the same time he takes it away from the reader in that subtitle which obliquely reminds him that the poem must have been spoken in Italian if it was spoken to Fortù. He must be reading a translation, something transposed into another language for the reader in his ignorance by some invisible ghost writer, perhaps the poet Robert Browning. This translator gives us all that Fortù has but at the same time takes it away by giving it in simulacrum. The poem gives it written, not spoken, and in the wrong language.

The law of the genre of the dramatic monologue, marked by *Piano di Sorrento*, is this multiple absurdity. It is a poem supposedly spoken but actually written, which has an auditor who by convention cannot answer, or whose answers cannot enter except indirectly into the notation of the poem. It is a poem in which something happens and yet nothing happens, since it happens, even within the fiction of the poem, only in a language marked by negatives, hypotheticals, various forms of non-presence. But might one not say that something is revealed through the language, and that this makes something happen? But to whom? To Fortù? To the speaker? To Browning? To the reader? It happens without happening, since the language is a facsimile of real language spoken in a real situation. The poem is like those sample checks in advertisements, signed John Doe, which no one would think of cashing. "The Englishman in Italy" exposes nothing, no mean feat. It is like one of J. L. Austin's etiolated performatives, for example, a wedding performed on stage in a play.[22] To put this another way, "The

---

[22] See J. L. Austin, "Conditions for Happy Performatives," *How To Do*

Englishman in Italy" exposes nothing but its own artifice of language.

Insofar as "The Englishman in Italy" uses its synecdoches symbolically, it is a magnificent act of recuperation or of interlocking unity, drawing the circle tight in all the ways I have discussed: metrical, figurative, textural, thematic. Against all this is the disintegrating momentum of the linguistic moment. This unsnaps the circle and unstrings the beads. It makes them like the splinters of stone the Englishman scrambles through or like the loose, broken teeth of some monster. Each item adds itself to the heap of dispersed fragments named one by one, in a speech-act in reverse that destroys them. This act of naming turns things not into symbols but into signs. It makes them memories in the sense of *Gedächtnis*. This second penchant of the poem works against the grain of the other at every point. It reveals itself in the inexhaustible power the poem has of beginning again, like Fortù's brother treading the grapes. Another item can always be added to the series without any hope of coming to a proper end.

The poem hovers in the space between these two mutually destroying penchants. It is unable to affirm one of them without at the same time affirming the other and so cancelling the first. Insofar as the Englishman, or the poem, succeeds in the first aim, the Englishman, or Browning, or the reader, vanishes into the "Oh" of the sublime moment where *I* names the locus of a universal experience Ulysses and all the other personages in the perpetual quest have had. Insofar as the second momentum dominates, the Englishman, Browning, and the reader are depersonalized by being drawn into the artifice of the poem. Within this artifice the *I* in "I see and I hear" is a function in an abstract notation capable of being reexperienced in a similar way by any reader. *I* is not the name of a specific person or self.

Things with Words, ed. J. O. Urmson and Marina Sbisà (Oxford, New York, Toronto, Melbourne: Oxford University Press, 1980), pp. 12-24.

At their vanishing points both penchants come together in this moment where impersonation becomes depersonalization. It is a feature of poetry, as I shall show in more detail in the chapter on Hardy, that it forces the reader to become another *I*, to cease to be himself.

"The Englishman in Italy" is not itself a failure. It is a magnificent verbal notation of failure, which is quite a different thing. Nor are the co-presence of two contradictory (though that is not quite the right word) forms of language, two kinds of memory, and a consequent openness to two radically different but inextricably intertwined readings, contingent facts about the poem. This doubleness is not something that might have been otherwise if Browning had not been two-minded himself, or if he had chosen to write a poem unequivocally affirming one or the other doctrine of language and of memory. It is impossible, I am arguing, to have one without the other, as the poem demonstrates. This is why the word *contradictory* is not quite right. It presupposes the possibility of a noncontradictory or unequivocal affirmation, which in this case is not the case. The linguistic moment in the form of some sign that a poem is made of signs, of inscribed notations, of the word *lentisk* and not of the lentisks themselves, will inhabit even the more exuberantly positive symbolic poem or poem of *Erinnerung*. The triumph of "The Englishman in Italy" repeats in its own way the triumph of Shelley's "The Triumph of Life." This triumph is to enact so brilliantly in words both the urge to symbolic appropriation and the inhibition of this by the medium itself, its memorial inscription in words.

Hopkins

In order to identify the linguistic moment in the work of Gerard Manley Hopkins I shall begin by way of a detour through a passage by Hopkins' tutor, Pater, and before Pater, through texts from Pater's not so hidden master, Hegel, then forward in time to Nietzsche. Though Pater seems appropriate enough, Hegel and Nietzsche will no doubt seem unlikely bedfellows for Hopkins, but the three together will establish an essential context for what I have to say about Hopkins. Roman Catholic through and through though he is, Hopkins is a man of the nineteenth century too. His poetry, like his conversion and like the special mode of Victorian Catholic thinking in his writing, is an attempt to resist the disassociation of self, nature, God, and language represented, in different ways, by Pater, by Hegel, or by Nietzsche, among many others. In Hopkins' relationship to Pater, both the influence and the opposition were often more or less explicit. Hopkins, for example, rejected Paterian evolutionary chromatism in favor of a theory that each created species exists as a fixed node at a distance from all other created things.[1]

Though not published until 1889, Walter Pater's essay, "Aesthetic Poetry," was written in 1868, six years before Hopkins composed "The Wreck of the Deutschland." In that essay Pater puts forth a definition of the poetry of his time that is developed to describe Pre-Raphaelite poetry, or, more narrowly, the poetry of William Morris. The latter is the overt subject of his essay. Nevertheless, Pater's def-

[1] See my discussion of this in *The Disappearance of God* (Cambridge, Mass.: The Belknap Press of Harvard University Press, 1963), pp. 277-279.

inition may be applied to much other Victorian poetry. Even more broadly, it may be taken to describe the sense of nature in many Victorian novelists and prose writers, too.[2] Pater brilliantly describes the situation in poetry out of which Hopkins wrote and against which he wrote:

> The "aesthetic" poetry is neither a mere reproduction of Greek or medieval poetry, nor only an idealisation of modern life and sentiment. The atmosphere on which its effect depends belongs to no simple form of poetry, no actual form of life. Greek poetry, medieval or modern poetry, projects, above the realities of its time, a world in which the forms of things are transfigured. Of that transfigured world this new poetry takes possession, and sublimates beyond it another still fainter or more spectral, which is literally an artificial or "earthly paradise." It is a finer ideal, extracted from what in relation to any actual world is already an ideal. Like some strange second flowering after date, it renews on a more delicate type the poetry of a past age, but must not be confounded with it. The secret of the enjoyment of it is that inversion of home-sickness known to some, that incurable thirst for the sense of escape, which no actual form of life satisfies, no poetry even, if it be merely simple and spontaneous.[3]

A comprehensive theory of poetry and of the history of poetry is implicit in these sentences. This theory and this history are somewhat like the ones in their possible source, Hegel's *Ästhetik*, but Pater presents a significant variation on Hegel. Poetry, for Pater, begins in a confrontation of

---

[2] See my "Nature and the Linguistic Moment," *Nature and the Victorian Imagination*, ed. U. C. Knoepflmacher and G. B. Tennyson (Berkeley, Los Angeles, London: University of California Press, 1977), pp. 440-451. This essay sketches (pp. 447-449) the interpretation of Hopkins proposed at greater length in this chapter.

[3] Walter Pater, *Appreciations* (London: Macmillan and Co., 1889), pp. 213-214.

nature, of "life." All poetry is an idealization, a transfiguration of the raw material of sensation. It takes the data of
the senses, things as they are, "the realities of its time," and
transforms them into an ideal world. This transfiguration
is something like the Hegelian *Aufhebung*, cancelling and
preserving at once. The ideal world of poetry exists only
in the words of the poem. It has been projected only there
and is accessible only there. By "modern poetry" Pater appears to mean what we should call "Romantic" poetry, including its Renaissance antecedents in Spenser and Milton.

The transposing, "sublating" activity of Greek, medieval,
and modern poetry remains the same, a direct operation
on the actual forms of life, but aesthetic poetry is another
matter. By "aesthetic poetry" Pater means Pre-Raphaelite
poetry and a major portion of high Victorian poetry, that
part of Tennyson or Browning which is already consonant
with Pre-Raphaelite practice. The peculiarity of "aesthetic
poetry" is that it no longer performs its act of transformation directly, as did Greek, medieval, and "modern" poetry. Nor does aesthetic poetry simply "reproduce" Greek
or medieval poetry, as, at one extreme, Rossetti's translations of early Italian poetry might appear to do. Aesthetic
poetry takes the world already transfigured into poetry—
Greek, medieval, or modern—and transforms that poetry
once more, rarefies it, "sublimates" it, as ice may pass to
vapor without pausing in the liquid state.

Pater's figures are characteristically decadent: "strange
second flowering after date"; "inversion of home-sickness."
This should not obscure the cogency of the distinctions he
makes. The figures are a powerful vehicle of his description
of the unnatural or even uncanny detachment from reality
of aesthetic poetry. Such poetry is like a flower blooming
out of season, or like a man who should perversely flee
from home rather than toward it. For Pater there are three
possible kinds of poetry: the "merely simple and spontaneous," made by direct transformation of experience; a
straightforward reproducing at a later time of an earlier

231

poetry; a poetry, finally, that performs its work of transformation not on experience but on earlier poetry, treating that earlier poetry in the same way that simple and spontaneous poetry treats life. Aesthetic poetry is at a double remove from life. It is poetry about poetry. It is the poetry of repetition with a difference rather than a repetition as identical reproduction either of the world or of earlier poetry. In aesthetic poetry the relation of sign to sign has displaced the relation of sign to referent. Such poetry uses allegorical signs rather than participative symbols, to use again the Hegelian distinction employed in the chapter on Browning here. Aesthetic poetry is based on a temporal rather than on a spatial relation, and it is based on the difference and distance of a sign from its referent rather than on their similarity.[4] The allegorical relation of sign to sign may be either "internal" or "external." If either is the case, the borders of the individual poem break down or tend to break down. The allegorical sign may draw its meaning from its reference to another sign in the same work. If so, it produces within the work the effect of a second flowering after date. Or it may refer to a sign in an earlier work, as by allusion or citation, incorporating within itself a fragment of the earlier work and drawing its meaning from the interaction set up. This structure is essentially temporal, even within the poem. It is a matter of early and late rather than of the spatial relation of elements within an arbitrary border.

Realistic art, "simple and spontaneous," satisfies a desire for a homecoming to the real or for a revelation of what in reality would otherwise remain covered, as in the speaker's credo of realism in Browning's "Fra Lippo Lippi." Aesthetic poetry, on the other hand, appeals to a strange inversion of homesickness. It puts a distance between us and

[4] The Hegelian distinction is developed by Paul de Man in "The Rhetoric of Temporality," *Interpretation: Theory and Practice*, ed. Charles S. Singleton (Baltimore: The Johns Hopkins Press, 1969), pp. 190-191, and in his essay on Hegel cited in note 18 of chapter 4 above.

the world. Aesthetic poetry satisfies a desire for escape from any actual form of life into some artificial realm or "earthly paradise," like that in William Morris's poem of that name.

One may doubt whether there may ever be a poetry that is "merely simple and spontaneous," or, on the other hand, a poetry that does no more than "reproduce" the poetry of a past time. As many recent critics have in different ways been arguing, and as poets have always known, poetry is mediated in its response to things as they are by the obstacle and stimulus of previous poetry. Even Homer's epics had predecessor poems, the presence of which may often be detected as ghostly palimpsest-like texts or as murmuring ancestral voices just beneath the surface of the words of the *Iliad* or the *Odyssey*. In the grand sequence from Homer to Virgil to Dante to Spenser to Milton to Wordsworth and from Shelley to Browning, Yeats, and Stevens, originality, in the sense of a merely simple and spontaneous relation to nature and to human life, is always mediated, however covertly, by the words of previous poets. Of all these poets one could say what Johnson, in a celebrated passage, says of Milton: "Whatever be his subject, he never fails to fill the imagination. But his images and descriptions of the scenes or operations of Nature do not seem to be always copied from original form, nor to have the freshness, raciness, and energy of immediate observation. He saw Nature, as Dryden expresses it, *'through the spectacles of books'*; and on most occasions calls learning to his assistance."[5] A poem belongs to the real world not in its initial inspiration but in its action on its readers and successor poets, after a longer or shorter "allegorical" wandering in the labyrinth of its deviations from the earlier poems that have generated it. It is impossible, moreover, to maintain and reproduce in a new time the poetry of an earlier tradition. Even translations—for example, those splendid translations from the

[5] Samuel Johnson, "Milton," *The Lives of the English Poets*, ed. G. B. Hill, I (Oxford: Oxford University Press, 1905), p. 178.

Italian by Rossetti—are interpretation, a bending or distortion of what is translated. *Dante and His Circle, With the Italian Poets Preceding Him* (1861) might paradoxically be taken as the model of what Pater means by aesthetic poetry, poetry that makes something new by a process of subliming earlier poetry.

It was this mediated and indirect relation of poetry to what is outside language, the veil poetry puts, rather than removes, between man and the world, which Hopkins was most concerned to combat. What Hopkins was fighting against may be more precisely defined by the exegesis of a passage in Hegel's *Lectures on Aesthetics*. This work proposes a development of art something like Pater's scheme, though not perfectly congruent with it. For Hegel, art moves by stages through history from Symbolic to Classical to Romantic modes. In the movement from one to the other there is increasing discovery of the independent being (*Insichseins*) of the spirit. Hegel's terminology here remains enclosed within a dialectic of subject and object. In the passage I cite below he pays little apparent attention to language as such. After all, his topic is art in general, the aesthetic as such, which includes sculpture, architecture, and painting, as well as poetry. The peculiarity of Hegel's definition of Romantic art is its divergence from the notion, still current in Anglo-American criticism today, that Romanticism is to be defined as Coleridge and Wordsworth seemingly defined it—that is, as the reconciliation of subject and object. For Hegel, Romanticism is precisely the opposite of this. It is based on the decisive and irremediable division of man and nature.

In this breaking apart, several events simultaneously occur. Spirit discovers its independent, inward existence and the impossibility of expressing itself in terms drawn from the external world. This means at the same moment the emergence of a new kind of nature. Nature now appears as it is in itself, naked, bare, without transfiguration by any kind of spiritual meaning. This allows the appearance in

Romantic art, says Hegel, of the most insignificant things—flowers, trees, household utensils, "the pans above the stove, the pots on the table, the tulips among them," as Wallace Stevens puts it.[6] As I have elsewhere argued,[7] this appearance of a denuded nature, bereft of any transcendent, or perhaps even human, meaning, is a crucial moment in many nineteenth-century novels, and of course for such a critic as Friedrich Schlegel, the typical expression of Romantic art is not lyric poetry but the novel. Here is Hegel's admirably condensed expression of this double simultaneous development in Romantic art. Such art uncovers the independent and irreconcilable distances of subject, on the one hand, and of objects, on the other. The reader will note that the passage turns on the opposition between inner and outer and on the spectrum of words for these categories:

> The external and phenomenal [*Das äußerlich Erscheinende*] is no longer able to express internality [*die Innerlichkeit*]; and if it is still called upon to do this, it retains only the task of proving that the external [*das Äußere*] is an incomplete existence, and must refer back to the internal [*das Innere*], to mind [*Gemüt*] and sensibility, as to the essential element. But for this very reason Romantic art allows externality [*die Äußerlichkeit*] to appear again freely on its own account, and in this respect permits each and every matter to enter unhindered into the representation, even flowers, trees, and the most ordinary household furniture, and this, too, in the natural accidentality of present existence.[8]

---

[6] "Large Red Man Reading," line 5, *The Collected Poems* (New York: Alfred A. Knopf, Inc., 1954), p. 423.

[7] In the essay cited in note 2 above.

[8] This and the following passages from Hegel are to be found in G.W.F. Hegel, *Vorlesungen über die Aesthetik*, II, *Werke in zwanzig Bänden*, XIV (Frankfurt am Main: Suhrkamp Verlag, 1970), pp. 140-141, my trans. modified from that by W. M. Bryant in *The Philosophy of Hegel*, ed. Carl J. Friedrich (New York: The Modern Library, 1954), pp. 364-365. I have also con-

The "natural accidentality of present existence" is, according to Hegel, deprived of any intrinsic connection to subjectivity or significance for it. This means the revelation of its baseness and meaninglessness: "This content, however," says Hegel, "bears with it at the same time the characteristic that as mere external matter [*als bloss äußerlicher Stoff*] it is insignificant and low." Destitute of any value in itself, it "only attains its true value when it is pervaded by human interest [*wenn das Gemüt sich in ihn hineingelegt hat*]." This pervasion, however, is accomplished across the gap between subjectivity and the base outer world. The mark made on nature that imbues it with human interest remains external and superficial, like that print of the hand or wear on a threshold of which Hardy speaks in a notebook entry: "An object or mark raised or made by man on a scene is worth ten times any such formed by unconscious Nature. Hence clouds, mist, and mountains are unimportant beside the wear on a threshold or the print of a hand."[9] Such a mark on nature or such an object erected on its surface leaves untouched the otherness and lowness of nature beneath. This giving of interest to nature presupposes the difference between subject and object rather than their harmony. Violence is done to nature when it is made over by the spirit into the signs of its own internality. Moreover, as Hegel recognizes, this violence must make natural things into an expression not merely of this or that aspect of the mind but of the mind in itself, as it is to itself in its solitary self-reflexiveness, in its *Insichseins*. Nature, says Hegel, "must express not only the inner [*das Innerliche*] but even internality [*die Innigkeit*] itself. Internality, far from blending itself with the outer world, appears reconciled only in and with itself."

Here occurs the most extraordinary moment of Hegel's

sulted the translation by T. M. Knox, *Aesthetics: Lectures on Fine Art*, I (New York: Oxford University Press, 1975), p. 527.

[9] Florence Emily Hardy, *The Life of Thomas Hardy: 1840–1928* (London: Macmillan; New York: St. Martin's Press, 1965), p. 116.

thought in this brief extract from the vast expanse of his writing. Neither language as such nor the medium of any other art is overtly mentioned here, though of course language is abundantly discussed by Hegel elsewhere and taken, not with entire consistency, into the dialectic of constantly self-transforming negativity whereby the spirit gradually fulfills itself.[10] A theory of language, or, more generally, of signs, is nevertheless implicit in the passage. The discovery of the otherness of external nature means the discovery of the inexpressibility of consciousness. There are no literal names or signs for subjectivity. It cannot be made visible in any outer form. It is in fact invisible, inaudible, intangible, without savor. It is incapable of being expressed outwardly. It can express itself only negatively, in its difference from anything external. This means that it can only express itself in signs that are taken, reflected, echoed, from nature, but that confess, in their formulation as signs, to the fact that they are figurative, not literal. They are fictions, arbitrary emblems, rather than substantial analogies or symbols. They do not participate in what they name, nor is the sign similar to its referent. They are, once more, catachreses, figures that do not substitute for any possible literal term. In Hegel, however, catachreses are not, as in Browning, personifications used to name nature, but nature words wrenched from their literal use and employed to name the unnamable, namely spirit, subjectivity.

It is not even possible to express this situation in literal or conceptual language. This impossibility is indicated in the fact that Hegel himself at this point falls back on figures to state his meaning. The invisibility of the mind can be expressed by visible things only negatively. It is like the

[10] See my discussion of Hegel's theory of signs and memory in the chapter on Browning above; see also the essays on Hegel by Paul de Man cited in notes 18, 19, and 20 to that chapter, and Jacques Derrida's discussions of Hegel's theories of language in "*Le puits et la pyramide,*" *Marges* (Paris: Les Éditions de Minuit, 1972), pp. 79-127, and in *Glas* (Paris: Galilée, 1974), pp. 14-17 and *passim*, left column.

fleeting outer shape matter may have, as water becomes momentarily a wave, though the wave shape has no intrinsic relation to its watery substance, or as a tone is an invisible and momentary modulation of air to make it express, in its vibration, something other than itself, or as sound or light reflected back from a natural object expresses not that object itself, though without the intervening object it would disperse in silence or darkness or empty space and remain inaudible or invisible. "Thus driven to extremity [*so auf die Spitze hinaustrieben*]," says Hegel, in this admirable formulation, "the inner at this point is externalization destitute of externality [*die äußerlichkeitslose Äußerung*]. It is, as it were, invisible and comprehended only by itself; a tone as such, without objectivity or form; a hovering over the waters [*ein Schweben über den Wassern*] a resounding through a world, which in and upon its heterogeneous phenomena can only take up and send back a reflected ray [*einen Gegenschein*] of this independent-being [*Insichseins*] of the soul."

For Hegel here, at least so it seems, consciousness is presumed to pre-exist its making visible in its invisibility by way of figures drawn, without the authority of any pre-established similarity, from an alien nature. Nietzsche, in a brilliant passage added in 1887 for the second edition of *Die Fröhliche Wissenschaft*, challenges this apparent assumption of Hegelian thought. Nietzsche's argument also expresses succinctly, in order to destroy it, the relation between nature, consciousness, and the names of natural things that Hopkins must preserve or re-establish at all costs. Hegel might be described as the climax or *Aufhebung* of the metaphysical tradition that Nietzsche patiently in all his works attempts to dismantle, or rather he attempts to show that the fabric of metaphysical assumptions unravels itself. One might argue that the development from Hegel to Nietzsche occurs by a remorseless logic because it is already latent in Hegel. If spirit is invisible, tasteless or colorless, nameless, and can only express itself in terms drawn from nature, may spirit not perhaps only exist in that activity of naming? Nietzsche takes the step to affirming this, though it is implicit already in Hegel. It might be said that the vast shifting edifice of Hegel's writing is an attempt to avoid taking this step while simultaneously taking it all the time. Once spirit, *Geist*, is detached from the idea of a personal God in whose image man is made, the unity of nature, consciousness, language, and absolute spirit falls apart at the slightest touch. Such a touch Nietzsche repeatedly administers in all his works, more or less gently, for example, in this paragraph from *The Gay Science*.

In the passage in question Nietzsche employs a characteristic strategy of deconstruction: the identification and reversal of the hidden tropes on which metaphysical assumptions depend. In this case the figures include metalepsis and synecdoche. The assumption that consciousness precedes the expression of it and could exist without that expression is, says Nietzsche, a fiction arising from the taking literally a metalepsis, the substitution of late for early. Consciousness is not the creator and manipulator of signs. Language rather creates consciousness. Language is necessarily social. It is an intersubjective phenomenon arising from the necessity for communication between human beings living together, especially when they live together in a relation of domination and subservience. A single isolated human being would not need either consciousness or language, which is to say he would not be human. Both minds and words arise together out of a collective need to have a superficial and simplified interpretation of the world about which men and women in their living together can agree. It arises especially from the need to make comprehensible signs of command and obedience. There is no consciousness without words and only so much consciousness as is allowed by the stage of development language at a given point has reached.

Not only is the notion of a prior and self-subsistent consciousness a metaleptic myth born of the illicit taking of effect for cause. There also is no such thing as an isolated consciousness, closed in on itself in its internality or *Insich-seins*. If language is necessarily intersubjective, so also is that effect of language called consciousness or self-consciousness. Consciousness always involves consciousness of others. It is an awareness, through the generative effects of a shared language, of the pressure of the presence of others. It arises from a battle for domination among conflicting wills to power. Even those wills to power, however, insofar as they require consciousness to exist, are generated by language and do not pre-exist its appearance:

> . . . I may now proceed to the surmise that *consciousness [Bewuβtsein] has developed only under the pressure of the need for communication [Mitteilungs-Bedürfnisses]*; that from the start it was needed and useful only between man and man (particularly between those who commanded and those who obeyed); and that it also developed only in proportion to the degree of this utility. Consciousness is really only a net of communication [*Verbindungsnetz*] between man and man; it is only as such that it had to develop; a solitary human being who lived like a beast of prey would not have needed it. . . . In brief, the development of language and the development of consciousness . . . go hand in hand. . . . The human being inventing signs [*Der Zeichenerfindende Mensch*] is at the same time the human being who becomes ever more keenly conscious of himself. It was only as a social animal that man acquired self-consciousness—which he is still in the process of doing, more and more.[11]

If the traditional notion of the relation of language and consciousness depends on the reification of a metalepsis, the assumption that thinking and consciousness are co-

[11] All the citations from Nietzsche here are from Friedrich Nietzsche, *Werke in Drei Bänden*, ed. Karl Schlechta, II (Munich: Carl Hanser Verlag, 1966), pp. 220-222. I have used, with slight alterations, the translation by Walter Kaufmann: *The Gay Science* (New York: Vintage Books, 1974), pp. 298-300.

terminous arises from the reification of a synecdoche. For Nietzsche thinking is the whole activity of interpretation, simplification, falsification, appropriation, and assimilation performed by any living organism. For Nietzsche, to live is to interpret, which means to misinterpret. By interpretation living creatures do violence to what is exterior in order to take possession of it safely, to reduce, however precariously, its dangerous otherness and unpredictability. Consciousness is only a part of this total activity of living, and a superficial part at that. It is the part that expresses itself in language as such rather than in other less articulate forms of appropriation and falsification: "Man," says Nietzsche, "like every living being, thinks continually without knowing it; the thinking that rises to *consciousness* is only the smallest part of all this—the most superficial and worst part [*der oberflächlichste, der schlechteste Teil*]—for only this conscious thinking *takes the form of words, which is to say signs of communication* [*Mitteilungszeichen*], with which the origin of consciousness reveals itself [*womit sich die Herkunft des Bewußtseins selber aufdeckt*]."

Consciousness is an effect of language. Language, in turn, is the instrument of that collective simplification of the world necessary to make the transmissible conventions essential to human society. Or rather language is that simplification. Consciousness is therefore superficial, a thin skin of ice over watery depths. Even in relation to the "unconscious thinking" of which it is a part, consciousness is at a ludicrous distance from the unknown and unknowable substratum of things as they are: "Owing to the nature of *animal consciousness*, the world of which we can become conscious is only a surface- and sign-world [*nur eine Oberflächen- und Zeichenwelt ist*], a world that is made common and meaner; whatever becomes conscious *becomes* by the same token shallow, thin, relatively stupid, general, sign, herd signal [*Herden-Merkzeichen*]; all becoming conscious is bound up with a great and thorough corruption, falsification, reduction to superficialities [*Veroberflächlichung*], and generalization."

For Nietzsche, nature vanishes into the signs for it. Those signs are not even the product of a single man's solitary misinterpretations. They are generated, along with consciousness itself, in the dangerously superficial living together of men and women in society. The private relation of subject and object, the "imagination of nature," is displaced to the relation of consciousness and language. In this relation, consciousness, including self-consciousness, is generated only as the interpersonal realm of signs develops. Those signs borrow the false or figurative names men make for natural things both to describe and to generate the various aspects of the intersubjective realm of consciousness. Far from being a substance or a source, consciousness is the figure of a figure, "like some strange second flowering after date." The harmonious and continuous world of subject and object, bound together by the symbol—as in a familiar misinterpretation of Romanticism, less perceptive than Hegel's—is replaced, in Nietzsche's formulation, by the discontinuities of figurative transfers. These are always wrenchings, distortions, misreadings, the taking of names in vain.

GERARD MANLEY HOPKINS begins in the human and poetic situation I have sketched with the help of Pater, Hegel, and Nietzsche. Hopkins' often negative comments in his letters on the English Romantic poets and on the Victorians corresponds, somewhat surprisingly, to those by Matthew Arnold—for example, in Arnold's letters to Clough.[12] For

[12] For Arnold on the Romantics see the preface above, p. 15. For Hopkins' comments on the Romantics, on the Victorians, on the Pre-Raphaelites, and on Whitman, see the multitudinous comments indexed in the three volumes of Hopkins' letters, *The Letters of Gerard Manley Hopkins to Robert Bridges*, ed. C. C. Abbott (London: Oxford University Press, 1955), henceforth cited as L–I followed by the page number; *The Correspondence of Gerard Manley Hopkins and Richard Watson Dixon*, ed. C. C. Abbott (London: Oxford University Press, 1955), henceforth L–II; *Further Letters of Gerard Manley Hopkins*, ed. C. C. Abbott (London: Oxford University Press, 1956), henceforth L–III. Perhaps especially important are the letter of

both Arnold and Hopkins Romanticism seeks "fulness without respect of the means"[13] and claims to have an ontological grounding it lacks. In this both Arnold and Hopkins agree with Hegel's characterization of Romanticism as the perhaps irrevocable splitting apart of nature, consciousness, God, and language. Both Arnold and Hopkins found this splitting apart intolerable, and both, in quite different ways, attempted to use language to bring the fragmented pieces back together, to revoke the irrevocable, with indifferent success, in Arnold's case at least, as I have shown in chapter 1. Hopkins' parallel attempt to reintegrate the disintegrated proposes a chiming of nature, man, and God as it may be affirmed in what he called the "inscapes" of language.

The primary motive for Hopkins conversion to Roman Catholicism from his native Anglicanism was the absence in the latter of any genuine belief in the "Real Presence" of Christ in the bread and wine of the Sacrament of Communion.[14] In that Presence nature, God, self, and Word come together. Poetry, if it is to have value, must repeat

---

September 10, 1864, to A.W.M. Baillie about "Parnassian" or uninspired verse in Wordsworth and Tennyson (L–III, 215-222), and the letter of October 18, 1882, to Robert Bridges about Whitman (L–I, 154-158). Hopkins' comments on the Romantics and the Victorians tend to emphasize their stylistic and technical shortcomings along with their moral failings, as in the famous statement about Whitman, made with who knows how much or how little irony: "I always knew in my heart Walt Whitman's mind to be more like my own than any other man's living. As he is a very great scoundrel this is not a pleasant confession" (L–I, 155).

[13] Matthew Arnold, *Letters . . . to Arthur Hugh Clough*, ed. H. F. Lowry (London and New York: Oxford University Press, 1932), p. 97.

[14] "The great aid to belief and object of belief," Hopkins wrote in a letter, "is the doctrine of the Real Presence in the Blessed Sacrament of the Altar. Religion without that is sombre, dangerous, illogical, with that it is . . . *loveable*" (L–III, 17). In the letter to his father announcing his conversion from Anglicanism to Roman Catholicism Hopkins says that belief in the incarnation and in its correlate, the Real Presence, is all that preserves his faith in God: "The belief once got is the life of the soul and when I doubted it I shd. become an atheist the next day" (L–III, 92).

that magical assimilation of the dispersed into one. Like the words of the priest in the Communion, poetry must not describe things as they are but make something happen. This presupposes that the initial situation in poetry is the dispersal Hopkins inherited from the Romantic and Victorian poets, just as his situation in religion was the lax Anglicanism, as he saw it, of his family and of his native land.

That this situation of separation was Hopkins' starting place is indicated in the melancholy eloquence of the celebrated opening of his commentary on the *Spiritual Exercises* of Saint Ignatius: "And this [my isolation] is much more true when we consider the mind; when I consider my selfbeing, my consciousness and feeling of myself, that taste of myself, of *I* and *me* above and in all things, which is more distinctive than the taste of ale or alum, more distinctive than the smell of walnutleaf or camphor, and is incommunicable by any means to another man (as when I was a child I used to ask myself: What must it be to be someone else?)."[15] Selfhood, each man's consciousness of himself, is incommunicable by any means to another man (a terrifying thought) because, just as Hegel said, it has no kinship with those things in nature all men share, for example, the taste of ale or alum or the smell of walnutleaf or camphor. This is true in spite of the fact that, for the man himself, the taste of "*I* and *me*" is "in all things," as well as "above" them. If I borrow figures from nature to attempt to express my sense of myself to others, I shall communicate not my taste of myself but what other people already know: the taste of ale or alum, the smell of walnutleaf or camphor. This conspicuously happens in the passage just quoted. The passage does not tell the reader anything at all about what it was like to be Gerard Manley Hopkins, except that it was a state

[15] Gerard Manley Hopkins, *The Sermons and Devotional Writings*, ed. Christopher Devlin (London: Oxford University Press, 1959), p. 123; henceforth S.

of desolate solitude. His state was like that of a man who has been shipwrecked in a country where no one knows his language. He was like Conrad's Yanko Goorall, for example, already invoked here apropos of Browning's "The Englishman in Italy." Or Hopkins' situation was like that of Dante's Nimrod, who can only babble in an utterly private language: *Raphel maì amècche zabì almi.* As Virgil explains to Dante, Nimrod is the one "through whose ill thought one language only is not used in the world [*per lo cui mal coto / pur un linguaggio nel mondo non s'usa*]," and there is no use talking to him, "for every language is to him as his is to others, which is known to none [*ché così è a lui ciascun linguaggio / come 'l suo ad altrui, ch'a nullo è noto*]."[16]

If Hopkins' isolation is like that of Yanko or Nimrod, it has a special twist, for Hopkins is a master of many languages, a teacher of Latin and Greek, a skilled translator, able to write poems in Latin, Greek, and Welsh. This is to say that Hopkins is a comparatist, engaged in the repair of the disaster of Babel, Nimrod's folly, according to the tradition Dante follows.[17] Nevertheless, for all his linguistic skill Hopkins is unable to communicate "by any means," that is, by means of any language or sign system, his taste of himself. If he speaks or writes in any language, he will communicate only what that language already says. If he speaks adequately of his self-taste, he will, like Nimrod, speak a private language and so communicate nothing: *Raphel maì amècche zabì almi.*

"The Wreck of the Deutschland," that first great burst of poetic language of Hopkins' maturity, speaks from such a condition of desolation and attempts to escape it. The

[16] *Inferno*, XXXI, 67, 77-78, 80-81, cited from Dante Alighieri, *The Divine Comedy, Inferno*, trans. Charles S. Singleton, 1, Italian Text and Translation (Princeton: Princeton University Press, 1970), pp. 330-333. My citations in English and in Italian manifest the situation the passage is about: the multiplication and dispersal of languages.

[17] See Singleton's discussion of this, *The Divine Comedy*, ed. cit., *Inferno*, 2, Commentary, pp. 570-573.

wreck is Hopkins' own, incarnated in his own flesh, blood, and self-taste, and it is at the same time the wreck he inherited from his immediate predecessors in poetry. Hopkins' attempted repair of the disaster of Babel had long been preparing, for example, in his early diaries and journals. It continues, of course, in all the poems written after "The Wreck." Hopkins' poetic problem was to find a way to communicate the incommunicable. It was an attempted rescue of the self and of language through language.

Kenneth Burke, in remarks about an earlier version of this essay,[18] argued that I should add something about the multiple meaning of the word *wreck* in the title. "The Wreck of the Deutschland," he said, is about Hopkins' wreck, as indeed in this present essay I am also affirming in my own way. Burke's statement was a powerful plea to relate the linguistic complexities, or tensions, back to their subjective counterparts. Much is at stake here. That the poem is a deeply personal document there can be no doubt. Its linguistic tensions are lived, not mere verbal play in the negative sense. It has always been Kenneth Burke's great strength, as opposed to some present-day structuralists or semiologists, never to neutralize literary language, never to make it into a tame conundrum or trivial crossword

[18] "On Literary Form," *The New Criticism and After*, ed. Thomas Daniel Young (Charlottesville: University Press of Virginia, 1976), p. 85. The secondary literature of commentary on "The Wreck of the Deutschland" is of course voluminous. See, for example, Elisabeth W. Schneider, *The Dragon in the Gate: Studies in the Poetry of G. M. Hopkins* (Berkeley and Los Angeles: University of California Press, 1968), which is primarily on "The Wreck"; Paul L. Mariani, *"The Wreck of the Deutschland*: 1875–1876," *A Commentary on the Complete Poems of Gerard Manley Hopkins* (Ithaca and London: Cornell University Press, 1970), pp. 47-73; Michael Sprinker, *"A Counterpoint of Dissonance": The Aesthetics and Poetry of Gerard Manley Hopkins* (Baltimore and London: The Johns Hopkins University Press, 1980); James Milroy, *The Language of Gerard Manley Hopkins* (London: André Deutsch, 1977). Sprinker's book contains a good chapter on "The Wreck of the Deutschland," pp. 96-119, and is also of great value for its discussion of Hopkins' theory of language in its historical connections.

puzzle. For Burke literature is always incarnated in the flesh and blood and nerves of its writer or reader. In this he is true to his great exemplar, Sigmund Freud.

Nor can there be any doubt that in "The Wreck of the Deutschland" Hopkins is speaking of his own wreck in the sense of personal disaster, fragmentation, or blockage (with the pun, elsewhere used by Hopkins, on *reck* as *beware of, take warning from*). Hopkins' experience of himself as a wreck was associated with his sense of impotence, with his inability ever to finish anything or to "breed one work that wakes,"[19] as in a moving late letter: "And there they lie and my old notebooks and beginnings of things, ever so many, which it seems to me might well have been done, ruins and wrecks" (L–III, 255).

The movement to resurrection and salvation in "The Wreck of the Deutschland" does not, I agree, fully counterbalance the extraordinary expression of unresolved tension. Resolution, in the sense of the final untying of a blocking knot, always remains a future event in Hopkins' writing, and necessarily so, on the terms of his own theology. The danger in Burke's suggestion, however, is, as always in such cases, the possibility of a psychologizing reduction, the making of literature into no more than a reflection or representation of something psychic that precedes it and could exist without it. Hopkins' personal wreck is rather his inextricable involvement, in flesh and blood, in a net of signs, figures, concepts, and narrative patterns. The exchanges, permutations, contradictions, latent aporias, untyings and tyings of these elements he had the courage and the genius to live through in his writing and in his experience. Subjectivity, with all its intensities, is in this case, too, more a result than an origin. To set it first, to make an explanatory

[19] Gerard Manley Hopkins, "Thou art indeed just, Lord," line 13, *Poems*, 4th ed., ed. W. H. Gardner and N. H. MacKenzie (London, Oxford, New York: Oxford University Press, 1970), p. 107; henceforth PHop. All of Hopkins' poems are cited from this edition.

principle of it, is, as Nietzsche says, a metalepsis, putting late before early, effect before cause.

Hopkins' attempt to rescue himself from language through language begins with a linguistic assumption, an assumption about the relation of individual words to the Logos—Christ the Word. Hopkins' religious thought is centered on an ultimately acentric analogy: the parallelism between the structure of language and the structure of the creation in relation to the creator. The most obvious way in which this analogy appears is in the systematic and of course wholly orthodox use of a metaphor drawn from language to describe the relation of the world to God. Christ, the second person of the Trinity, is the Logos, the word or utterance of God. The world with all its multitude of creatures, including man, is spoken into existence in the name of Christ, modeled on Christ, just as all the multiplicity of words in a language might be considered as the product of an increasingly elaborate differentiation of a primal word, an ur-word. The structure of language is the vehicle of the metaphor that is the irreplaceable means by which Hopkins expresses his conception of God in his relation to the creation. One might say that his theological terminology is logocentric. Language itself, however, is also a primary theme in Hopkins' writings, not only in the brilliant etymological speculations in the early diaries or in the early essay on words,[20] but also in the mature poetry itself, for example, in "That Nature is a Heraclitean Fire and of the comfort of the Resurrection," and in "I wake and feel the fell of dark, not day." The theme of language is most elaborately developed in Hopkins' masterpiece, "The Wreck of the Deutschland." This motif runs all through "The Wreck," not just as a metaphor but as a theme treated directly, for itself.

[20] See Gerard Manley Hopkins, *The Journals and Papers*, ed. H. House and G. Storey (London: Oxford University Press, 1959), pp. 4-73, 125-126; henceforth J.

248

Hopkins affirms three apparently incompatible theories of poetry. Each is brilliantly worked out in theory and exemplified in practice.[21] Poetry may be the representation of the interlocked chiming of created things in their relation to the Creator. This chiming makes the pied beauty of nature. Poetry may explore or express the solitary adventures of the self in its wrestles with God or in its fall into the abyss outside God. Poetry may explore the intricate relationships among words. These three seemingly diverse theories of poetry are harmonized by the application to all of them of a linguistic model. This model assumes that all words rhyme because all are ultimately derived from the same Logos. Nature, for example, is "word, expression, news of God" (S, 129) because God has inscribed himself in nature. The structure of nature in its relation to God is like the structure of language in relation to the Logos, the divine Word. Christ is the Logos of nature, as of words. The linguistic model also applies to the changes within the self. The permutations of language, as in the final two lines of "That Nature is a Heraclitean Fire," mime the permutations of the self as it is changed by grace from a Jackself, steeped in sin, turned from God, to a more Christ-like, Logosimilar, self. The lines solve a linguistic puzzle. How to get from "Jack" to "immortal diamond" with the smallest number of changed or added sounds. The solution to the puzzle corresponds to Hopkins' escape from the incommunicable solitude of his self-taste. He escapes from it in the only way possible, by the transformation of what is altogether particular, his self-taste, to the altogether general—Christ the ubiquitous Word. He makes this change without ceasing to be himself, as carbon may be changed, with enough fire and pressure, into its allotropic form, diamond, though it is still carbon:

[21] See my essay on Hopkins in *The Disappearance of God* (Cambridge, Mass.: The Belknap Press of Harvard University Press, 1963), pp. 270-359.

I am all at once what Christ is | since he was what I am, and
This Jack, joke, poor potsherd, | patch, matchwood, immortal diamond,
    Is immortal diamond.
                        (PHop, 106)

Since the structure of language is the indispensable metaphor by means of which Hopkins describes nature or the
self, the nature of language is a matter of fundamental
importance to him. From his early diaries to the last poems,
Hopkins shows his fascination with language as such. One
can see why, since everything else, his vision of nature and
of the self in their relations to God, hangs on the question
of the nature of language and of the adequacy of the linguistic metaphor.

In all three realms—language, nature, and self—the notion of rhyme, the echoing at a distance of entities that are
similar without being identical, is essential. The exploitation of rhyme in this extended sense may be seen operating
throughout "The Wreck of the Deutschland" as its fundamental organizing principle. Rhyme operates in "The
Wreck" both on the microscopic level of local poetical effect
and on the macroscopic level of the large structural repetitions organizing the whole.

On the local level there are repetitions with a difference
of word sounds, word meanings, and rhythmical patterns.
As is indicated by the etymological speculations in Hopkins'
early diaries, the basis of Hopkins' interest in the labyrinth
of relations among the sounds of words is the assumption
that if words sound the same they will be similar in meaning. Each sequence of words with the same consonant pattern but with different vowels—for example, *flick, fleck, flake*—
is assumed to be a variation on a single ur-meaning from
which they are all derived. All words whatsoever, all permutations of all the letters of the alphabet, are assumed to
have a common source in the Word, "him that present and
past, / Heaven and earth are word of, worded by," as Hopkins puts it in "The Wreck" (lines 229-230). This attention

to sound similarities in their relation to similarities of meaning is perhaps most apparent in the emphatic use of alliteration throughout the poem (breath/bread; strand/sway/ sea; bound/bones); but there are many other forms of sound echo—assonance, end rhyme, internal rhyme, recurrences of vowel sequences, and so on—which the attentive reader will follow as threads of embodied meaning in the tapestry of the poem. In all these cases the underlying assumption is theological as well as technical. The fact that Christ is the Word, or Logos, of which all particular words are versions, variations, or metaphors, allows Hopkins even to accommodate into his poem words that are similar in sound though opposite in meaning. Christ underlies all words and thereby reconciles all oppositions in word sound and meaning: "Thou art lightning and love, I found it, a winter and warm" (line 70).

The same assumptions ground the various forms of repetition with difference of word meaning in the poem. The complex fabric of recurring metaphors is not mere verbal play to unify the poem. This pattern is based on the assumption that metaphorical comparisons reflect ontological correspondences in the world. Such correspondences are placed there by the God whom heaven and earth are word of, worded by. Fire, water, sand, and wind are the primary elements of this "metaphorology." To the recurrence of metaphors may be added the repetition of metaphorical elements by thematic motifs that exist on the literal level of narrative in the poem. It is no accident that the poet's experience of grace in the first part of the poem is described in terms of figures of fire, sand, and water. These anticipate the elements literally present in the lightning, sandbar, and ocean waves of the shipwreck.

Hopkins' frequent use of puns assumes that a single sound may be a meeting place, crossroads, or verbal knot where several distinct verbal strands converge. This convergence is once more evidence of ontological relations among the various meanings layered in a single word. Man's condition

251

as sullenly fallen, stubbornly "tied to his turn" away from God ("Ribblesdale," line 11, PHop, 91), for example, may be expressed by calling him "dogged in den" (line 67). Here, *dogged* is a quadruple pun meaning sullenly determined, doglike, twisted down (as a *dog* is a kind of bolt), and hounded (as a wild animal is chased by dogs into its den and kept at bay there). There may also be an expression of the mirroring of God by man in the fact that *dog*, man's epithet here, reverses the letters that spell *God*.

Hopkins' use of sprung rhythm, a distinctive feature of "The Wreck of the Deutschland," is discussed in a letter of October 5, 1878, to R. W. Dixon. Hopkins' prosodic practice is a complex matter, since most of his verse combines sprung rhythm with elements from the ordinary accentual rhythm of English poetry, but the basic principle of sprung rhythm is simple enough. Each foot or measure has a single strong beat, but there may be "any number of weak or slack syllables" ("Author's Preface," PHop, 47), so that a foot may have only one syllable or many, though the time length of all feet is the same. This gives the great effect of tension, or "springing," to such verse. Hopkins insisted that sprung rhythm is the "rhythm of common speech and of written prose, when rhythm is perceived in them" (PHop, 49). Hopkins expected his poetry to be recited aloud with the emphases and rhythms of common speech. A note written apropos of "The Wreck of the Deutschland" makes explicit the way Hopkins wanted the poem to be spoken out:

Be pleased, reader, since the rhythm in which the following poem is written is new, strongly to mark the beats of the measure, according to the number belonging to each of the eight lines of the stanza, as the indentation guides the eye, namely two and three and four and three and five and five and four and six; not disguising the rhythm and rhyme, as some readers do, who treat poetry as if it were prose fantastically written to rule (which they mistakenly think the perfection of reading), but laying on the beat too much stress rather than too little, nor caring whether one, two, three, or more syllables go to a beat, that is to say, whether two or more beats follow running—as there are three running in the third line of the first stanza—or with syllables between, as commonly, nor whether the line begin with a beat or not; but letting the scansion run on from one line into the next, without break to the end of the stanza: since the dividing of the lines is more to fix the places of the necessary rhymes than for any pause in the measure. . . . And so throughout let the stress be made to fetch out both the strength of the syllables and the meaning and feeling of the words. (PHop, 255-256)

The rhythmical complexities in "The Wreck" are not ends in themselves. They are another form of repetition with variation. They are another way to set down or to specify a given sound pattern, which is then differentially echoed in later units of the poem, according to the fundamental principle of all poetry, which Hopkins identified in "Poetry and Verse" (1873 or 1874) as "repetition, *oftening, over-and-overing, aftering*" (J, 289).

The sprung rhythm of "The Wreck" has as much a theological basis as any of the other forms of rhyme. As Hopkins says in the letter to Dixon of 1878, he "had long had haunting [his] ear the echo of a new rhythm which now [he] realized on paper" (L–II, 14). The strategic use of the metaphor of music in "The Wreck" makes it clear that the rhythm echoed in the poet's ear and then embodied in the words of the poem is no less than the fundamental rhythm or groundswell of the creation—the ratio, measure, or Logos that pervades all things, as a fundamental melody may be varied or echoed throughout a great symphony. This rhythm is not "*I* and *me* above and in all things" but God above and in all things. The long Platonic and Christian tradition connecting the notion of rhythm to the Logos or underlying principle of things, "Ground of being, and granite of it" (line 254), as Hopkins calls it here, is subtly integrated into the texture of thought in this poem as well as into its rhythmical practice. When the poet is at the point of affirming the attunement of the tall nun with the name of Christ, worded everywhere in the creation, he affirms that His name is "her mind's" "measure" and "burden" (lines 215-216), where *measure* is musical measure and *burden* is fundamental melody, as in Shakespeare's "Come Unto these Yellow Sands"; "and, sweet sprites, the burden bear." The sprung rhythm of "The Wreck" is not merely a device for achieving a high degree of tension and patterning in the poem. It is based on the belief that God himself is a rhythm that the poet may echo in his verse. The poet's breath in its modulations and tempo may answer God's "arch and original Breath" (line 194).

To these small-scale forms of organization corresponds the way in which the large-scale dramatic or narrative structure of the poem is put together. If the poem is an ode, it is also an elegy for the dead, part of the long tradition of elegies in English stretching from "Lycidas" to *The Waste Land* and "The Owl in the Sarcophagus." Like "Lycidas," "Adonais," or *In Memoriam*, "The Wreck of the Deutschland" is only nominally about the dead whom it memorializes. The poet's response to the death of another is the occasion for a personal affirmation about the poet's inner life and his sense of vocation.

Once again repetition with variation is the basis of Hopkins' poetic practice. The key to the overall structure of "The Wreck of the Deutschland" is given in stanza 18. There the poet describes his tears when he reads of the death of the nuns in his safe haven "away in the loveable west, / On a pastoral forehead of Wales" (lines 185-186): "Why, tears! is it? tears; such a melting, a madrigal start!" (line 142). The poet's tears are a madrigal echo or rhyme of the nun's suffering, that is, an echo of the same melody on a different pitch, as in the basic musical structure of a Renaissance madrigal, canon, or round. This canonlike response leads the poet first to re-enact in memory an earlier experience in which he felt God's grace, then, in the second part of the poem, to re-enact in his imagination the death of the nuns. The narrative doubling, the memory of his own experience doubling his vivid picture of the shipwreck, causes a redoubling in a new experience of God's presence to the poet. This new experience of grace occurs within the poem itself and is identical with the writing of it. The poem is addressed directly to God in the present tense, and this immediate reciprocity between the poet and the God who "masters" him is the "now" of the poem generated by its doubling and redoubling of the two earlier "nows" that it iterates.

The various techniques of "rhyme" in "The Wreck of the Deutschland," though perhaps based on methods Hopkins had learned from Pindar's odes, from Old English verse, or from the complex Welsh system of poetry called *cynghanedd*, are in fact a magnificent exploitation of the general properties of language as they may be put to a specifically poetic use. This use Roman Jakobson calls the set of language towards itself.[22] This formulation occurs in an essay in which Jakobson quotes with approval Hopkins' expression of the same idea. In the passage in question Hopkins defines poetry as repetition. As he puts it, "poetry is in fact speech only employed to carry the inscape of speech for the inscape's sake," and "in this light poetry is speech which afters and oftens its inscape, speech couched in a repeating figure" (J, 289).

Hopkins' exploitation of the manifold possibilities of repetition in language is based then throughout on the theological notion that God is the Word. The divine Word is the basis of all words in their relations of similarity and

[22] Roman Jakobson, "Concluding Statement: Linguistics and Poetics," *Style in Language*, ed. Thomas A. Sebeok (Cambridge, Mass.: The M.I.T. Press, 1960), p. 356: "The set (*Einstellung*) toward the MESSAGE as such, focus on the message for its own sake, is the POETIC function of language."

255

difference. The play of phonic, verbal, and rhythmical texture in "The Wreck of the Deutschland" is controlled by the idea of a creator who has differentiated himself in his creation. The world is full of things that echo one another and rhyme. The same God is also the Word behind all words, the "arch and original Breath" that modulates itself into all the words that may be said. The branches and twigs of the tree of language are divided and derived forms of the initial Word. Word and world in this happily correspond because they have the same source.

This theory of poetic language is not only exemplified in "The Wreck." It is one of the chief thematic strands in the poem. Repeatedly, in one way or another, throughout "The Wreck," the question of language comes up, for example, in "I did say yes" and "truer than tongue" as early as the second stanza (lines 9, 11). One theme of the poem is its own possibility of being. "The Wreck of the Deutschland," like many great poems of the nineteenth and twentieth centuries, is, in part at least, about poetry. In this, in spite of Hopkins' Catholicism, he may be seen as a poet in the Romantic tradition, a poet who belongs in the great line leading from Wordsworth, Blake, and Hölderlin through Baudelaire, Tennyson, and Rimbaud to poets of our own century like Yeats, Rilke, and Stevens. All in one way or another make the powers of poetry a theme of their poems.

In exploring this aspect of "The Wreck," however, the reader encounters what is most problematic about it, both in its form and in its meaning. In a letter to W. M. Baillie of January 14, 1883, Hopkins develops a theory that in classical literature—for example, in Greek tragedy—the overt meaning may be matched by a covert sequence of figures or allusions constituting what he calls an "underthought." This will be an "echo or shadow of the overthought . . . an undercurrent of thought governing the choice of images used." "In any lyric passage of the tragic poets," says Hopkins, ". . . there are—usually; I will not say always, it is not likely—two strains of thought running together and like counterpointed; the overthought that which everybody, editors, see . . . and which might for instance be abridged or paraphrased . . . the other, the underthought, conveyed chiefly in the choice of metaphors etc used and often only half realized by the poet himself. . . . The underthought is commonly an echo or shadow of the overthought, something like canons and repetitions in music, treated in a different manner" (L–III, 252-253). If the overthought of "The Wreck of the Deutschland" is the story of the tall nun's salvation and the story of the musical echoes of that salvation both before and after by the poet's parallel experiences of grace, the underthought of the poem is its constant covert attention to problems of language. This linguistic theme is in a subversive relation of counterpoint to the theological overthought.

One important thematic element in "The Wreck of the Deutschland" is the image of a strand, rope, finger, vein, or stem. This image is Hopkins' way of expressing the link between creator and created. One form of this motif, "tongue," is present in the poem in "truer than tongue" (line 11), in "past telling of tongue" (line 69), with its reference to the gift of tongues, which descended at Pentecost on the Apostles in tongues of flame (Acts 2:1ff.), in "a virginal tongue told" (line 136), and in the conflation of God's finger and the tongue which rings the tall nun as if she were a bell (stanza 31). The creative "stem of stress," in Hopkins' phrase, between God and his creatures is a tongue that speaks by modulating or dividing the arch and original breath, the undifferentiated word that is Christ, as the tongues of fire at Pentecost were "cloven."

Christ, the second Person of the Trinity, the link between God the Father and the creation, is a principle of unity. He is the only means by which man may return to the singleness of the Godhead. At the same time He is the principle of differentiation. Christ is the model for the multiplicity of individual things in the world, including that most highly individuated creature, man. This is one mean-

257

ing justifying Hopkins' epithet for Christ in stanza 34: "double-naturèd name" (line 266). Christ is both God and man, both one and many. He is the avenue by which man loses his individuality in God, in imitating Christ or, like the tall nun, in reading Christ as the single word of the creation. At the same time Christ is the basis of puns in language. He is also the explanation of the fact that God manifests himself as both lightning and love, as winter and warm—that is, in things named by words that sound alike but have opposite meanings. The devil is in this diabolical imitation of Christ, as Abel and Cain are brothers, or as Deutschland is "double a desperate name" (line 155), the name both of the ship and of a country, a country that is itself double. Germany has given birth both to a saint, Gertrude, lilylike in her purity, and to Luther, the "beast of the waste wood" (lines 157-158).

The theme of language in "The Wreck" moves toward the ambiguous vision of a God who is single but who can express himself in language and in his creation only in the multiple. Though it takes a "single eye" to "read the unshapeable shock night" (lines 226-227)—that is, to see the unitary presence of God in the storm—this insight must be expressed by the poet in multiple language. There is no masterword for the Word, only metaphors of it, for all words are metaphors, displaced from their proper reference by a primal bifurcation. When the tall nun "rears herself" (line 150), like "a lioness . . . breasting the babble" (line 135), she is moving back through the multiplicity of language (by way of the pun on *Babel*) to the Word—Christ. But what the nun says must be interpreted: "the majesty! What did she mean?" (line 193). Ultimately her word must be moved back into the babble, the confusion of tongues introduced by Babel and confirmed as well as repaired by the gift of tongues at Pentecost.

In the same way the straightforward linear narrative of Hopkins' poem is continuously displaced by all the echoes and repetitions that turn the language of the poem back on itself in lateral movements of meaning. These lateral relationships proliferate in multitudinous echoes. If Hopkins' basic poetic strategy, as Geoffrey Hartman has noted, is a differentiation of language that attempts to say the Word by dividing the word, these divisions are controlled by no central word that could be enunciated in any language.[23]

Striking evidence of Hopkins' awareness of this tragic eccentricity of language appears in two crucial places in "The Wreck" where the poet presents an ornate series of terms or metaphors for the same thing. In one case, significantly enough, the series names the act of writing, that act whereby God's finger inscribes his own name on those he has chosen, "his own bespoken" (line 173). The stanza (22) presents a series of metaphors for the act of stamping something with a sign, making it a representation or metaphor for something else, as grace makes man a metaphor of Christ. These are metaphors for metaphor:

> Five! the finding and sake
> And cipher of suffering Christ.
> Mark, the mark is of man's make
> And the word of it Sacrificed.
> But he scores it in scarlet himself on his own bespoken,
> Before-time-taken, dearest prizèd and priced—
> Stigma, signal, cinquefoil token
> For lettering of the lamb's fleece, ruddying of the rose-flake.

Finding, sake, cipher, mark, word, score, stigma, signal, cinquefoil token, lettering—each is only one more word for the act of wording, in the physical sense of carving and inscription. The series of terms is controlled by no unmoving word in any human language that would be outside the play of differences.

The other such list appears at the climax of the poem,

[23] See Geoffrey Hartman, "Hopkins Revisited," *Beyond Formalism* (New Haven: Yale University Press, 1970), p. 239.

the appearance of Christ to the nun at the moment of her death. It comes just after a passage in which the poet's syntactical control breaks down (the ellipses are Hopkins'): "But how shall I . . . make me room there: / Reach me a . . . Fancy, come faster—" (lines 217-218). Then follows a list of names for Christ. Significantly, this is the only place in the poem, and one of the few places in all Hopkins' English poetry, where the poet speaks with tongues himself and inserts a word not in his native language: "There then! the Master, / *Ipse*, the only one, Christ, King, Head" (lines 220-221). The tragic limitation of poetic language lies in the fact that the Word itself cannot be said. Far from having a tendency to fall back into some undifferentiated ground of phonemic similarity (as Hartman affirms), a word by the very fact that it is just that pattern of vowels and consonants which it is, cannot be the Word. The words of human language, for Hopkins, seem to have been born of some primal division, a fall from the arch and original breath into the articulate. This fall has always already occurred as soon as there is any human speech. Words have therefore a tendency to proliferate endlessly their transformations by changes of vowel and consonant, as if they were in search for the magic word that would be the Word.

In the example already given of the permutations of vowels and consonants in the series turning a mere "Jack" into Christ in "That Nature is a Heraclitean Fire," the endpoint is not some triumphant uttering of the Word as such. It is only another metaphor, and a metaphor tautologically repeated at that: "immortal diamond, / Is immortal diamond." It seems as if such a series can only be arbitrarily ended by being turned back on itself in a locution that in its punning doubleness confesses to its inadequacy as a name for the Word. "Immortal diamond," uttered as an epithet for the hardest and most indestructible of natural substances, is then thrown out as a figure for what has no literal name, the self turned into supernatural brilliance, transparency, hardness, and permanence: "Immortal diamond / Is immortal diamond." The language remains still as far as it was when it began with "Jack" from speaking the Word literally.

In the same way, the dramatic climax of "The Wreck of the Deutschland" is also the climax of its treatment of the theme of language. Its dramatic climax is the tall nun's saying the name of Christ and thereby being saved, transformed into Christ at the moment of her death. The linguistic climax is the implicit recognition, in stanzas 22 and 28, that there is no way of speaking of this theological mystery except in a cascade of metaphors whose proliferation confesses to the fact that there is no literal word for the Word. Since these "metaphors" do not replace a literal term, they are, strictly speaking, not metaphors but catachreses, names thrown out toward the unnamable Word and more covering it in human noise than revealing it or speaking it out.

A confirmation of the eccentricity, or irremediable distance from the center, of natural language is the fact that the original meaning lying behind most of the word lists in Hopkins' early diaries is one form or another of the gesture of dividing or marking. Hopkins' insight into the nature of language is a complex matter, but here, as in other areas of his thought, he had the insight of genius. The center around which Hopkins' linguistic speculations revolve, the unsettling intuition that they approach and withdraw from, is the exact opposite of his theological insight. It is the notion that there is no primal word, that the divisions of language have always already occurred as soon as there is language at all. If this is so, there is no word for the Word, only displaced metaphors of it. In the word lists in Hopkins' early onomatopoetic etymological speculations, each list goes back to an ur-gesture, action, or sound. In each case this is an act of division, marking, striking, or cutting. Here are examples of these lists: "grind, gride, gird, grit, groat, grate, greet," "flick, fleck, flake," "skim, scum, squama, scale, keel," "shear, shred, potsherd, shard."

Of the first list Hopkins says, "Original meaning to *strike, rub*, particularly *together*." Of the second list, "*Flick* means to touch or strike lightly as with the end of a whip, a finger etc. To *fleck* is the next tone above flick, still meaning to touch or strike lightly (and leave a mark of the touch or stroke) but in a broader less slight manner. Hence substantively a *fleck* is a piece of light, colour, substance etc. looking as though shaped or produced by such touches. *Flake* is a broad and decided *fleck*, a thin plate of something, the tone above it. Their connection is more clearly seen in the applications of the words to natural objects than in explanations." The third list involves the notion of "the topmost flake what [sic] may be skimmed from the surface of a thing," and the fourth list is of words playing variations on the act of division, as "the *ploughshare* [is] that which divides the soil." For Hopkins, "the onomatopoetic theory has not had a fair chance" (J, 5), and all these word lists lead back to an original sound or sound-producing act of differentiation. For Hopkins, as for modern linguistics, the beginning is diacritical. Even the intimate life of the Trinity, in which Hopkins was much interested, is characterized, for him, by the act whereby God divides himself from himself, goes outside himself, "as they say *ad extra*" (S, 197).

The metaphor of language, moreover, has a peculiar status in Hopkins' poem. It seems to be one model among others for the relation of nature to Christ or for the relation of the soul to Christ. A chain of such metaphors exists in Hopkins' poems and prose writings: music, echo, visible pattern or shape as figures for nature's interrelations of "rhyme" in the connection of one item in nature to another and of each item to its model, Christ; cleave, sex, threshing, pitch (with a triple pun) for the action of grace on the soul. Along with the other items in the first sequence is the metaphor that says nature is interrelated in the way the words in a language are interrelated. This is one reason why Hopkins is so insistent that words should be onomatopoetic in origin. The second sequence includes the metaphor that says the transformations of grace are like the changes from one word to another in the chain that goes from *Jack* to *diamond*. Christ is the Word on which all other words are modeled.

The difficulty raised by these figures of language is double. In the first place there is something odd about using as a model what in other cases has to be assumed to be a transparent means of naming. Language about language has a different status from language about pomegranates being cloven, about threshing, or about sexual intercourse. Insofar as language emerges as the underthought of "The Wreck of the Deutschland," language in general and figure in particular are made problematic. They no longer can be taken for granted as adequate expressions of something extralinguistic. Second, this metaphor, like the others, asks to be followed as far as it can be taken. When this happens in Hopkins' case, the whole structure of his thought and textual practice—theological, conceptual, or representational—is put in question by the fact that there is no master word, no word for the Word, only endless permutations of language. For Hopkins these permutations are not based on an emanation from a primal unity. The "origin" of language is a nonorigin, a bifurcation. This bifurcation has always already taken place as soon as there is language at all. This split, not unity, is reached by a backward movement to the origin of language, as in Hopkins' etymological speculations, just as it is not "the Word" that is reached in "The Wreck of the Deutschland" or in "That Nature is a Heraclitean Fire," but only another word or a tautology.

There are indeed two texts in Hopkins, the overthought and the underthought. One text, the overthought, is a version (a particularly splendid version) of Western metaphysics in its Catholic Christian form. In this text the Word governs all words, as it governs natural objects and selves. Like Father, like Son; and the sons, all the particular words, are a way back to the Father. "No man cometh to the Father but by me" (John 14:6). On the other hand, Hopkins' underthought is a thought about language itself. It recognizes that there is no word for the Word, that all words are metaphors. Each word leads to another word of which it is the displacement, in a movement without origin or end. Insofar as the play of language emerges as the basic model for the other two realms (nature and the effects of grace within the soul), it subverts the theological harmony of both nature and supernature. The individual natural object and the individual self, by the fact of their individuality, are incapable of ever being more than a metaphor of Christ—that is, split off from Christ. They are incapable by whatever extravagant series of sideways transformations from ever becoming more than another metaphor. On the one hand, then, "No man cometh to the Father but by me," and on the other hand, to vary John's formulation, in accordance with Hopkins' darker insight, "No one comes to the Father by imitating me, for I am the principle of distance and differentiation. I am the principle of a splitting or punning which is discovered to have already occurred, however far back toward the primal unity one goes, even back within the bosom of the Trinity itself."

If the tragedy of language is its inability to say the Word, the mystery of the human situation, as Hopkins presents it, is parallel. The more a man affirms himself, the more he affirms his eccentricity, his individuality, his failure to be Christ, or Christ-like, an "AfterChrist," as Hopkins puts it (S, 100). It is only by an unimaginable and, literally, unspeakable transformation, the transformation effected by grace, such as the nun's "conception" of Christ at the moment of her death in "The Wreck of the Deutschland," that the individual human being can be turned into Christ. The fact that this transformation is "past telling of tongue" in any words that say directly what they mean is indicated not only by the fact that the action of grace (both in this poem and throughout Hopkins) is always described in metaphor, but also by the fact that such a large number of incompatible metaphors are used: forging (lines 73, 74), sexual reproduction, speaking, eating and being eaten, threshing, rope-twisting, armed combat, change of pitch or angle ("she rears herself," line 150).

To put this in terms of the linguistic metaphor: if Hopkins' poetic theory and practice are everywhere dominated by wordplay based on a recognition that the relation of rhyme is the echoing at a distance of entities that are similar but not identical, the change of man through grace into Christ is a transcendence of that distance and difference into identity, a change of play into reality in which the image becomes what it images. "It is as if a man said," writes Hopkins, "That is Christ playing at me and me playing at Christ, only that it is no play but truth; That is Christ *being me* and me being Christ" (S, 154). "The Wreck of the Deutschland," like all the great poems of Hopkins'maturity, turns on a recognition of the ultimate failure of poetic language. Its failure is never to be able to express the inconceivable and unsayable mystery of how something that is as unique as a single word—that is, a created soul—may be transformed into the one Word, Christ, which is its model, without ceasing to be a unique and individual self.

Rather than being in happy correspondence, Hopkins' theological thought and its linguistic underthought are at cross-purposes. They have a structure of chiasmus. The theological thought depends on the notion of an initial unity that has been divided or fragmented and so could conceivably be reunified. The linguistic underthought depends on the notion of an initial bifurcation that could not by any conceivable series of linguistic transformations, such as those that make up the basic poetic strategies of Hopkins' verse, reach back to any primal word. There is no such word. Hopkins' linguistic underthought undoes his Christian overthought.

After all his efforts, Hopkins remains, as far as language goes, where he was in the beginning, imprisoned within a self-taste that can be communicated by no means to another man, not even when it undergoes that transformation by grace which turns it into an AfterChrist, that is, into another utterance of the aboriginal Word. Though Hopkins seems so different from Pater, Hegel, or Nietzsche, and though he makes every effort to escape the poetic and personal impasse of Romanticism, he is forced, in his linguistic insight and in his linguistic practice, to express another version of the detachment from one another of self, nature, God, and language that Pater, Hegel, and Nietzsche in their different ways express. For Hopkins, too, language is a medium of separation, not of reconciliation. For Hopkins, too, all things come together within language only to disperse.

Hardy

In the chapter on "The Triumph of Life" something has already been said about the paradoxical relation of Hardy's work to Shelley's. Hardy sometimes almost seems to be Shelley's dark precursor, and Hardy's work offers a double reading of Shelley. It sees him alternately as both idealist and as skeptic. Something of the same sort might be said of Hardy's relation to Wordsworth. Hardy often affirms as his own a subversion of Romantic pantheism that Wordsworth himself has already abundantly performed in his own poetry, for example, in Book v of *The Prelude*. Once more the later poet seems to need to misread the earlier poet in order to assert as his own something the earlier poet had already said. I have cited in chapter 5 the passage in *The Life of Thomas Hardy* in which Hardy affirms that the wear on a threshold or the print of a hand are worth ten times as much as any mark made by unconscious Nature. That Hardy sides with Hegel and Nietzsche against any assumption that nature and consciousness can be reconciled is clear enough, not only in Hardy's poetry but also in his novels. *Tess of the d'Urbervilles* (1891), for example, contains a running commentary that sardonically rejects what Hardy apparently understands to be Wordsworth's pantheism or spiritualization of nature. It seems to Tess, as she goes through the night toward the fatal convergence of the twain that will end poor Prince's life, that "the occasional heave of the wind" is "the sigh of some immense sad soul, coterminous with the universe in space, and with history in time." In a bitter parody of the Romantic union of subject and object, each of Tess's drunken companions on the moonlit night of her violation feels that he or she is the center of a harmonized universe:

267

. . . as they went there moved onward with them, around the shadow of each one's head, a circle of opalized light, formed by the moon's rays upon the glistening sheet of dew. Each pedestrian could see no halo but his or her own, which never deserted the head-shadow, whatever its vulgar unsteadiness might be; but adhered to it, and persistently beautified it; till the erratic motions seemed an inherent part of the irradiation, and the fumes of their breathing a component of the night's mist; and the spirit of the scene, and of the moonlight, and of Nature, seemed harmoniously to mingle with the spirit of wine.

Here moonlight and the "correspondent breeze," two major Romantic symbols for the harmony of man and nature, are ironically mocked. The sense that there is one life within us and abroad is reduced to a sleepy illusion or to a drunken deception. That the reference is to Wordsworth, as Hardy understood or misunderstood him, is suggested by a passage earlier in the novel in which, apropos of the sufferings of the shiftless Durbeyfield family, Hardy explicitly challenges Wordsworth's affirmation, in "Lines Written in Early Spring," of a providential harmony of man and nature. "Some people," says the narrator, "would like to know whence the poet whose philosophy is in these days deemed as profound and trustworthy as his song is breezy and pure, gets his authority for speaking of 'Nature's holy plan.' "[1] Rather than being of value in itself, nature for Hardy has meaning and value only when it has been marked by man's living in it and so has become a repository of signs preserving individual and collective history. The shift from nature to subjective or intersubjective life and then to language is enacted, for Hardy, not only in spoken or written words as such, but in the shift of interest to the embodied signs of himself man imprints on nature in his passage

[1] My three initial citations are from Thomas Hardy, *Tess of the d'Urbervilles*, chaps. 4, 10, 3, The New Wessex Edition (London: Macmillan London Ltd., New York: St. Martin's Press Inc., 1978), pp. 60, 101-102, 51.

through life. As for Hegel, so for Hardy, the substratum so marked remains indifferent and aloof, the patient bearer of meanings man has inscribed on it, meanings with which it has nothing to do. In my discussion of the linguistic moment in Hardy's poetry, I shall circle around this question of the relation of a sign to the material base on which it is written, carved, or projected.

It is generally agreed today that Thomas Hardy is one of the greatest of modern poets writing in English. He is worthy to rank with Yeats or Stevens. Less clearly agreed upon is how to identify that greatness, how to talk intelligently and comprehensively about Hardy's poetry. If the interpreter chooses the road of "close reading," the sheer abundance of the poetry is daunting, not to speak of the special difficulties his poems oppose to explication. More than much great lyric poetry, Hardy's poems seem to slip away from commentary. They defy the techniques of analysis or do not seem to need them. Each poem seems to say clearly what it means. Even distinguished critics like Blackmur or Ransom are sometimes reduced to discussing such relatively impalpable topics as "tone," "texture," and "diction,"or abstractions like "crossed fidelities."[2] Moreover, it

---

[2] See John Crowe Ransom, "Introduction," *Selected Poems of Thomas Hardy* (New York: The Macmillan Company, 1961), pp. ix-xxxiii, and "Honey and Gall," *The Southern Review* VI (Summer 1940), 2-19; R. P. Blackmur, "The Shorter Works of Thomas Hardy," *Language as Gesture* (New York: Harcourt, Brace and Company, 1952), pp. 51-79. Recognition of Hardy's greatness as a poet has been accompanied by a growing list of books all or in part on the poetry; for example, Samuel Hynes, *The Pattern of Hardy's Poetry* (Chapel Hill: The University of North Carolina Press, 1961); Kenneth Marsden, *The Poems of Thomas Hardy: A Critical Introduction* (London: Athlone Press, 1969); J. O. Bailey, *The Poetry of Thomas Hardy: A Handbook and Commentary* (Chapel Hill: The University of North Carolina Press, 1970); Jean Brooks, *Thomas Hardy: The Poetic Structure* (Ithaca: Cornell University Press, 1971); Paul Zietlow, *Moments of Vision: The Poetry of Thomas Hardy* (Cambridge, Mass.: Harvard University Press, 1974); *Essays on the Poetry of Thomas Hardy*, ed. Patricia Clements and Juliet Grindle (London: Vision Press, 1980); Dennis Taylor, *Hardy's Poetry, 1860–1928* (New York: Columbia University Press, 1981). In addition, see the perceptive com-

is hard to imagine a book consisting of over nine hundred close readings, while all attempts that I know of to reduce Hardy's poetry to manageable size by selection are unsuccessful, including of course my own here discussing only a handful of Hardy's poems. All selections, even the best and biggest, perhaps best because biggest, that of T.R.M. Creighton,[3] leave out poems that seem to me as important and admirable as the ones left in. We need all of Hardy's poetry, and we need it in the odd and to some degree haphazard order in which it was published in Hardy's successive volumes of poems. We need it all, even though there is a sense in which there is too much of it, too much to hold in one's mind at once, too much to reduce to an orderly mapping.

If individual close readings are unsatisfactory, so are attempts to survey the whole and organize it thematically, or phenomenologically, by noting similarities from poem to poem and generalizing on that basis. One of the themes of Hardy's poetry, as of his fiction, is the uniqueness of each moment of experience, as well as of each record in words

---

ments on Hardy's *Winter Words* by Harold Bloom in *A Map of Misreading* (New York: Oxford University Press, 1975), pp. 19-26; and for an essay following some of my own trajectory through Hardy's verse, see the fine essay by Mary Jacobus, "Hardy's Magian Retrospect," *Essays in Criticism* XXXII, 3 (July 1982), 258-279. It is remarkable how many of the good essays on Hardy's poetry are by those who are poets themselves; for example, the essays by W. H. Auden, Delmore Schwartz, John Crowe Ransom, R. P. Blackmur, and Allen Tate gathered with other essays in the Thomas Hardy Centennial Issue of *The Southern Review* IV (Summer 1940); or the essay by C. Day Lewis, "The Lyrical Poetry of Thomas Hardy," *Proceedings of the British Academy* XXXVII (1951), 155-174; or the introduction by John Wain to *Selected Shorter Poems of Thomas Hardy* (London: Macmillan, 1966), pp. ix-xix; or Donald Davie's, *Thomas Hardy and British Poetry* (New York: Oxford University Press, 1972). I have always remembered a remark made by Dylan Thomas in the course of an eloquent recitation of several of Hardy's poems. "I like the bus that Hardy misses," he said, "better than the bus some other poets catch."

[3] *Poems of Thomas Hardy: A New Selection*, ed. T.R.M. Creighton (London: The Macmillan Press Ltd., 1977).

of such a moment. Each moment, each text, is incommensurate with all the others. To see an experience or a poem as like others or as repeating them and to begin to make grand interpretative patterns on that basis is to perform just the sort of falsifying simplification that the poems themselves repeatedly warn against.

In the characteristically defensive, thin-skinned, but nonetheless defiant "Apology" of 1922 to *Late Lyrics and Earlier*, Hardy calls attention to these problems. He apologizes for the lack of unity in his poems but does not promise to mend his ways. "I have sinned," he says in effect, "and I am sorry for it, but I am going to go on sinning." Hardy begins the "Apology" by explaining that the volume mixes some quite recent verse, some "unusually far back poems" overlooked in gathering previous collections, and some relatively recent poems held over from past volumes published during the second decade of the century for no more reason than that the volumes were full enough already. The result of this mixture of chronological incompatibles is identified a little later in the "Apology." The paragraph is Hardy's most important statement about the effect the juxtaposition of his poems has on their meaning:

... there is a contingency liable to miscellanies of verse that I have never seen mentioned, so far as I can remember; I mean the chance little shocks that may be caused over a book of various character like the present and its predecessors by the juxtaposition of unrelated, even discordant, effusions; poems perhaps years apart in the making, yet facing each other. An odd result of this has been that dramatic anecdotes of a satirical and humorous intention following verse in graver voice, had been read as misfires because they raise the smile they were intended to raise, the journalist, deaf to the sudden change of key, being unconscious that he is laughing with the author and not at him. I admit that I did not foresee such contingencies as I ought to have done, and that

271

people might not perceive when the tone altered. But the difficulties of arranging the themes in a graduated kinship of moods would have been so great that irrelation was almost unavoidable with efforts so diverse. I must trust for right note-catching to those finely-touched spirits who can divine without half a whisper, whose intuitiveness is proof against all the accidents of inconsequence. In respect of the less alert, however, should anyone's train of thought be thrown out of gear by a consecutive piping of vocal reeds and jarring tonics, without a semiquaver's rest between, and be led thereby to miss the writer's aim and meaning in one out of two contiguous compositions, I shall deeply regret it.[4]

The reader will see that the old man (he was 82 in 1922) remained cheekily indomitable to the last. What scorn there is in that word *journalist*! It is Hardy's word for all bad readers, for all those "deaf to sudden changes of key" and "less alert" than the "finely-touched spirits" (the phrase is an echo of the "Finale" of *Middlemarch*) whom Hardy hopes to have as readers. A volume of his verse, says Hardy, is like a piece of music that constantly changes key, tempo, tone, and timbre, so that it is "jarring" and "discordant." What is needed to make the sudden leaps required from poem to poem is an ability to suspend the demand for consecutiveness of logical thought. The reader needs instead an "intuitive" "note-catching" that is alogical in the sense that it does not expect one poem necessarily to be in tune with the ones on either side. If the right critics are like those with an intuitive gift for following the inconsequences of a certain kind of music, the wrong critics are amusingly compared to those who blindly follow a me-

[4] Thomas Hardy, *The Complete Poems*, ed. James Gibson (New York: Macmillan Publishing Co., Inc., 1978), pp. 559-560. All poems and prefaces will be cited from this edition, henceforth CPH, followed by the page number.

chanical "train of thought." Such a train is "thrown out of gear" when it meets something that does not fit.

Various critics are studying the effect on meaning of the organization of separate volumes of verse by lyric poets: Keats, Stevens, Yeats, or Lowell, for example.[5] Hardy, in the "Apology" and in other prefaces, consistently warned his readers (and his journalistic reviewers) against trying to do that with his books of poems, though the warning has not been much heeded. Critics, myself included, tend to go on speaking of "Hardy" or of "the mind of Hardy" as a single entity, and of his *Complete Poems* as if they must form some kind of unity. Reason, in the sense of the need for a logical train of thought in criticism, demands this. Any such train of thought, Hardy affirms, will be continually thrown out of gear by the poems themselves, if the critic actually reads them. This does not mean that the ordering of each book of poems by Hardy or of *The Complete Poems* as a whole is not significant. I am using the question of this significance here as my entry into Hardy. I hold, moreover, that a selection of the poems arranged by category or topic, even the admirable one by T.R.M. Creighton, however helpful it may be as a preliminary way of reading Hardy's poetry, falsifies the meaning of that poetry by giving it a spurious order. The poems should be read in all the ostentatious disorder of *The Complete Poems*. This ordering in disorder is a matter of radical discord and "irrelation." The discord is radical in that it cannot be reduced to concord or unity by going down to the roots. At least that is what Hardy says. The country of "Hardy's mind,"or of the texts that record the topography of that mind, cannot be charted. It is unmappable.

Several sorts of discord are simultaneously present in a book of Hardy's poems or in the whole collection taken

[5] Most consideration of this aspect of Hardy's verse has been focused on the series of elegies for his first wife, the "Poems of 1912–13" (CPH, 338-358). See, for example, Taylor, *Hardy's Poetry, 1860–1928)*, pp. 22-29.

together. One is a discord of time. This is an irrelation resulting from the strange fact that the records of diverse times—for example (but it is only an example), in the form of poems—can be set side by side in a single volume. There they are like contiguous plots of ground on a landscape or on a map of that landscape. Hardy tacitly assumes, in the paragraph quoted above, that "poems perhaps years apart in the making" will necessarily be "unrelated, even discordant." Time, for Hardy, at least in this passage, is the medium of a necessary discontinuity. Space, in the literal sense of a landscape, a map, a book of musical compositions, or of poems on sequential pages in *Late Lyrics and Earlier*, is the realm of "juxtaposition," of "contiguity." This curious incompatibility of time and space makes possible those "chance little shocks" produced by the accidental juxtaposition of spatial records of diverse times. The mind of the critic or journalist tries to reconcile them. He tries to make them related in meaning as well as in physical location. It cannot be done. The discord produced by the chance juxtaposition in space of diverse times is a property of texts as such. A text is for Hardy here the physical notation of an "impression." It is a strange fact about texts, as of, say, the notations of a piece of music, that they, or any parts of them, can be moved around at will, rearranged. They can be put together in any order. The result is that a collective text like a book of Hardy's poems, organized, so he says, by "chance," as a "miscellany," is almost certainly going to be cacophonous.

To the discords of time and space and of the fact that a text is an object as well as a meaning must be added a discord of thought and a discord of the self. Hardy always insisted, most overtly in the prefaces to his successive volumes of verse, that it is a mistake to look for "cohesion of thought" or a coherent philosophy in "fancies written down in widely differing moods and circumstances, and at various dates" (CPH, 84). His poems, he says, do not present a single unified "view of life" but are "really a series of

fugitive impressions which I have never tried to co-ordi-
nate" (CPH, 558). Discord of thought follows naturally from
the discords of time, space, and accidental textual contiguity. Any conceptual or ideological consistency ascribed
to Hardy by a critic is a falsifying construction. It is a product of that irresistible desire to smooth out rough edges.
The critic wants to make everything in an author fit so that
he can with a clear conscience utter sentences that take the
form, "For Hardy, such and such is the case," or "In Hardy's
poems, so and so is the regular law." No such uniformities,
the poet tells his readers, exist, except perhaps a law of
discrepancy or difference, the regularity of a consistent
failure to consist, to hang together, to fit.

Many critics who recognize this and use it to challenge
attempts by others to talk about the coherence of Hardy's
ideas in his poetry nevertheless still cling to another form
of unity, that of Hardy's self or personality. "Thomas Hardy,"
such critics tacitly assume, persists as the same person from
one end of his work to the other. This form of unity is
rejected as categorically by Hardy as are the others. Hardy
is here the inheritor of that native British tradition of skepticism about the unity of the self which is most notoriously
present in David Hume. Even if Hardy is not directly influenced by Hume's argument against "personal identity"
in the famous section 6 of Book I of Part IV of *A Treatise
of Human Nature*, he uses Hume's terminology, for example,
the word *impression*. He makes the same assumptions and
draws the same conclusions. Even if he did not read this
part of Hume carefully, he would have had access to Hume's
ideas and to his terminology through contemporaries such
as Leslie Stephen, with whom his intellectual and personal
friendship was close. Hume is mentioned once by name in
Hardy's poetry, in "Drinking Song" from *Winter Words*. In
that poem Hume is included with Thales, Copernicus, Darwin, Cheyne, and Einstein as one of the sages who has failed
to solve the riddle of the universe. In particular, Hume's
disbelief in miracles is cited, though hardly with unqualified

approval since the poem debunks the efforts of deep think-ers generally. In a letter of 1911 Hardy is more explicit. "My pages," he writes, "show harmony of view with Darwin, Huxley, Spencer, Hume, Mill, and others, all of whom I used to read more than Schopenhauer."[6]

For Hume, "if any impression gives rise to the idea of self, that impression must continue invariably the same, thro' the whole course of our lives; since self is suppos'd to exist after that manner. But there is no impression con-stant and invariable." Therefore each "person" is "nothing but a bundle or collection of different perceptions, which succeed each other with an inconceivable rapidity, and are in a perpetual flux and movement. . . . The mind is a kind of theatre, where several perceptions successively make their appearance; pass, re-pass, glide away, and mingle in an infinite variety of postures and situations. There is properly no *simplicity* in it at one time, nor *identity* in different; what-ever natural propension we may have to imagine that sim-plicity and identity. The comparison of the theatre must not mislead us. They are the successive perceptions only, that constitute the mind; nor have we the most distant notion of the place where these scenes are represented, or of the materials, of which it is compos'd."[7] Hume's extreme nominalism or atomism, his adherence to a principle of indiscernibles for the entities of the mind, leads him to disintegrate the self. The self for Hume is pulverized into innumerable separate entities, each entirely unique, each without resemblance to any other, each cut off from all the others except that they occur either simultaneously or in

[6] Cited in Carl J. Weber, *Hardy of Wessex*, 2 ed. (New York: Columbia University Press; London: Routledge & Kegan Paul, 1965), pp. 246-247.

[7] David Hume, *A Treatise of Human Nature*, ed. L. A. Selby-Bigge, 2d ed., revised by P. H. Nidditch (Oxford: Clarendon Press, 1978), pp. 251-253; henceforth THN. On this aspect of Hume in its relation to literary studies, especially studies of autobiography, see Robert H. Bell, "David Hume's Fables of Identity," *Philological Quarterly* LIV, 2 (Spring 1975), 471-483.

succession within the same empty, indefinable chamber, the "theatre"of the mind. "[E]very distinct perception, which enters into the composition of the mind," says Hume, "is a distinct existence, and is different, and distinguishable, and separable from every other perception, either contemporary or successive" (THN, 259). Each perception is not only different and separable. It is in fact separated and by an unbridgeable gap: "[E]very distinct object is separable by the mind, and may be separately consider'd, and appears not to have any more connexion with any other object, than if disjoin'd by the greatest difference and remoteness" (THN, 260).

How then do we come to have the false idea of the unity, simplicity, and identity of the self? The villains are memory and the mind's propensity to create mental fictions by what Hume calls the "association of ideas": "As memory alone acquaints us with the continuance and extent of this succession of perceptions, it is to be consider'd, upon that account chiefly, as the source of personal identity. Had we no memory, we never shou'd have any notion of causation, nor consequently of that chain of causes and effects, which constitute our self or person" (THN, 261-262). Causation is one of the three basic operations in the association of ideas. Hume of course notoriously rejects causation. It is a mental fiction lacking any external evidence. The other two modes of association are resemblance and contiguity. Resemblance too depends upon memory. It is that error whereby we ascribe identity to two things that in one way or another are similar, as when we think of the mind as a theatre and then go on to reason falsely about the mind on the basis of the theatre's properties of unity and continuation through time. Hume says the third mode, contiguity, "has little or no influence in the present case" (THN, 260). This is a somewhat dubious claim since a causal connection is often suggested for two events that are merely contiguous in time. Even spatial contiguity may be said to operate when we assume that because a group of perceptions or impressions occur side by side in the same mind, that mind has the sort of unity and identity we mean by "selfhood."

The errors based on causality, resemblance, and contiguity create the fiction of personal identity. These are in fact linguistic errors. These errors might be defined as the taking literally of figures of speech. Just as Freud's fundamental operations of dreamwork, condensation and displacement, are names for metaphor and metonymy, so Hume's "resemblance" and "contiguity" are other names for the same figures. Hume is therefore correct to say that the "nice and subtile questions concerning personal identity ... are to be regarded rather as grammatical than as philosophical difficulties" (THN, 262). Such problems are "verbal," that is, they have to do with the production of fictions through words or other signs. "All the disputes concerning the identity of connected objects are merely verbal, except so far as the relation of parts gives rise to some fiction or imaginary principle of union" (THN, 262). There is little in Nietzsche's dissolution of the idea of selfhood, for example, in Book Three of *The Will to Power*, that is not already present in Hume, including even the figure of the republic or commonwealth for the constantly changing, warring, negotiating forces in the "self" (see THN, 261).[8] Both Hume and Nietzsche dissolve the self by seeing it as a verbal fiction based on taking figures of speech literally.

Hardy experienced in his own life a form of this dissolution. One of the fundamental burdens of his poetry is to testify scrupulously to it. At the same time he testifies to the almost irresistible force of those linguistic fictions which lead us to think that the self exists as an entity and goes on being in some fundamental sense the same. The same elements are present in Hardy's rejection of the idea of con-

[8] I have discussed this aspect of Nietzsche's thought in "The Disarticulation of the Self in Nietzsche," *The Monist* LXIV, 2 (April 1981), 247-261.

tinuous identical self as in Hume, but they are arranged somewhat differently. Hardy's poems are, he says, "the juxtaposition of unrelated, even discordant, effusions," and this is so simply because they are "unadjusted impressions," "a series of fugitive impressions which I have never tried to coordinate," and which were produced by "humbly recording diverse readings of [life's] phenomena as they are forced upon me by chance and change" (CPH, 84). If this is so, the incoherence of the poems presupposes not only the incoherence of the various "philosophies of life" expressed in the poems, the cacophony of their tunes and tones, but also the disintegration of the self that made the diverse "readings" of the phenomena of life. If Hardy had gone on being the same person the readings would have been in harmony. The fact that they are not demonstrates that there is no such thing as Thomas Hardy or the mind of Thomas Hardy, if one means by that something continuously identical with itself. Hardy is, like each human mind for Hume, a null place where diverse impressions happen to have congregated. The value of Hardy's poems lies in their truthful recording of the immediate moment in which a given impression occurred. Their value lies in the fact that each impression remains "unadjusted," "uncoordinated." All have been thrown together pell-mell in each volume of verse without any attempt to give them a factitious order—not a chronological order, nor a logical order, nor the order of musical "gradation." This disorder reflects the way they exist in "Hardy's mind" (though calling it that falsely unifies the disparate), and in the place where he keeps the physical pieces of paper, in his desk drawer or wherever.

It is in this context that the reader must understand the curious and mostly ignored claim Hardy repeatedly makes that his poems in the first person are dramatic monologues. In the brief preface to the first book of his lyrics, *Wessex Poems* (1898), Hardy affirms that "the pieces are in a large degree dramatic or personative in conception; and this even where they are not obviously so" (CPH, 6). The same phrasing is repeated in the preface to *Poems of the Past and Present* (1902), though with the substitution of "not explicitly so" for "not obviously so" (CPH, 84), meaning, I suppose, that most of the poems, even where there is no textual indication—for example, in the title or in a certain use of the first person—are to be thought of as spoken by an imaginary person, not by Thomas Hardy himself. In the preface to *Time's Laughingstocks and Other Verses* (1909) the same disclaimer is made, this time with an overt claim that the incoherence of the poems is explained by the fact that they are "personative": "the sense of disconnection, particularly in respect of those lyrics penned in the first person will be immaterial when it is borne in mind that they are to be regarded, in the main, as dramatic monologues by different characters" (CPH, 190).

Many readers probably consider these claims as more or less disingenuous, an attempt to hide the autobiographical character of Hardy's poetry by an illicit appeal to the Browningesque cover of the genre of the dramatic monologue, just as the claim that "no harmonious philosophy is attempted in these pages" (CPH, 834) is often seen as an attempt to avoid responsibility for a "philosophy" that *is* "dark," "skeptical," or "pessimistic," appellations Hardy hated. The notes and annotations to Hardy's poems by such experts as J. O. Bailey and T.R.M. Creighton assume without question that Hardy's poems are not dramatic monologues at all, but can be more or less directly related back to specific moments in Hardy's personal history. Though this is true, it is also true that Hardy's poems *are* dramatic monologues, though in a different way from Browning's "Fra Lippo Lippi" and "The Englishman in Italy." For Browning the dramatic monologue is a means of expressing, one by one, various potentialities of a mind and heart that, as the speaker of his "Pauline" says, want to "be all, have, see, know, taste, feel, all,"[9] want to experience all the possible ways of being a person on the stage of private life or of public history. For Hardy, on the other hand, strict and humble fidelity in lyric poetry to the "impression" of each passing moment means becoming in turn a whole series of disconnected persons. The result is books of poems that are "personative," spoken first by this person, then by that, however much they can also be said to be spoken in the first person by the person Thomas Hardy for the moment is. Hardy does not, like Browning, expand himself by becoming in imagination first this person and then that person from history or from fiction. "Hardy," rather, is a sequence of disconnected evanescent persons. Each is called into being by the impression of the moment, then "recorded" in a poem that personifies the impression. Each person then vanishes, never to return except when the poem is reread, or when the past impression is remembered. What is for Browning a means of expansion and of reaching toward wholeness is for Hardy a principle of impoverishment and of disintegration. "Thomas Hardy" is not who he is. He is no one, no one but the vacant place, without walls, margins, or location, in which these fugitive persons take shape momentarily and then disappear. They leave behind only their textual silhouettes in the form of those slips of paper with poems on them which Hardy kept, sometimes for forty or fifty years, before he published them.

I have said that the past impression may be remembered. It may be remembered, for Hardy, even without the "memory aid" of the written text of a poem. Hardy has the worst of both possibilities in the temporal dimension of his existence. On the one hand he cannot remain the same person, have the same thoughts, feel the same feelings, for more than a moment. An irresistible fugacity forces him

---

[9] Robert Browning, *The Complete Works*, ed. Roma A. King, Jr. *et al.*, ɪ (Athens, Ohio: Ohio University Press, 1969ff.), p. 19.

to be unfaithful to himself however hard he tries to remain the same, as the poem called "The Wind's Prophecy" brilliantly demonstrates. On the other hand, he cannot, however hard he tries, forget those earlier selves to whom he has been unfaithful, those earlier feelings he no longer feels. They return at intervals, suddenly and unpredictably, mutely reproaching him for his infidelity. "I have a faculty (possibly not uncommon)," he says, "for bearing an emotion in my heart or brain for forty years, and exhuming it at the end of that time as fresh as when interred. . . . Query: where was that sentiment hiding itself during more than forty years?"[10] In spite of the similarities between Hardy and Hume, the concept of memory is different in each case. For Hume memory is the agency of a falsification that makes similarities seem identities. Memory is beguiled by figures of speech and makes the different appear the same. The grand fiction of continuous personal identity is fabricated by memory and impossible without it. For Hume, "Memory alone . . . [is] the source of personal identity." For Hardy, on the other hand, memory preserves the different in its difference. It brings back impressions as fresh as when they first occurred, or at least seemingly so. It brings them back as forceful reproaches, evidence of how different "Hardy" has become. At the same time he is unfortunately still able with extreme vividness to remember exactly what he was and no longer is.

If all these forms of discontinuity operate to produce discord and irrelation among Hardy's poems, the critic can, in this emergency, best follow Hardy's own advice. He must hope that he has that mental agility "for right note-catching" Hardy demands in his readers. He must move from poem to poem trying to identify as exactly as possible just what fugitive reading of life's phenomena each one makes.

[10] Florence Emily Hardy, *The Life of Thomas Hardy: 1840–1928* (London, Melbourne, Toronto: Macmillan; New York: St. Martin's Press, 1965), p. 378.

He must resist as much as possible the temptation to link poem with poem in some grand scheme. He must keep as much as possible (it will never be wholly possible) to the close-up view that maps a single field at a time, without ever trying to attain the aerial perspective that sees the whole of the difficult terrain as a single country. As Hardy categorically says, his poems taken together are in principle not to be considered a unified country of the mind or the linguistic notation of such a mind. They are rather a congeries not open to any integration except a falsifying one.

I SHALL concentrate, in my attempt to be faithful to Hardy's advice to his readers, on a group of poems that explore, each in a different way, the relation between matter, whether as landscape, as household objects, or as writing material, and the notations inscribed on that matter. It might be thought that in taking a group of poems together I am being unfaithful to my claim that the poems must be read one by one. Their incommensurability one with another, however, can best be demonstrated through the unsuccessful attempt to make them all fit. A reader making his way slowly through Hardy's poems is likely to group them in bunches according to some apparent similarity and then read one against another within that group, a group small enough to be held all at once within the mind. The model for this might be the way persons and episodes from the poet's past are confronted as ghosts by the speaker of "Wessex Heights" or of "In Front of the Landscape."[11]

The poems I choose to show this in action are the following: "Beyond the Last Lamp," "The Place on the Map," "Under the Waterfall," "At Castle Boterel," "The Re-En-

---

[11] See my "History as Repetition in Thomas Hardy's Poetry: The Example of 'Wessex Heights,' " *Victorian Poetry*, Stratford-upon-Avon Studies, 15, ed. M. Bradbury and D. Palmer (London: Edward Arnold, 1972), pp. 222-253, and "Topography and Tropography in Thomas Hardy's 'In Front of the Landscape,' " forthcoming in *The Identity of the Literary Text*, ed. M. J. Valdes (University of Toronto Press).

actment," "In the British Museum," "The Obliterate Tomb," "Old Furniture," "The Wind's Prophecy." I give the poems in the order in which they appear in *The Complete Poems*. All but the last two are from *Satires of Circumstance* (1914). Those last are from *Moments of Vision* (1917). These poems should now all be read through so they may be present together in their dissonant chiming within the mind of the reader of my commentary. It is not clear that they should be read aloud, as one might think must occur in a proper performance of any lyric poem. It may be that Hardy's poems speak best as the phantoms of "In Front of the Landscape" do, that is, as silent features dumbly pleading, as marks on the page to be read mutely by the eye and placed before what Hardy calls "the intenser / Stare of the mind" (CPH, 304), not echoed within the living ear.

The poems seem a miscellaneous lot enough. All have something to do with the relations of event to place and with the role of signs or of inscriptions in a form of perpetuation that perhaps only for convenience is called "memory." In "Beyond the Last Lamp" the speaker affirms that a certain street near Tooting Common "does not exist" for him without the scene he saw take place there. In "The Place on the Map" a map is the *signe mémoratif* that vividly recalls an episode from the poet's past that occurred in the spot the map represents. In "Under the Waterfall" the speaker is a woman for whom plunging her arm in a basin of water always brings back an episode of courtship from her past. With the affective memory of that episode returns the knowledge that the glass they drank from together, which she lost while washing it, is still there under the little waterfall. In "At Castle Boterel" the poet claims that what some rocks by a road in Cornwall "record in colour and cast / Is—that we two passed" (CPH, 352). In "The Re-Enactment" a new pair of lovers are inhibited from their courtship by the fact that an earlier scene of courtship had been enacted there:

. . . something in the chamber
        Dimmed our flame,—
An emanation, making our due words fall tame,
    As if the intenser drama
        Shown me there
    Of what the walls had witnessed
        Filled the air,
And left no room for later passion anywhere.
                                    (CPH, 364)

In "In the British Museum" the broken base of a pillar
from the Areopagus, empty of any inscription, in "ashen
blankness," is said nevertheless to signify that the sound of
St. Paul's preaching was centuries ago echoed back from it
(CPH, 381-382). In "The Obliterate Tomb" a man refrains
from his odd intention to renew the carvings on the tombstone of a family who are his hereditary enemies. He refrains because he meets a member of that family who declares that *he* intends to restore "each letter and line" of
the inscriptions. The family member does not do so. The
tombstone is eventually "obliterated," broken up as path-
paving, and the family wholly forgotten (CPH, 383-388).
In "Old Furniture," a beautiful and powerful poem, pos-
sessions of the dead are haunted by the dead:

I see the hands of the generations
    That owned each shiny familiar thing
In play on its knobs and indentations,
    And with its ancient fashioning
        Still dallying:

Hands behind hands, growing paler and paler,
    As in a mirror, a candle-flame
Shows images of itself, each frailer,
    As it recedes, though the eye may frame
        Its shape the same.
                    (CPH, 485-486)

In "The Wind's Prophecy" a journey, a displacement across the landscape, becomes the coercive agent of a displacement of the speaker's affections. He will love the girl he meets at the journey's end, however hard he tries to remain faithful to the girl he leaves behind:

> "I roam, but one is safely mine,"
> I say. "God grant she stay my own!"
> Low laughs the wind as if it grinned:
> "Thy Love is one thou'st not yet know."
> (CPH, 495)

This brief recapitulation of a handful of poems is meant to mime the way they might exist in the mind of a reader of *The Complete Poems* as he gropes his way from page to page trying to reduce their abundance to some kind of harmony. The poems I have chosen display various forms of genealogical resemblance. They are like a group of photographs of members of the same family. Each has similarities in feature with at least one of the others. Faced with such an assemblage, the mind—my mind at least—is likely to try to superimpose them all in a stack, poem behind poem, in order to make them in some way congruent. To the poems I have cited might be added four other poems by Hardy I have elsewhere discussed, "Wessex Heights," "The Pedigree," "The Torn Letter," and "In Front of the Landscape." They too can be seen as in one way or another members of this family. The figure of repeating mirror images, one behind the other, appears, for example, in both "The Pedigree" and "Old Furniture." "In Front of the Landscape," like "At Castle Boterel," "Under the Waterfall," and "In the British Museum," has to do with the way a scene or some object from a scene is inscribed, however covertly, with the signatures of the past.

The minds of most readers or critics will try in one way or another to get these poems to sing parts of the same tune. The reader does this instinctively, through an intrinsic need for order, or by training in one form or another of the expectation that literature will be logical and conform to some model of coherence. The attempt at reconciliation or at justification (in the sense in which the right hand margin of a printed page is justified) may take, as I have said, the form of relating all the poems back to Hardy's life story or of saying they are in any case expressions of a single mind or sensibility. It may take the form of finding thematic, formal, tonal, or conceptual concordances.

The first of these strategies has been, not surprisingly, tried with many of the poems in my little anthology, just as there have been attempts to identify the ghosts in "Wessex Heights" or "In Front of the Landscape." "The one of the broad brow / Sepulture-clad" in the latter has been identified as Hardy's friend Horace Moule or perhaps as William Barnes. "Beyond the Last Lamp" has been related to the time in Hardy's life when he and Emma, his first wife, lived near Tooting Common, or perhaps to an earlier time when Tryphena Sparks was at Stockwell College, three miles from Tooting Common, and may have met Hardy at the scene of the poem. "The Place on the Map" has been taken as evidence that Hardy got his cousin Tryphena pregnant and as referring to an episode in their love affair. The speaker in "At Castle Boterel" appears to be Emma, and the reference is to a picnic she and Hardy had when he was courting her. "The Wind's Prophecy" has been taken as a description of Hardy's first journey to Cornwall, his journey away from Tryphena toward his first meeting with Emma.[12] Such biographical explanations are wonderfully appeasing to the mind. "Ah ha," the reader says to himself, "so that's what the poem is about." He then feels more or less exempt from any effort at exegesis. The poems become luminous and coherent as they are referred back to the unified narrative of Hardy's life as it might be told in a formal biography.

[12] For such identifications see, for example, the entries on these poems in J. O. Bailey, *The Poetry of Thomas Hardy.*

As for taking the poems as expressions of a single consciousness or sensibility, or as manifesting a thematic coherence, my own earlier work on Hardy provides good examples of that.[13]

None of these strategies works to satisfaction. The biographical mode of obtaining unity is at once too deep and too superficial. It is too deep because it makes the error of referring the poems back to a ground that is presumed to underlie them all, to unify them, and to explain them as their cause and meaning, their *logos* in all the senses of that word. But no reference is made to Horace Moule or to William Barnes in "In Front of the Landscape." "Beyond the Last Lamp" was in its original publication, in *Harper's Monthly Magazine* (New York), December 1911, called "Night in a Suburb." "The Place on the Map" in its appearance in the *English Review*, September 1930, had as subtitle, "A Poor Schoolmaster's Story." In all these titles any autobiographical reference is carefully effaced. Nor do any of these poems, even the most anecdotal of them, "The Obliterate Tomb," tell a complete story with beginning, middle, and end. They are episodes without before and after, detached from their contexts and hanging in the air or on the page. Who the sorrowful lovers are in "Beyond the Last Lamp," for example, why they are sorrowful, what happened to them afterward—of this nothing is given or can be known. All the reader knows is the fragmentary episode itself. He knows that episode, and he knows that it has a strange power to go on happening, to iterate itself. Hardy's poems are mostly bare of autobiographical reference. Even if the reader hypothesizes that Hardy carefully expunged such references, it is unjustified extrapolation to relate the poems to details of Hardy's life that are known from other sources. They may have such relation or they may not. It is impossible to tell. The poems, moreover, make sense in them-

[13] See *Thomas Hardy: Distance and Desire* (Cambridge, Mass.: Harvard University Press, 1970).

selves to a reader ignorant of Hardy's life. Biographical explanations, though they may be too deep in the sense that they refer the poem to a false underlying *logos*, are also too superficial in that they divert the mind from exploring what the poems really say. This exploration requires an effort many readers are only too happy to escape from, if they can do so with a clear conscience, that is by the short circuit of a premature explanation.

Nor do explanations based on Hardy's consciousness or on thematic coherences among the poems work any better. They too are the projection of a spurious unity on what remains diverse, discrepant, clashing. There is more than one "Hardy." "He" affirms now one belief—for example, belief in an "akasic" realm where all memories are stored—now another, the contrary belief that only accidental traces of the past, artifacts, marks, or texts, preserve it.

Hardy is right. His poems are fugitive glimpses, transient readings of life. The candid reader, if there is such, must always confess, when he tries to harmonize even a relatively small group of seemingly concordant poems, as I am doing in this case, that there is at least one poem which confounds his generalizations or disintegrates the neat story he tries to make the poems in one way or another tell. The reader is made to feel like a man trying to pick up a miscellaneous bundle of objects. His fingers will not hold them all. The effort to pick up the last one always causes one already picked up to drop. Nevertheless, the reader goes on trying. This nightmare of a failure to comprehend or to be comprehensive, while nevertheless being compelled to go on attempting to do it, is the *malconfort* of interpretation in the case of Hardy's poems. If the critic succeeds in being coherent in what he says, then he has falsified the poems. He has let something important in them slip away. If he succeeds in being comprehensive then he will by necessity be illogical or incoherent himself. Nor shall I be exempt from committing these sins of interpretation in what follows, even though my goal is to account logically for the necessary failure of logic in this case. There is no doubt that this still remains a form of the search for coherence and a form of the search for comprehensive mastery over the poems. My effort remains an attempt to encompass Hardy's poems in a unified interpretation.

The constant in Hardy's poems is their inconstancy. Their coherence is their presentation of a peculiar kind of incoherence and of the patient, lifelong, ever renewed attempt to record this accurately and to account for it. What is peculiar in this case is the combination of fragmentation and a partial hanging together. Poems, moments of experience, states of mind, the self from one time to another, are for Hardy neither wholly disintegrated nor are they wholly integrated. This is the cause of much suffering.

Why is it that for Hardy no unit of life can be either wholly detached or wholly assimilated? The incoherence derives from certain properties of language or of signs generally. All the poems in my list in one way or another explore these features of language. For Hardy, between the intention and the deed, between moment and moment, between the self and itself, between mind and landscape, falls the word. This descent of the word is the linguistic moment in Hardy. All these poems in one way or another have to do with the power of language or of signs to be generated in the first place and to go on functioning. Signs have a coercive effect. They repeat that effect indefinitely or without term, in detachment from any conscious intent either human or divine, in one direction, and in detachment from the material substratum on which they are written, in the other direction. Moreover, these bits of language cannot be made to form a system. Each has meaning in itself, as the kind of detached monad Hardy calls an "episode" (see "The End of the Episode" [CPH, 226-227]), but a given collection of them, for example, the group I have chosen, do not hang together to form a totality, except perhaps as a series of diverse demonstrations of the fact that there can be no rational totality, only discordant conglomerations. One such conglomeration is all Hardy's poems in their disparity going on side by side in the volume of *The Complete Poems*.

Nor do any of these episodes (even if they are detached from those next-door episodes in the book that seem to belong to other life stories) form coherent wholes with their own befores and afters. Each was most often initiated as the betrayal of an earlier commitment. Each in its turn in one way or another betrayed by what comes after. In spite of the fact that the episode in no way forms part of a coherent series, it does not vanish. It goes on happening in the traces of itself it has left behind when it is over. These traces have the power of iteration that cannot be stopped. They have a power to intervene in new contexts where they do not fit, almost certainly with destructive effect. The earlier love affair inscribed on the walls of the room in "The Re-Enactment" "leaves no room for later passion anywhere." It destroys the new liaison that has begun there. The old episode, once it has occurred, can neither be abolished, nor will it, given time, "obliterate" itself as the inscription on a tombstone is gradually effaced by the weather. The old episode, or rather the mark it makes—its signature, so to speak—goes on repeating itself in new contexts in which it does not fit and to which it can by no effort of trimming or reinterpretation be assimilated (in the root sense of made "like"). The episode just goes on blindly happening over and over, like a locomotive without a driver plunging down the track.

Let me try to specify the way this works in the not wholly harmonious set of variations on this theme my group of poems constitutes. In a passage in *Tess of the d'Urbervilles* that I have more than once cited before, as if in response to what it says about the irresistible tendency of signs to be repeated, Tess is said to be unusally sensitive to music and never to cease to wonder at the power a composer has, even after his death, to make later generations experience again a series of emotions that he alone had originally felt (chap.

13). A similar idea is expressed in *Jude the Obscure* when Jude goes to visit the composer of a hymn that greatly moves him. The composer tells Jude that he has given up hymn writing because it does not pay and is going into the wine business (part 3, chap. 10). In one case the composer is dead, in the other a changed man, but in both cases the musical notation has the power to go on producing its effect in detachment from any conscious intent on the part of the one who originally put those notes down on paper.

In "An Imaginative Woman," one of those strange short stories Hardy wrote in such abundance, a married woman falls obsessively in love with a young poet not so much by reading his poems, though she does that, as by living in rooms he has occupied. His personality has impregnated not only the poems he has written but the very rooms he has lived in. He is able to act at a distance, by an odd species of telepathy. The poet makes the woman feel with or for him, by an irresistible coercion, though of course he has never consciously intended anything of the sort: "She was surrounded noon and night by his customary environment, which literally whispered of him to her at every moment. . . . No, he was not a stranger! She knew his thoughts and feelings as well as she knew her own."[14] Though she never meets the poet, she bears her husband a child who looks like the poet. A purely imaginative act of generation comes to be incarnated in the flesh. Here Hardy echoes, perhaps without knowing it, a striking episode in Goethe's *Elective Affinities*. Hardy calls this strange form of infidelity (or of fidelity to a dream) "a known but inexplicable trick of Nature": "There were undoubtedly strong traces of resemblance to the man she had never seen; the dreamy and peculiar expression of the poet's face sat, as the transmitted idea, upon the child, and the hair was of the same hue" (p. 31).

[14] In *Life's Little Ironies, Writings*, Anniversary Edition, VIII (New York and London: Harper & Brothers [1920]), pp. 11, 16.

In another variation on this idea, Bathsheba, in *Far From the Madding Crowd*, commits on a whim one of those strange acts that has neither forethought, nor after it is done, afterthought—no expectation of consequences. The act almost passes out of her mind when it is finished. It was hardly in her mind when she did it. Guided in part by what Hardy calls the "sortes sanctorum" of random prophecy by turning a key on a Bible, in part by pure chance, she sends Farmer Boldwood a valentine: "Marry Me." The effect, as readers of the novel will remember, is devastating. Boldwood falls hopelessly in love with Bathsheba, and his life is ultimately destroyed. He becomes the person the valentine invited him to be. He mistakenly assumes that the valentine expresses the deliberate intent of the person who has sent it, though nothing could be further from the case. As the narrator says: "Since the receipt of the missive in the morning, Boldwood had felt the symmetry of his existence to be slowly getting distorted in the direction of an ideal passion." The valentine acts autonomously, on its own, in detachment from any conscious mind. It produces deadly effect, just as the pieces of music and the poet's room and poems, in the other examples cited, act to make something happen. In all three instances, signs function to determine the feelings of their fortuitous recipients.[15]

All my examples from the poems can, with more or less of trimming, be assimilated to this pattern. In "Beyond the Last Lamp (Near Tooting Common)," for example, a single event thirty years past, two sad lovers slowly pacing back and forth the length of a dreary suburban street on a wet rainy evening, has so marked the spot, at least for the speaker of the poem, that the "lone lane" has become a permanent sign of the event. The lane has become inextricably connected with what occurred there, as though the event were inscribed on the place. Or rather the existence of the place

---

[15] See *Far From the Madding Crowd*, Anniversary Edition, II, chap. 14, p. 112.

is dependent on the event, as though the figure brought its background into the open and maintained that merely contiguous scene in being. This does indeed often seem to be the case with the scenes and backgrounds or with inscriptions and the matter on which they are inscribed. In one sense the event and its surroundings have nothing to do with one another, just as an inscription may be transferred from place to place, transcribed, translated, copied, duplicated, and reduplicated. The writing seems to have no necessary relation to the material ground on which it was originally carved. In another sense the two seem indivisibly connected. Each is dependent on the other for its existence, however absurd this may seem. This absurdity and its coercive power over the mind is admirably dramatized in "Beyond the Last Lamp." The apparently fortuitous rhyming of the last two words in the last stanza seems to express this contingent and yet implacably operative echoing of scene and event. *Pain, lane, remain*: the chiming of these encapsulates the poem in miniature:

> ... And yet
> To me, when nights are weird and wet,
> Without those comrades there at tryst
>   Creeping slowly, creeping sadly,
>   That lone lane does not exist.
> There they seem brooding on their pain,
> And will, while such a lane remain.
>   (CPH, 315)

In one sense "Beyond the Last Lamp" is a poem supporting the idea that Hardy is a poet of causal rigor. The episode imposes itself on the scene and on the accidental spectator of the scene. It becomes the irresistible cause of its own re-enactment, long after the couple has gone. The re-enactment occurs in the scene, in the mind of the spectator who cannot think of the scene without the two sad lovers, in the poem the spectator-poet is impelled to write, and in the mind of any reader of the poem. In all these places the two lovers pace again as on that rainy night in the dreary lane beyond the last lamp near Tooting Common. The sequence forms a rigorous causal chain, with each link determining the next and determining that the episode will go on happening, in one form or another, indefinitely, again and again, as it is happening now again in the mind of whoever is reading these words.

Various other links of causal connection, however, are decisively broken in this poem. The episode is cut off from what preceded it and from what followed it. The reader is never told why the lovers were so unhappy, what had happened to bring them to this pass, nor what happened afterwards. If determinism in Hardy is supposed to mean stories with beginnings and middles following step by step according to implacable causes toward a predestined end, neither this poem, nor indeed most of Hardy's other poems, would support such generalizations. The episode does not tell a story but a moment in a story. The moment is detached from a before and an after that seem irrecoverable. These were perhaps consistent with the moment, "caused" in the ordinary sense of a narrative causally connected, perhaps not. There is no way to tell. Moreover, though the episode seems to have the power to cause the scene in which it is enacted to become a sign for the episode, this is without the intent or knowledge of the unhappy pair of lovers. For them the scene is contingent. It is just what happens to be there. It has nothing to do with their plight.

This poem expresses a familiar paradox of Hardy's poetry, present in a different way, for example in, "In Front of the Landscape." People are usually so preoccupied with before and after, particularly in moments of crisis or of intense feeling, that they are unable to notice the present moment or the place where they are at that moment. That place is nonetheless becoming so marked by their passion that it will forever after be associated with it. The place will be able to recall the episode even for someone who comes on that place again unawares, as the new lovers do on the place of the old lovemaking in "The Re-Enactment." In "Beyond the Last Lamp" the downcast lovers are so absorbed in "a misery / At things which had been or might be" that they do not see the present dreary scene at all: "Some heavy thought constrained each face, / And blinded them to time and place" (CPH, 314). Nevertheless, they are unwittingly inscribing the scene with their misery so that their suffering may be read back from it later on. The relationship is that peculiar form of causality or of acausality (it is neither quite one nor the other) always involved in the transformation of an innocent bit of matter, an object, a scene, a sheet of paper, into the bearer of a sign or set of signs, the fragment of a story, a cryptic message: "Hardy was here."

The function of the circumstantial subtitle of "Beyond the Last Lamp," "(Near Tooting Common)," is, among other things, to invite the reader to try it out for himself or herself. It is as though the subtitle were saying: "Tooting Common exists. It is a real place to be found on any map of the region. Go there on a rainy night and see for yourself. If you find the right lane and go beyond the last lamp you will find the sad lovers still pacing back and forth there. Or at any rate you will do so if you have read this poem." And who could say that this would not be the case? Go and see for yourself.

In "At Castle Boterel," to turn to another poem, Hardy sees again a long past episode of courtship that had occurred on a certain steep lane in Cornwall. He sees it again when he returns to the spot. Though the episode "filled but a minute," and though many other things have occurred in that place, "to one mind," at any rate, the mind of the speaker of the poem, the scene records or expresses that event alone. The scene has become like an inscription from which the event can be reread and thereby resurrected, as the scenes and personages in a novel come alive in the mind of its reader when he or she follows the words on the page. The paradox here is that in fact nothing at all is written on the rocks. They are blank but act as if they were inscribed, as if in fact this poem had been carved on them. The rocks act like a text though they are not a text:

> Primaeval rocks form the road's steep border,
>   And much have they faced there, first and last,
> Of the transitory in Earth's long order;
>   But what they record in colour and cast
>   Is—that we two passed.
>   (CPH, 352)

In the "same way"—though the placement of Hardy is quite different in each case, in one as passionate participant, in the other as casual and accidental witness—the words of "Beyond the Last Lamp," in whatever copy of Hardy's poems they are found and by whatever reader, have the potential of raising again the phantoms of those two lovers and of turning the reader into a duplicate of Hardy. The reader too would now be unable to visit the scene without seeing the lovers "in his mind's eye" or without reading the shabby lane "near Tooting Common" as a memorial sign of the long-vanished episode. The elements in question here form a chain, each link of which keeps a certain pattern alive. That pattern is capable of generating itself anew in whatever mind happens to encounter any version of it. Any of these links may be substituted for any of the others. They are interchangeable. From the original episode to the indifferent scene in which the episode happens to occur, to the mind of the participant or casual witness of the scene who is forced to associate the two because they happen to be there side by side, to the poem, words written down on paper, perhaps many years later, by the witness or participant, to the reader who happens to encounter that poem in whatever circumstances and in whatever copy it may have been disseminated, broadcast here and there throughout the world like scattered seed, and who then will see the real scene, if he or she visits it, as the sign of the episode—the pattern proliferates itself.

The reader, in this chain, is the helpless recipient of the pattern. He cannot help but raise the phantoms once again. He cannot help, if he reads the poem, but feel again the emotion Hardy once felt, by a sort of telepathy or feeling at a distance. He cannot help being dispossessed of his own self. He cannot help becoming, in a manner of speaking, the self of Hardy in that aspect or incarnation of it which is invaded at this time or at that time by these particular phantoms, the sad estranged lovers in "Beyond the Last Lamp," the happy lovers in "At Castle Boterel." This invasion and this reincarnation occur without respect of the situation, intent, or state of mind of the one who is invaded. The possession or dispossession has nothing to do with his own before or after. It may interfere with his life, deflect it, or even destroy it, so that he becomes henceforth malignly inhabited by ghosts who originally belonged to another person. There is great power, but not necessarily power to do good, in an innocent-looking book of poems, as there may be power in a place that happened to be the scene of some passionate encounter, as in "The Re-Enactment," or as the unmarked stone that echoed Paul's words in "In the British Musuem," in spite of being blank, brings those words back to the mind of someone who encounters the stone centuries later. St. Paul's words were "in all their intimate accents / Patterned upon / That marble front, and were wide reflected, / And then were gone." Though they left no traces of themselves on the stone, that stone still can retransmit them again, at least to the mind of the imaginative "labouring man" who speaks the second half of the poem and who stands with rigid stare looking at the stone in the British Museum, "as if [he] heard" Paul's words again (CPH, 382). Like a sheet of printed paper or like the walls of a room or like a blank stone, any object or set of objects may harbor phantoms, as does for example, the glass in "Under the Waterfall." The glass keeps the lovers' picnic in being. In a similar way, the clock, the old viol, and the tinderbox in "Old Furniture" are inhabited by ghosts of all the generations who have used them, "hands behind hands, growing paler and paler."

In "The Place on the Map," not words about a place but a conventional representation of that place has power to raise ghosts. The schematic sign of the scene brings back the episode that occurred there. The map perpetuates the scene just as effectively as the place itself or as the poem that recounts the experience of seeing the map: "So, the map revives her words, the spot, the time, . . . / And its episode comes back in pantomime" (CPH, 322). From episode to scene to map of the scene to Hardy's mind to the words of the poem on the page to the mind of the reader of the poem, the pattern is perpetuated, adapting itself with seeming effortlessness to the different substances that must serve as its medium, just as a family face is passed from generation to generation by a genetic code, and just as the ostentatiously complex and artificial rhyme and metrical schemes of so many of Hardy's poems proliferate themselves from stanza to stanza and shape whatever material they express to their own form. The awkward complexity of these stanzaic forms, their individual idiosyncrasy, the great number of different ones, and the fact that many are used only once make the form of the poems the parabolic expression of their content. The uniqueness of each episode or moment of vision, the incommensurability of each with all the others, corresponds to the unique stanzaic pattern used, even if that stanzaic pattern does not seem particularly appropriate to the thematic material it shapes.

"The Obliterate Tomb" may appear to be a poem about one instance in which an inscription is destroyed and with it the pattern it perpetuated. Neither the enemy of the family nor its descendent succeeds in keeping intact the family tombstone that "records a luminous line whose talents / Told in their day" (CPH, 386). The stone, its inscription all but effaced, is broken up, the "family forgotten," its "deeds unknown." The paradox of the poem (it is not the same paradox as the one in "Beyond the Last Lamp") is that the poem itself does what neither friend nor foe of the family succeeded in doing. The poem perpetuates the pattern. It substitutes for the obliterate tomb and functions anew to perpetuate the memory of the "luminous line" every time it is read again. It does this in a characteristically partial and unsatisfactory way. The reader is not told the names of any family members, nor indeed anything about them except that they hated the protagonist of the poem, weighed him falsely and wronged him bitterly. In one sense the family has "shrunk away into the silence / Like a lost song" (CPH, 383), but in another sense the family is maintained still in existence, like fragments of a tune heard faintly at a distance, as if to demonstrate once again that for Hardy no pattern can be wholly obliterated. All find some way to keep themselves in being, in however displaced and partial a form.

"The Wind's Prophecy" differs from the poems so far discussed in orienting toward the future Hardy's interrogation of the power of signs to act at a distance. In this case it is not so much telephony, television, or telepathy, as prevision, foresight, "forephony," or "forepathy," if there were such words. If, as in "The Pedigree" or in many others of the poems I have singled out, I, now in the present, can pick up signals transmitted from the past, relayed from one incarnation to another and reaching me finally with a power to determine the way I think, feel, act, even what I am, it would follow that patterns of signs generated now in the present will have a curious power of self-fulfilling prophecy. What the pattern says will come true because the pattern itself will make it come true. In "I Said and Sang Her Excellence (Fickle Lover's Song)," a poem not so far mentioned here, the fickle lover overpraises his present beloved. His consciously hyperbolic love song is fulfilled, item for unlikely item, with another girl he meets months later:

Strange, startling, was it then to learn
I had glanced down unborn time,
  (Have your way, my heart, O!)
And prophesied, whereby I knew
That which the years had planned to do
  In warranty of my rhyme.
                              (CPH, 466)

"In warranty of my rhyme"—the phrase is a striking formulation of the idea that time acts to justify or to confirm
the most unlikely of conceptual schemes. This is so even if
those schemes are conscious fictions or are directed in the
present toward persons they do not fit. The heart can con-
fidently expect to "have its way." The years are like a company that guarantees a product, in this case a "rhyme," to
go on working and fixes it up to work if it happens to fail.

"The Wind's Prophecy" is a more subtle and more powerful poem on the same theme, though the tune it sings is
not quite in harmony with that of the fickle lover's song.
In "The Wind's Prophecy" the journeying lover affirms and
reaffirms his fidelity to the black-haired beloved he leaves
behind, but instinctively he personifies the gale winds blowing up from the sea and over the land he traverses. To him
the winds seem a loud, hoarse, shrieking voice, or sometimes, in a lull, a low laughing one. That voice foretells that
"Thy love is one thou'st not yet known." The wind proph-
esies that the journeyer will betray the black-haired girl and
fall in love with a girl with "tresses flashing fair!" (CPH,
494). Prosopopoeia in Hardy is a projection of man's own
voice and person, not a response to some personality in-
habiting the inanimate. This will be known to careful readers of the famous opening chapter of *The Return of the
Native*. There Egdon Heath is personified, but as the reflex
of the spectator's person. The phrase at the end of *Tess of
the d'Urbervilles* about the "President of the Immortals," Hardy
said, personifies the impersonal. It is not a name for a

conscious deity within or behind nature. The speaker in "The Wind's Prophecy" projects into the wind his fore-knowledge of his fated infidelity. It is not necessary to relate the poem to Hardy's journey away from Tryphena toward his first meeting with Emma to know that what the speaker projects into the wind, against every conscious wish and intent, will come true, word for word. The ominous tone of the poem indicates this well enough. The prophecy itself breaks the speaker's fidelity to the black-haired girl and prepares for its fulfillment when he meets the fair-haired one.

As was perhaps inevitable, I have come to speak of Hardy as a single person and of his writings as a single unit capable of being marshalled under a single law. This assimilation, however, has been under the law of the inassimilable, the incongruous, the discordant. A strange combination of connection and disconnection characterizes Hardy's work in the various dimensions I have explored. These include the not quite congruous similarity between one poem and another, as well as the presence in those poems of many selves and of many readings of the phenomena of life by the diverse selves. These selves and readings cannot quite be assimilated to one another, and yet they have a family resemblance. In addition there are the not quite harmonious analogies in the poems among the following: the scene or landscape, the episode that takes place there, objects, minds and their contents, and the words of the poem, there on the page as physical marks. Then there is the way an object or a scene that is not strictly speaking a sign and may be as blank as a piece of paper on which nothing is yet written functions as if it were inscribed with language. For Hardy, furthermore, a sign or pattern of signs, a program, is detachable from its material substratum. It may be transmitted from substratum to substratum. It may be written on rocks, rooms, drinking glasses, musical instruments, minds, paper, and yet go on functioning. On the other hand, a given pattern of signs may be inextricably associated with a substratum that remains indifferent to it, unmarked by it. Finally, language or signs have for "Hardy" a curious power to generate themselves, to proliferate or disseminate themselves according to a self-perpetuating power of iteration. This happens without the direction of any conscious mind or will. Minds intervene only later on as recipients of signs that are already there. All these features of Hardy's poetry are only to be assimilated under the law of the inassimilable. That law can only be expressed anomalously, as I have expressed it here, that is, as a string of not quite parallel anomalies.

I have said that Hardy's abiding topic in his poems is the ability of language or of signs to be generated, to function, and to go on functioning without conscious intent. Another way to put this is to say that Hardy's work constitutes a long, patient, faithful exploration of the consequences for man of the absence of the *logos*, in all the systematically interconnected senses of that word, as mind, voice, ground, word, meaning, reason, message, measure, ratio, logic, concord, gathering. If there is no *logos* in the sense of transcendent conscious directing power, God in short ("I have been looking for God for fifty years," Hardy wrote, "and think that if he had existed I should have discovered him."),[16] then there is no ontological ground guaranteeing the coherence of beginning, middle, and end, either of collective history or of individual histories. Nor is there a support for the coherence of the mind of the single self—"Thomas Hardy," for example—as it persists through time. Nor is there, finally, a support for the coherence of language, neither language taken as a whole, the English language, for example, nor individual language systems within that whole, *The Complete Poems* of Hardy, nor any single poem from that collection, the text of "The Wind's Prophecy" or

[16] Cited in H. C. Duffin, *Thomas Hardy* (Manchester: University Press, 1967), p. 196.

of "The Obliterate Tomb." The notion of the coherence of language is also a logocentric concept through and through. It vanishes with the vanishing of confidence in the *logos*. For Hardy there is no *logos*, neither in the sense of a conscious transcendent mind, nor in the sense of an immanent reasonable force making for order, nor in the sense of the unified mind of the poet as order-giving perspective, nor in the sense of language itself as a pre-existing order. In place of these forms of unity and coherence only a legion of warring fragments of selves, stories, groups of signs is left. Each of these unsuccessfully attempts to impose itself on the whole in order to become the *logos* of that whole. Each fragmentary urge toward order is neutralized by the force of the others. The whole remains in pieces, like squirming bits of a snake chopped in segments. Hardy's work is an admirable exploration of these various forms of fragmentation, though with many waverings, hesitations, and nostalgias for what is lost. This is appropriate, since when the *logos* is lost, much is lost. It is in this sense that Hardy may be called, in the strictest terms, a poet of "fierce unreason" (CPH, 303).

He is often, on the contrary, said to be a poet and a novelist of reason or *logos* in the sense of causal rigor. The successive episodes in his works, it is said, form an irresistible chain of cause and effect. Each effect becomes in its turn an efficient cause. All taken together lead the protagonist step by step to his or her doom, as Tess, in *Tess of the d'Urbervilles* is led to the scaffold, where the President of the Immortals finishes his sport with her. Of Tess's whole life the same thing may be said that the country folks say about her deflowering: "It was to be."[17] To efficient cause may be added first cause, in the sense of some initial impetus starting the whole chain, like the push to the first of a row of dominoes (Tess's father's accidental meeting with Parson Tringham in *Tess of the d'Urbervilles*); final cause in

[17] *Tess of the d'Urbervilles*, ed. cit., chap. 11, p. 108.

304

the sense of a *telos* or goal (the doom drawing Tess or anyone else in Hardy's world toward his or her end); and underlying cause, in the sense of ground, *Grund, logos*, or *ratio* as base. To the latter Hardy, it appears, gives the name Immanent Will. That term also names the other three aspects of cause as well, since all four causes are parts of the same coordinated energy, before, behind, beneath, present here and now.

There would be, then, grounds for finding all four of the traditional Aristotelian vectors of causality at work in Hardy's writing, as he could have encountered them, for example, in Arthur Schopenhauer's *On the Four-fold Root of the Principle of Sufficient Reason*, which he read carefully in 1889 or 1890 in Mrs. Karl Hillebrand's translation.[18] There is no doubt that Hardy was attracted by this kind of thought. He experiments both in his poetry and in his fiction with the ways thinking according to cause makes sense of human life, makes human life reasonable. There is no doubt that for Hardy "nor God nor Demon can undo the done" (CPH, 310). What is done not only cannot be undone; its power to do, to go on doing, cannot be neutralized. Once something has happened, it goes on happening in one way or another. Its causal power echoes irrevocably down through the years. It may unexpectedly pop up decades hence, as an ancestral face may reappear in the collateral line of a pedigree after generations of absence. Both the poems and the novels offer many examples of this.

On the other hand, the penchant toward reason and cause in Hardy's thought is constantly countered by a contrary penchant toward seeing the world as the arena of senseless discontinuity. One form of unreason in Hardy's work is the co-presence of these two impulses, nostalgia for the old metaphysical way of thinking along with the need to testify that his experience offers no firm support for

[18] See Weber, *Hardy of Wessex*, pp. 246-247.

such thinking—far from it. A book of poems by Hardy presents the "fierce unreason" of a heterogeneous collection of detached moments, scenes, and episodes all going on side by side, interfering with one another, inhibiting one another, contradicting one another, refusing to form a coherent series. Each moment is an irrevocable cause, but none has the power to organize the whole into a reasonable causal chain.

The "reason" for this is easy to identify. It is hinted at in my word *irrevocable*. What functions as cause for Hardy is not mind, force, or deliberate will but voice in the sense of words spoken or written. More broadly, causes for Hardy are almost always signs of some sort. These are generated and go on operating in detachment from any conscious mind, universal or particular. For Hardy, once a sign has been emitted, in however accidental and undeliberate a way, it goes on forcing the meaning that is programmed within it on whatever is around, as a genetic code produces a similar face intermittently. Since these signs are not the product of one cause in the sense of a single designing mind, since they are not the product of any mind at all if one means the deliberate use of words by a single self to communicate a message or to produce a desired effect, they do not form an orderly whole, and their effects are unpredictable, fortuitous. For Hardy, it is not minds that generate signs, but minds that are generated, shaped, and coerced, done and undone, by signs. The Immanent Will for Hardy names the unconscious forces that make things happen as they happen. The phrase expresses a tautology: What happens, happens. The appellation "President of the Immortals," Hardy firmly said, was a figure of speech, a prosopopoeia, the personification of the impersonal energies that make things occur as they do happen to occur.[19]

---

[19] F. E. Hardy, *The Life of Thomas Hardy*, p. 244: ". . . the forces opposed to the heroine were allegorized as a personality (a method not unusual in imaginative prose or poetry) by the use of a well-known trope, explained

Among the most important of these forces are fortuitously generated words or other signs. Among the most important themes of Hardy's work is an exploration of this fact, for example, in the handful of poems I have transmitted to the reader here.

Though Hardy wavered and was inconsistent on this point (as on all the others, as he says himself), it may be that the definition of the universe as a whole that tends to occur more often than the others, is not "energy," material or spiritual, nor "will," nor any form of "mind," conscious or unconscious, but a communication system. The totality of what is, is a web of signs or of language, like that of the postal and telegraph service. Along the fibers of this web messages are constantly transmitted. These make and un-make, willy-nilly, minds that happen to come in the way of one or more of the transmission lines. This may happen, for example, when someone receives a letter, or reads a poem, or sees a map, or finds himself or herself in a place where a certain episode has occurred, even if the place is not visibly marked or inscribed by the story it tells. This immense web of signs is not immaterial or spiritual. It is a result of the strange propensity of matter to be marked by notations and so to turn itself into proliferating signs and ever-extending systems of signs.

In certain forms of mental disorder it seems to a person that he is unwittingly a transmitter of radio or television signals. All he sees and feels, his most secret thought, is being sent out against his will, then picked up and recorded by some sort of "thought police," spies from whom nothing can be hidden. This pathological disorder, it may be, is nothing more than an extrapolation from what we all take for granted as objectively the case. We are transfused, pierced, invaded, inundated every moment of the day and night by an unimaginable complexity of various sorts of

in that venerable work, Campbell's *Philosophy of Rhetoric*, as 'one in which life, perception, activity, design, passion, or any property of sentient beings, is attributed to things inanimate.' "

307

signals on different wave lengths. Why should we not be transmitters, too? One remembers the story of the man whose teeth-fillings accidentally functioned as a crystal radio receiver, so that, until the doctors figured out what was wrong, he was forced to hear all day and all night the broadcasts from the most powerful local station—music, news, commercials, soap operas, the works. It may be that Jacques Derrida is right, in "Télépathie" and in *La carte postale*, to see significance in the fact that the evidence Freud uses in his curious essays on telepathy "is almost always written, literal, not to say solely epistolary (letters, postcards, telegrams, visiting cards)."[20] Derrida sees the Freudian theory of the unconscious, too, as belonging to the age of the modern postal system and of telegraphic communication, impossible without them as models. Modern communication networks are not so much figures of the workings of telepathy and of the unconscious as they are objective incarnations and proofs of them. Telepathy depends on writing. It is an effect of writing. A man happens to get plugged into the network and, behold!, he gets messages at a distance. Radio, television, sonar, radar, information storage, retrieval, and manipulation on tapes, discs, and in ever more compact and more powerful computers are no more than extensions of the human ability to feel, see, hear, and receive messages at a distance. All these are no more than modifications of the "miraculous" gift of writing, the recording on matter of some kind of sign. The latter has been with us for a long time now, though there has been a quantum leap in its technological powers in the last one hundred and fifty years. Hardy's poetry also belongs to this epoch of telepathy, telephone, television—far-feeling, far-hearing, and far-seeing. The most generalized description of Hardy's universe, it may be, is that it is a vast array of lines along which pass in every direction messages, voices, visions, in incoherent and proliferating multiplicity. These

[20] Jacques Derrida, *"Télépathie," Furor*, 2 (February 1981), 20, my trans.

signals are not controlled by an all-powerful, all-knowing "central." They are broadcast automatically, undirected by any comprehensive logical program. They are products of a "fierce unreason," an unreason that encompasses the totality of what is.

Hardy's most comprehensive expression of this vision of things is in the admirable "Fore Scene" of *The Dynasts*. There the universe is compared to the lines, nerves, filaments, and webs of a vast dreaming brain:

> A new and penetrating light descends on the spectacle, enduing men and things with a seeming transparency, and exhibiting as one organism the anatomy of life and movement in all humanity and vitalized matter included in the display.

SPIRIT OF THE PITIES
(*after a pause*)

Amid this scene of bodies substantive
Strange waves I sight like winds grown visible,
Which bear men's forms on their innumerous coils,
Twining and serpentining round and through.
Also retracting threads like gossamers—
Except in being irresistible—
Which complicate with some, and balance all.

SPIRIT OF THE YEARS

These are the Prime Volitions,—fibrils, veins,
Will-tissues, nerves, and pulses of the Cause,
That heave throughout the Earth's compositure.
Their sum is like the lobule of a Brain
Evolving always that it wots not of;
A Brain whose whole connotes the Everywhere,
And whose procedure may but be discerned
By phantom eyes like ours; the while unguessed
Of those it stirs, who (even as ye do) dream
Their motions free, their orderings supreme;
Each life apart from each, with power to mete

Its own day's measures; balanced, self complete;
Though they subsist but atoms of the One
Labouring through all, divisible from none . . .[21]

In this passage, as in so much else in *The Dynasts*, pre-suppositions that are latent in Hardy's novels and lyric poems surface in figures of great generalizing power. What the novels and poems present by synecdoche, this passage presents whole. Basing himself, no doubt, on nineteenth-century formulations of the wave theory of light and of electromagnetism, Hardy envisions a universe not too different from the one the science of the 1980s presents: an enormous field of vibrations on different frequencies penetrating everything and coercing each thing irresistibly according to the messages encoded along each line of force. The universe is in this like a giant brain with its encoiled nerve fibers and tendrils. The Immanent Will operates not by physical force but as a universal field of signs traversing all the lines in every direction, in unimaginable abundance and diversity. The paradox is that this brain is not conscious. It is mind without mind. The brain remains in deep sleep, evolving always that it wots not of. It is implacably functioning language without any waking mind to be aware of that language, perhaps in this not wholly different from the seemingly self-generating proliferation of language in *Finnegans Wake*. The universal dreaming brain, for Hardy, works much as, on a small scale, the genetic material in a virus transmits its message to the cell it has invaded. Consciousness is not necessary on either side of the deadly agon, in spite of the fact that the battle is carried on with signs. Consciousness, in man, for example, is a mere ripple on the surface of this all-powerful communications network sending messages ceaselessly to its own unconscious self. If the brain is an oxymoron, a mind without mind, human minds are conscious without being able to know that of

[21] Thomas Hardy, *The Dynasts* (London, Melbourne, Toronto: Macmillan; New York: St. Martin's Press, 1965), pp. 6-7.

which they are the unwitting instruments. The brain is "the while unguessed / Of those it stirs." Human minds are minds unable to be mindful of what they most should mind and do nevertheless mind whatever they intend.

The figure of the universe as a sleeping brain appears to be the image of a fixed simultaneous spatial array. In fact it is an image of time or of temporality, with its anticipations, recollections, delays, detours, postponements, and indefinite suspensions. Once more, as in Wordsworth, Shelley, or Browning, in fact as in all the poets included in this book, space becomes time, or time expresses itself in what appears to be a spatial image. The network of Hardy's all-encompassing, unwitting brain programs and coerces the individual persons who are nodes within the web (Napoleon, for example), to act and think as they do, and so generates stories extended through time. Each individual may appear to himself to be conscious and to be able to choose, will, and act autonomously. In fact, each is subject to the messages that reach him accidentally along this line or that. Each man or woman acts somnambulistically, by rote, as Tess in *Tess of the d'Urbervilles*, for example, conspicuously does at the crises of her life. It is as though each person were hypnotized, though seemingly awake, subjected constantly to an irresistible telepathic coercion. Each person is programmed from without by a vast circumambient network of language that invades the self from all sides in incoherent abundance and forces her or him to act, think, and feel in certain ways. This web of signs is a discordant conglomeration of various fragmentary messages—thoughts, stories, texts—passing of their own accord back and forth along whatever lines of transmission are open to them. These are in no way capable of being organized into a logical or coherent whole, except as reasonable images of unreason, the law of a lack of lawfulness, may be formulated, as I have tried to do here. If the universal conglomeration of texts is incoherent, that inco-

311

herence will be programmed in any receiver or retransmitter of one or more of them.

For Hardy too, though in a way unlike that for any of the other poets discussed here, the linguistic moment has such momentum or force that it tends to spread out to dominate and redefine everything else. The "sufficient reason" of Hardy's fierce unreason, the *logos* of his illogic, is the ability of the *logos* as language to be generated and to operate without the presence of the *logos* as mind. For Hardy too there is a priority of word over mind. Consciousnesses or selves are reduced to momentary epiphenomena within the vast tidal sweep of a ceaseless proliferation of signs, like "waste waters / Stretching around," occupying all time and space in every direction (CPH, 303).

Such a vision of the universe reappears as such in many of Hardy's lyrics. In "The Absolute Explains," for example, Hardy speaks of all the events of the past as being "Coiled like a precious parchment fell, / Illumined page by page, / Unhurt by age" (CPH, 756), ready to be uncoiled, reread and so brought back into existence again. A single kiss, in another poem, acts according to that propensity of objects, sounds, places, to behave like signs or words, especially in their iterability, and to speak, to go on speaking: "It cannot have died; that know we well. / Somewhere it pursues its flight, / One of a long procession of sounds / Travelling aetherial rounds / Far from earth's bounds / In the infinite" (CPH, 467). For Kafka written kisses never reach their destinations because they are signs for kisses, not real kisses,[22] but for Hardy even a real kiss is a sign. It therefore goes

[22] See Franz Kafka, *Briefe an Milena* (Frankfurt am Main: S. Fischer Verlag, 1965), p. 260: "*Geschriebene Küsse kommen nicht an ihren Ort, sondern werden von den Gespenstern auf dem Wege ausgetrunken.*" The whole letter is of great interest. It is relevant, moreover, to what I am saying about Hardy. For further discussion of it, see my essay on Hardy's poem, "The Torn Letter," in *Taking Chances: Derrida, Psychoanalysis, and Literature*, ed. Joseph H. Smith and William Kerrigan, *Psychiatry and the Humanities* 7 (Baltimore and London: The Johns Hopkins University Press, 1984), pp. 135-145.

on past the lips it momentarily joins and wanders about the vast empty spaces of the universe along with all the other signs. In "In a Museum," to give a final example, which I transcribe here in its entirety, two separate articulated sounds are joined together in that vast crisscrossing system of intercommunication along with all the other sounds, signs, scenes, words, texts, episodes:

In a Museum

I

Here's the mould of a musical bird long passed from
    light,
Which over the earth before man came was winging;
There's a contralto voice I heard last night,
That lodges in me still with its sweet singing.

II

Such a dream is Time that the coo of this ancient bird
Has perished not, but is blent, or will be blending
Mid visionless wilds of space with the voice that I heard,
In the full-fugued song of the universe unending.

Exeter

(CPH, 430)

This poem is a synecdochic miniature of Hardy's universe as a whole. The careful reader will remember the figure of music as it is used in Hardy's prefaces and will know that the "full-fugued song of the universe" here is the "blending" of discordant notes. The universe is an immense chorus of musical themes or fragments of themes all playing themselves over and over at once without composer or score or conductor. If "In a Museum" offers a miniature model of this, a given copy of Hardy's *Complete Poems*, in its superabundance of unreconciled "moments of vision," is not so much a slightly larger replica of Hardy's universe as it is in itself. The book is rather a physical object made of paper, glue, cardboard, and cloth, with inked words imprinted on the paper, that functions as one of the relay stations in that universe. A copy of Hardy's *Poems* is receiver and transmitter at once. It is a point of intersection where a large number of the linguistic events making up the universe have happened to come together and take the form of printed words on paper. There they wait to be retransmitted and thereby to take other forms again, most obviously in the mind of someone who reads the words. The reprinting of the book would do this in another way. A reader may become a relay station in his or her turn. He or she may be impelled, for example, to write a critical essay. Such an essay passes the patterns once more on to others. They would go on happening anyhow even if there were no mind anywhere to be aware of them, just as a radio, a television, a telegraph, or a telephone signal does not depend on being received for its existence, and just as a computer silently stores whatever is put in it. That someone becomes conscious of one of the patterns a poem by Hardy records is accidental, contingent, intermittent, in no way essential to its nature.

This, to come full circle, will give the answer to Hardy's "query" about where that emotion has been hiding in his heart and brain for forty years waiting to be exhumed at the end of that time, "as fresh as when interred." Hardy's heart and brain are part of the totality of the sleeping brain of the universe. That all-encompassing brain functions like a computer within which all programs are stored as on memory tapes waiting to generate again the emotions that correspond to them whenever they happen to be encountered again by a conscious mind. For Hardy nothing dies or can die that has had the good or ill luck to inscribe itself in some way on matter, on someone's heart and brain, on paper or stone, on walls or utensils, on the landscape, or on the mere circumambient air.

I have in this chapter intercepted the signals emitted by a small handful out of the almost one thousand poems stored in Hardy's *Complete Poems*. I have then retransmitted them with more or less, probably with more rather than with less, of static, interference, or, as the French call it, "parasites," in the retransmitted signal. Or, to vary the figure, I have acted as a medium. I have resurrected or disinterred a few of the ghosts imprisoned within the covers of that book as within a tomb. I have allowed them to walk again in my mind, on these pages, and in your minds again when you read these pages.

Yeats

> How can we include in a discourse, *any* discourse, that which, being the very condition of discourse, would by its very essence *escape* discourse? If non-presence, the core and ultimate reason behind all discourse, becomes speech, can it—or should it—make itself heard in and through self-presence?
>
> Nicolas Abraham,
> "The Rind and the Core"[1]

> ... it is quite hopeless to try to penetrate directly to the nucleus of the pathogenic organization.
>
> Sigmund Freud,
> *Studies on Hysteria*[2]

My topic here is the topography of Yeats's "Nineteen Hundred and Nineteen." This topography is a certain structure of places, in both the spatial and rhetorical senses of that word. The structure incorporates also a non-place, not so much utopian as atopical, a place that is both there and not there. It is a certain crossroads to which all roads lead and yet which can be reached by no road. What can this mean?

Topography—the word indicates both an arrangement of places that is already there and the activity of graphing them, mapping them, transposing them from the real to its representation. This activity Yeats's poem already per-

[1] Cited by Jacques Derrida in "Fors," trans. Barbara Johnson, *The Georgia Review* XXXI, 1 (Spring 1977), 93.

[2] Sigmund Freud, *The Complete Psychological Works*, st. ed., trans. James Strachey *et al.*, II (London: The Hogarth Press, 1953–66), p. 292.

forms. It puts a multitude of elements within the space of the poem, laid out on the page as a map. The critic repeats that activity in his turn. He makes a new map of his own. These topographies are also topologies. They are a mapping that is a search for meaning, a search for the central *logos* that gives significance to the whole place and to the separate places within the place. This chapter makes its search in part through the implicit superimposition on Yeats's poem of several other "similar" spatial structures—a painting by Paul Klee, *Danceplay of the Red Skirts*; a poem by Wallace Stevens, "A Primitive Like an Orb"; an essay by Friedrich Nietzsche, "On Truth and Lies in a Nonmoral Sense"; and two passages by Sigmund Freud, one in *Studies on Hysteria*, the other in *The Interpretation of Dreams*.[3] These might be thought of as transparent maps laid over the ground plan of "Nineteen Hundred and Nineteen," or perhaps projected there in an imaginary version of the Hinman collating machine. Their shadowy presence will allow me to raise in another way the question of what is meant by calling the poet's mapping a "transposition." They also raise the question of what is meant by saying two texts have "similar" spatial structures. The goal of this chapter is to reach the center of the labyrinth of the Yeats's poem, but since reaching this goal directly is impossible, I have tried to get there by way of detours through other corridors in a group of analogous labyrinths. When the way is blocked by one route, one seeks another way in.

The implicit superimposition of diverse examples will also allow the raising of several more general questions. A

[3] I say "implicit" because the necessary economy of space forbids inclusion here, except in the case of Klee, of more than brief indications of what might be said about these alternative examples of the structure in question. The full texts of these detours have been or will be published elsewhere, as parts of this book remaining outside the book. For the discussion of the essay by Nietzsche see my "Dismembering and Disremembering in Nietzsche's 'On Truth and Lies in a Nonmoral Sense,'" *Boundary 2*, ix, 3, and x, 1 (Spring/Fall 1981), 41-54.

lyric poem, for example, "Nineteen Hundred and Nine-teen," has a temporal structure. Word follows word when we read it silently or aloud. Why do such poems so often use spatial figures to describe their own activity, just as the critic, in his turn, is so often drawn to spatial images in his mapping? This spatialization may be especially easy to in-vestigate in a lyric poem of moderate length, such as "Nine-teen Hundred and Nineteen" or "A Primitive Like an Orb." Is such a poem a separate genre, with its own form, dif-ferent from the brief lyric poem, for example, a sonnet, "Leda and the Swan," say, or different from the group sequence, like Yeats's "A Woman Young and Old," or dif-ferent from the long lyric philosophical poem, like Stevens' "An Ordinary Evening in New Haven"? If so, what are those formal properties? Why is it, finally, that this spa-tialization, which seems so effective as a means of inter-preting the poem, tends ultimately to break down? It fails to account for the poem unless the image or the concept (it is both and neither) of the atopical is introduced. This introduction ruins the reader's initial enterprise of topo-graphical mapping as a way of accounting for the poem.

That "Nineteen Hundred and Nineteen" raises the most urgent metaphysical, moral, historical, aesthetic, and po-litical questions, there can be no doubt. Written as a re-sponse to the Black and Tan violence in Ireland and more generally to the disillusionment in the West after the First World War, it joins such works as Paul Valéry's "*La crise de l'esprit*" and *Regards sur le monde actuel*, Oswald Spengler's *The Decline of the West*, T. S. Eliot's *The Waste Land*, and Virginia Woolf's *Mrs. Dalloway*, in asking why it is "no work can stand, / Whether health, wealth or peace of mind were spent / On master-work of intellect or hand, / No honour leave its mighty monument."[4] Yeats's poem asks also the

4 W. B. Yeats, "Nineteen Hundred and Nineteen," lines 35-38, *The Variorum Edition of the Poems*, ed. Peter Allt and Russell K. Alspach (New York: Macmillan Publishing Co., Inc., 1977), p. 429; henceforth VPY. Further citations from Yeats's poems will be made from this edition and will be identified by line numbers.

ethical question: In the light of such knowledge, what should we now do? Knowing no work can stand, how should we then spend our time, from moment to moment, before we die?

The reader of a lyric poem raises certain questions, instinctively or by training in one version or another of the long Western tradition of rhetoric, of which Anglo-American New Criticism is only one of the latest. Who is speaking, from what place, and to whom? What form of order or unity does the poem have, allowing the reader to organize every detail around a beginning, middle, end, and generative center? What, finally, is the poem "about"? What is the literal, nonlinguistic thing, situation, event, state of mind, or supernatural reality to which it refers as to its center? This center is assumed to govern all the figurative language in the poem and to make the figures, figures of something or other nonfigurative.

In the case of Yeats, critics have tended to assume that it is Yeats himself speaking. He speaks directly from his real personal and historical situation, or he speaks by way of a persona, Crazy Jane or Ribh. The persona is a transposition of that real self of Yeats and may be translated back again. Critics have tended to assume that a poem by Yeats, like any good poem, will have an "organic unity"— leaf, blossom, and bole rooted in the particularities of Yeats's sense of his own life. Yeats's own early critical prose, in *Ideas of Good and Evil*, contains many powerful restatements of the Romantic doctrine of organic unity. For Yeats a poem must be a living whole, like a flower, or a tree, or the body of a beautiful woman dancing. Critics, finally, have tended to assume that the literal center which controls all those figures is either the objective historical world, or Yeats's subjectivity, his sense of that world, or the supernatual powers in which Yeats believed and of which all those figures are emblems. It is in this latter area that Yeats's critics have most disagreed, for example, Denis Donoghue or Richard Ellmann on the one hand and F.A.C. Wilson or Kathleen Raine on the other. It is here, also, that Yeats himself appears to be most vacillating and contradictory, to offer his critics most scope for disagreement.

It will be my position here, presented hypothetically in terms of a reading of one poem standing by synecdoche for them all, that Yeats, in "Nineteen Hundred and Nineteen" at least, speaks as no one, from nowhere, at no time, to no identifiable listeners; that "Nineteen Hundred and Nineteen" can by no effort be shown to have an organic unity; and that there is no identifiable central, literal thing of which all else is figure. The poem, in short, is a "labyrinth of the wind" (line 121). This labyrinth has no center that can ever be named literally or be present, here and now, to perception or to experience. This absence redefines all the named elements in the poem and makes them neither literal nor figurative, neither emblems nor things. Such figures take place, in Joyce's phrase, "at no spatial time." The absence of an identifiable center disqualifies all the conceptual oppositions that the critic needs to interpret the poem but at the same time gives the poem its enigmatic power, as though it were that "stump on the Acropolis," the "ancient image made of olive wood" (lines 46, 6), both sign and thing, therefore neither unequivocally.

What are the elements that enter into the poem? What is their placing, and within a space of what shape? What the elements are, the basic alphabet of the poem's code, we know. Previous critics have identified them.[5] Though the competent reader of Yeats will steer his way among them without difficulty, they appear, when the reader stands back a little and surveys the group, an amazingly heterogeneous lot. They represent by synecdoche the material that enters into Yeats's work generally. In fact each detail of the poem ("Phidias' famous ivories," "the circle of the moon" [lines 7, 3], and so on) tends to stand for an entire context—

[5] Among annotative commentaries on the poem see, for example, A. Norman Jeffares, *A Commentary on the Collected Poems of W. B. Yeats* (Stanford: Stanford University Press, 1968), pp. 273-281, and Harold Bloom, *Yeats* (New York: Oxford University Press, 1970), pp. 356-363.

Greek civilization as a whole, Yeats's visionary phases of the moon, or whatever. The concentration and explosive intensity of the poem is achieved by this bringing together in abrupt juxtaposition detached parts that stand for large wholes. The parts have been cut by violence from these wholes and mutilated. Each stands for its context, across the gap of its incisive separation from it. This form of synecdoche is appropriate, since the emblems are uniformly of acts of violence by man against the cherished monuments of his own constructive power. An example is the burning, by incendiary or bigot, of "that stump upon the Acropolis," the "ancient image made of olive wood," already given an ironically diminishing epithet that suggests mutilation, as of a hand or leg cut off. What was already a stump is then burned, though it was the emblem, in its making, in its preservation, and in its destruction, of Athenian civilization. It was created by Athene to counter Erechtheus' spring of salt water, in their rivalry over who was to become deity of the city. Each image of Yeats's poem in complex ways records an act of violence and is put into the text by another act of sundering. The images are then placed side by side with more violence. They are heterogeneous materials yoked together by violence.

The poem contains events from 1919, "the present time" of the poem: "A drunken soldiery / Can leave the mother, murdered at her door, / To crawl in her own blood, and go scot-free" (lines 26-28). This material is placed side by side with the Greek details from Sophocles, Thucydides, and Herodotus, the "ancient image made of olive wood," "Phidias' famous ivories / And all the golden grasshoppers and bees" (lines 6, 7-8). The latter images open the poem and precede the present-day material. To both of these are added elements from those "mummy truths" of *Per Amica Silentia Lunae* and *A Vision*, the latter at that moment still in progress: the circle of the moon, the "Platonic Year" that "Whirls out new right and wrong, / Whirls in the old instead" (lines 55-56), the notion that after death the soul sometimes cannot free itself from the habits of life. This idea also has a specific source in Blake's *Milton* and is as much literary as esoteric or Neoplatonic. Blake's "Mock on" is echoed in the fifth section of the poem: "Come let us mock at the great . . ." (lines 93ff.). Then there are "Loie Fuller's Chinese dancers" (actually Japanese), with all their context of Art Nouveau decor and the Mallarméan symbolism of dancer and dance. Juxtaposed with all that is the image of the swan. This may come from Shelley's *Prometheus Unbound* or from Spenser, as well as from Yeats's experience of real swans in Ireland, those wild swans at Coole. He had also seen there weasels fighting in a hole, mentioned in line 32. The final stanza mixes Herodias' daughters, with their context of Oscar Wilde's *Salomé* and Arthur Symons' "The Dance of the Daughters of Herodias," Yeats's own plays for dancers on the theme of the severed head, and material from Irish history and folklore. The latter include the whirling wind of the hosting of the Sidhe, those apparitional riders on horses with flowers on their heads, and the story of the fourteenth-century witch, Dame Alice Kyteler, and her "insolent" incubus, Robert Artisson, "Robin son of Art."

Finally, there are elements that are in the poem, apparently, only as passing figures of speech: the sun ("as it were wax in the sun's rays" [line 12]; "now but gape at the sun" [line 102]); the dragon ("It seemed that a dragon of air" [line 51]); the labyrinth ("A man in his own secret meditation / Is lost amid the labyrinth that he has made / In art or politics" [lines 69-71]; "the labyrinth of the wind" [line 121]). Or are they only passing figures of speech? If so, of what literal things are they the figures? What meaning do those weasels have? Are they merely a figure of the unbridled ferocity, now, of that *we* who speaks the poem, we "who are but weasels fighting in a hole"? This is just the question. What center, literal reference, or *logos*, in the sense of chief meaning, organizes all the heterogeneous material of the poem—esoteric, historical, Hellenic, Biblical, literary, traditional, and biographical—making it an integrated whole? What stands outside the dance and controls it, in the sense that all the emblems of the poem are emblems for that "what"? Is it Yeats himself, the mind of the poet, who names himself in the first person twice in the poem ("I am satisfied with that"; "What my laborious life imagined" [lines 61, 82])? Is it a collective consciousness, the *we* of Ireland or of Europe at this moment of history? Is it material, historical, objective "reality"? Is it some transcendent spiritual center or force? Could it be all four, or some vanishing point where they coincide?

The *now* of the poem seems firmly located in the year named in the title, and its *here* seems to be Ireland, the speaker the poet. "Now days are dragon-ridden, the nightmare / Rides upon sleep" (lines 25-26): "I am satisfied with that . . ." That *I*, however, appears only briefly in the poem. It emerges as the separate subjectivity of the poet who thinks of destroying even "the half-imagined, the half-written page" (line 83), the page, it may be, we are at that moment reading in printed copy. The "image" (line 80) of the wild swan leaping into the desolate heaven brings a savage rage to destroy what he has half-imagined, even the image that has generated the wildness and rage, in a self-dismantling torsion whereby the image is the means of taking "the solitary soul" to a place where that image is an impediment to achieving the act or state of the soul of which it is an image. The soul cannot get there without the image, but cannot get there with the image either.

This drama of the solitary soul emerges only briefly in the third part of the poem from a speaking consciousness that is consistently collective, a *we*. That *we* at first seems to be *we Irish*, but even by the third stanza of the first part must include the English, too, by implication all Europeans who have endured the great war. Gradually, as the poem progresses, the consciousness becomes an absolutely all-inclusive *we*, a *we* any man or woman joins when he or she reads the poem and looks back over the panorama of world history. The poem is spoken by no one in particular. It is uttered by a vast, visionary, all-inclusive voice within which the personal *I* of the poet only momentarily identifies itself.

Passages from Yeats's prose, for example, from the position-taking summary essay of 1937, "A General Introduction for My Work," have often been cited to support the claim that Yeats's poems should be thought of as the intense speech of Yeats himself in a particular time, place, and situation. "I tried," says Yeats, "to make the language of poetry coincide with that of passionate, normal speech. I wanted to write in whatever language comes most naturally when we soliloquise, as I do all day long, upon the events of our own lives or of any life where we can see ourselves for the moment."[6] One need only read on to the next page, however, to discover that this "passionate, normal speech" in poetry is in fact not private and particular to the poet. It is not personal at all but another voice, universal, anonymous, depersonalizing, a voice speaking through the poet. It is the voice of human experience generally, of literary and philosophical tradition. It is the voice ultimately of "nothing," of that no one and no place from which the desolate winds blow in "Nineteen Hundred and Nineteen": "If I wrote of personal love or sorrow in free verse, or, in any rhythm that left it unchanged, amid all its accidence [sic], I would be full of self-contempt because of my egotism and indiscretion, and foresee the boredom of my reader. I must choose a traditional stanza, even what I alter must seem traditional. I commit my emotion to shepherds, herdsman, camel-drivers, learned men, Milton's or Shelley's 'Platonist,' that tower Palmer drew. Talk to me of originality and I will turn on you with rage. I am a crowd, I am a lonely man, I am nothing" (p. 522).

The speaker of "Nineteen Hundred and Nineteen" is not the private person William Yeats, but Yeats as a part

[6] W. B. Yeats, *Essays and Introductions* (London: Macmillan Co., Ltd., 1961), p. 521.

of that *we* who is a crowd, a lonely man, nothing. The time and the place of the poem undergo a similar expansion. As the poem progresses the now of the poem reveals itself to be not the historical now of 1919 but a perpetual now in which the dance of history has always already occurred and yet is always occuring again, as the "Platonic year / Whirls out new right and wrong, / Whirls in the old instead." In the last section of the poem "Herodias' daughters have returned again" and Robert Artisson "lurches past" (lines 118, 126), brought back from the fourteenth century into the perpetual present of the poem. Within that present all things, and the loss or "vanishing" of all things, are contemporary because all things are "image."

The place of the poem undergoes a similar expansion. At first it is Ireland at a certain moment in history, but the place rapidly becomes a vast all-inclusive space of visionary image large enough to contain Greece, Phidias' famous ivories and all the golden grasshoppers and bees, that swan, Loie Fuller's Chinese dancers, those weasels, Robert Artisson and Lady Kyteler. It is big enough also to contain the vanishing of all these, according to the universal law of the poem: "Man is in love and loves what vanishes, / What more is there to say?" (lines 42-43). It seems as if that hole in which the weasels fight must be a black hole.

The voice of the poem is the voice of the poem. The time of the poem is the time of the poem. The place of the poem is the place of the poem. What person, time, and place are these? What is the topography of this space? What are its loci, the *lieux* within its milieu?

The shape of the poem, it is easy to see, is a round. The poem is a circular labyrinth in which the various elements of each of the six sections rotate around a center that is never named (except in figure), in a constant double process of substitution. This spatial design of a whirlwind or maze is reinforced throughout the poem in overt images: in the "circle of the moon" at the opening, in the circular whirling of the dancers and of the great year, in the word *round*, with its rhyme, *enwound*, which echoes through the poem ("But wearied running round and round in their courses," etc., lines 43, 49, 52, 116), in the labyrinth that is twice named (lines 70, 121), in the circular movement, in the last section, first of the apparitional horsemen and then of the dance of Herodias' daughters. The latter are seen by countrymen in Ireland in those miniature cyclones of dust that blow across the fields and roads.

This overt naming of a certain topography is reinforced first by the structure of each separate section. Each section is circular. A small set of elements is set in relation in each: Greek ivories, grasshoppers, and bees are placed against details from contemporary history in the first, dancers are set against the Platonic year in the second, and so on. Each section is a circular round of displacements in which each element or category of elements gives way to another set to which it is figuratively compared. The swan is set against a solitary soul in the third poem; the *we* of the poem against weasels fighting in the third; the great, the wise, the good, and the mockers are juxtaposed in the formally symmetrical mocking stanzas of the fifth section; the ghostly riders, Herodias' daughters, Robert Artisson and Lady Kyteler are put side by side in the sixth. The actual form of figurative equivalence among the elements in each section is uncertain since it depends in each case on their common relationship to the absent center. All one can see is that each new element rapidly replaces the one before. Their relation is as much antagonistic as harmonious. They are opposites living one another's death, dying one another's life, old right and wrong against new, weasels fighting in a hole. As the images interact in their whirling, they almost immediately consume one another and vanish. This occurs most strikingly in the fourth section, which exhausts its elements in four brief lines:

> We, who seven years ago,
> Talked of honour and of truth,

Shriek with pleasure if we show
The weasel's twist, the weasel's tooth.
(lines 89-92)

"Nineteen Hundred and Nineteen" is a discontinuous poem. It must constantly start again from nothing, the nothing of the blank space between each section, so rapidly do the elements in each section destroy one another and exhaust what can be said of them in their relationship. The reader feels in the poem a great urgency to say what can be said before that gong's "barbarous clangour" (line 58) announces the end of a given effort of articulation. The speaking or writing constantly destroys itself, and this necessitates a constant new beginning.

The second form of substitution in the double circular form of the poem is that whereby each new section replaces the one before. All the sections are related to one another as the elements of each separate section are related. It seems as if the poet is forced to reach again and again the point, a point that is also a moment, a moment-point, "at no spatial time," in which he must say "Man is in love and loves what vanishes, / What more is there to say?" The space of the poem collapses in a moment and in a point that can be given no spatial location, can be mapped by no image placed in its rightful home in a visible topography.

Does the poem continuously self-destruct, or is its scattering caused by some force outside itself? The new elements in each section rapidly take on the whirlwind or labyrinth shape that dominates the whole. They then vanish in their turn in a new mutually destroying agon, to be replaced by a new whirlwind structure in symmetrical juxtaposition. Or are they symmetrical? By what law or by what right, in the name of what common measure, may they be called "analogous"? Does the reader know that it is a "new whirlwind," or is it perhaps the same wind levelling whatever it encounters? This wind may be revealed only in its acts of destruction, since in itself it is invisible.

327

It constantly needs new material, so hungry is it for annihilation, and so insatiable, it may be, to display its power.
What is that wind? From what center or periphery, from
what cave of the winds or "center on the horizon," to use
Stevens' phrase, does it blow?

THE INTERPRETER, at this crucial point of the analysis, when
he has encountered a crossroads or a blind alley in the
labyrinth of the wind, may be helped by following the threads
of other, analogous, versions of the "same" structure—in
art, in poetry, in philosophy, and in psychoanalytic theory.
The topology of a whirlwind or of a whirlpool, a swirling
of elements around a missing or veiled center, is a common
one in all these forms of expression, though of course it is
not the only one. The abyssal structure of Stevens' "The
Rock" is not the same as this whirlwind form, nor is the
self-generating linear sequence of vision within vision of
Shelley's "The Triumph of Life" the same, nor are the
complex temporal reversals and substitutions of Hardy's
lyrics the same. Each of my chapters here explores a different spatial representation of temporality. Just as the relation between the successive sections of Yeats's "Nineteen
Hundred and Nineteen," across the blank spaces dividing
each from each, stays problematic as long as the central
ratio by which they may all be measured remains uniden-
tified, so the sense in which topographical structures by
different workers in different media may be said to be
analogous is even more problematic. The notion of analogy, whether this is thought of as a logical or as a figurative
relation, is precisely what is in question here. What is the
logos in the name of which we may say that *A* is like *B*, or
falls within the "same" conceptual category, or in the name
of which we may create one of those ratios Aristotle finds
at the base of one class of metaphors: *A* is to *B* as *C* is to
D, "wild swan" is to "the solitary soul" as "we," these days,
are to "weasels fighting in a hole," or as Lady Kyteler and
Robert Artisson are to—to what? The dance of Herodias'

daughters? The latter, however, is not quite the "same" relationship. Or is it? This is just the question. In any case, the whirlwind always turns on those little words *is* and *as*.

In the case of Stevens' "A Primitive Like an Orb," the invisible and unnamable power at the center of the labyrinth of words making up the poem is the rising or setting sun, "at the center on the horizon,"[7] but the rule of the poem is that the word *sun* may not appear. As the sun may not be looked in the eye without blinding the looker, so the non-presence, the core and ultimate reason behind all discourse, what Stevens here calls "the poem at the center of things," can only be named evasively, as something that "is and it / Is not and, therefore, is" (lines 13-14).

To give another example, one of the earliest great theoretical or metapsychological passages in Freud's work, in section 4 of *Studies on Hysteria*, presents a dazzling series of incompatible metaphorical models, each contradicting the one before, to express the fact that the "pathogenic nucleus" at the source of a given case of hysteria may not be reached or brought unchanged into the light of day, there to be seen and literally named. The work of the analyst is like that of the explorer of a labyrinth that has a center, but one that may by no procedures be reached as such. It has the nature of language or of signs and is the condition of the discourse of the hysteric, but it cannot be named directly, neither by the patient nor by the analyst.[8] A more famous passage in *The Interpretation of Dreams* names this unreachable and unidentifiable "black hole" at the center of the maze of psychic life with the figure of the mushroom mycelium:

> Even in the best interpreted dreams, there is often a place that must be left in the dark because in the process of interpreting, one notices a tangle [*ein Knäuel*] of dream-

[7] Wallace Stevens, "A Primitive Like an Orb," line 87, *The Collected Poems* (New York: Alfred A. Knopf, Inc., 1954), p. 443; henceforth CPSt.

[8] See Freud, *Works*, st. ed., II, pp. 288-291.

thoughts arising, which resists unravelling but has also made no further contributions [*keine weiteren Beiträge*] to the dream-content. This is the dream's navel, the place where it straddles the unknown [*dem Unerkannten aufsitzt*]. The dream-thoughts, to which interpretation leads one, are necessarily interminable [*ohne Abschluß*] and branch out on all sides into the netlike entanglement [*in die netzartige Verstrickung*] of our world of thought. Out of one of the denser places of this meshwork [*Geflechts*], the dream-wish rises like a mushroom out its mycelium.[9]

This dark place, or a "similar" one at the center of his own thought, Friedrich Nietzsche, in "On Truth and Lies in a Nonmoral Sense," calls "the mysterious X [*das rätselhafte X*]."[10] Perception is already a metaphor of this *X*. Language is therefore a metaphor of a metaphor, twice displaced. If language, in Nietzsche's celebrated formulation here, is "a movable host of metaphors, metonymies, and anthropomorphisms" (Eng. 84; Ger. 314), these are not substitutes for literal names that could be given. All are, strictly speaking, catachreses, figures drawn from some other realm and transferred as the improper names for what has no proper name in any language. If lies are immoral because the truth should be given whenever possible, according to a categorical imperative, the "lies" of which Nietzsche speaks in this essay are "nonmoral" (*außermoralischen*) because it would

[9] Std. ed., v, p. 525: German: *Gesammelte Werke*, II-III (London: Imago Publishing Co., Ltd., 1952), p. 530. See Samuel Weber's discussion of this passage and of the misleading aspects of Strachey's translation in "Remarks on Freud's *Witz*," *Glyph* I (1977), 1-27, esp. 8ff. I have followed Weber's revision of Strachey's translation to bring it closer to Freud's German. Weber's analysis of the passage about the mushroom mycelium is also to be found as "The Meaning of the Thallus," *The Legend of Freud* (Minneapolis: University of Minnesota Press, 1982), pp. 75-78.

[10] "On Truth and Lies in a Nonmoral Sense," *Philosophy and Truth: Selections from Nietzsche's Notebooks of the Early 1870's*, trans. Daniel Breazeale (Atlantic Highlands, New Jersey: Humanities Press, Inc., 1979), p. 84. For the German see Friedrich Nietzsche, "*Über Wahrheit und Lüge im Außermoralischen Sinn*," *Werke in Drei Bänden*, ed. Karl Schlechta, III (Munich: Carl Hanser Verlag, 1966), p. 314.

not be possible for anyone to give the true formulations of which they are the figurative deformations. How can it be immoral to tell a lie when there is no possibility of telling the truth?

The image of the labyrinth does not appear as such in Nietzsche's essay. Its place is taken by the figures of the beehive, the columbarium, the stratified pyramid, the spider web, the stately and apparently impregnable fortress, an astrological map of the heavens, and the design made in sand in response to musical vibrations. These reticulated patterns are figures for the edifices of thought philosophers and other conceptual thinkers make to "bar the foul storm out." At the same time they are figures for artistic constructions, motivated by feeling, in musical tones, in paint, or in poetic words. Art and philosophy at first seem rigorously opposed in Nietzsche's argument, but in the end they are seen as coming to the same thing, or to different versions of the same thing. However solid any one of these architectural constructions may appear, each is no more than a frail spider web over a rushing stream. Both artist and philosopher are, in Nietzsche's famous formulation, "as if hanging in dreams on the back of a tiger [*gleichsam auf dem Rücken eines Tigers in Träumen hängend*]" (Eng. 80; Ger. 311).

In place of a full exploration of these analogous examples of the strange maze this chapter attempts to map, the maze whose center is "only . . . an X which remains inaccessible and indefinable for us [*nur ein für uns unzugängliches und undefinierbares* X]" (Eng. 83; Ger. 313), I limit myself to a somewhat more complete discussion of a single case. This is a graphic rather than verbal representation of the structure I claim is common to all these examples, the design of the labyrinth without attainable or representable center.

Paul Klee's *Tanzspiel der Rotröcke* [Danceplay of the Red Skirts] (1924)[11] seems almost like a negative version of Stevens' "A Primitive Like an Orb." Klee's painting presents

[11] The painting is oil and paper on panel, 35 x 44 cm. It is in a private collection in Zollikon, Switzerland.

a spiral, whirlpool, or labyrinth design with a dark core rather than a bright one. What better representation in graphic form of the topographical structure that is my topic here than a dark orb where vision fails, as eyesight is blinded when it looks directly at the sun? Is that central region in the painting a hollow tunnel or is it a solid object, absorbing all the light, a kind of black hole? What can be seen, the red skirts, seems to have come from the dark sun or to be returning to it, so that the center is clearly hot enough and bright enough, dark with excessive bright. The dark orb at the center of the painting can be thought of as made of

Paul Klee, *Tanzspiel der Rotröcke*, 1924.119. Private collection. (©1984 COSMOPRESS, Genève & ADAGP, Paris)

the superimposition of all the colors distributed across the surface of the painting: the browns, grays, greens, and yellows, as well as the reds.

The word *Tanzspiel* in the title suggests both dance and play, the latter in the sense of interplay or fluctuation (as one says, "there is play in this wheel"), as well as in the sense of game. Klee's painting is literally spatial, as no poem can be, except in the sense that the words are distributed spatially on the page. Nevertheless the topography of this painting is in its own way as enigmatic as that of "Nineteen Hundred and Nineteen." The figures in Klee's painting are clearly signs of some sort, not representations of some ballet that might be photographed. As enigmatic signs they must be interrogated. When they are interrogated they reveal themselves to create, in their play, there on the surface of the painting, a space that is as illogical, as disoriented, as unchartable, as the space of any poem.

One irreducible difference between any poem and any painting is that a painting is after all spatial. There it is, all at once, on the canvas, however complex the patterned echoes from one part of the painting to another may be. The basic resource of poetry, on the other hand, is repetition of the same structure with different materials along a temporal axis, as in "Nineteen Hundred and Nineteen." Klee presents only one version of his whirlpool pattern in this painting. He employs as elements only the repeated and fragmented doll-figure in the red skirt plus the architectural elements, perhaps real buildings, perhaps a stage set for a ballet: walls, roof, windows, and doors swirling with the skirts. What corresponds, in Klee's use of his medium, to the chainlike series of images in apposition in Stevens' "A Primitive Like an Orb," or to the sequence of sections, each developing its own set of figurative elements, in Yeats's poem, is of course the long sequence of Klee's paintings. Many, though not all, of these have the same topographical arrangement as *Tanzspiel der Rotröcke*. Each such painting develops with different elements the same

333

enigma of the relation of visible and yet peripheral hieroglyphic figures, halfway between writing and representational mimesis, to an invisible center.

The puzzle, in Klee, lies also sometimes in the relation
between the purely graphic elements in the painting and
Klee's witty and poetic title for it. These titles often name
the paintings only by figurative displacement. At any rate,
since they are language, they are open to the kind of interpretation appropriate for language rather than for graphic
figures. The title of *Tanzspiel der Rotröcke*, for example, not
only contains the doubling play between dance and play in
Tanzspiel. It also suggests that it is not the women who are
dancing but the red skirts. It is either as though there were
some compulsion in the skirts themselves that whirls them
around without human intent, or as though some dragon
of air had fallen among the skirts and whirled them and
their wearers around on its own furious path, to put it in
terms drawn from Yeats's "Nineteen Hundred and Nineteen."

The problems for interpretation in Klee's painting lie in
this either/or and in related undecidable alternatives. Do
the skirts impel themselves to dance or are they seized by
the rotating force that spirals out from the center? Are the
dancers, whole and fragmentary, along with the bits and
pieces of buildings or scenery, coming out of the central
obscurity, or are they going into it? Are they dispersing
centrifugally and taking form as they get further from the
formless center, or are they being sucked by centripetal
force into the maelstrom? Are they being broken and dismembered more and more as they reach nearer to the
center, until at last they vanish altogether in that dark core
where all colors and shapes are combined? Are there in
fact a multitude of red skirts, as the plural in the title suggests, or is there only one dancer shown simultaneously at
different times and at different loci on the spiral leading
toward and away from the center? Even if the skirts are
plural, they are clearly representations of the same process

at different stages. All the skirts are subject to the same forces. They are signs of that invisible energy from which they all come or to which they all return. This energy creates them or they create it, since the center draws its meaning from the peripheral signs for it. At the same time those signs, the indentifiable shapes of dancers in red skirts, wholes or parts, draw their meaning from the central dark primitive core of which they are the signs. They create and reveal it at once, make it and are made by it, in an oscillation of meaning like that in Stevens' "A Primitive Like an Orb."

However the critic chooses to interpret the dynamic topology of Klee's painting, it is clear that he must in one way or another recognize that its meaning is generated by the alogical correspondence between the red-skirted figures and the central orb around which they dance. Since that orb cannot be represented visually except in figures that both falsify it and yet are the only kind of representation it can have, it may be said that Klee's painting is a visual representation of a catachresis. It presents signs that are neither figurative nor literal. They refer by displacement to something that could not be represented literally and so do not substitute for a literal picture that just does not happen to have been given.

This strange relation between visible articulated form and formless all-absorbing orb is reinforced by the way the distinctness of the red-skirted figures fades again as they get too far away from the center, just as they seem to be fragmented by proximity to it. Examples of this are the yellow patch or blob in the upper right-hand corner of the painting and the large wispy tatters of upside-down red skirt in the upper left-hand corner. The most distinct figure is the upright one with arms akimbo and right knee at a jaunty angle near the center of the painting. It seems as if the red skirts achieve fullest distinction, come briefly into focus, so to speak, when they are exactly the right distance from the source, that patron of origins, the egg-shaped or helmet-shaped blurred brown patch at the center, with one quadrant obscured. This patch both generates the skirts and is the mortal enemy of their appearance in visible, sharp-edged form. The red skirts then disperse and disappear again when they get too far from the center that both makes and unmakes them and of which they are the only perceptible signs. Or, if they are moving toward the center, they come into focus briefly, coagulate, crystallize, or condense out of cosmic debris when they move into just the right distance from that center. They then disappear again in an instant when they cross the final threshold and plunge into the black hole, having briefly, in transit, manifested indirectly its existence. Klee's *Tanzspiel der Rotröcke*, in whichever way it is read, is a splendid example of the strange topographical structure I am mapping here.

These brief detours through maze-like displacements in Stevens, in Klee, in Freud, and in Nietzsche have left still hanging unanswered the questions I posed about Yeats's "Nineteen Hundred and Nineteen." The detours were in search of answers to the questions: What is that destructive wind that blows through Yeats's poem, levelling everything, even, repeatedly, the constructions of the poem itself? From what cave of the winds does it blow? Is that cave at the center or at the periphery, at the center on the horizon? Violence is the human and transhuman law. That law breaks all political codes of law to fragments, as those ivories, golden grasshoppers and bees, images of the gods, symbols of longevity and patiently constructed work, are turned into objects for sale or broken into bits. If no work of hand or intellect can stand, what then should man do?

The detours have identified a certain topographical pattern. This pattern is duplicated, always with a difference, from poem to poem and within each of the poems by Yeats and Stevens. It appears also in Klee, in Nietzsche, and in Freud. The difference is that different materials, in each case, are brought into proximity with an unnamable center. The various topologies are also analogies for one another. To say that this topographical structure is duplicated from text to text or from medium to medium must be taken in a special sense, "anasemically," as Jacques Derrida or Nicholas Abraham would say, that is, against the grain of the usual meaning of *analogy*.[12] That word traditionally suggests a circumferential similarity in wording between diverse verbal elements. This similarity is justified by the common relation of the elements to a presiding central word or *logos*—father, sun king, patron of analogies. This center is the guarantee of the sibling kinship of what is on the periphery. Do they not all have the same father? In the spatial design mapped in various examples here there is no patronizing king, no sun, at best a dark sun that is also an endless tunnel. The design is a topology without any *logos* at the center. This means that the relation of analogy among peripheral elements or between superimposed versions of the "same" design must be redefined. The relation is an ana-analogy of elements that do not really belong together in the same space. The most heterogeneous elements can be brought together in the same place, as they conspicuously are in Yeats's poem. Their relation to one another is governed not by their reference to a common *logos* but by the fact that they are all catachreses for an unknown X around which they circle. The X is something that both makes them emblems and at the same time undermines their referential validity. It also separates them from one another across fissures that do not allow the resonances of analogy in the traditional metaphysical sense of that term. This means that the spatial model breaks down. This breaking down reveals the model to be the indispensable means of thinking about the structure in question, but indispensable only if it is carried to the point where it

[12] See Nicholas Abraham, "*L'écorce et le noyau,*" *Critique* xxiv, 249 (February 1968), 162-181. And see Derrida's discussion of Abraham's use of this word in "*Fors,*" prefatory essay to Nicholas Abraham and Maria Torok, *Cryptonymie: Le Verbier de l'Homme aux Loups* (Paris: Éditions Aubier Flammarion, 1976), pp. 7-82, esp. p. 11. The English translation by Barbara Johnson of this essay is cited in note 1 above.

no longer functions and must be dispensed with. Why must we represent to ourselves in spatial terms what is not spatial but verbal and temporal? Why must this topographical structure always fail in the encounter with something that cannot be spatially located, that has no *topos* and no proper name?

This *it* is at a center that is no center but is missing there, and at the horizon but missing there, too. It is dispersed everywhere, not just outside, beyond the last wall, nor inside, at some inner core, like a hidden tomb or a corpse in a pyramid. Nor is this *it* in a transcendent realm. For Yeats as for Stevens, "the light / Of it is not a light apart, up-hill."[13] Yeats chooses firmly for the whirlpool, the gyre of immanent powers as against the waterfall of Platonic or Neoplatonic emanations dropping from the One in regular gradations. *It* is neither word, nor force, nor thing, nor subjective energy, nor spiritual entity, but all those "things" at once in a confusion that confounds the clear distinctions and binary oppositions between subject and object, between word and thing, between literal and figurative language, between this world and a supernal one, which are necessary to clear thought, whether in poetry, in philosophy, or in literary criticism. If the *it* is the cave of the wind that blows through the labyrinth of Yeats's poem, the thinking or the linguistic structures that lead to the intuition of this *it* must not be confused with any sort of trancendentalism, Platonic or otherwise, any thinking governed by the presence of presences, occult or otherwise, nor with a certain false Heideggerianism of the immanence of Being, nor with a nihilism of the abyss, the idea that nothing exists at the base but empty and factitious structures of signs. If the *it* is neither thought, nor thing, nor spirit, nor word, it is not nothing either. In the encounter with this *it*, the validity of the notion of the linguistic moment reaches its limit and dissolves before something that is not language, though it

[13] Stevens, "A Primitive Like an Orb," lines 47-48, CPSt, p. 441.

both motivates and disrupts language. This "something" nevertheless can only be approached through that language it disrupts when the final step across the threshold, the step that can never quite be taken, begins to be taken.

What I am calling the linguistic moment is the moment when a poem, or indeed any text, turns back on itself and puts its own medium in question, so that there is a momentum in the poem toward interrogating signs as such. This momentum may make a casual moment spread out to take up all the time of the poem, or to suspend time in a ceaseless hovering. This moment, when language is foregrounded, is indispensable to the putting in question of the presupposed structures of logocentric metaphysics: beginning, middle, end, organic unity, and underlying extralinguistic ground—whether that ground in a given case is called being, consciousness, will, self, physical object, absolute spirit, presence, or whatever. In the end, however, having performed this deconstructive function, the linguistic moment reaches the term of its usefulness as a term or as an endpoint. Beyond this boundary, though encountered only through words, the linguistic moment dissolves before the *it*. The unknown X is beyond language, though it is what all language "names," in the gap which may not be closed between all words and any fixed identifiable referent, subjective, objective, natural, or supernatural. This *it* is what undermines all thinking, performing, and constructing, in art, poetry, science, politics, or philosophy, all the monuments made by the great, the wise, the good, and the mockers of all those in Yeats's poem. Because of the *it* all these monuments are inhabited from the beginning by the leveling wind. They are woven or molded of wind, for "A man in his own secret meditation / Is lost amid the labyrinth that he has made / In art or politics," and that labyrinth is "the labyrinth of the wind."

I have spoken of an intuition through language of what is beyond language but on which language rests, like a spider web on a roaring river or like a man asleep on the back of a tiger. In what way, exactly, is this "intuition" (this word too must be read here against the grain of its ususal sense) expressed in the language of Yeats's "Nineteen Hundred and Nineteen"? The poem as a whole is not only written for the sake of its final section but rather leads up to its final section or reaches its climax in the final section. This section attains closest to the *it* from which the levelling wind blows. With a discussion of that section I shall conclude this chapter.

First a word should be said about the presence in Yeats's poem of the image of the sun that is the "central" figure in Stevens' "A Primitive Like an Orb." The sun is the basis of the "photological" tradition in Western thought from Plato on, for example, at the end of Book VI and the beginning of Book VII of the *Republic*. If the labyrinthine wind is the pervasive emblem in Yeats's poem, the sun is also twice mentioned, in ways that implicitly equate the levelling wind with the levelling sun. "Nineteen Hundred and Nineteen" is heliocentric too, as Yeats's work as a whole often is, as well as "centered" on that cavern from which the wind blows. It is as if the sun and the wind source were two foci of an ellipse, like one another and yet different. Around these foci the elements of the poem whirl like planets in their orbits.

If the wind levels all, there is something a little ominous, in spite of its benign action, about the way the sun works in the second stanza of the first section of the poem. "We too had many pretty toys when young," says the poet, among them "habits that made old wrong / Melt down as it were wax in the sun's rays." If the strong sun can so easily melt old wrong, might it not, almost by accident as it were, in its ubiquitious force, also melt old or new right, as the Platonic Year, a little later in the poem, with absolute indifference, "Whirls out new right and wrong, / Whirls in the old instead." The wax is implicit in that image of the golden bees, emblem in the opening stanza of the poem of the constructive power of Greek culture. What the bees in their architectural genius make, they make of wax, and Yeats has scarcely mentioned the bees before he reminds the reader in a seemingly casual simile of the vulnerability of wax to the sun's rays.

The second mention of the sun comes in the second stanza of the fifth section, the mocking poem. There the sun has its full function as the blinding center that cannot be looked at directly, or can be looked at directly only by blinded eyes. These eyes have been blinded, like those of Oedipus, by excess wisdom and gape open now like empty mouths, or like wounds. Though the sun cannot be looked at, all the calendars of seasonal and annual changes, all that can be known and studied, rotates around that dazzling invisible center:

> Come let us mock at the wise;
> With all those calendars whereon
> They fixed old aching eyes,
> They never saw how seasons run,
> And now but gape at the sun.
> (lines 98-102)

In the last section of the poem three images follow one another, each replacing the last when that last has hardly been presented, in the most rapid and most violent sequence of all. The sequence leads to the final violence of the last two lines: "To whom the love-lorn Lady Kyteler brought / Bronzed peacock feathers, red combs of her cocks" (lines 129-130), after which the poem, which has started and stopped and started again throughout, abruptly stops for good. The first image, of the apparitional horsemen, is replaced by that of the dance of Herodias' daughters, and that in turn by the insolent fiend, Robert Artisson, and the love-lorn Lady Kyteler. "I have assumed in this sixth poem," Yeats writes of the first image in his notes on the poem, "that these horsemen, now that the times worsen, give way to worse" (VPY, 433): "But wearied running round and round in their courses / All break and vanish, and evil

341

gathers head" (lines 116-117). What this "evil" is, the reader knows, both from earlier passages in this poem and from Yeats's interpretation of our times elsewhere. Evil is the increase in violence and unreason threatening all orders of law and art, but preparing, it may be, a new annunciation, a reversal of the gyres whirling out new right and wrong, whirling in the old instead. As the poem moves from section to section and from image to image, the reader moves also closer and closer to the center of the labyrinth, whirlpool, or circling gyres. The final three images, in the last section, whirl the fastest and are closest to the absolute violence of the center, that unnamed crossroads where Lady Kyteler makes sacrifice to her incubus. That center is also at the periphery. According to Yeats's image of the turning, intersecting gyres, the approach toward the center on one gyre is accompanied by the furthest centrifugal receding out to the edge on the other, as "Things fall apart; the center cannot hold" (VPY, 402).

None of the three final images is interpreted within the poem. Each is only presented, "concretely described." Each is a vehicle with a missing tenor. The three images are figures, but there are no named or namable literals that they replace. In this they are what Yeats calls "emblems" and what traditional rhetoric calls "catachreses." They hang, hover, or turn in the void as signs of what cannot be signified directly. Their interpretation therefore cannot be, as with ordinary figurative images, by way of the relation of the figurative vehicle to the literal tenor it replaces. The interpretation must be lateral, around the chambers or corridors of the labyrinth. This displacement from figure to figure is allegorical in the sense in which Walter Benjamin or Paul de Man use the term.[14] The meaning of a Yeatsian

[14] See Walter Benjamin, *"Allegorie und Trauerspiel," Ursprung des deutschen Trauerspiels* (Frankfurt am Main: Suhrkamp Verlag, 1969), pp. 174-268; Eng. trans. by John Osborne, "Allegory and Trauerspiel," *The Origin of German Tragic Drama* (London, NLB, 1977), pp. 159-235; Paul de Man, "Allegory and Symbol," in "The Rhetoric of Temporality," *Interpretation:*

emblem can be identified not in relation to what the emblem signifies, in a sign-thing structure (that "thing" remains absent and without a literal name), but in relation to other emblems, whether in the same poem or in other texts in the tradition, in a sign-sign relation. This relation is characterized by the temporal gap between the two emblems and by their heterogeneity in relation to one another. They cannot be assimilated to some common essence or archetype. Distance and unlikeness separate emblem from emblem. Across that gulf the interpreter must leap. Moreover, the critic is also bound by the law that prohibits the poem from naming the *it* directly. His language can have at best the same status of perpetual displacement as the language of the poet. The critic can only move in his turn from emblem to emblem around the periphery, troping one in terms of the other. The critic's language may be defined as the continuous translation of what cannot be by any means ever given, by poet or critic, in the original language. The emblematic or allegorical method, for both poet and critic, is always the translation of what is already a translation rather than ever being the translation of an original. There is no original language for the *it*.

The final three images of "Nineteen Hundred and Nineteen" are a splendid example of Yeats's emblematic strategy and of the implicit invocation of an appropriate method for the interpretation of such emblems. The first image is that of the ghostly horsemen, "ancient inhabitants of the country," or "fallen angels" seen by Irish country people, according to Yeats's note (VPY, 433). This image seems to make a reference back to the real horsemen and soldiers of the Black and Tan atrocities in section 1. The reader may at first mistakenly think the "violence upon the roads:

Theory and Practice, ed. Charles S. Singleton (Baltimore: The Johns Hopkins Press, 1969), pp. 173-191. See also my "The Two Allegories," *Allegory, Myth, and Symbol*, ed. Morton W. Bloomfield, *Harvard English Studies* 9 (Cambridge, Mass.; London: Harvard University Press, 1981), pp. 355-370.

violence of horses" is the same as that historical violence. In fact this image marks the transition to the overtly supernatural emblems of the final section. These are no earthly horsemen and riders. Such emblems are made of the transfiguration of natural objects, a certain way of seeing them as signs, as the countrymen see in those miniature whirling dust storms the dance of Herodias' daughters or the hosting of the Sidhe. "They [the Sidhe] journey in whirling winds,". wrote Yeats in a note to "The Hosting of the Sidhe," "the winds that were called the dance of the daughters of Herodias in the Middle Ages, Herodias doubtless taking the place of some old goddess" (VPY, 800).

The ultimate key to unlock the farthest door before the final cryptic barrier of silence protecting the *it* within the labyrinth of the wind is the allegorical relation between the two final images. Both of these combine the erotic and the supernatural in a way characteristic of Yeats. The two images, however, are related in crisscross or chiasmus. From one image to the next the sexes or their relations change place, and there is also a displacement from center to periphery of the perpetrator of violence.

The *it* is given the allegorical name first of the absent and unattainable center of the dusty labyrinth of the wind made by the dance of Herodias' blind daughters:

> Herodias' daughters have returned again,
> A sudden blast of dusty wind and after
> Thunder of feet, tumult of images,
> Their purpose in the labyrinth of the wind;
> And should some crazy hand dare touch a daughter
> All turn with amorous cries, or angry cries,
> According to the wind, for all are blind.
>
> (lines 118-124)

Here the female comes from the center and the male is captivated by her, drawn fatally into the maelstrom. Herodias' daughters, of whom Salomé of course is one, are themselves mutilated, blinded as the old wise men who gape at the sun are blind. The context here is Yeats's own work in his late plays, *A Full Moon in March, The King of the Great Clock Tower,* and *The Death of Cuchulain,* and in addition his sources for the figure of this dance: the Bible, Heine, Oscar Wilde's *Salomé,* and Arthur Symons' poem, "The Dance of the Daughters of Herodias."[15] Although these daughters are mutilated, they are for Yeats also emblems of a mutilating power in women, a power to unman and decapitate the men who love them as in the beheading of John the Baptist. Only a crazy hand would dare touch one. The daughters are emblems of the absence of any "head" meaning, underlying support for the meaning of all other signs. This meaning does not exist as something that can ever be named directly or confronted directly. It can only be named or confronted as an absence, like a missing head or a missing phallus. Herodias' daughters are, in Yeats's precise phrase, a "tumult of images," a storm of figures without ascertainable polar center.

This erotic relation is reversed in the final emblem. Now the male, Robert Artisson, comes from the center, and the enamored female, Lady Kyteler, is at the edge, drawn by infatuation toward that center. The mutilation or dismembering is now performed by the mortal woman in homage to her supernatural incubus, not by supernatural woman on mortal man. Lady Kyteler, though mortal, was a witch. She was as fatal to men as any of Herodias' daughters, having, it is supposed, killed by poison or enchantment four husbands, one after the other. Her own doom came in her submission to Robert Artisson, "an evil spirit," according to Yeats's note, "much run after in Kilkenny at the start of the fourteenth century" (VPY, 433). Lady Kyteler is supposed to have "had carnal knowledge" of Artisson. This demon, "named Son of Art, or Robin son of Art," was attracted into the natural world from his dwelling place in the supernatural by sacrifices made at crossroads, tradi-

---

[15] See Yeats's "Commentary on 'The Great Clock Tower,' " (VPY, 840).

345

tionally associated with ghosts, witches, and demons. Cross-roads are in folklore at the borderland between the canny and the uncanny. Here, that crossroad, or those crossroads, since they are a multiple and ubiquitous focus, may be taken as the emblem of the absent center itself. It or they are never named in Yeats's poem, only in his sources. Dame Alice and her "band of heretical sorcerers," these sources say, "offered in sacrifice to demons living animals, which they dismembered, and then distributed at cross-roads to a certain evil spirit of low rank, named the Son of Art."[16] In Yeats's poem Lady Kyteler dismembers peacocks, symbol for Yeats of annunciation ("the cry of Juno's peacock"), and cocks, offering to her insolent fiend bronzed peacock feathers starred or eyed, and red combs of her cock, images of unmanning once more, like the blindness of the gaping old men.

This act of dismembering causes Robert Artisson to manifest himself as the next emblem when Herodias' daughters vanish. Artisson is the version here of that "rough beast" in "The Second Coming" who "slouches towards Bethlehem to be born" (VPY, 402), or of that "brazen winged beast" of "laughing, ecstatic destruction" Yeats came to see "as always at my left side just out of the range of the sight":[17]

> But now wind drops, dust settles; thereupon
> There lurches past, his great eyes without thought
> Under the shadow of stupid straw-pale locks,
> That insolent fiend Robert Artisson
> To whom the love-lorn Lady Kyteler brought
> Bronzed peacock feathers, red combs of her cocks.
> (lines 125–130)

The beheading, mutilation, or castration is performed first by supernatural women on mortal men, then by a

[16] Jeffares, *Commentary*, p. 281.
[17] "Introduction to *The Resurrection*," from *Wheels and Butterflies, Explorations* (New York: Macmillan Publishing Co., Inc., 1962), p. 393.

mortal woman in homage to her supernatural lover. This reversible act of violence occurs across the barrier between the sexes. This is also the barrier between natural and supernatural, and between system, order, beauty, reason, on the one hand, and disorder, the foul storm, on the other. The reversal from Herodias' daughters to Lady Kyteler shows that the foul storm, which seems to blow from outside the human and natural world, is always already inside, intimate to man and to all his constructions, intrinsic to everything he has made.

"Nineteen Hundred and Nineteen" is a poem that systematically dismantles itself as system. It lacks the closed order of "organic unity." It keeps stopping and starting again and cannot be rationally integrated by interpretation. Also, it is about the ruination of system or order. It is about the way the "foul storm" cannot be barred out because it always gets incorporated into any system of art, of love, of politics, law, or philosophy and makes that system self-destruct, as "Nineteen Hundred and Nineteen" continually destroys itself.

This gives the answer to the questions I proposed at the beginning: "Why is it no work can last?" and "What should man do when he sees no monument of art or intellect can stand?" No work can last because any work is inhabited, undermined, by the *it* which destroys it. What one should do is some action like Yeats's in writing the poem. Destroying the half-imagined, the half-written page would accomplish nothing. To write a poem is a constructive act that at the same time participates in the destruction, as does Lady Kyteler in offering bronzed peacock feathers, red combs of her cocks. Such an act of mutilation as the poem performs does not end all things, but it approaches as close as possible to that cave of the winds by incorporating the wind's power into the labyrinth of the poem, in the words on the page. Things are preserved only in their destruction, by being turned into emblems, where they are in the closest proximity of signifying to the wind that destroys them. This means, for all the elements that enter into the poem—human, natural, and supernatural—being cut up and cut off from one another and from their natural contexts. Each is destroyed and renewed by being made into a sign that stands for that which there is no standing and no standing for.

Williams

In memory of my mother

C'est donc aussi en luttant pour la présence
(en acceptant de se faire naïvement le
mémorial de quelque chose qui s'y présente)
que le langage la détruit perfidement. Cela
arrive par l'écriture.

Maurice Blanchot, *Le pas au-delà*

William Carlos Williams' poetry scarcely seems to offer any
handles to interpretation.[1] The critic at first hardly knows
what to say of it, so transparent is it in meaning, so lacking
in conceptual words or in anything like the self-commen-
tary characteristic, for example, of Wallace Stevens' poetry.
In Williams' poems the mimesis is straightforwardly performed, not conceptualized. To put this another way, there
seems at first to be no form of the linguistic moment in
Williams. The reader, it may be, is reduced to saying how
beautiful a poem by Williams is, how admirably delicate its
prosody. As in certain traditions of Chinese literary criticism, the critic is reduced to saying something like "Wow!"
On the other hand, readers habituated to romantic or symbolist poetry may feel Williams' work fails to provide them
with the qualities they expect. Like a late eighteenth-century reader encountering the *Lyrical Ballads*, many present-
day readers of Williams "will look round for poetry, and
will be induced to inquire by what species of courtesy these

[1] The early pages of this chapter are a revision of the "Preface," pp. 1-
14, by J. Hillis Miller, from the book WILLIAM CARLOS WILLIAMS:
A COLLECTION OF CRITICAL ESSAYS, ed. J. Hillis Miller, © 1966
by Prentice-Hall, Inc. Published by Prentice-Hall, Inc., Englewood Cliffs,
NJ 07632.

attempts can be permitted to assume that title."[2] Take for example "Young Sycamore," from Williams' *Collected Poems 1934*:

Young Sycamore

I must tell you
this young tree
whose round and firm trunk
between the wet

pavement and the gutter
(where water
is trickling) rises
bodily

into the air with
one undulant
thrust half its height—
and then

dividing and waning
sending out
young branches on
all sides—

hung with cocoons
it thins
till nothing is left of it
but two

eccentric knotted
twigs
bending forward
hornlike at the top[3]

---

[2] Wordsworth's phrasing, in the "Preface" to *Lyrical Ballads, Poetical Works*, ed. E. de Selincourt, II (London: Oxford University Press, 1952), p. 386. The epigraph for this chapter is from Maurice Blanchot, *Le pas au-delà* (Paris: Gallimard, 1973), p. 47.

[3] William Carlos Williams, *The Collected Earlier Poems* (New York: New Directions, 1951), p. 332; henceforth CEP. The following books by Williams are also cited in this chapter. Each citation is followed by the acronym

The words of this poem sit there on the page (or hang in the air if it is read out loud) somewhat enigmatically. Word follows word with a curious particularity and detachment, as if each word had been at least partially separated from both its immediately surrounding grammatical

used, and the page numbers in parentheses. For *Imaginations,* all citations, unless otherwise noted, are from the full text of *Spring and All,* as reprinted there. KH is *Kora in Hell* as reprinted in *Imaginations. Poems* (Rutherford, NJ: privately printed, 1909): P [1909]; *In the American Grain* (New York: New Directions, 1956): IAG; *The Autobiography of William Carlos Williams* (New York: Random House, 1951): A; *Selected Essays* (New York: Random House, 1954): SE; *Selected Letters,* ed. John C. Thirlwall (New York: McDowell, Obolensky, 1957): SL; *I Wanted to Write a Poem: The Autobiography of the Works of a Poet,* reported and edited by Edith Heal (Boston: Beacon Press, 1958): IWWP; *Many Loves and Other Plays* (New York: New Directions, 1961): ML; *Pictures from Brueghel and Other Poems* (New York: New Directions, 1962): PB; *The Collected Later Poems* (New York: New Directions, 1963): CLP; *Paterson* (New York: New Directions, 1963): P; *Imaginations,* ed. Webster Schott (New York: New Directions, 1970): I. For an authoritive recent critical biography of Williams, see Paul Mariani, *William Carlos Williams: A New World Naked* (New York: McGraw-Hill Book Company, 1981). See also Thomas R. Whitaker, *Williams* (New York: Twayne, 1968); Bram Djikstra, *The Hieroglyphics of a New Speech: Cubism, Stieglitz, and the Early Poetry of William Carlos Williams* (Princeton: Princeton University Press, 1969); Sherman Paul, "A Sketchbook of the Artist in his 34th Year," *The Shaken Realist: Essays in Modern Literature in Honor of Frederick J. Hoffman,* ed. Melvin J. Friedman and John B. Vickery (Baton Rouge: Louisiana State University Press, 1970), pp. 21-44; Linda W. Wagner, "*Spring and All:* The Unity of Design," *Tennessee Studies in Literature* xv (1970), 61-73; James Breslin, *William Carlos Williams: An American Artist* (New York: Oxford University Press, 1970); Joseph N. Riddell, *The Inverted Bell: Modernism and the Counter-poetics of William Carlos Williams* (Baton Rouge: Louisiana State University Press, 1974); Rod Townley, *The Early Poetry of William Carlos Williams* (Ithaca: Cornell University Press, 1975); Hugh Kenner, *A Homemade World: American Modernist Writers* (New York: Alfred A. Knopf, 1975), esp. pp. 54-56, 57-67, 85-90, 102-104; David Jauss, "The Decent, the Dance, and the Wheel: The Aesthetic Theory of William Carlos Williams' *Kora in Hell,*" *Boston University Journal* xxv, 1 (1977), 37-42; Thomas P. Joswick, "Beginning with Loss: The Poetics of William Carlos Williams' *Kora in Hell: Improvisations,*" *Texas Studies in Literature and Language* xix, 1 (Spring 1977) 98-118; Gerald L. Bruns, "De Improvisatione," *The Iowa Review* ix, 3 (Summer 1978), 66-78; Richard J. Morgan, "Chaos and Order: The Cycle of Life and Art in Williams' *Spring and All,*" *Interpretations* xi (1979), 35-51; Henry M. Sayre, and syntactical connections and from the larger context of its place in the English lexicon. Each is proffered for a power to say something it brings in itself, something slightly alien and coercive that belongs intrinsically to that word, as a sign on the page, or in oral utterance as an acoustic shape. This power to say something does not seem to be invested in the word by its speaker or writer, or by a personified transcendent power, "God," or by its referent, since this power belongs as much to articles, to prepositions, to those anonymous "shifters," the pronouns, and to auxiliaries or parts of the verb *to be* as to adjectives, adverbs, or nouns. Each word, as Williams says, must be separated from others "in such a way that it will remain scrupulously itself, clean perfect, unnicked beside other words in parade" (SE, 128-129).

The identification of this curious separate intrinsic energy in words is accomplished by the placing of the words on the page, by rhythmical devices that lead the reader to pronounce the words one by one with almost separate and equal emphasis, the little, usually unnoticed words as much as the verbs, adjectives, and nouns, and by a spareness or purity in the grammar, along with an almost (but not quite) complete avoidance of figures of speech: "between . . . the . . . wet"; "is . . . trickling . . . rises"; "into . . . the . . . air . . . with"; "but . . . two." Each of these sequences is a separate line. Williams here achieves that ability to purify words, cleanse them and detach them from all else, as though they had been "separated out by science, treated with acid to remove the smudges, washed, dried, and placed right side up on a clean surface" (SE, 128), for which he praises Marianne Moore, Gertrude Stein, and Laurence Stern:

> Miss Moore gets great pleasure from wiping soiled words or cutting them clean out, removing the aureoles that

"Ready-Mades and Other Measures: The Poetics of Marcel Duchamp and William Carlos Williams," *Journal of Modern Literature* VIII, 1 (1980), 3-22; Joseph N. Riddel, " 'Keep Your Pecker Up'—*Paterson Five* and the Question of Metapoetry," *Glyph 8* (1981), 203-231.

352

have been pasted about them or taking them bodily from greasy contexts. For the compositions Miss Moore intends, each word should first stand crystal clear with no attachments; not even an aroma. (SE, 128)

The feeling [in Stern and Stein] is of words themselves, a curious immediate quality quite apart from their meaning, much as in music different notes are dropped, so to speak, into repeated chords one at a time, one after the other—for themselves alone. (SE, 114)

The result of this purification and separation is that the words seem to speak of themselves or to speak for some radical otherness or alien power of enunciation that the words as such evoke. It is as though the words were calling "Come" and that call were answered by the entry into the words of something nameless that comes at the call. Among the words that work this way is the personal pronoun *I*, which opens "Young Sycamore," after its title: "I . . . must . . . tell . . . you." It would be a mistake to identify this *I* with the man William Carlos Williams, however plausible and even irresistible the temptation to do so is. The *I*, too, is depersonalized. It is rather some anonymous power of or in language that is urgently affirming its need to establish a strange sort of "I-thou" relation to the reader and to tell him or her something obligatory; "I *must* tell you." This message is not something about the external world as such but something only these words detached from all subjective and objective ligatures can convey. It is as though the words themselves were saying "I," or were using (and depersonalizing, dispossessing) the "I" of the poet to say what they must say. This compulsion to write or to allow the words to write themselves through the poet is a little like glossolalia, a speaking in tongues, or it is like one of those strange and terrible linguistic disorders, half physical, half psychological, breaking down the borders between the two, in which some other self within the self uses the vocal chords of the victim to bark or crow or to utter obscenities, against all efforts at propriety, something beyond the volition of the speaker, in a frightening parody of the "I must tell you." Williams' greatness as a poet is his ability to allow the words themselves to speak in this way. This is the linguistic moment in his work.

What is this strange obligation, an odd kind of categorical imperative, that seems to take possession of the words or of the poet who uses the words and speaks through both poet and the words with an irresistible urgency or coercion: "I must tell you." Why must he tell me, and what, exactly, must he tell me? The reader too, you or I, as if caught up in the necessity of this *must*, becomes subject in his or her turn to another categorical imperative, what I have elsewhere called the "ethics of reading." This imperative is the necessity of hearing or of reading the words of the work and of responding to them, willy-nilly. The critic too responds to the gratuitous call, to the demand of interpretation. The critic too must pass on the message. Though modern American poetry is not my "field," though no person, no institution, no professional obligation has ever demanded that I write on William Carlos Williams, I have now five times responded to some imperious *must* in Williams' work that seems to impel me once more to try to get him right and to tell others what I hear in his work. I too must say, "I must tell you." Each new essay has revised or modified the position about Williams taken in the one before. If the *I*, who is no longer Williams, but someone or something speaking through Williams or through the words, must tell you or me, you and I must listen, must understand, and must tell in our turn.

Or must we, he, you, I? Is this strange multiple serial obligation, passed from person to person, in a kind of perpetual round of the pronouns that seems to deprive them gradually of their distinctness, one that ever can be fulfilled, the debt paid off? If the *I* must tell the *you*, does he or she ever succeed in doing so? How would one know for sure the obligation had been fulfilled, the note "payable on demand" paid off when it was called in (and it is constantly being called in)? All Williams' work, from *Kora in Hell* and *Spring and All* to "Asphodel, That Greeny Flower," the latter with its constant renewal of speech against death, holding off death, is inhabited by this peculiar urgency and is a response to this call. No reader of Williams' poems from beginning to end or of the adjacent prose—for example, the prose parts of *Spring and All*—no reader of the *Autobiography*, or of the letters, can doubt that Williams was driven all his life by an imperious need to write, which took precedence over his obligations as a doctor, as husband, as father, as member of various communities. That need persisted into his old age, beyond those debilitating strokes, when the body could hardly any longer function as a medium for that voice or that power of putting words on paper. That power worked constantly through him, using him as its instrument for writing:

> There is something
>   something urgent
> I have to say to you
>   and you alone
>   but it must wait
> While I drink in
>   the joy of your approach,
>   perhaps for the last time.
> And so
>   with fear in my heart
>   I drag it out
> and keep on talking
>   for I dare not stop.
>   Listen while I talk on
> against time.
>   It will not be
>   , for long.
> I have forgot   .
>   (PB, 154)

Once more, and for the last time, the poet here speaks of something urgent he must say, and once more he forgets it, or does not get it said, but keeps on talking and writing anyhow, in the space between the imminence of the end and the end that never quite comes in the words, in the space, that is, between the flash of the bomb and the shock-wave thunder crack.

I now must return to "Young Sycamore" to see in more detail how the necessity to tell functions in this particular poem. Such a poem as "Young Sycamore" seems recalcitrant to analysis. The sycamore in the poem is not a symbol. "No symbolism is acceptable," says the poet (SE, 213). The tree does not stand for anything or point to anything beyond itself. Like the red wheelbarrow, or the sea trout and butterfish, or the flowering chicory in other poems by Williams, the young sycamore turned into language is itself, means itself. It is an object in verbal space, separated from other objects in verbal space, with its own sharp edges, its own innate particularity. The tree in the poem stands "between" the pavement and the gutter, but there is no assertion of an interchange between the three objects, no flow of an ubiquitous nature-spirit binding all things together. Things for Williams stand side by side in the world of the words, and the poet here locates the sycamore by reference to the things closest to it.

The avoidance of symbolism in Williams' poetry is related to the absence of another quality—the dimension of depth. In Romantic poetry, space frequently leads out to a "behind" or "beyond," which the poet may reach through named objects, or which the objects in the poem signify at a distance. In the Christian and Platonic traditions, things of this world in one way or another stand for things of the other world. Romantic poets inherit or extend this tradition, as in the thoughts too deep for tears, which for Wordsworth are given by the meanest flower that blows, or as in the attraction of the "Far-far-away" for Tennyson, or as in Yeats's reaffirmation of the hermetic tradition in "Ribh denounces Patrick": "For things below are copies, the Great Smaragdine Tablet said." In Williams' poetry this kind of depth has disappeared and with it the symbolism appropriate to it. Objects for him exist in a poem within a shallow space, like that created on the canvases of the American abstract expressionists. "Anywhere is everywhere" (P, 273), and there is no lure of distances that stretch out beyond what can be immediately seen. Nothing exists but what stands in the poem just before the speaker's wide-awake senses, and "Heaven seems frankly impossible" (SL, 147).

For this reason there is no need to go anywhere or to do anything to possess the plentitude of existence. Each of Williams' poems, to borrow the title of one of them, is "the world contracted to a recognizable image" (PB, 42). The poet has that power of "seeing the thing itself without forethought or afterthought but with great intensity of perception" that he praises in his mother (SE, 5), and all his poems have the quality that he claims for "Chicory and Daisies": "A poet witnessing the chicory flower and realizing its virtues of form and color so constructs his praise of it as to borrow no particle from right or left. He gives his poem over to the flower and its plant themselves" (SE, 17). While a poem lasts, nothing exists beyond it—nothing but the chicory, in one poem, or bits of broken glass on cinders, in another, or the young sycamore between pavement and gutter, in another. Immediacy in space, and also immediacy in time. The present alone is, and the aim of the poem must therefore be "to refine, to clarify, to intensify that eternal moment in which we alone live" (I, 89). "Young Sycamore" is written in the present tense. It records the instant of the *I*'s confrontation of the tree: "I must tell you / This young tree . . ."

There can also be for Williams little figurative language, little of the creation of a "pattern of imagery" that often unifies poems written in older traditions. Metaphors compare one thing to another and so blur the individuality of those things. For Williams the uniqueness of each thing is more important than any horizontal resonances it may have with other things: "Although it is a quality of the imagination that it seeks to place together those things which have a common relationship, yet the coining of similes is a pastime of very low order, depending as it does upon a nearly vegetable coincidence. Much more keen is that power which discovers in things those inimitable particles of dissimilarity to all other things which are the peculiar perfections of the thing in question" (SE, 16). "Young Sycamore" contains a single overtly figurative word, *hornlike*, and though this word is of great importance in the poem, spreading its implications backward to pick up the overtones of words like *bodily* or *thrust*, and suggesting that the sycamore has an animal-like volition and power (or perhaps, as Wallace Stevens has said, the lithe sinuosity of a snake), nevertheless the personification is attenuated. The poem is made chiefly of a long clause that in straightforward language describes the tree from trunk to topmost twig.

Such poetry provides problems not only for the analyst, but also for a reader concerned about the uses of poetry. Poetry of the Romantic and symbolist traditions usually at least appears to be dramatic or dialectical in structure. It often appears to presuppose a double division of existence. The objects of this world are separated from the supernatural realities they signify, and the consciousness of the poet is separated both from objects and from their celestial models. A poetry based on such assumptions will be a verbal act attempting to bring about a change in man's relation to the world. In uniting subject and object it will try to give the poet momentary possession of that distant reality the object symbolizes. Such a poetry is the enactment of a journey that may take the poet and his reader to the very bourn of heaven. Mallarmé's work provides a symbolist version of this poetry of dramatic action. He avoids that direct description Williams so willingly accepts. He writes a poetry of indirection in which the covert naming of things is the annihilation of those things so that they may be replaced, beyond negation, by an essence that is purely notional, an aroma "absent from all bouquets."

Nothing of this sort, it seems, happens in Williams' poetry. "Young Sycamore" does not go anywhere or accomplish any new possession of the tree. There is no gradual approach of subject and object that leads to their merger in an ecstatic union. The reader at the end is apparently where he was at the beginning—standing in imagination before the tree. The sycamore and the poem about the sycamore are separate things, side by side in the world in the same way that the tree stands between the pavement and the gutter detached from both. Romantic and symbolist poetry is usually an art of willed transformation. In this it is, like science or technology, an example of that changing of things into artifacts which assimilates them into the human world. Williams' poetry, on the other hand, is content to let things be. A good poet, he says, "doesn't *select* his material. What is there to select? It is."[4]

No symbolism, no depth, no reference to a world beyond the world, no pattern of imagery, no dialectical structure, no interaction of subject and object—just description, just the placing of words on the page so the intrinsic virtue of each may best operate, borrowing no particle from right or left. How can the critic analyze such a poem? What does it mean? Of what use is it? How can the critic justify the urgency of the first line: "I must tell you"? If the poem does not make anything happen, or give the reader something she or he did not have before, it seems of no more use than a photograph of the tree.

The answers to these questions can be given only if the reader places himself or herself within the context of the assumptions that underlie the poem. Anywhere is everywhere for Williams not because all places are indifferent, so that one place is as good as another, each one confessing

[4] "Introduction" to Byron Vazakas, *Transfigured Night* (New York: The Macmillan Company, 1946), p. xi.

the same failure of mind, objects, and their meanings to become one. Quite the opposite is the case. Williams' poetry can give itself to what appears to be no more than calm description because all objects are already possessed from the beginning, in what he calls an "approximate co-extension with the universe" (I, 105). The co-extension need be only approximate because that concentration on naming a single object or group of objects so habitual to Williams confirms his virtual identification with all things. In order to attain that concentration, other things, for the moment, must be set aside, but they are no less there, no less latently present in the realm of co-extension the poet has entered. A primordial union of subject and object is the basic presupposition of Williams' poetry.

In assuming such a union, his work joins in that return to the facts of immediate experience that is a wide-spread tendency in twentieth-century thought and art. This tendency is fundamental in the movement in art, literature, and thought called modernism, though of course like everything else in modernism it has a long tradition and is more the ringing in of the old again than the appearance of the altogether new. The return to immediacy may be identified in painters from Cézanne through cubism to abstract expressionism. It may be seen in poets like René Char, Jorgé Guillen, Charles Olson, and Robert Creeley. It is visible in that transformation of fiction which generated the French "new novel," the *romans blancs* of Alain Robbe-Grillet or Nathalie Sarraute. It may be found in the linguistic philosophy of Wittgenstein in the *Philosophical Investigations*, and in different ways in the tradition of phenomenology from Husserl through Heidegger and Merleau-Ponty. Williams' poetry has its own unique structure and assumptions, but if any milieu is needed for it, this tradition is the proper one. Though the connection between his work and modern painting is one of the main topics of the prose parts of *Spring and All*, and though Williams admired, for example, the poetry of Char, the similarities between his writing and other work should not be thought of in terms of influences. The similarities are rather a matter of independent responses to assumptions about art everywhere in the air when Williams wrote.

Williams differs from some other recent English and American poets in the timing of his acceptance of the new relation to the world. Yeats, Eliot, and Stevens, for example, also move beyond dualism, but this movement fills the whole course of their lives. It is accomplished only in their last work—in the explosive poetry of the moment in Yeats's "High Talk" or "News for the Delphic Oracle," or in the poetry of Incarnation in Eliot's *Four Quartets*, or in the fluid improvisations, joining imagination and reality, of Stevens' "An Ordinary Evening in New Haven." Williams, however, begins his career with the abandonment of his separate ego. Only in the unfinished narrative poem written during his medical studies[5] and in his first published volume, the *Poems* of 1909, does he remain within the tradition of a poetry dramatizing the relation of subject and object. Themes of spatial distance and of the isolation of the self are dominant there. With his next long poem, "The Wanderer," Williams takes the step beyond this. The poem ends with the protagonist's plunge into the "filthy Passaic." He is swallowed up by "the utter depths of its rottenness" until his separate existence is lost, and he can say, "I knew all—it became me" (CEP, 12). This "interpenetration, both ways," (P, 12) is assumed in all Williams' later poetry. His situation may be defined as "the mind turned inside out" into the world (KH, I, 75), or, alternatively, as the world turned inside out into the mind, for in the union of poet and river both his separate ego and the objective world disappear. An important letter to Marianne Moore describes this union of inner and outer and the "security" that resulted from it. It is, he says, "something which occurred once when I

[5] See the *Autobiography*, pp. 59, 60, for Williams' description of this poem.

was about twenty, a sudden resignation to existence, a despair—if you wish to call it that, but a despair that made everything a unit and at the same time a part of myself. I suppose it might be called a sort of nameless religious experience. I resigned, I gave up" (SL, 147).

"Young Sycamore," like the rest of Williams' mature poetry, is written on the basis of this act of resignation. In the poem there is neither subject nor object, but a single realm in which all things are both subjective and objective at once: the tree, the pavement, the gutter, the poem, the poet. Or rather, it is a region in which names from all these realms are borrowed to name an *it* that is none of them. The reader is included too, the *you* of the first line. The poet's address to the reader assimilates him or her into the realm of interpenetration. In Williams' poetry there is no description of private inner experience. There is also no description of objects that are external to the poet's mind. Nothing is external to his mind. His mind overlaps with things; things overlap with his mind. For this reason "Young Sycamore" is without dramatic action and can limit itself to an itemizing of the parts of the tree. There is no need to do anything to possess the tree because it is already possessed from the beginning. Language itself is the realm of this interpenetration, beyond the opposition of subject and object, person and person.

The imaginary space generated by the words of "Young Sycamore" is not that space of separation, primarily optical, which the reader enters, for example, in the poetry of Matthew Arnold. Williams' poem creates a space appropriate to the more inward senses whereby the body internalizes the world. Such a space is characterized by intimacy and participation. It denies the laws of geometrical space, in which each thing is in one place and is limited by its surfaces. So Williams describes, for example, that aural space in which each sound permeates the whole world, like the pervasive tone in "The Desert Music," which is everywhere at once, "as when Casals struck / and held a deep cello tone"

362

(PB, 119). Or in "Queen-Ann's-Lace" he experiences a woman and a field of the white flower not as metaphors of one another, but as interpenetrating realities. The poet's body, for Williams, is the place where subject and object are joined, and so, in "Young Sycamore," the tree is described as though its life were taking place inside his own life. The poem is a characteristic example of Williams' minimizing of eyesight and his emphasis on the more intimate senses—hearing, tasting, smelling, and above all touch, that *tactus eruditus* (CEP, 63) which it is proper for a physician to have. The assimilation of the world by the senses makes of the body a kinesthetic pantomine of the activity of nature. "A thing known," says Williams, "passes out of the mind into the muscles" (KH, I, 74). "Young Sycamore" affirms this possession not only in the tactile imagery of *round and firm trunk* and *bodily*, but also in the pattern of verbs or verbals that makes up the framework of the poem: *rises, undulant thrust, dividing and waning, sending out, hung, thins, knotted, bending*. These words articulate the way the poet lives the life of the tree.

The sequence of verbal forms also expresses the special way in which "Young Sycamore" takes place in a single moment. The poetic pseudo-instant for Williams is a field of forces in tension. In one sense his poetry is static and spatial. The red wheelbarrow, the locust tree in flower, the young sycamore, even all the things named in long poems like *Paterson* or "Asphodel, That Greeny Flower," stand fixed in their poems, on the page, in the span of an instant. It is therefore appropriate that Book Five of *Paterson*, for example, should be organized according to the spatial imagery of a tapestry. Nevertheless, there is in every moment a dynamic motion. "Young Sycamore" exemplifies one of the most important modes of this in Williams' poetry: flowering, or growth. According to the cosmology of three elements that underlies Williams' poetry, things rise from the "unfathomable ground / where we walk daily" (CLP, 23), take form in the open air, and in that openness uncover a glimpse of the "hidden flame" (IAG, 204), the universal beauty each formed thing both reveals and hides. This revelation takes place only in the process of growing, not in the thing full grown. For Williams the momentary existence even of a static thing like a wheelbarrow contains future and past as horizons of the present. In its reaching out toward them it reveals the non-presence of things present, something which dislocates things temporally, that "strange phosphorus of the life" (IAG, [vii]) liberated between the words. Williams' poetry is not primarily spatial. Time, for him, is the fundamental dimension of existence. The dynamic motion of the non-present in words creates space, unfolding it in the energy that brings form out of the ground so that it may, for the moment, reveal the "radiant gist" (P, 133). Though the young sycamore is all there in the non-present of the poem, from trunk to topmost twig, the poet experiences this stasis as a growth within the moment. It is an "undulant thrust" taking the tree up out of the dark ground as a bodily presence that pushes on into the air, "dividing and waning," until it thins out in the last two eccentric knotted twigs bending forward with the aggressive force of horns.

A grammatical peculiarity of the poem may be noted at this point. When the undulant thrust from trunk to twigs has been followed to its end, the sycamore seems to stand fixed, its energy exhausted, the vitality that urged it into the air now too far from its source in the dark earth. But this is not the case. The inexhaustible force of the temporal thrust of the tree is expressed not only in the cocoons that promise a renewal of the cycle of growth, but also in the fact that there is no main verb in the second clause of the long sentence that makes up the poem. The poem contains so much verbal action that this may not be noticed, but all these verbs are part of a subordinate clause following *whose*. Their subject is *trunk* not *tree*, and *trunk* is also the apparent referent of *it* in line 18. All the movement in the poem takes place within the confines of the subordinate clause.

The second line, "this young tree," still hovers incomplete at the end of the poem, reaching out toward the verb that will complement its substantiality with an appropriate action. The poem names not the presence of the present but an imminence. If the subordinate clause is omitted the poem says: "I must tell you / this young tree"—and then stops. This is undoubtedly the way the poet wanted it. This grammatical incompletion makes the poem give the reader a glimpse of that never present beauty which is revealed in the tree turned poem, just as, in one of Williams' last poems, "Asphodel, That Greeny Flower," the moment of the poem is the endless space of time between a flash of lightning and the sound of thunder, or between the explosion of the world-ending atomic bomb and the coming of the shock wave:

> The light
> for all time shall outspeed
> the thunder crack.
> (PB, 181)

"Young Sycamore," too, prolongs indefinitely the moment between beginning and ending, birth and death, in the always-not-quite-yet characteristic of modernist apocalypse.

There is, however, a contradiction in what I have said so far about the poem. To say the poem "expresses" Williams' experience of the temporality of objects is more or less the same thing as to say it pictures or represents or describes this. Such a notion presupposes a quadruple division of existence. The poet is in one place and looks at a tree that is outside himself. On the basis of his experience with the tree he makes a poem that mirrors in language his experience. The reader re-creates the experience through the mediation of the poem. This is precisely the theory of poetry that Williams emphatically denies. Repeatedly he dismisses the representational theory of art. Like Charles Olson, he avoids all "pictorial effects" (ML, 9), all that

365

" 'evocation' of the 'image' which served us for a time" (I, 100-101). Poetry, for him, is "not a mirror up to nature" (I, 150), "not a matter of 'representation' " (I, 117), "nor is it description nor an evocation of objects or situations" (I, 149). The poet must deny such notions of poetry if his writing is to be true to that union of subject and object he gains with his plunge into the Passaic. But if the sycamore is already possessed in perception of it, of what use is the poem? And yet Williams says that the aim of poetry is "to repair, to rescue, to complete" (SL, 147). What can this mean? The answer is suggested by another passage from the letters: "To copy nature is a spineless activity; it gives us a sense of our mere existence but hardly more than that. But to imitate nature involves the verb: we then ourselves become nature, and so invent an object which is an extension of the process" (SL, 297). "Young Sycamore" is an object, like the tree itself, and it grows out of the poet's identification with nature. Like the tree again, the poem exists as an activity, not as a passive substance. For this reason it must be a dynamic thing, primarily verbal.

What it means to think of a poem as a thing rather than as a picture of something is revealed not only by Williams' constant poetic practice, but, most explicitly, in the prose sections of *Spring and All*. To turn to these will also allow a further going beyond the more or less straightforward phenomenological, thematic, or mimetic reading of "Young Sycamore"—and of Williams' work generally—that I have for the most part been giving so far. My initial comments on the curious immediacy, beyond their referential meaning, of words as Williams places them on the page already suggest something incompatible with such a reading. *Spring and All* was printed at Dijon in 1923 and published by the Contact Publishing Company, one of Williams' joint enterprises with Robert McAlmon. It is a handsome little book bound in blue paper covers, dedicated to Williams' friend, the painter Charles Demuth. *Spring and All* in its integral form is perhaps the most important single work by Williams. "Nobody ever saw it," he says,"—it had no circulation at all—but I had a lot of fun with it" (IWWP, 36). It contains two of Williams' most famous lyrics, "By the road to the contagious hospital" and "The Red Wheelbarrow," along with twenty-five others. The poems are dispersed among passages of prose, some of which are prose poems in the manner of Williams' earlier *Kora in Hell* (1920) or of Rimbaud's *Illuminations*, and some of which are Williams' fullest statements of his theory of poetry.

In spite of the absolute value Williams here and elsewhere puts on making it new in America, *Spring and All* is self-consciously imitative of Rimbaud and the surrealists. "Thank you," says Williams at one particularly Rimbaudian moment, "I know well what I am plagiarizing" (I, 92). Moreover, the book doubles back on itself and contains its own interpretation. Just as *Kora in Hell* is made up of prose poems and "interpretations" of them written later, so in *Spring and All* the prose passages present the theory of imaginative action exemplified in the poems. The latter are strewn throughout the prose like gemstones in clay. "Who am I," asks Williams, "but my own critic?" (I, 111). The poems sometimes come with fine dramatic suddenness. Such interaction between the prose and the poetry is lost in the publication of the poems alone in *The Collected Earlier Poems*, but with the publication of *Imaginations* by New Directions in 1971 the integral text of *Spring and All* was made generally available again. If *Spring and All* has its pre-texts, it is also divided within itself between text and interpretation. The critic adds his interpretation to the text as one more link in a chain. His reading inserts itself in the texture of words that is already there and follows one thread or another in the weaving as he tries to identify a fundamental pattern. In this case the background design is a network of contradictions and tensions in aesthetic theory as old as Plato and Aristotle. Apparently without full awareness of its lineage, Williams has knitted this pattern into his text. The poems that matter and the interpretations that matter are not the ones that dissolve such contradictions, for they cannot be unravelled, but those that "elucidate" them, to use one of the key words of *Spring and All*.

Spring and All, like the self-consciously modernist tradition to which it belongs, is seemingly based on an affirmation of the supreme value of presence and of the present, and on a repudiation of all that is derived, repetitive, and copied. This opposition is initially given an overtly temporal expression. Authentic life exists only in the present moment of immediate experience, but most people live detached from that moment. They remain lost in memory of the no longer real past, or in anticipation of the not yet existing future, or in thoughts about some distant place. They are unable to concentrate on what is here and now, before the senses. According to Williams:

> There is a constant barrier between the reader and his consciousness of immediate contact with the world. . . . [T]he whole world is between: Yesterday, tomorrow, Europe, Asia, Africa,—all things removed and impossible, the tower of the church at Seville, the Parthenon. . . . The reader knows himself as he was twenty years ago and he has also in mind a vision of what he would be, some day. Oh, some day! But the thing he never knows and never dares to know is what he is at the exact moment that he is. And this moment is the only thing in which I am at all interested. (I, 86-89).

Among the most impenetrable substances standing as a screen between man and the present moment is traditional art, the art of "illusion," "representation," and the "copy after nature." "[N]early all writing, up to the present," says Williams, "if not all art, has been especially designed to keep up the barrier between sense and the vaporous fringe which distracts the attention from its agonized approaches to the moment. It has always been a search for 'the beautiful illusion' " (I, 89). Art adds itself in "layers of demoded words and shapes" (I, 100) to the vaporous fringe of the

past, the future, and the distant to double the barrier between consciousness and the luminous center of the moment. Art is, like past and future, like all things removed
and distant, a form of the mediate, the secondary. A resolute repudiation of the tradition of mimetic art runs as a
continuous filament through *Spring and All*. Representational artists are "the traditionalists of plagiarism" (I, 97).
They commit themselves to "the falseness of attempting to
'copy' nature" (I, 107). Such copying is the "crude symbolism" of "strained associations" (I, 102). It is "plagiarism
after nature" (I, 111):

> I suppose Shakespeare's familiar aphorism about hold-
> ing the mirror up to nature has done more harm in
> stabilizing the copyist tendency of the arts among us than—
> [T]he mistake in it . . . is to have believed that the
> reflection of nature is nature. It is not. It is only a sham
> nature, a "lie." (I, 121)

Williams recognizes the indissoluble connection of the
art of mimesis with symbolism, with subjectivism, and with
the notion that the origin of the objective world, of man's
subjectivity, and of artistic forms is located in another world.
Williams rejects as "crude symbolism" the traditional universe of hierarchical levels in participation. According to
this personifying symbology, things of the outer world are
properly symbols of qualities in man's subjective world.
This correspondence is validated by the resonance of both
with the supernatural center that is their source. Williams
rejects this personification as firmly as he rejects metaphor.
"Crude symbolism," says Williams, "is to associate emotions
with natural phenomena such as anger with lightning, flowers with love . . . Such work is empty" (I, 100). Elsewhere,
speaking of the way the paintings of Juan Gris detach the
things of everyday experience and present them in unfa-
miliar juxtapositions, making it impossible for the onlooker
to think of the canvas as a photographic representation of
reality, Williams brings to the surface the association of

369

representational art with subjectivism and with belief in an extraterrestrial center:

> This [the "distortion" of Juan Gris] was not necessary where the subject of art was not "reality" but related to the "gods"—by force or otherwise. There was no need of the "illusion" in such a case since there was none possible where a picture or a work represented simply the imaginative reality which existed in the mind of the onlooker. (I, 111)

In rejecting the art of imitation, Williams wants also to reject those other elements—symbolism, metaphor, prosopopoeia, subjectivism, and supernaturalism—with which it is systematically connected. All these aspects of art stand between man and the living moment. The whole fabric must go.

What, for Williams, would be the instrument of this prodigious act of demolition? What power in man can blow up all the barriers and return man to the moment? The answer is unequivocal: "To refine, to clarify, to intensify that eternal moment in which we alone live there is but a single force—the imagination. This is its book" (I, 89). The prose of *Spring and All* centers on a definition or redefinition of this traditional romantic term. The imagination is the only power that can reach through all obstacles to the reality of the present moment. Williams uses language drawn from physics to describe how this happens:

> [T]he imagination is an actual force comparable to electricity or steam, it is not a plaything but a power that has been used from the first to raise the understanding of—[Here, as often, Williams leaves the reader to fill in the missing words, in this case, I suppose, "Life," "nature," "reality," "the moment."] . . .
>
> [T]he work of the imagination [is] not "like" anything but [is] transfused with the same forces which transfuse the earth—at least one small part of them. (I, 120, 121)

The imagination is that energy in man through which flows the same force as that outside man which creates weeds, stone, trees, and white chickens. The imagination, for Williams as for Stevens, is part of nature.[6] By its means the poet can cast out all the past, all inherited and demoded forms. He can then turn directly to nature, activating his liaison with it.

Turn to nature in what way? What, in fact, is the work of the imagination? Here Williams' thought turns curiously back on itself and then even redoubles that doubling. The imagination is, in one sense, a creative force linking man to nature. The poems and paintings produced by the imagination grow from nature and remain rooted in it. The compositions of great writers like Homer, says Williams, "have as their excellence an identity with life since they are as actual, as sappy as the leaf of the tree which never moves from one spot" (I, 101). In another sense, the imagination is a destructive force, perhaps the most powerful explosive of all. It has power to annihilate everything. Though it is part of nature, its essential function is to destroy nature. The opening pages of *Spring and All* express a joyous dedication to the destruction of the world. The instrument of this destruction is the imagination: "The imagination, intoxicated by prohibitions, rises to drunken heights to destroy the world. Let it rage, let it kill. The imagination is supreme. . . . To it now we come to dedicate our secret project: the annihilation of every human creature on the face of the earth. . . . None to remain; nothing but the lower vertebrates, the mollusks, insects and plants. Then at last will the world be made anew" (I, 90-91).

It is easy to see the logic according to which the imagination must be destructive as well as creative. As Williams

[6] The same thing could be said for Kant, for example, or, in a different way, even for Aristotle. For Stevens and Aristotle, see chap. 1, above, pp. 5-10, and for Kant see Jacques Derrida, "*Economimesis*," in Sylviane Agacinski *et al.*, *Mimesis: Desarticulations* (Paris: Aubier-Flammarion, 1975), pp. 57-93.

371

says in the fifteenth poem of *Spring and All*, "destruction and creation / are simultaneous" (I, 127). If dead forms of language stand between man and the novelty of the moment, so also do those objects in nature already there a moment or a decade ago. The first movement of the imagination must therefore be violently anarchistic, the "destruction of what is," to borrow the slogan of the Professor in Joseph Conrad's *The Secret Agent*. The precursor text here is Rimbaud's *Illuminations*. In "Conte," for example, a bored prince dedicates himself to sadistic cruelty: "All the women who had known him were assassinated; what havoc in the garden of beauty! . . . He amused himself cutting the throats of rare animals. He set palaces on fire. He would rush upon people and hack them to pieces."[7] Like Rimbaud, Williams must break down all cultural and natural forms, kill everyone and destroy everything in order to return things to the primal formlessness from which new forms without antecedents may spring. Williams shares here with Rimbaud the artist's wish to be himself the cause of the apocalypse, the last end. This notion that genuine art brings the apocalypse rather then just describing its imminence is a frequent motive in so-called modernist writers.

As in the case of Conrad's Professor, Williams' destructive rage must be directed especially against mankind. Human beings most remember the past or anticipate the future and therefore are the least real. "I love my fellow creature," says Williams. "Jesus, how I love him: endways, sideways, frontways and all the other ways—but he doesn't exist! Neither does she. I do, in a bastardly sort of way" (I, 89). Since the subjectivity of ordinary humankind is per-

[7] Arthur Rimbaud, *Illuminations and Other Prose Poems*, trans. Louise Varese, rev. ed. (New York: New Directions, 1957), pp. 17, 19. For a good discussion of the influence of surrealism on Williams, see Marjorie Perloff, " 'Lines Converging and Crossing': The 'French' Decade of William Carlos Williams," *The Poetics of Indeterminacy: Rimbaud to Cage* (Princeton: Princeton University Press, 1981), pp. 109-154.

haps the most recalcitrant way in which the unreal corrupts the real, it must be the special target of imaginative action. It can be erased first by being merged in the imagination of the poet-protagonist. He does exist, in a bastardly sort of way, because he lives in the imagination: "In the imagination, we are from henceforth (so long as you read) locked in a fraternal embrace, the classic caress of author and reader. We are one" (I, 89). Williams' readers must abandon their separate selves and lose themselves in the imagination of the poet, sharing with him there in the action whereby every man, woman, and child on the face of the earth is annihilated. In this annihilation all the separate unreal minds are merged in a single real soul: "This final and self inflicted [sic] holocaust has been all for love, for sweetest love, that together the human race, yellow, black, brown, red and white, agglutinated into one enormous soul may be gratified with the sight . . ." (I, 91).

Once this monstrous act of demolition has been completed, the world will be new, and the imagination can then turn from acts of destruction to acts of authentic creation. Here, however, Williams turns back on himself unexpectedly a second time. The world after its destruction is not new at all. It repeats itself exactly again from the beginning, down to the last detail. If an art of mimesis is bad because it is sterile copying, there is in nature a similar tendency toward plagiarism. Williams' hyperbolic act of imaginative destruction leads him only to witness the comedy of a nature that, destroyed so that spring may begin, repeats itself exactly as it was, as if it had not wit or energy enough to be different:

> It is spring! But miracle of miracles a miraculous miracle has gradually taken place during these seemingly wasted eons. Through the orderly sequences of unmentionable time EVOLUTION HAS REPEATED ITSELF FROM THE BEGINNING. . . .
>
> Every step once taken in the first advance of the human

373

race, from the amoeba to the highest type of intelligence, has been duplicated, every step exactly paralleling the one that preceded in the dead ages gone by. A perfect plagiarism results. Everything is and is new. Only the imagination is undeceived. (I, 93)

The imagination is undeceived because it can see that nothing has been accomplished. There has been no return to a primal novelty. Nature is capable only of a dead imitation of what already was. This doubling brings into the open nature's sterility. Nature cannot return to an origin that is other than a repetition of something that has already happened innumerable times before.

This barrenness in nature is also a limitation in the imagination, since the imagination is no more than a derived force of nature. The enormous energy of the imagination is able to destroy everything, but can man create on the basis of the resulting debris not "the unheard of work [*l'oeuvre inouïe*],"[8] but only a repetition of what was there before: "Yes, the imagination, drunk with prohibitions, has destroyed and recreated everything fresh in the likeness of that which it was" (I, 93). In the same way, the Prince's murders and burnings in Rimbaud's "Conte" leave things untouched: "The throngs, the gilded roofs, the beautiful animals still remained."[9] Williams has followed through the same line of imaginative thought as Rimbaud and has come face to face once more with the same blank wall. He repeats Rimbaud's celebrated failure to use the poetic imagination as a revolutionary force. For Williams as for Rimbaud, it seems, "There is no sovereign music for our desire."[10] For him, too, the longed-for immediacy and novelty of the present moment turns out to be secondary, stale, an old game.

Only a language beyond imagination can break this impasse. Left alone, nature repeats itself. Destroyed by the

[8] Rimbaud, *Illuminations*, ed. cit., p. 40.
[9] *Ibid.*, p. 19.
[10] *Ibid.*

imagination, it repeats itself again. Only when it is repeted in a certain way in words is it new: "The only means [the poet] has to give value to life is to recognize it with the imagination and name it; this is so. To repeat and repeat the thing without naming it is only to dull the sense and results in frustration" (I, 115). This act of naming is the linguistic moment in Williams. It disrupts or dislocates the perceptual or phenomenological vocabulary within which the prose of *Spring and All* for the most part remains caught, just as something beyond mimesis disrupts almost imperceptibly the language of a poem like "Young Sycamore."

What is the difference between repeating with the imagination and "naming"? It would seem that naming could only be another form of the aesthetic of imitation Williams is making every effort to reject. In elucidating the distinction between naming and repeating, Williams finds a way out of the dilemma he faces. The poems in *Spring and All* are presented as examples of the power of imaginative naming. To put this another way, Williams finds a way to go beyond those three irreconcilable and yet inextricably connected theories of art that have dominated Western thought since the Greeks. These are discussed above in my opening section on Stevens in the first chapter. They also unobtrusively govern the argument of *Spring and All*. Art as mimesis, art as revelation, art as creation *ex nihilo*—these three regal ideas are present in the distinction Williams makes between words as repetition, words as names, and words as pure sounds. Though he rejects the first and last and chooses the second, he cannot free his theory or his practice from the contradictory inherence of each of these notions in the others. What the words of his poem do is ultimately compatible with none of them.

In developing his version of the traditional patterns of thought about poetry, Williams makes use implicitly of two concepts of repetition. On the one hand, there is the sterile imitation of the exact copy. This form of repetition is integral to the Platonic system Williams rejects. Platonism connects the idea of repetition as the eternal return of the same with the idea of art as mimesis. Both are to be associated with the notion of a divine center that is principle and model. The cosmological image of the universe as a circle or ring in which the same eternally returns because nature is a copy of fixed ideas in the mind of the One is doubled in an aesthetic theory of art as the copy of a copy, as a mirror held up to nature. In both cases, legitimacy lies in the exactness of the duplication, since both nature and art are valid only insofar as they imitate a divine model.

Against this form of repetition, Williams sets the notion of a repetition based on difference. On this concept he builds his theory of imaginative naming. The poem must not be an exact repetition in words of the object it describes. On the other hand, it cannot be made of nonsense sounds— that is, of words freed from their usual function as names of objects. Poetry cannot be words turned into sounds approaching pure music: "According to my present theme the writer of imagination would attain closest to the conditions of music not when his words are disassociated from natural objects with specified meanings but when they are liberated from the usual quality of that meaning by transposition into another medium, the imagination" (I, 150).

The key to Williams' theory of imagination is the idea that the imagination is a natural force that goes beyond nature when it becomes imaginative naming. Naming makes possible the re-creation of physical objects in a different form—that is, in their names. The object is a thing. It really exists. The poem is another real, existing thing. The two things echo one another at a distance, but with a difference. In a world where there is no divine center to control the production of meaning out of the juxtaposition of differences, the thing and its name create resemblance out of difference. The destruction of nature by the imagination is both good and bad. It is bad because it accomplishes nothing. Nature repeats itself exactly after being destroyed. The destruction of nature is good because it is necessary to the naming that uses another form of the energies running through nature to re-create it in a new form.

Imaginative naming is creative repetition in a double sense. The verbal form duplicates what it names with a difference, and the different elements that imagination gives rise to echo one another. From this echoing, meaning is created. This generation of meaning through resonance is present in *Spring and All* in two ways. In even the simplest of the poems, multiple objects from multiple sources rise through language into the realm of imaginative naming. So much depends on the red wheelbarrow, to cite one example, not because it is supremely important in itself, but because it can momentarily be taken as the center of a miniature world of words with other objects set beside it (in this case, the white chickens). Meaning arises from the juxtaposition of wheelbarrow and chickens. Other poems in *Spring and All* often work even more obviously according to a technique of the juxtaposition of the disparate: the mixture of natural and urban details in the eighth poem, the series of "unrelated" images in the eleventh, the montage of seascape and cityscape in the thirteenth, the naming of the crowd at a ball game in the twenty-sixth poem, with its multitude of the unthinking masses that are "beautiful" "in detail" (I, 148, 149).

In all these poems the underlying assumption is the same: "Anywhere is everywhere." Williams' universe, unlike the Platonic cosmos, has no center, no reservoir of eternal models. There are only the strange anonymous forces in names. These give rise to resonating differences in objects appearing within their names side by side or in sequence from an infinity of centers. Out of the resemblances in difference that occur among these named objects, meaning is created. No one place is the center or origin in this nonhierarchical world. The center is everywhere. This is why Williams pays such loving attention to naming random, ugly, "anti-poetical" objects. The wheelbarrow, the scrawny magnolia raising "its straggling branches of ivorywhite flowers" by the millworker's shack (I, 91), street signs or posters (I, 146-147), "the broken pieces of the city" (I, 115), "the small / yellow cinquefoil in the / parched places" (I, 118), "a girl with one leg / over the rail of a balcony" (I, 120)—all are important, all equally important, because all exist, all have sprung up from the "unfathomable ground" (CLP, 23) to manifest themselves in their naming in the poems. "It is only in isolate flecks that / something / is given off" (I, 133). Any one of these flecks released by language may be taken as the point on which everything depends and around which it turns.

This creation of meaning by the resonance of the names of adjacent objects is confirmed by the theory of language on which these poems are based. Words are for Williams part of the already existing furniture of the world. They are objects, just as the red wheelbarrow, the bits of green glass, the sycamore tree are objects. As a painting is made of paint, or music of sounds, so a poem is "a small (or large) machine made of words" (SE, 256). Words differ from bits of green glass or a sycamore not because meanings are inherent in one case and ascribed in the other. Both a word and a tree have their meanings as inextricable parts of their substances. But the meaning that is intrinsic to a word is its power of referring to something beyond itself. Williams has no fear of the referential power of words. It is an integral part of his theory of imagination. On the one hand he rejects those poets who "use unoriented sounds in place of conventional words" (I, 150), that is, words not pointing toward real things. On the other hand, he also rejects the notion that things depend on words. The thing "needs no personal support but exists free from human action" (I, 150). To think of words as too close to the objects they name would be a return to that kind of description in which "words adhere to certain objects, and have the effect on the sense of oysters, or barnacles" (I, 149). A further sentence from the prose of *Spring and All* expresses in admirably exact language Williams' way of avoiding these extremes. "The word is not liberated, therefore able to communicate release from the fixities which destroy it until it is accurately tuned to the fact which giving it reality, by its own reality establishes its own freedom from the necessity of a word, thus freeing it and dynamizing it at the same time" (I, 150).

Once words have been given reality and energy by their distant attunement to the things they name, an interaction among words analogous to the interaction among things in nature creates meaning in the poem. Words set side by side are forces that jostle one another. Out of this jostling of differences grows a new energy exceeding the sum of forces going into it. This dynamism gives the poem as a whole an exorbitant movement in one direction or another, all the words rising together to create that sense of enlargement or alleviation, the essential effect for Williams of a successful poem. This movement of the words together affirms simultaneously the reality of the objects named and the separate reality of the poem. It also liberates something beyond or between the words that only those words can free: "Either to write or to comprehend poetry the words must be recognized to be moving in a direction separate from the jostling or lack of it which occurs within the piece. . . . As bird's wings beat the solid air without which none could fly so words freed by the imagination affirm reality by their flight" (I, 146, 150). Bird and air are both real, both equally real, but the bird cannot fly without the air whose solidity it reveals in its flight. So the poem about the sycamore both depends on the tree and is free of it. In its freedom it allows the tree to be itself, at the same time as it confirms its own independent existence.

What exactly does Williams mean when he says that in poetry words "affirm reality by their flight"? He has repeatedly asserted that "reality needs no personal support but exists free from human action" (I, 149-150). The imagination seems no more than a mode of the life force that has the power to create "new forms as additions to nature"

379

(I, 140). Therefore it must be subject to the same law of spontaneous self-plagiarism, the return of the same to the same, that governs nature as a whole. Williams in fact grants the imagination a special, one might even say an "extra-natural," function. Once more, his thought is traditional, its roots reaching back to the beginnings of Western thought, and present throughout its history, for example, in Kant or in Heidegger. Like the tradition lying behind it, his theory of art is unable to free itself from the theories it rejects. For Aristotle, in mimesis the underlying *logos* of nature is destroyed in its sovereign oneness by being differentiated into the multiplicity of individual words. In the metaphoric interaction of words, the *logos* is brought into the open by mimetic repetition, but it is uncovered in a transferred form. In metaphor, the *logos* is destroyed and revealed at once. A similar structure of thought organizes the prose of *Spring and All*, in spite of the violence of Williams' attack on the aesthetic of imitation. The key terms he uses to describe the action of imagination—*value, life, truth*—are again traditional. Though there may be an echo of Wordsworth's "Preface" to *Lyrical Ballads* in his formulation, Williams' claim that reality is revealed and therefore brought into existence for man only in the work of art is no more Romantic than it is Aristotelian:

> Taught by the largeness of his imagination to feel every form which he sees moving within himself, he must prove the truth of this by expression. . . . Only when this position is reached can life proper be said to begin since only then can a value be affixed to the forms and activities of which it consists. . . . It is not necessary to count every flake of the truth that falls; it is necessary to dwell in the imagination if the truth is to be numbered. . . . [I]n great works of the imagination A CREATIVE FORCE IS SHOWN AT WORK MAKING OBJECTS WHICH ALONE COMPLETE SCIENCE AND ALLOW INTELLIGENCE TO SURVIVE. . . . [L]ife becomes

actual only when it is identified with ourselves. When we name it, life exists. (I, 105, 106, 112, 115)

Only in the poem or in the painting is the truth of nature "elucidated" in the sense of being "brought to light," made available to human intelligence. This elucidation, in a recurrent theme of *Spring and All*, produces the "enlargement" or lightening men feel "before great or good work, an expansion" (I, 107). It is as if men had been released from a great burden and had come into an open space—it is the opening of revelation. Though value, life, and truth are already in nature, they are hidden. They come into visibility only when the poet names natural objects. This naming brings objects into that domain of the imagination where they may, in their jostling, transcend themselves in the creation of meaning. Such an art is at once mimesis, for "the same things exist, but in a different condition when energized by the imagination" (I, 138), and *aletheia*, for in art alone is the hidden truth of nature uncovered. It is also an act of creation, since in art a new object is brought into existence. In being all three, it is something more than any of them separately or in combination. The "truth" exists only when it is "numbered," named, "invented," and given compositional form. In its naming it becomes "actual"— that is, present. In poetic naming Williams at last takes possession of the presence of the present, that eternal moment in which we alone live. It is a present, however, that is not perceptual but linguistic, a present not present except in words. The poet takes possession of this present-not-present in imaginative naming—that is, as translated into the secondary reality of its verbal image. This new or secondary linguistic reality performs the essential function of poetry, which for Williams, as for so many writers before him, is to be a mediator between man and primary reality. Great works of art "stand between man and nature as saints once stood between man and the sky" (I, 112). The authentic art work "is new, immediate—It is so because it is

actual, always real. It is experience dynamized into reality"
(I, 134).

Now it is possible to see why Williams makes verbs and
verb forms the axis of "Young Sycamore." The poem is not
a picture of the tree. It is an object that has the same kind
of life as the tree. It is an extension of nature's process. In
order to be such an object it must have "an intrinsic movement of its own to verify its authenticity" (SE, 257). The
pattern of verbs creates this movement. "The poem is made
of things—on a field" (A, 333), but words, like other things,
exist primarily as energies, directed forces. Words are nodes
of linguistic power. This power is their potentiality for combining with other words to form grammatical structures.
When words are placed side by side against the white field
of the page they interact with one another to create a space
occupied by energies in mobile tension.

Poems are more than objects added to the store of objects
already existing in nature. The words of a poem "affirm
reality by their flight." Language is so natural to man and
so taken for granted as part of his being that it is difficult
to imagine what the world would be like without it. Nevertheless, language may become soiled or corrupted. Then
it will no longer affirm reality, but hide it. Language will
become part of the "constant barrier between the reader
and his consciousness of immediate contact with the world"
(I, 88). The theme of the degradation of language runs all
through Williams' writing, from the prose of *Spring and All*
and *The Great American Novel* through the analysis of American civilization in *In the American Grain* to the passages on
the speech of urban man in *Paterson*: "The language, the
language / fails them" (P, 20). Even though man's language
is corrupt, the sycamore will still be there and will still be
a revelation of beauty. The failure of language, however,
means necessarily a failure of man's power to perceive the
tree and to share its life. The loss of a proper language
accompanies man's detachment from the world and from
other people. Authentic speech sustains man's openness to

the world. It is in this sense that "we smell, hear and see with words and words alone, and . . . with a new language we smell, hear and see afresh" (SE, 266). As Williams puts it in a phrase, the poem alone "focuses the world" (SE, 242). Like Aristotle's mimesis, Williams' imagination is both part of and more than nature, both immediate and mediating—imitation, revelation, and creation at once. Like the long tradition he echoes, Williams remains seemingly caught in the inextricable web of connection among these concepts.

Or does he? Williams in the prose parts of *Spring and All* and elsewhere in his prose makes strenuous but unsuccessful efforts to think through and escape from the programmed machine of the concepts of mimesis that has governed the West since Aristotle and Plato. He is as much self-consciously aware as Wallace Stevens of the impasse to which thinking that poetry returns the same to the same will lead. He too thinks that poetry must present and rescue the presence of the present. He too is aware of the inextricable complicity of the concepts of poetry as revelation and poetry as autonomous creation in the concept of poetry as imitation. And for him, too, as much as for Stevens, for example, in "The Red Fern," there is a repetition of nature by itself or within itself even before the poet tries to repeat it in his poetry.

The work of such a "plagiarist" poet is, in a way, not too different from Plato's idea of it, not just sterile and useless repetition but repetition of a repetition. Nature plagiarizes itself even before it is plagiarized by the poet. If the poet eschews mimesis as imitation and tries to think of his poetry as uncovering the hidden "radiant gist" he only cooperates in that periodic renewal wherein nature, even if it is deliberately and totally destroyed in a vast apocalypse making a clear place for the revelation of the new, only repeats itself exactly. On the other hand, a poetry of autonomous sounds, cut off wholly from nature, is sterile. Words must be made dynamic by reality to have power.

Williams escapes from this impasse not in thought or in theory, for no theoretical thinking can escape it, but in *praxis*, in something that occurs in or between the words of his poems. This something is difficult to identify. It exceeds the poems' paraphrasable meanings. At the moment when the repetition in nature is complete and the universe has returned to exactly the point where it was before, so that the two natures can be superimposed exactly, like two maps made to the same grid or "grate," suddenly the repetitive cycling ends:

> [L]ife has now arrived for the second time at that exact moment where in the ages past the destruction of the species *Homo sapiens* occurred.
>
> Now at last that process of miraculous verisimilitude, that grate [sic in original text] copying which evolution has followed, repeating move for move every move that it made in the past—is approaching the end.
>
> Suddenly it is at an end. THE WORLD IS NEW. (I, 94-95)

The repetition ends and the world is new, however, not in nature, which, left to itself, repeats itself endlessly, and not in the theoretical ruminations and parodic hijinks of the prose, which repeat or plagiarize Rimbaud and the surrealists. Nor does repetition end in the presence of the present of perception, however much Williams seems committed to the idea that only the present moment is. In the end, or intermittently along the way, he recognizes that the present moment is not, or is only the mimesis of what has already happened over and over. The present, too, only returns the same to the same. It is another form of sterile repetition. Repetition ends and spring begins only in the words of the poem as they follow one another on the page, with just that spacing they have, or as they follow one another in the air if the poem is spoken aloud. The spring so far unsuccessfully sought occurs, for example, in "By the road to the contagious hospital," which in *Spring and*

All follows just after the prose passage quoted above. I cite it only in part:

> All along the road the reddish
> purplish, forked, upstanding, twiggy
> stuff of bushes and small trees
> with dead, brown leaves under them
> leafless vines—
>
> Lifeless in appearance, sluggish
> dazed spring approaches—
>
> They enter the new world naked,
> cold, uncertain of all
> save that they enter. . . .
>
> One by one objects are defined—
> It quickens: clarity, outline of leaf
> But now the stark dignity of
> entrance— . . .
>   (I, 95-96)

"By the road" is one of Williams' most admirable fulfillments of his project of naming rather than repeating. Here, as in "Young Sycamore," Williams does what he says a good poet must: "The word must be put down for itself, not as a symbol of nature but a part, cognizant of the whole— aware—civilized" (I, 102). The imperious obligation of the "I must tell you" is never fulfilled in the present. In spite of Williams' apparent commitment to the presence of the present and to the fact that only the present moment is, the ethical obligation to the words or in the words is never paid off now. It is always never quite yet fulfilled in that just-about-to-be future that dislocates or detemporalizes the words. That future makes words anachronistic. It puts them temporally beside themselves. It makes, for example, the words of "Young Sycamore" not a picture of the young tree in the present moment (there is no present indicative verb but *must* in the poem), but the naming of a non-present

presence. This non-presence is a strange otherness inhab-
iting language and imposing the unfulfillable obligation of
the "I must tell you" on the poet. There is no present or
presence either in words or between words. There is only
a relation to something that has always already occurred
in them and that the *I* must always promise that he is about
to tell by means of the words in the just-about-to-be future.
The poem tells the reader nothing, nor does it make anything happen in the "real" world. In the fulfillment of this
other *must* ("The word must be put down for itself."), something happens in the words, or between the words. What
Williams calls elsewhere a "desert music" is liberated. Here,
too, as in Stevens, but in a different way, the word is not
a repetitive label or mimesis of something in nature but a
part of nature. The awakening newborn weeds of spring
in "By the road," the artist figure of the farmer in "The
farmer in deep thought" (I, 199), the young sycamore in
"Young Sycamore," are not what these poems are about.
The rooted natural objects or persons are figures for the
energy, life, and movement independently possessed by the
words. The poem is not a symbol for nature. Nature is a
"symbol" for a "nameless" action within or between words,
or rather, not a symbol, since that word implies similarity
and participation. If "no symbolism is acceptable," "the strong
phosphorus of the life" is "nameless under the old misappellation" (IAG, [vii]), but no new appellation can be
other than a misappellation. Nor can it name the phosphorus of the life directly. It can only be named between
the words, as in that strange image of Marianne Moore's
words as "white circular discs grouped closely edge to edge
upon a dark table [which] make black six-pointed stars"
(SE, 129). The starry design is not the words themselves
but the black space between them shaped by the words or
brought by them into a kind of negative visibility. This is
an odd kind of figuration by displacement. The nameless
is named, or at least exposed, not by the words but by the
shape of the black and wordless interstices between the

words in their syntactical grappling with one another. This is troping as turning away, naming by not naming.

Nothing obliges anyone to read between the lines of Williams' poems, nothing or almost nothing, something so evanescent as to be scarcely present as a kind of non-present, interrupting ever so slightly the presence of the words on the page. Nothing or almost nothing obliges the reader to interpret Williams as other than entirely encompassed within the phenomenal metaphysics of the presence of the present to which his self-analysis in *Spring and All* seems almost wholly, but not quite wholly, committed. If nature in "By the road" or in "Young Sycamore" is not a symbol, it is another example of that figure-no-figure encountered so often in this book—catachresis. And once more catachresis is contaminated, as so often, by that kinesthetic personification of nature and of language that is the one figure Williams cannot expel from his words. As the weeds in "By the road" are newborn creatures, the young sycamore makes a bodily thrust, and words are projected or proffered like newborn babies into the physician-poet's care: "The physician enjoys a wonderful opportunity actually to witness the words being born. Their actual colors and shapes are laid before him carrying their tiny burdens which he is privileged to take into his care with their unspoiled newness" (A, 360-361).

If in poetry, as Williams says, something nameless is given off, it can only be by the operation of this nonfigurative figure—catachresis—not in the words, but beside them, between them, or around them. What I have called the "curious immediacy" in the words of Williams' lyrics exceeds the conceptual circles from mimesis to revelation to autonomous creation within which his "theorizing" is apparently caught. The words on the page liberate a "nameless" otherness that they seem to copy, generate, and reveal all at once, though it is none of these, either separately or in combination. The poet's cry of "I must tell you" in answer to this wordless cry is continuous with the echoes of the "Come"

387

of the book of *Revelation* in one of Williams' earliest poems, "To simplicity": "Where art thou hid? Cry, cry again: I come! I come! I come!" (P [1909], 9). Williams writes eloquently in his *Autobiography* of this strange something present as a non-presence not in the meanings of words but beyond or between them as a ubiquitous force:

> We catch a glimpse of something, from time to time, which shows us that a presence has just brushed past us, some rare thing—just when the smiling little Italian woman has left us. For a moment we are dazzled. What was that? We can't name it; we know it never gets into any recognizable avenue of expression; men will be long dead before they can have so much as ever approached it. . . . It is actually there, in the life before us, every minute that we are listening, a rarest element—not in our imaginations but there, there in fact. It is that essence which is hidden in the very words which are going in at our ears and from which we must recover underlying meaning as realistically as we recover metal out of ore. (A, 360, 362)

Having shown spring to be impossible, in nature or in concept, except as repetition, Williams makes spring happen in the poem that comes next, as literal word follows literal word, there on the page, with that strange rhythmical flatness of the words put down on paper, each for its own sake, which is characteristic of Williams: *purplish, forked, upstanding, twiggy; But, now, the, stark, dignity, of.* This detached immediacy of individual words in Williams' work is quite different from the savage vatic singsong of Stevens of which I have written in Chapter 1 here, but in Williams, too, there is something odd in the words, something recalcitrant to analysis, incommensurate, arhythmical, or at any rate something not measurable by the repetitions of traditional meter. This quality is Williams' distinctiveness as a poet. It breaks through the conceptual impasses of his theories of poetry and is not reducible to any one of them or to all three together. It interrupts or disrupts the literal representational sense of his poems. Only the spring without spring, the words energized by nature but detached from nature, no longer a symbol of it, can be "cognizant of the whole," and so, by a strange species of synecdoche, give the poet and the reader not just spring beyond spring but "spring and *all*," or rather, the words seem always just about to do that.

It is as if the words of such poems as "Young Sycamore" or "By the road," proffered one by one, were each an invocation. Each word is different, but each asks for the same hidden otherness, the "radiant gist," to appear. Each is like that echoing "Come," "Come," "Come," relayed from speaker to speaker, in the last chapter of *Revelation*, each "Come" inviting the ever imminent but never quite yet present apocalypse. If nothing comes, in this false verbal appearance of a present spring, the spring beyond spring, or spring not spring, therefore spring and all, it seems always, in Williams' best poetry, almost about to come.

CHAPTER NINE

Stevens

In Memory of William K. Wimsatt
(1907-1975)

This book begins with Stevens. It has returned to Stevens intermittently throughout. Now I come full circle back to Stevens again in a concluding discussion of "The Rock," followed by a brief postface on the relation of the linguistic moment to the eternal return. The discussion of the figure of the *mise en abyme* completes the repertoire of spatial images for temporality. Each chapter has provided a different example, the image of a moving across the landscape toward "something ever more about to be" in Wordsworth, the image of the enveloping scene enveloped in Shelley, and so on.[1]

I begin with a citation from "The Rock" (1950):

It is not enough to cover the rock with leaves.
We must be cured of it by a cure of the ground
Or a cure of ourselves, that is equal to a cure

Of the ground, a cure beyond forgetfulness.
(lines 28-31)[2]

---

[1] See the fuller discussion of this in the preface, above pp. xv-xviii.

[2] Wallace Stevens, *The Collected Poems* (New York: Alfred A. Knopf, Inc., 1954), p. 526; henceforth CPSt. "The Rock" is CPSt, pp. 525-528. Citations are also made in this chapter from Wallace Stevens, *Opus Posthumous* (New York: Alfred A Knopf, Inc., 1957); henceforth OPSt. For a discussion of "The Rock," see Harold Bloom, *Wallace Stevens: The Poems of Our Climate* (Ithaca: Cornell University Press, 1977), pp. 338-351. For Stevens' poetry generally, see Frank Kermode, *Wallace Stevens* (New York: Grove Press, 1961); *Wallace Stevens: A Collection of Critical Essays*, ed. Marie Borroff (Englewood Cliffs, New Jersey: Prentice-Hall, Inc., 1963); *The Act of the Mind: Essays on the Poetry of Wallace Stevens*, ed. Roy Harvey Pearce and

"A cure of the ground"? What can this mean? "Progress," Stevens says in the *Adagia*, "is a movement through changes of terminology" (OPSt, 157). *Rock, ground*, and even *forgetfulness*, readers of Stevens will be able to interpret from other poems by him, from works in his immediate tradition, the tradition of Whitman and Emerson, or from the common language of poetry and philosophy. Such readers will remember, among other rocks in Stevens, "this tufted rock / Massively rising high and bare" in "How to Live. What to Do" (CPSt, 125), the Leibnizian "thought-like Monadnocks" of "This Solitude of Cataracts" (CPSt, 424), the rocky mountain who speaks in "Chocorua to Its Neighbor" (CPSt, 296-302), the rock of "The Poem that Took the Place of a Mountain," "The exact rock where his inexactnesses / Would discover, at last, the view toward which they had edged" (CPSt, 512), and that ecstatic meridian rock of "Credences of Summer":

J. Hillis Miller (Baltimore: The Johns Hopkins Press, 1965); Joseph Riddel, *The Clairvoyant Eye: The Poetry and Poetics of Wallace Stevens* (Baton Rogue: Louisiana State University Press, 1965); Frank Doggett, *Stevens' Poetry of Thought* (Baltimore: The Johns Hopkins Press, 1966), and *Wallace Stevens: The Making of the Poem* (Baltimore and London: The Johns Hopkins University Press, 1980); Robert Buttel, *Wallace Stevens: The Making of "Harmonium"* (Princeton: Princeton University Press, 1967); Ronald Sukenick, *Wallace Stevens: Musing the Obscure* (New York: New York University Press, 1967); James Baird, *The Dome and the Rock: Structure in the Poetry of Wallace Stevens* (Baltimore: The Johns Hopkins Press, 1968); Helen Hennessy Vendler, *On Extended Wings: Wallace Stevens' Longer Poems* (Cambridge, Mass.: Harvard University Press, 1969); A. Walton Litz, *Introspective Voyager: The Poetic Development of Wallace Stevens* (New York: Oxford University Press, 1972); Michael Benamou, *Wallace Stevens and the Symbolist Imagination* (Princeton: Princeton University Press, 1972), and *L'Oeuvre→Monde de Wallace Stevens* (Paris: Librairie Honoré Champion, 1975); Isabel G. MacCaffrey, "A Point of Central Arrival: Stevens' *The Rock*," *ELH* XL, 4 (Winter 1973), 606-633; *Wallace Stevens: A Celebration*, ed. Frank Doggett and Robert Buttel (Princeton: Princeton University Press, 1980); Janet McCann, "'The Celestial Possible': Wallace Stevens' Last Poems," *Southwest Review* LXVI, 1 (Winter 1981), 73-82; Leonora Woodman, *Stanza My Stone: Wallace Stevens and the Hermetic Tradition* (West Lafayette, Indiana: Purdue University Press, 1983).

> The rock cannot be broken. It is the truth.
> It rises from land and sea and covers them.
> It is a mountain half way green and then,
> The other immeasurable half, such rock
> As placid air becomes.
> (CPSt, 375)

Forgetfulness, or its converse, memory, is also a motif elsewhere in Stevens, inextricably entwined with the theme of time, as in "The Owl in the Sarcophagus," where the fleeting present moment, the presence of the present, "the mother of us all," cries in her vanishing, "Keep you, keep you, I am gone, oh keep you as / My memory" (CPSt, 432).

Ground, too, is a common word in Stevens. To follow it through his poetry is to observe its modulation from the everyday use of it as the solid earth we stand on ("The jar was round upon the ground" [CPSt, 76]), to ground as background upon which a figure appears, to the more "metaphysical" use of the term to mean foundation, basis, source, mind or consciousness, reason, measure. The rock, in "The Rock," "is the habitation of the whole, / Its strength and measure" "the main of things, the mind" (lines 70-71, 75), in short, a Monadnock, according to Stevens' pun. Ground and rock, in "The Rock," are apparently not the same, since a cure of the ground is necessary to cure us of the rock, though what the difference is between ground and rock remains, at this point, something still to be interrogated. The means of this interrogation, however, as of the investigation of *forgetfulness*, would, it seems, be the familiar one of following these words in their interplay with other words as they gradually weave together in a single grand intertextual system, a polyphonic harmony of many notes—"The Whole of Harmonium," as Stevens wanted to call his *Collected Poems*.

What, then of *cure*? It has little resonance in philosophic or poetic tradition, and according to the *Concordance to the Poetry of Wallace Stevens*, the word is used only once, in a more or less unpregnant way, prior to its decidedly pregnant use in "The Poem as Icon," the middle of the three sections of "The Rock." "The Poem as Icon" is in fact partly a meditation on the multiple sense, "the new senses in the engenderings of sense," of the word *cure* in its relation to certain other terms and figures. The word thereafter disappears from Stevens' poetic canon, not even being used in the third poem of "The Rock," though it does appear in the *Adagia*: "Poetry is a health"; "Poetry is a cure of the mind" (OPSt, 176). In formulations of the workings of intertextuality, the weavings of word with word, of figure with figure, in the canon of a writer, or of that canon in relation to tradition, the theorist would need to allow for the emergence of a word that is played with, turned this way and that, mated with other words, used as an indispensable means of that progress which takes place through changes of terminology, and then dropped.

To think of the whole work of a writer as being based on a permanent ground in an underlying system or code of terms—conceptual, figurative, "symbolic," mythical, or narrative—is an error, just as it is an error to suggest, as I. A. Richards does in his admirable *How to Read a Page*, that there may be in our Western languages a finite set of key words of multiple senses whose mastery would give approximate mastery of Western thought and literature. The repertoire of such words, big with antithetical and irreconcilable meanings, is very large, finite still (there are only so many words in the *O.E.D.*) but virtually inexhaustible. Any poet's vocabulary is to some degree irreducibly idiosyncratic. The most unexpected words, for example *cure*, may become momentarily nodes, at once fixed rock and treacherous abyss of doubled and redoubled meanings, around or over which the thought of the poet swirls or weaves its web. Such words are not the equivalents or substitutes for other terms. Each has its own proper laws and so may not be made an example of some general law. Such words may not be translated, thereby made transparent,

393

dispensed with, evaporated, sublimated. They remain stub-bornly heterogeneous, inassimilable, impervious to dialec-tic sublation, rocks in the stream, though the rock is air. The vocabulary of a poet is not a gathering or a closed system, but a dispersal, a scattering.

What, then, of *cure*? The first section of "The Rock," "Seventy Years Later," is, at least until the last two stanzas, as bleak and cold a poem as any Stevens wrote. It is a poem about forgetting. The old man of seventy has forgotten not the illusions of his past but the affective warmth of those illusions, "the lives these lived in the mind" (line 8). When that warmth goes, the illusions come to be seen as illusions and so are undermined, annihilated. Not only are their validity and vitality rejected. Their very existence is denied: "The sounds of the guitar / Were not and are not. Absurd. The words spoken / Were not and are not" (lines 9-11). *Absurd*: from *ab*, away, an intensive here, and *surdus*, deaf, inaudible, insufferable to the ear. The sounds of the gui-tar—those, for example, played by Stevens' man with the blue guitar—were not only an inharmonious jangling mask-ing as harmony. They did not even exist at the time. They were inaudible when they most seemed audible. They did not exist because they were pure fiction, based on noth-ingness. A *surd* in mathematics is a sum containing one or more irrational roots of numbers. The square root of two is an irrational number. There is a square root of two, but it is not any number that can be said, rationally. A *surd* in phonetics is a voiceless sound, that is to say, a sound with no base in the vibration of the vocal chords. The original root of the word *surd, swer*, means to buzz or whisper, as in *susurration* or *swirl*, which I used above. The Latin *surdus* was chosen in medieval mathematics to translate an Arabic term that was itself a translation of the Greek *alogos*: speech-less, wordless, inexpressible, irrational, groundless.

The first six stanzas of "Seventy Years Later" record a radical act of forgetting. This disremembering annihilates everything that seems most vital in the poet's past, most solidly grounded. Such forgetting annihilates the past by uprooting it, by seeing its roots as nonexistent, "alogical." Then in the final three stanzas the dismantled illusion is put together again. Though the base may be "nothingness," this nothingness contains a "métier," a craftsmanlike power of working, "a vital assumption" (lines 19, 20). It contains a desire for illusion so great that the leaves come and cover that high rock of air, as the lilacs bloom in the spring, cleansing blindness, bringing sight again to birth, and so starting the cycle of illusion over again. Blindness is parallel to the deafness of *absurd*, and the power of seeing again is here expressed as "a birth of sight" (line 25). The lilacs satisfy sight. They fill the eye, as the sounds of the guitar filled the ear, saturated it, so hiding the "permanent cold" at the base, "the dominant blank, the unapproachable," as Stevens calls it in "An Ordinary Evening in New Haven" (CPSt, 477). A cure of ourselves equal to a cure of the ground would make us sound, heal us of our deafness, our absurdity. We could then hear again the sounds of the guitar, as springtime makes us see again, like a blindness cured, or scoured.

The cure of the ground called for in the beginning of the second poem of "The Rock," "The Poem as Icon," must be "a cure beyond forgetfulness" (line 31). It must be a cure not subject to the periodic cycles of annihilation revealing the illusion to be illusion and so negating it. Or, perhaps, it must be a cure that reaches beyond forgetfulness, that repression disabling present affirmations. This repression has caused us to forget the something lacking in earlier satisfactions, something missing even when we "lived in the houses of mothers" (line 2). To remove this repression would, perhaps, make it possible to get to something solid behind, or to make something solid behind not based on a forgetting and so vulnerable to forgetting. After the cure we would live in a permanent state of illusion known as illusion, therefore "beyond forgetfulness." This illusion would be known in such a way that the abyss, the

Abgrund, would appear as the truth of the ground, without undermining the illusion, so that the illusion might never be forgotten. Or does Stevens mean that the cure beyond forgetfulness would permanently cover or solidify the abyss? Then the illusion might never again be scoured away and the abyss never again be seen: "The poem makes meanings of the rock, / Of such mixed motion and such imagery / That its barrenness becomes a thousand things / And so exists no more" (lines 55-58). The possibility of each of these alternatives is suggested by Stevens' often cited adage: "The final belief is to believe in a fiction, which you know to be a fiction, there being nothing else" (OPSt, 163).

A similar uncertainty (but what is the status of similarity here?) is expressed in the relation between rock and ground. Ground and rock are each the base of the other. The rock is the truth, but the rock is air, nothingness, and so must be grounded on something solid beneath it. The ground, on the other hand, is itself not ground. It is an abyss, the groundless, while the rock remains visible in the air as "the gray particular of man's life / The stone from which he rises, up—and—ho, / The step to the bleaker depths of his descents . . ." (lines 61-63). The rock is the solid of the ground, the ground the base of the rock, in a reversal, interchange, doubling, or abyssing that Stevens elsewhere calls "an insolid billowing of the solid" ("Reality Is an Activity of the Most August Imagination" [OPSt, 111]).

A cure of the ground would be a caring for the ground, a securing of it, making it solid, as one cures a new fiberglass hull by drying it carefully. At the same time the cure of the ground must be an effacing of it, making it vanish as a medicine cures a man of a disease by taking it away, making him sound again, or as an infatuated man is cured of a dangerous illusion. *Cure* comes from Latin *cura*, care, as in *curate* or *a cure of souls*. The word *scour*, which I used above, has the same root. A cure of the ground would scour it clean, revealing the bedrock beneath. Such a curing would be at the same time—according to an obsolete meaning of the word, with a different root, Middle English *cuuve*: cover, conceal, protect—a caring for the ground by hiding it. Stevens might even have known (why should he not have known?) the word *curiologic*, which means, according to the *O.E.D.*, "of or pertaining to that form of hieroglyphic writing in which objects are represented by pictures, and not by symbolic characters." The root here is neither *cura* nor *cuuve*, but the Greek *kuriologia*: use of literal expressions, speaking literally; from *kurios*, as an adjective: regular, proper; as a noun: lord, master. A curiological cure of the ground would find proper names for that ground, make a mimetic icon of it, copy it exactly, appropriate it, master it. The cure of the ground proposed in the poem is the poem itself. The poem is an icon, at once a "copy of the sun" (line 40) and a figure of the ground, though the relation of sun and ground remains to be established. The icon (image, figure, resemblance) at once creates the ground, names it properly, reveals it, and covers it over. The poem annihilates the rock, takes the place of it, and replaces it with its own self-sufficient fiction—the leaves, blossom, and fruit that come to cover the high rock. At that point its barrenness has become a thousand things and so exists no more.

The multiple meanings of the word *cure*, like the meanings of all the key words and figures in "The Rock," are incompatible. They may not be organized into a logical or dialectical structure but remain stubbornly heterogeneous. They may not be followed, etymologically, to a single root that will unify or explain them, explicate them by implicating them in a single source. They may not be folded together in a unified structure, as of leaves, blossom, and fruit from one stem. The origin rather is bifurcated, even trifurcated, a forking root that leads the searcher for the ground of the word into labyrinthine wanderings in the forest of words. The meanings of the passages in "The Rock" turning on the word *cure* vibrate uneasily within the reader's mind. However hard he or she tries to fix the word in a single sense it remains indeterminable, resisting his or her attempts to end its movement. Cover the abyss, or open it up, or find the bottom, the ground of the rock, and make it a solid base on which to build—which is it? How could it be all three at once? Yet it is impossible to decide which one it is. To choose one is to be led to the others and so to be led by the words of the poem into a blind alley of thought, though the suspense of meaning hovers between specific and identifiable alternatives.

Since it is a question here of the abyss of the absurd and of the grounding or filling of that abyss, one may borrow from the French an untranslatable name for this impasse of language: *mise en abyme*. *Abyme* is an older variant of the modern French *abîme*, from late Latin *abyssus*, from Greek *abussos*, without bottom. The circumflexed *i, i* deprived of its head or dot, and given a hat or tent instead, indicates a dropped *s*. This *i* is then dropped in turn to be replaced by a *y, i grec*, Greek *i*. In fact the late Latin *y* was an equivalent both for Greek *u, upsilon*, "bare *u*," and for the *y*, or *u*, with a tail, that is, an *i* sound, as in French *ici*. The Greek *u*, which became Roman *y*, is only one of the two letters deriving from the Phoenician *waw*, which is itself derived from *v*. The other descendent is *f*, Greek *digamma*, "double *gamma*." The *gamma* is of course also *y*-shaped. The word *abyme* is itself a *mise en abyme*, hiding and revealing the hollow of the *u* by the masculine addition of the tail, but leaving no sign of the absent *s*. The word *abyme* contains dropped letter behind dropped letter, in a labyrinth of interchanges figured by the doubling shape of the *y*: a path leading to a fork, Hercules at the crossroads, or Theseus at one of the infinitely repeating branchings of the Daedalian labyrinth.

Mise en abyme is a term in heraldry meaning a shield that has in its center a smaller image of the same shield and so, by implication, *ad infinitum*, ever smaller and smaller shields receding toward the central point. The nearest equivalent in the English language of heraldry is the admirably suggestive term, "escutcheon of pretense." The arms to which a knight pretends to have a claim are *mise en abyme* on his own shield. As in the case of a bar sinister, the implication is of some possible illegitimacy, some break in the genetic line of filiation. I have, in *The Form of Victorian Fiction*, called this structure "the Quaker Oats box effect." To name it or to give examples of it is not to create a concept, a general structure that all the examples exemplify, since it is a question, in this case, of what has no concept, no literal name. Therefore it can only be figured, each time differently, and by analogies that are not symmetrical to one another. What is the meaning of the terms *figure, icon, analogy*, here, if there is no literal name on which they are based? Here, from Michel Leiris's autobiography, *L'âge d'homme* (1939), is a splendid "example" of a *mise en abyme*:

> I owe my first precise contact with the notion of infinity to a box of cocoa of Dutch manufacture, raw material [*matière première*] for my breakfasts. One side of this box was decorated with an image representing a peasant girl with a lace headdress who held in her left hand an identical box decorated with the same image and, pink and fresh, offered it with a smile. I remained seized with a sort of vertigo in imagining that infinite series of an identical image reproducing a limitless number of times the same young Dutch girl, who, theoretically getting smaller and smaller without ever disappearing, looked at me with a mocking air and showed me her own effigy painted on a cocoa box identical to the one on which she herself was painted.[3]

The paradox of the *mise en abyme* is the following: Without the production of some schema, some "icon," there can be no glimpse of the abyss, no vertigo of the underlying

---

[3] Michel Leiris, *L'âge d'homme* (Paris: Gallimard, 1973), pp. 36-37, my trans. On the *mise en abyme* as a narrative structure, see Lucien Dällenbach, *Le récit spéculaire: Essai sur la mise en abyme* (Paris: Éditions du Seuil, 1977).

nothingness. Any such scheme, however, both opens the chasm, creates it or reveals it, and at the same time fills it up, covers it over by naming it, gives the groundless a ground, the bottomless a bottom. Any such figure almost instantaneously becomes a trivial mechanism, an artifice. It becomes something merely made, confected, therefore all-too-human and rational. Examples would include the Daedalian labyrinth—product, after all, of a human artificer, however "fabulous"—and the Borgesian labyrinths of words, products of a visible manipulation of verbal effects. Another example is the cunning wordplay of Stevens' "The Rock," with its sagacious and somewhat covert use of the full etymological complexity of a word like *cure*. If Stevens is right to say that "poetry must be irrational" and that "poetry must resist the intelligence almost successfully" (OPSt, 162, 171), the moment when the intelligence triumphs over the poem, encompassing its *mise en abyme*, with human reason, is the moment of the poem's failure, its resolution into a rational paradigm. The *mise en abyme* must constantly begin again. "The Rock" is, accordingly, a running *mise en abyme*. It repeatedly takes some apparently simple word, a word not noticeably technical or tricky: *found, exclaiming, ground,* or *cure.* The poem plays with each such word in turn, places it in such a context of surrounding words that it gives way beneath its multiplying contradictory meanings and reveals the chasm below, a chasm that the word, for example, the word *cure*, cures in all senses of the word.

There are other ways in which "The Rock" is a *mise en abyme*. One is the sequence of phrases in apposition. This is a constant feature of Stevens' poetic procedure. It is a basic linguistic resource, for example, of "A Primitive Like an Orb," referred to briefly in chapter 7 above. "The Rock" provides further examples: "The blooming and the musk / Were being alive, an incessant being alive, / A particular of being, that gross universe"; "They bud the whitest eye, the pallidest sprout, / New senses in the engenderings of sense, / The desire to be at the end of distances, / The body quickened and the mind in root" (lines 25-27, 46-49). The relation among the elements in such a series is abyssed. Since the phrases often have the same syntactical pattern and are objects of the same verb (most often the verb *to be*), it seems as if they must be equivalents of one another, or at least figures for one another, but can *eye, sprout, senses, desire, body,* and *mind* really be equivalent? Perhaps the phrases form a progression, a gradual approximation through incremental repetition ("being alive, an incessant being alive"), reaching closer and closer to the desired meaning in what Stevens in "An Ordinary Evening in New Haven" calls "the edgings and inchings of final form" (CPSt, 488)? Perhaps each new phrase cancels the previous one? Sometimes the parallel in syntax is misleading, as "that gross universe," in my first example, is in apposition with "being" in the phrase before, not with "particular." The sequence plays with various incongruent senses and grammatical functions of the word *being.* Sometimes the established syntactical pattern misleads the reader into interpreting the grammar incorrectly or at any rate leads him or her into a fork in the labyrinth where he or she cannot decide which path to take, as when the parallelism of "And yet the leaves, if they broke into bud, / If they broke into bloom, if they bore fruit, / And if we ate the incipient colorings / Of their fresh culls might be a cure of the ground" (lines 32-35) makes *colorings* appear to be simultaneously the object of *ate* and the subject of *might be* which it cannot, logically, be. The actual subject of *might be* is *leaves,* three lines above. The phrase seems alogical, absurd, with no root in a single sense.

Such sequences, with their tantalizing half-parallelisms and asymmetrical analogies, with their suggestions that the series might continue indefinitely without exhausting itself or "getting it right," are *mises en abyme.* They are like those nursery rhymes that work by variation and incremental repetition, such as "The House That Jack Built." John Ruskin in the twenty-third letter of *Fors Clavigera* (1872), compares "The House That Jack Built" to the Daedalian maze:

"the gradual involution of the ballad, and necessity of clear-mindedness as well as clear utterance on the part of its singer, is a pretty vocal imitation of the deepening labyrinth."[4] Like Stevens' sequences of phrases in apposition, "The House That Jack Built" turns back on itself. It is a snake with its tail in its mouth, or a snake almost succeeding in getting its tail in its mouth. Just as that "gross universe" comments on or defines the word *being*, which has been the theme varied in the sequences of phrases in Stevens' sentence until then, so the *mise en abyme* of the potentially endlessly mounting series in "The House That Jack Built" is broken when "the farmer sowing his corn" is reached, since that corn is presumably the source of the malt that lay in the house that Jack built. This takes the listener back to the second item in the sequence and so makes the infinitely receding series, the labyrinth within the house that Jack built, an infinitely rotating circle instead. In the same way the diminishing sequence described in the passage from Leiris quoted above is blocked by the end that turns back to remind the reader that the "first" girl is herself an image painted on a box. The series, moreover, is asymmetrically balanced by a second paragraph describing the multiplying of erotic reflections in facing mirrors: "I am not far from believing that there was mixed in this first notion of infinity, acquired at about the age of ten (?), an element of a distinctly disturbing sort: the hallucinatory and genuinely ungraspable character of the young Dutch girl, repeated to infinity as libertine visions can be indefinitely multiplied by means of a carefully constructed play of mirrors in a boudoir."[5]

This structure of not quite congruent parallelism is characteristic of all forms of the *mise en abyme*. This is one of the ways this pattern keeps open the chasm while filling it,

[4] John Ruskin, *Fors Clavigera*, Letter XXIII, *Works*, ed. E. T. Cook and Alexander Wedderburn, XXVII (London: George Allen, 1907), p. 402.

[5] Leiris, *L'âge d'homme*, ed. cit., p. 37, my trans.

resists the intelligence almost successfully. An admirable example of this asymmetry is that cartoon by Charles Addams showing the receding reflections in doubled mirrors of a man in a barber chair, facing frontwards, then backwards, then frontwards again, in endless recession. One figure in the midst of the sequence, five images back into the mirror's depths, is a wolfman with fangs and a hairy face. The wolfman is the terrifying item that is part of the series but does not fit it, though he is neither its beginning, nor its end, nor its base. Another more complex example of the mirror as *mise en abyme* is Thomas Hardy's admirable poem, "The Pedigree," which would merit a long analysis.[6] As Ruskin astutely saw, "Jack's ghostly labyrinth [meaning the mythical Daedalian maze, with its Charles Addams monster as inhabitant] has set the pattern of almost everything linear and complex, since."[7]

Also characteristic of such structures is some play with the figure of container and thing contained or with an inside/outside opposition that reverses itself. Inside becomes outside, outside inside, dissolving the polarity. The house that Jack built contains all the elements in the nursery rhyme, though they are mostly outside the house. As Ruskin suggests, the cunning artifice of the poem is the house itself, just as the Daedalian labyrinth is at once an enclosure and a place of endless wandering. A labyrinth is a desert turned inside out. In a similar way the passage from Leiris's autobiography turns on the cocoa box that is a container of the *matière première* of the child's breakfast, while the girl who offers the box is also offering herself, in a troubling erotic opening, which is another characteristic of the *mise en abyme*. Eating and sex are interchanged, as also in "The Rock," which has in its first section an embrace at noon at the edge of a field and moves on to the image of curing

[6] See pp. 276-278 of the essay by Mary Jacobus cited above in chapter 6, footnote 2, for a brief discussion of this poem.

[7] Ruskin, *Works*, ed. cit., xxvii, p. 407.

the ground and curing ourselves by eating the fruit grown from the rock. That eating, with its disturbing echoes of Milton and the Bible, is also a transgression with erotic and Satanic overtones. These involve seeing and knowing, in various punning ways, knowledge of the whole and of the base of the whole by an incorporation of a synecdochic part: "In the day ye eat thereof, then your eyes shall be opened, and ye shall be as gods, knowing good and evil" (Genesis 3.5); "They bear their fruit so that the year is known, / As if its understanding was brown skin, / The honey in its pulp, the final found, / The plenty of the year and of the world" (lines 51-54). Like the passage from Leiris, "The Rock" contains a complicated play on the figure of container and thing contained. It is a version of what Kenneth Burke calls "the paradox of substance." The rock is the base from which things rise up, therefore it is outside. At the same time it is the habitation of the whole, that in which space and all the contents of space are contained. This enigmatic structure is repeated with the houses of mothers, with the sun, with the fruit, and with the poem itself. To read the poem or to eat the fruit is to incorporate the whole as it is contained in the part, to incorporate even the ground of that whole, and so to become oneself whole, sound, cured, knowing all in a final "found."

The *mise en abyme* is likely also to contain some puzzling play with the intertwined notions of representation, on the one hand, and, on the other, of figure, metaphor. The girl on the cocoa box offers smilingly a picture of herself, an image, an effigy, but she is herself only an image. The image within an image tends both to affirm the literal reality of the outside image and to undermine it, as in another, more recent, *New Yorker* cartoon showing a middle-aged couple watching on television a representation of themselves watching a televised picture of themselves watching television, and so on. In "The Rock" this turning back of representation on itself enters by way of the contradictory meanings of the word *icon*, as it has already entered more obscurely in the word *shadow* in the first section. The poem as icon is both curiological, a mimetic copy of the whole, and at the same time a figure, similitude, or metaphor of the whole. The poem is an icon in both senses, in a coming and going between literal and figurative. This enigmatic interchange between proper and improper uses of language, in a bewildering multiplication of different chains of figurative terminology superimposed, juxtaposed, interwoven, is a final form of *mise en abyme* in "The Rock."

"The Rock" contains at least four distinct linguistic "scenes," repertoires of terms each adding up to a distinct pattern. The poem is like those paintings by Tchelitchew that are simultaneous representations of several different objects, superimposed or interwoven, or it is like those children's puzzles in which the trick is to see the five monkeys hidden in the tree or, more grotesquely, the sailboats in the vegetable garden. The poem contains a scene of love, even a love story: "the meeting at noon at the edge of the field ... , an embrace between one desperate clod / And another"; "as a man loves, as he lives in love" (lines 12-14; 50). The poem also presents a geometrical diagram. This diagram is described and analyzed with appropriate mathematical and logical terminology: *absurd, invention, assertion, a theorem proposed, design, assumption, figuration, predicate, root, point A / In a perspective that begins again / At B, adduce.* The poem presents in addition a natural scene, the rock that in the turn of the seasons and in the diurnal warmth of the rising and setting sun is covered with leaves, blossoms, and fruit. Man shares in this natural cycle as he eats of the fruit, or as he becomes himself a natural body rooted in the ground, his eye growing in power like the sprouting eye of a potato: "They bud the whitest eye, the pallidest sprout, / New senses in the engenderings of sense" (lines 46-47). "The Rock," finally, describes and analyzes itself. It presents a theory of poetry, with an appropriate terminology: *icon, copy, figuration, imagery,* and so on.

The question, it would seem, is which of these scenes is

405

the literal subject of the poem, the real base of which the others are illustrative figures. This question is unanswerable. Each scene is both literal and metaphorical, both the ground of the poem and a figure on that ground, both that which the poem is centrally about and a resource of terminology used figuratively to describe something other than itself, in a fathomless reversal. The structure of each scene separately and of all four in their relation is a dramatization, or articulation, or iconic projection of the uncanny relation, neither polar opposition, nor hierarchy, nor genetic filiation, between figurative and literal uses of language.

In one sense the description of all four of the scenes is entirely literal. They are icons in the sense of being mimetic pictures of things that for most practical purposes and for those living within the terminology of English or American communities are supposed to exist as independent objects. There really are rocks, leaves, flowers, fruit, and the seasons of the year. A man and a woman have no doubt met in the real world at the edge of a field at noon to embrace. This may well be an autobiographical reference to some episode in the old poet's past. There really are geometrical diagrams with points A and B, theorems, and so on. A poem's self-referentiality is just that, a form of reference or mimesis, as realistic as a description of the weather.

On the other hand, no reader of "The Rock" can remain long under the illusion that it is a poem about the weather or indeed a poem about geometry or about love or about poetry. When the reader focuses on any one of these scenes, that scene both emerges in full mimetic vividness, as the chain of words describing it is culled out of the mesh of other words in the poem, and, at the same time, the reader sees that the scene cannot be copied, made into an icon, without the use of terms drawn from the other scenes. The embrace at noon at the edge of the field, for example, is, mathematically, "a theorem proposed between the two" (line 16). At the same time each scene, though it must borrow

406

names from the others to name itself, becomes a resource of figurative language for the other scenes. The leaves bud, blossom, and make fruit, "as a man loves, as he lives in love." Each scene is both ground and design on that ground, both literal and figurative, icon in both senses of the word, in an oscillation that forms and re-forms itself with each word, phrase, or image throughout the poem. As the reader tries to rest on each element in the poem or on a chain of elements forming a single scene, as he seeks a solid literal ground that might be the curiological basis of the other figurative meanings, that element or chain gives way. It becomes itself a verbal fiction, an illusion, an icon in the sense of similitude not in the sense of mimetic copy. The element becomes an *Abgrund*, not a *Grund*. The reader is forced then to shift sideways again, seeking to find somewhere else in the poem the solid ground of that figure, seeking, and failing, or falling, and seeking again.

Another way to put this is to say that the reader can make sense of the poem by assuming any one of the scenes to be the literal ground on the basis of which the others are defined as analogical, figurative, iconic. By that definition, however, the base, when examined, must be defined as itself analogical. That which must necessarily be taken as literal in order to define the figurative is itself figurative, and so the distinction breaks down. In order for the fruit, the man, lovers, poem, and geometric design to be defined as figurative, the leftover term, the sun in its turnings, must be taken as literal. If, however, fruit, man, poem, and so on are figurative, so, necessarily, must be the sun, since it is, like the others, an icon of the ground. Analogy cannot be defined except with the use of analogies. The defined enters into and so contaminates the definer, annulling the validity of the definition. Figure must always be defined figuratively. There is always a remainder, something alogical left over that does not fit any logical scheme of interpretation. Something has to be left out, assumed to be marginal, in order to make a completely coherent interpretation. The word *cull* in "The Rock" carries this ambiguity. A cull (from *culligere*, to gather) is a fruit chosen, collected, or separated out from the rest, but chosen because it does not fit. A cull is imperfect or inferior. That act of decision, of differentiation, establishes the criteria of fitness or perfection. Without the culling out of the culls there can be no gathering of what is left as examples of a uniform grade. The figurative, as in the example I have just given, defines the literal rather than the other way around. Whichever scene is taken as figurative implicitly defines some scene as literal, but that scene, when it is looked at directly, turns out to be itself clearly figurative. The reader must then seek the literal base elsewhere, in a constant lateral transfer with nowhere a resting place in the unequivocally literal, mimetic—the "exact rock," cured at last.

Each of the scenes in "The Rock" is, as a "particular of being," the equivalent of all the others. Each holds an equivalent status as simultaneously both figure and ground, in a chain of chains that is articulated in the poem around the verb *to be*: "The fiction of the leaves is the icon / Of the poem, the figuration of blessedness, / And the icon is the man" (lines 36-38); "This is the cure / Of leaves and of the ground and of ourselves. / His words are both the icon and the man" (lines 59-60). Extending these chains of equivalence, or linking them together, one would get the following affirmation: The icon is the man is the poem is the fruit is the sun is a theorem or geometrical design is the relation of love is . . . the rock.

The structure of each of these scenes is the same. It is, in fact, the traditional metaphysical structure of *aletheia*, the appearance of something visible out of the abyss of truth. Truth is, for Stevens too, evasive, veiled, feminine, and dwells at the bottom of a well. The revelation or unveiling of what has been hidden brings the truth momentarily into the open, out of Lethean forgetfulness, and displays it. This revelation expands to become a container of the whole or a means of appropriating the whole, and then instantaneously hides the abyss, or ground. It quickly becomes a fiction, an illusion, something hollowed out, a mere "rind," or "cull." It becomes something that never was, and so vanishes. The lovers appear at noon and create a relation between one another, a theorem that makes them "Two figures in a nature of the sun, / In the sun's design of its own happiness" (lines 17-18). A geometrical design appears in the open as an appropriation of space. Fruit grows out of the leaves and blossoms that come and cover the high rock. That fruit then encompasses the whole year and becomes "the final found, / The plenty of the year and of the world" (lines 53-54). The fruit is a gathering of the whole, a cull. To eat the fruit would be to possess the whole and so to cure the ground. It would be to understand the ground, in the etymological sense of reaching the base and standing there, in a "final found," with a multiple pun on *found* as discovery, invention, and foundation. The man in turn grows like the fruit. His maturing is a birth and extension of sight, "new senses in the engenderings of sense" (line 47). These new senses allow him to encompass space. This equivalence of seeing and symbol making goes back, in Stevens' case, to Emerson, as in the formulation of Charles Sanders Peirce: "The symbol may, with Emerson's Sphynx, say to man, 'Of thine eye I am the eyebeam.' "[8] All the symbols or icons of "The Rock" are a means of seeing, an extension of sight, "like a blindness cleaned" (line 23). The poem itself rises as an icon that is the equivalent of leaves, blossom, and fruit, and so cures the ground.

The reader is tempted to arrange these items in some kind of hierarchy. Surely, he or she thinks, one item in the series can be recognized to be the base of the others, thereby grounding the sequence and putting a stop to the discomfort caused by their oscillation. No doubt the prime can-

[8] Charles Sanders Peirce, "The Nature of Symbols," *Elements of Logic, Collected Papers*, ed. Charles Hartshorne and Paul Weiss, II (Cambridge, Mass.: The Belknap Press of Harvard University Press, 1960), p. 169.

didate for the first in the series is the self, the self of the poet or speaker, the self in general of each individual included in the collective *we* of the poem. The reader wants to find in the poem a personal voice and a personal drama, the voice and drama of Stevens himself in old age. The experience of reading the poem would then have the security and enclosure of an intersubjective relation. In such a relation my self as reader would respond through the words to the self of the poet and communicate with him beyond the grave. After all, does not the poem assert that "a cure of ourselves" would be "equal to a cure / Of the ground, a cure beyond forgetfulness" (lines 30-31)? The affirmative substitutions and translations of "The Poem as Icon" seem to come to rest in the ecstatic certainty of a poem that would found and be founded on the solid rock of the self, the man's words being the man and rooting him:

> This is the cure
> Of leaves and of the ground and of ourselves.
> His words are both the icon and the man.
> (lines 58-60)

The poem's many echoes of its immediately preceding American tradition, the Whitman of "Song of Myself," the Emerson of "Experience," would seem to confirm this priority of the self over the other icons in the poem. In Whitman there is the same return to the self as the base of all experience, and the same universalization of the self to enclose all events, things, and persons, as the reader is tempted to find in "The Rock." It is surely in honor of Whitman that Stevens chooses to have lilacs come and bloom, like a blindness cleaned, to cover the high rock. Stevens' leaves grow up from chthonic depths, as signs, like the inscribed leaves of a book, just as do Whitman's leaves of grass: "I bequeath myself to the dirt to grow from the grass I love"; "Or I guess the grass is itself a child, the produced babe

of the vegetation. / Or I guess it is a uniform hieroglyphic."[9]
The equivalence, in Stevens' poem, between the leaves covering the rock, the man, and the poem as icon is sanctioned by Whitman. Whitman's pun on leaves as the leaves of a book surfaces most in "The Rock" when Stevens says "The fiction of the leaves is the icon / Of the poem" (lines 36-37). Whitman's "Song of Myself," moreover, like Stevens' "The Rock," is governed by the repeated movement of *aletheia*, the appearance from the dark ground of some "particular of being" that manifests itself in the sunlight. "I find," says Whitman, "I incorporate gneiss, coal, long-threaded moss, fruits, grains, esculent roots." Rocks and earth are part of these figures of descent and return in Whitman's song of himself: "the mica on the side of the rock," a shining from the depths, "the plutonic rocks" that "send" "in vain" "their old heat against [his] approach," "voluptuous cool-breath'd earth," "earth of departed sunset." There is even a striking anticipation of Stevens' embrace of two desperate clods at the edge of the field at noon in Whitman's: "I believe the soggy clods shall become lovers and lamps."[10]

From Whitman the reader moves back one further step to Whitman's immediate precursor, Emerson. The sequence forms its own *mise en abyme* of successive influence and misinterpretation, from Emerson to Whitman to Stevens. For Emerson, in "Experience," the strong affirming of self is the bedrock fiction beneath which one cannot and should not go. The self is the one power remaining when all else has been peeled off and cast away, like dead husks. Though the self is illusion too for Emerson, it is illusion that constantly reforms itself, however often it is expelled. The illusion of the self or the fact that the self is an illusion

[9] Walt Whitman, "Song of Myself," lines 1339, 105-106, *Leaves of Grass*, Comprehensive Reader's Edition, ed. Harold W. Blodgett and Sculley Bradley (New York: New York University Press, 1965), pp. 89, 34.
[10] *Ibid.*, lines 670, 383, 675, 438, 440, 658, ed. cit., pp. 59, 46, 59, 49, 59.

411

is the bleak truth that is the source of all power, as if nothingness contained a vital métier forming a base for all practical purposes as solid as the divine rock. Such a self would be a substance in the etymological sense, a ground beneath on which all the experiences or affirmations of the self may be based. Once again the governing figure is that of descent and ascent into solar prominence:

> The great and crescive self, rooted in absolute nature, supplants all relative existence and ruins the kingdom of mortal friendship and love. Marriage (in what is called the spiritual world) is impossible, because of the inequality between every subject and every object. The subject is the receiver of Godhead, and at every comparison must feel his being enhanced by that cryptic might. Though not in energy, yet by presence, this magazine of substance cannot be otherwise than felt; nor can any force of intellect attribute to the object the proper deity which sleeps or wakes forever in every subject. . . . And we cannot say too little of our constitutional necessity of seeing things under private aspects, or saturated with our humours. And yet is the God the native of these bleak rocks. That need makes in morals the capital virtue of self-trust. We must hold hard to this poverty, however scandalous, and by more vigorous self-recoveries, after the sallies of action, possess our axis more firmly. The life of truth is cold and so far mournful; but it is not the slave of tears, contritions and perturbations. It does not attempt another's work, nor adopt another's facts. It is a main lesson of wisdom to know your own from another's. . . . [I]n the solitude to which every man is always returning, he has a sanity and revelations which in his passage into new worlds he will carry with him. Never mind the ridicule, never mind the defeat; up again, old heart!—it seems to say,—there is victory yet for all justice; and the true romance which the world exists to realize will be the transformation of genius into practical power.[11]

[11] Ralph Waldo Emerson, "Experience," *Essays: Second Series, The Com-*

This ringing affirmation, central in the American tradition of the strong self, makes the scandalous poverty of that self a radiating power and of its fictive and perspectival insubstantiality, a godlike rock. Stevens' "The Rock," on the other hand, in spite of its discovery of a cure of the ground in the equivalence of self, leaves, ground, and rock, is a thorough deconstruction of the Emersonian bedrock self. Stevens' poem, in one of its aspects, is an interpretation of Emerson and Whitman that undermines their apparent affirmations (though of course both Emerson and Whitman had, each in his own way, already annihilated his own seemingly solid grounding). Stevens' poem further hollows Emerson and Whitman out, gives their key figures one final twist that shatters the structure based on them and shows it to have been baseless. For Stevens, Emerson's bleak rocks are not a beginning below or before which it is impossible to go. The self, for him, is deprived of its status as ground by being shown to be a figure on that ground. The self has the same status as the other elements to which it is equated. The self exists, but in the same fragile and groundless way as fruit, sun, poem, and geometrical diagram. It exists as icon, as image, as figure for the underlying nothing. The self is not the rock but an insubstantial substitute for the absent rock, something that was not, and is not, absurd. Moreover the self for Stevens is not the base of the sequence. It is only one link in a chain. This link has the same status as the others in the sense that it is inscribed in a horizontal series of displacements. In this series each item depends on the others for its definition and therefore for its existence. The self, for Stevens, is generated by this play of linguistic substitutions, vanishing itself if they vanish, depending for its illusory existence on figurative borrowings from them: "His *words* are both the icon and the man" (line 60, my italics).

Moreover, there is a significant difference between Ste-

plete Works, Concord Edition, III (Boston and New York: Houghton, Mifflin and Company, 1903), pp. 77, 81, 85-86.

vens' use of the collective *we* and Emerson's. When Emerson says, "We must hold hard to this poverty," he means something not too different from Whitman's "I incorporate gneiss, coal," or from his "We also ascend dazzling and tremendous as the sun, / We found our own O my soul in the calm and cool of the daybreak."[12] For both Emerson and Whitman each self must affirm itself, if not in isolation, then as the axis of all, the incorporator of all: "I am large, I contain multitudes."[13] One of the crucial moments of Emerson's "Experience" is his rejection of any confrontation of another, or equal relation to another, even in love. The other can only be an image or icon of the self and so not its equal. All doubling or imaging must be rejected as introducing chaos into the spherical and all-inclusive unity of the self. Subject can only marry object, that is, not something its equal or fellow but something that can be devoured, wholly mastered: "There will be the same gulf between every me and thee as between the original and the picture. The universe is the bride of the soul. . . . Life will be imaged, but cannot be divided nor doubled. Any invasion of its unity would be chaos. The soul is not twin-born but the only begotten, and though revealing itself as child in time, child in appearance, is of a fatal and universal power, admitting no co-life."[14]

Who, in contrast, is the "we" of Stevens' "The Rock," the "we" of whom the first two lines say, "It is an illusion that we were ever alive, / Lived in the houses of mothers . . ." (lines 1-2)? Husband and wife? Poetic *we*? The general collective first person plural standing for all men and women together, all old folk of seventy? There is a bleak impersonality of tone and locution in Stevens' poem that forbids thinking of it or feeling it as the autobiographical statement of a recognizable person, the man Wallace Stevens, Vice

[12] Whitman, "Song of Myself," lines 562-563, ed. cit., p. 54.
[13] *Ibid.*, line 1326, ed. cit., p. 88.
[14] Emerson, "Experience," ed. cit., III, pp. 77-78.

President of the Hartford Accident and Indemnity Company, author of *Harmonium*. This impersonality is thematized in the way the personal self in the poem dissolves into a plural self, all mankind and womankind, the *ourselves* of "a cure of ourselves," and that *ourselves* into a collective impersonal consciousness, "the main of things, the mind, / The starting point of the human and the end" (lines 75-76), and that mind, beyond any personality, into the rock, the rock into nothingness. Self in the sense of individual personality is one of the major illusions dissolved by the poem. This dissolution, paradoxically, takes place not by a movement into a more and more vacuous solipsism, as is sometimes said to be Stevens' fate as a poet, but by incorporating that doubling of self and other which Emerson so resolutely, and by the necessity of his more genuinely solipsistic definition of the strong self, rejects. Stevens is more open to the existence of others, more in need of them, and so, in the end, more vulnerable, than Emerson and Whitman to an abyssing or dissolution of the self. This dissolution comes through the doubling of the self or through its attempt to found itself on a relation to another. For Stevens the self-enclosed sphere of the self is broken. It is thereby engulfed in the chasm of its own bifurcation. This conflict between an attempted self-subsistent enclosure and the doubling, breaking apart, and abyssing of that enclosure is present in all four of the chief scenes of "The Rock."

All four take the form or attempt to take the form of a rounded, unified whole that is soundly based. Poem, fruit, sun, geometrical diagram or logical system, single man rooted in the earth, child enclosed in the house of his mother, lovers embraced at noon—all strive to take that form. Each of these figures, however, divides itself by scissions both horizontal and vertical and so becomes not an enclosed finite figure but an endlessly receding series. The geometrical design appears at first to be a closed logical system based on solid predicates that may secure the proposition of theorems generating figures in the sun's design of its own happiness. This closed figure turns into an infinitely repeating sequence, like that cartoon by Charles Addams, with the rock, "that which is near," functioning not as a base but as "point A / In a perspective that begins again / At B" (lines 71-73). Starting at *A*, motivated by the desire to be at the end of distances, one reaches on a line toward the horizon point *B*. At *B* the receding perspective begins again, and so on, ad infinitum, without ever reaching the end of distances. No solid starting place exists, but only an arbitrary beginning that constantly begins again at points *B, C, D*, and so on, and there is no reaching the horizon. This endlessly receding geometrical figure is asymmetrically balanced, in "Forms of the Rock in a Night-Hymn," by the enfolded figure of the rock as "The starting point of the human and the end, / That in which space itself is contained, the gate / To the enclosure" (lines 76-78). Which figure can be built on the rock? The question is unanswerable. The circumscribed design constantly turns into the labyrinthine *mise en abyme*, as the enclosure of the last lines is abyssed by their opening into the alternations of day and night, night with its midnight-minting fragrances exhaling or coining chasms of darkness.

The same transformation dismantles the human scene of the poem. To "live in the houses of mothers" rather than in the masculine labyrinth of the house that Jack built was to dwell in a warm embracing enclosure that at the same time allowed an idyllic openness and freedom of movement. In the houses of mothers, says Stevens, we children "arranged ourselves / By our own motions in a freedom of air" (lines 2-3). The doubling of that relation in a meeting of lovers at noon at the edge of the field produced a schism that in retrospect undermines both scenes and makes them like a perspective starting at *A* that begins again at *B*. If the *mise en abyme* has something uncanny about it, one can also often relate this, as in the passage cited above from Leiris or in the present poem, to a shadowy psychodrama involving the differences of the sexes and of generations,

416

the prohibition against incest, and narcissistic mirroring. In one version of the myth of Narcissus he is in love with his twin sister, who dies and is searched for, vainly and fatally, in the mirror image. The doubling of brother or sister or of any man and woman of the same generation is the embrace of two desperate clods, detached bits of the substantial earth beneath, trying to recover a lost unity, trying to make a global whole that would encompass space in a theorem proposed between the two. This theorem would generate a finite diagram, a closed logical system, in a warm house: "Ah, love, let us be true / To one another!"[15] Let us recover together what we thought we had in the houses of mothers but have lost. Once the division has occurred, however, and it has always already occurred as soon as the child is born, the chasm between self and other remains unfilled.

The desire to be at the end of distances can never be satisfied. The division perpetuates itself in whatever expedients are chosen to close or cure the wound. In "a fantastic consciousness" (line 14) I face my sister self, that other desperate clod. I see in her a substitute for the lost mother, but the failure of that substitution reminds me that the mother was herself the abyss I have forgotten. The warmth in the mother's house was an illusion, something that never was. Her house stands "rigid in rigid emptiness" (line 6). My narcissistic relation to my double of the other sex is an affective movement seeking to find a bedrock for the self or in the self. It discovers only a perspective that begins again at B, a perpetually receding horizon. Stevens dismantles Emerson by insisting on the doubling or imaging of the self in the other, by seeing the self, against Emerson's prohibition, as twin-born, a schismatic or schizoid *we*. The relation to my mirror image doubles my relation, across a generation gap, to my mother and reveals that relation,

[15] Matthew Arnold, "Dover Beach," lines 29-30, *Poems*, ed. Kenneth Allott (London: Longmans, Green and Co., Ltd., 1965), p. 242.

417

too, to have been an empty image, an icon of nothing. Though it seemed an enclosure, solidly based, it was already the abyss, since there was something missing that was suppressed or veiled. This absence has now been revealed in the annihilating, after the fact, both of that warm enclosure and of the security of its repetition in the embrace at noon at the edge of the field. Both the relation to the mother and the relation to the beloved are the experience of a perpetual distance, desire, dissatisfaction, an "emptiness that would be filled" ("An Ordinary Evening in New Haven," CPSt, 467). They are figures, not realities, "Two figures in a nature of the sun, / In the sun's design of its own happiness" (lines 17-18).

Perhaps if the self, for Stevens, is no Emersonian or Whitmanian rock, a solid foundation may be found in that which is imaged by the self in its doublings, that is, in the sun's rising and setting, in the sequence of the seasons, in that universal manifestation of permanence in change of which Whitman said, "there are millions of suns left."[16] Poem, man, lovers, fruit, geometric figure are heliotropic, "copies of the sun," "figures" or "shadows" cast by the sun (lines 40, 17, 7). The poem is a sun. The fruit is a little sun, a mango. Both the man alone and the man in relation to his beloved are suns or figures of the sun. This poem is governed, like so many of Stevens' poems, by the annual and diurnal movements of the sun, as it shifts with the seasons, causing them, and as it rises and sets each day, appearing like man from the ground and disappearing into the rock, that "stone from which he rises, up—and—ho, / The step to the bleaker depths of his descents" (lines 62-63).

Is the sun, then, the literal, of which all the other icons are figures, the bedrock that supports and validates them? No, the sun is the figure par excellence, both in the Western tradition generally and in Stevens' work as a whole. The

---

[16] Whitman, "Song of Myself," line 34, ed. cit., p. 30.

sun is that which cannot be looked at directly but is the source of all seeing, the designer of the figures of its happiness. The sun is the visible, invisible figure for the invisible and unnamable, for the base of the intelligible, "the main of things, the mind." The sun is the traditional icon for occulted being, for the good, for the real, in short, for the rock. The rock in turn is a figure for the ground, and vice versa, in a perpetual displacement.

If the structure of the various scenes in "The Rock" is a repetition of the act of manifestation, it is also a deconstruction of that structure. The rhetorical name for this is *catachresis*. Catachresis is the violent, forced, or abusive use of a word to name something that has no literal name. The word also means, in music, a harsh or unconventional dissonance. "The Rock" seems based on the search for a name that would be an icon for the hidden truth, the figure for a covert literal. All the terms in the poem, however, are at once literal and figurative. Each is a catachresis. According to the logic of a theory of language that bases meaning on the solid referentiality of literal names for visible physical objects, open to the light of the sun, the referent of a catachresis does not exist, was not and is not, absurd. Each term in "The Rock," including *rock* and *ground*, is a catachresis for something that has not, cannot have, a proper name. That something is the abyss, the *Abgrund* or *Ungrund*, the chasm, "the dominant blank, the unapproachable" ("An Ordinary Evening in New Haven," CPSt, 477), which the poem, in all the ways I have identified, encounters. The cure of the ground in a curiological picturing, which Stevens says we *must* have, remains necessarily a future imperative. This imperative can never be fulfilled. To name the abyss is to cover it, to make a fiction or icon of it, a likeness that is no likeness. What is a likeness of the sun? Of what is the sun a likeness?

All the catachreses in the poem re-form the fiction of the referential, the illusion that the terms of the poem refer literally to something that exists, some physical rock or ground, some psychological entity, even some metaphysically existing nothing, the "nothing that is" ("The Snow Man," CPSt, 10). In fact all these terms refer to the blind spot, to the perpetually absent, to the sun when it is below the horizon, "grounded." For this invisible sun, as Aristotle said, there is no name and therefore no substance, no *logos*. The sun in its risings and settings is alogical, the father of all *mises en abyme*. The word *sun* itself is deprived thereby of full propriety. It is a catachresis, since the word cannot be based on a full perception by the senses of what it names. Since all referentiality in language is the aboriginal trope or turning away from the abyss, the blind spot, the referentiality of language is its fall, its unconquerable penchant toward fiction.

All words are initially catachreses. The distinction between literal and figurative language is an alogical deduction or bifurcation from that primal misnaming. The fiction of the literal or proper is therefore the supreme fiction, and all poetry and all language are attempts to fill the abyss, since all language is "based" on catachresis. The continuity of Western thought on this point and Stevens' congruity with that tradition in his use of the rising and setting sun as the prime example of an iconic structure that disarticulates itself are indicated by the applicability to "The Rock" of a passage in Aristotle's *Topics*: "he who has stated that it is a property of the sun to be 'the brightest star that moves above the earth' has employed in the property something of a kind which is comprehensible only by sensation, namely 'moving above the earth'; and so the property of the sun would not have been correctly assigned, for it will not be manifest, when the sun sets, whether it is still moving above the earth, because sensation then fails us."[17]

Where is the sun after it sets, after it disappears into the

---

[17] Aristotle, *Topica* 5.3.131b 25-31, trans. E. S. Forster, Loeb Classical Library (London: William Heinemann Ltd.; Cambridge, Mass.: Harvard University Press, 1960), pp. 503, 505.

ground? The sun becomes the ground, vanishes into the rock, where sensation fails and where blindness is substituted once more for sight and insight. Of that blind spot nothing "true" or "proper" can be said, and so about it we must be silent, deaf and dumb, absurd. The end of Stevens' poem is a brilliant illustration (darkness made visible, silence given speech) of this doubleness of the sun, its visibility and invisibility as the dissolution of rock. Like the poem, the man, and the fruit, the sun rises from the rock as the rock's visible embodiment or icon, while the rock is a night-sun, shining with its fragrant black light on what "night illumines." The rock as "the habitation of the whole" encloses the sun and all things under the sun. The rock, though it may appear to be the literal thing of which all else is a figure, is itself another catachresis. At the farthest or deepest point of the *mise en abyme*, at the end of the poem, the perspective begins again with a further glimpse, a scene that is no scene, into the chasm of night. The rock is:

> The starting point of the human and the end,
> That in which space itself is contained, the gate
> To the enclosure, day, the things illumined
>
> By day, night and that which night illumines,
> Night and its midnight-minting fragrances,
> Night's hymn of the rock, as in a vivid sleep.
>> (lines 76-81)

"As in a vivid sleep"! The final quiet displacement by way of the *as* to another figure expresses once more and for the last time the cadence that has governed the poem. Like a voice of the voiceless, or like an ability to hear the soundless, or like a seeing, with blindness cleaned, of what can be only illusion, a vivid sleep is an oxymoron. It is a sleep that is yet acutely conscious, though with a consciousness not grounded in sensation. A vivid sleep is a clear consciousness of nothing, as night's hymn of the rock is darkness visible. That hymn is the final icon of blessedness, the last appearance of religious terminology in the poem. These religious terms, like the other chains of terms, are also catachreses. This hymn creates what it praises in naming it. It creates what it worships in the displacements figuring that which has no proper name and so has only a poetic existence. "After one has abandoned a belief in God, poetry is that essence which takes its place as life's redemption"; "God and the imagination are one" (*Adagia*, OPSt, 158, 178).

Beginning with the word *cure* in "The Rock," the interpreter is led further and further into a labyrinth of branching linguistic connections going back through Whitman and Emerson to Milton, to the Bible, to Aristotle, and behind him into the forking pathways of our Indo-European family of languages. Stevens' poem is an abyss and the filling of the abyss, a chasm and a production of icons of the chasm. Its textual richness opens abyss beneath abyss, beneath each deep a deeper deep, as the reader interrogates its elements and lets each question generate an answer that is another question in its turn. Each question opens another distance, a perspective begun at *A* that begins again at *B*, without ever reaching any closer to the constantly receding horizon. Such a poem is incapable of being encompassed in a single logical formulation. It calls forth potentially endless commentaries, each one of which, like this essay, can only formulate and reformulate the poem's receding abysses. The linguistic momentum of the poem generates a corresponding momentum in commentaries on the poem.

Between Practice and Theory

> ... entre le désir et l'accomplissement, la
> perpétration et son souvenir: ici devançant,
> la remémorant, au futur, au passé, *sous une*
> *apparence fausse de présent.*
>
> Mallarmé, "Mimique"[1]

The task of criticism at the present time remains what it
has always been: the further exploration, as much by practical essays of interpretation as by theoretical speculation
(though of course they always go together), of that coming
and going in quest and in questioning of the ground which
my preface above identified and which Wallace Stevens
pursued, as the chapter just concluded shows. All the readings in this book have been offered as a contribution to the
fulfillment of that perennial task of criticism.

This brings my trajectory back, by a noncircular circle
or nonspiraling spiral, to my beginning, to the preface and
to questions of exemplarity and sequential coherence raised
there. If each of these readings has been exemplary only
of itself, the string of them together has not formed a
pathway from here to there—neither a triumphant construction of that bridge from theory to practice, from epistemology to ethics, which Kant's third critique tries to build,
nor the completion of a hermeneutical circle or circles, nor
the ordered spiralings of an Hegelian *Aufhebung*, which
returns to itself at a higher level, nor the tracing out of a
progressive or regressive historical development. At the
end we remain just where we began, suspended between

---

[1] Stéphane Mallarmé, *Oeuvres complètes*, éd. de la Pléiade (Paris: Éditions
Gallimard, 1945), p. 310.

practice and theory, though the scenery of the place may look a little different now, in this moment.

It may look different now, in this moment, because the series of readings will perhaps allow in this postface a drawing together of three themes or topics identified in the preface but left more or less separate, like fragments of a structure not yet gathered into one, bridgeheads without the bridge. These three topics are, first, the linguistic moment, the moment of the foregrounding of language in poetry; second, the presentation in poetry of various spatial images for temporality; third, the fact that both poetry and discourse about poetry tend to be a search for grounds, for what in German is called a *Satz vom Grund*, a principle of reason. What is the relation among these topics? What, if anything, draws them together into one? I suggest that the place of convergence knotting or knitting them together is that trope-no-trope encountered so often in this book, that form of language that hovers between literal and figurative and so breaks down the distinction between them: catachresis. To see how catachresis brings together my three topics it will be necessary, with the help once more of Friedrich Nietzsche, to show that catachresis is another name for what Nietzsche called "the thought of the eternal return" [*der **Ewige-Wiederkunfts-Gedanke***].[2]

The image of the Janus-faced gateway appears more than once in my preface, once as an image for the preface itself as located simultaneously at beginning and end and as facing both ways, marked entrance and exit at once; once more in my citation from Nietzsche about the way "good reading, slow reading" looks cautiously before and aft, with doors left open; once more in the concluding citation from Emerson's "Seashore." That image of the gateway (*Torweg*), at

[2] Friedrich Nietzsche, *Ecce Homo* (with *On the Genealogy of Morals*), trans. Walter Kaufmann, slightly altered (New York, Vintage Books, 1967), p. 295; German: *Ecce Homo, Werke in Drei Bänden*, ed. Karl Schlechta, II (Munich: Carl Hanser Verlag, 1966), p. 1128. Further citations from *Ecce Homo* will be from these editions.

once passageway and barrier, appears again in the crucial section on the eternal return in *Also Sprach Zarathustra*, "On the Vision and the Riddle" (*Vom Gesicht und Rätsel*).[3] The *Torweg* is Nietzsche's image for the moment (*Augenblick*), not for the presence of the presence, but for the "false appearance of the present," that blink of the eye in which one sees that all things have returned and will return eternally, including that moment. The moment is so slender and evanescent as never to be experienced as such, any more than we are aware of experiencing the darkness and obliteration of vision that occurs whenever we blink our eyes. Nevertheless, the moment divides before and after, differentiating the one from the other with a wall as impenetrable as a locked door of adamant (though it is as transparent as glass and though all things pass through it as if it were not there), becoming quick as a wink no longer not-yet but already no-longer.[4] The gateway of the moment faces two ways, preface and postface, opening at once toward the past and toward the future. The moment stands as the imperceptible interruption that divides past and future eternally from one another and yet brings them together face to face or, as Nietzsche's German idiom puts it, head to head (*vor den Kopf*). This confrontation is an endless contradiction whose strangeness lies in the fact that though the same things happen in past and in future they happen in different and contradictory modes, as always already and as always not yet.

There are in fact four faces face to face at the barrier of the moment. The gateway faces both ways, and past and

[3] Friedrich Nietzsche, *Thus Spoke Zarasthustra*, *The Portable Nietzsche*, trans. Walter Kaufmann (New York: The Viking Press, 1954), pp. 267-272; German, *Werke in Drei Bänden*, ii, pp. 406-410. Further citations will be from these editions.

[4] I thought this play on *Augenblick* as wink or blink of the eye was original with me, but I find it has already been thought of by Jacques Derrida. See "The Principle of Reason: The University in the Eyes of its Pupils," *Diacritics* xiii, 3 (Fall 1983), 20.

future face one another across that double-faced gateway, just as my preface and postface can either be thought of as a double document encompassing the main body of the book, hedging it in at beginning and ending, or as a single continuous text that is implicitly present at every moment during the reading of the book, dividing what has already been read from what has not yet been read. Or the whole body of the book (since it all has to do with the moment, with the linguistic moment, with the *Augenblick* as a self-suspending, self-duplicating sign, breaking the forward movement of poems) could be thought of as an extended form of that interruption of the moment, separating past and future. The latter are represented here by preface and postface, the "you are about to read" and the "now you have read." This continuously reversing structure, in which inside becomes outside, outside inside, envelope letter and letter envelope, enfolder enfolded, has been encountered here before, especially in the chapter on "The Triumph of Life." The structure is one of those spatial images for time as moving forward to come back to itself, or moving back to reach the future, that is, for time as the eternal return. The relation of my preface and postface to the text "proper" of the main chapters is, then, another version of that enigmatic turning, inturning, out-turning, returning, self-enfolding, so that my book itself is another example of the form it discusses. This is appropriate, since the form cannot be "discussed," only exemplified, or only discussed by being exemplified anew, just as, for example, parables can only be talked about adequately in parable. The parabolic contaminates even the most resolute attempts to analyze parable in purely literal or conceptual terms.

In order to show how the face-to-face encounter of past and future across the moment brings together my three topics, Zarathustra's enigmatic vision of the gateway marked "Moment" must be cited as one final text to be read, the final passageway to the end of this book. The passage is certainly not another poem, but it is not a philosophical or a critical text either, at least not in the sense of presenting what it says conceptually or logically. It is, in Nietzsche's precise terminology, vision and riddle at once, that is, "the riddle that I saw [*das Rätsel das ich sah*]" (Eng. 268; Ger. 406), or, to give it another of Nietzsche's names for it, this visionary riddle or riddling vision is a "parable [*Gleichnis*]" (Eng. 272; Ger. 410). It will be remembered that Hegel, in his discussion in the *Ästhetik* of "The Symbolic Form of Art," includes the riddle (*das Rätsel*) along with fable, parable, proverb, apologue, allegory, metaphor, image, and simile as one of the modes of "the comparative art-form [*der vergleichenden Kunstform*]" among which he discriminates.[5] A parable is a riddle that one sees, both in the sense that it is presented not in conceptual terms but in enigmatic image, as a story about things one might see with one's own eyes that nevertheless has a further meaning, and also in the sense that he who has eyes to see will understand it. As opposed to the ordinary riddle, as Hegel defines it, a visionary or parabolic riddle does not begin with its meaning, and its enigmatic quality is not dissolved by its "solution." A visionary riddle, like a parable, is an extended or narrative catachresis. Like catachresis it is neither literal nor figurative but both or neither at once. Such a form of language is the only mode in which what it says can be said and so does not substitute for any conceptual language that could be given, while at the same time it means more than it says. A parable or visionary riddle is a metaphor (another meaning of *Gleichnis*), and yet it does not substitute for any literal expression that could be presented.

Zarathustra tells his parable to the sailors on board a ship during a sea voyage, "embarked with cunning sails on terrible seas" (Eng. 268), not on a ship next to the shore, as in the case of Christ's parable of the sower in Matthew 13.

[5] G.W.F. Hegel, *Aesthetics: Lectures on Fine Art*, trans. T. M. Knox, I (Oxford: Clarendon Press, 1975), pp. 378-426; German: *Vorlesungen über die Ästhetik, Werke in zwanzig Bänden*, XIII (Frankfurt am Main: Suhrkamp Verlag, 1970), pp. 486-546.

Zarathustra tells the sailors the story of a vision he had when climbing a mountain carrying a dwarf who is the embodiment of the spirit of gravity. It is a story within a story, visionary gateway within mountain climb within sea voyage, a vision within a vision within a vision, according to that propensity for duplication, encapsulation, or pocketing, narrative region within region within region, intrinsic to the parabolic, just as it is an intrinsic tendency of parables to be about their own functioning, to be in one way or another parables of parable. Here is Zarathustra's parable of the gateway:[6]

> "Behold this gateway, dwarf!" I continued. "It has two faces [*zwei Gesichter*]. Two paths meet here; no one has yet followed either to its end. This long lane stretches back for an eternity. And the long lane out there, that is another eternity. They contradict each other, these paths [*Sie widersprechen sich, diese Wege*]; they offend each other face to face [*sie stoßen sich gerade vor den Kopf*]; and it is here at this gateway that they come together. The name of the gateway is inscribed above: 'Moment' ['*Augenblick*']. But whoever would follow one of them, on and on, farther and farther—so you believe, dwarf, that these paths contradict each other eternally?"
>
> "All that is straight lies," the dwarf answered contemptuously. "All truth is crooked; time itself is a circle [*die Zeit selber ist ein Kreis*]."
>
> "You spirit of gravity," I said angrily, "do not make things too easy for yourself! Or I shall let you crouch where you are crouching, lamefoot; and it was I that carried you to this *height*.
>
> "Behold," I continued, "this moment! From this gate-

---

[6] Among previous interpretations of *Vom Gesicht und Rätsel*, see Martin Heidegger, *Nietzsche*, I (Pfullingen: Verlag Günther Neske, 1961), pp. 289-297; Werner Hamacher, "*pleroma — zu Genesis und Struktur einer dialektischen Hermeneutik bei Hegel*," in G.W.F. Hegel, *Der Geist des Christentums* (Frankfurt am Main, Berlin, Vienna: Verlag Ullstein, 1978), pp. 313-316.

way, Moment, a long, eternal lane leads *backward*: behind us lies an eternity. Must not whatever *can* walk have walked on this lane before? Must not whatever *can* happen have happened, have been done, have passed by before? [*Muß nicht, was geschehn **kann** von allen Dingen, schon einmal geschehn, getan, vorüberlaufen sein?*] And if everything has been there before—what do you think, dwarf, of this moment? Must not this gateway too have been there before? And are not all things knotted together so firmly that this moment draws after it *all* that is to come? *Therefore*—itself too? [*Und sind nicht solchermaßen fest alle Dinge verknotet, daß dieser Augenblick **alle** kommenden Dinge nach sich zieht? **Also**— —sich selber noch?*] For whatever *can* walk—in this long lane out *there* too, it *must* walk once more.

"And this slow spider, which crawls in the moonlight, and this moonlight itself, and I and you in the gateway, whispering together, whispering of eternal things—must not all of us have been there before? And return and walk in that other lane, out there, before us, in this long dreadful lane—must we not eternally return [*—müssen wir nicht ewig wiederkommen?*]"

Thus I spoke, more and more softly; for I was afraid of my own thoughts and the thoughts behind my thoughts [*meinen eignen Gedanken und Hintergedanken*]. (Eng. 269-270; Ger. 408-409)

Here, if there ever was one, is one more spatial image for time, or rather, two, and certainly both are among the most traditional of such images. Time is a pathway (*Weg*), a lane (*Gasse*) extending backward into the past and forward into the future. Things occur in time by walking somewhere along that lane. Or, on the other hand, time is a circle, according to the dwarf, spirit of gravity. According to a long, long tradition he repeats,[7] time turns back on itself after however extended a detour. Much is at stake in the disagreement between Zarathustra and the dwarf. The op-

---

[7] See Georges Poulet, *Les métamorphoses du cercle* (Paris: Plon, 1961).

position between Zarathustra and the dwarf is expressed in another spatial image: the opposition between the lightness, rapid tempo, and freedom from all weight of Zarathustra's climb to the mountaintop and, on the other hand, the dwarf's gravity, in the double sense of a pull downward, as of a stone falling toward the center of the earth, and of a ponderous solemnity and seriousness in thought, a pedantic *lento*, which is the opposite of Zarathustra's *allegro* or *presto*, thinking as lightening, levitation, thinking as music or dance.

For the dwarf, time is a circle. It turns back on itself because it is governed by the gravitational pull of the center. This image expresses a theory of the eternal return as determined by a central reservoir of archetypes that is outside the movement of time and of which all things are copies, representations, images. All things that move into time are modeled on those extratemporal originals. They draw their authenticity from their resemblance to the fixed originals standing in the center.[8]

For Zarathustra, on the other hand, time is a straight line stretching infinitely in both directions, as time tended to be seen by nineteenth-century geology, physics, and astronomy. That time is infinite not only means it is long enough, since it is endless, for all things that might occur to have occurred. It also means that all things have reoccurred and are destined to re-occur again and again. If time is a straight line, this also means that it is not governed by any center of gravity pulling it around back on itself and serving as a ground for all things. In Nietzsche's thought of the eternal return there is nowhere a middle point along that infinitely long lane stretching toward the past, toward the future, nor outside that line either. There is nowhere any first moment, head of the line, no origin, end, or ground,

---

[8] See Mircea Eliade, *Le Mythe de l'éternel retour: archétypes et répétition* (Paris: Librairie Gallimard, 1949) and the revised and enlarged English translation, *Cosmos and History: The Myth of the Eternal Return*, trans. Willard R. Trask, Harper Torchbooks (New York: Harper & Brothers, 1959).

therefore nowhere any present or presence of the present in temporality. There is only the infinite series of moments themselves, each not presence but image, since each has already occurred innumerable times before. The past, in such a view of time, is not a set of things that once were present and are no longer present, the future a set of things that have not yet occurred but will come to be present. Nothing exists, has existed, or will exist but the infinite series of those hollowed out moments, the eternal repetition of the moment as image. If all things recur for Zarathustra as well as for the dwarf, they recur for Zarathustra with the lightness and lack of gravity of images without original. No original or originating version of any event exists, since any version is the repetition of an earlier version that has always, however far back or forward one goes, already occurred innumerable times before and will occur innumerable times again. There is nowhere any starting place, only image and image of image.

This lack of ground in any original originals for those "all things" that eternally recur explains why Nietzsche can say in *Ecce Homo* that the thought of the eternal return is "the fundamental conception" of *Also Sprach Zarathustra* ("*die Grundkonzeption des Werkes*") (Eng. 295; Ger. 1128) and at the same time have Zarathustra tell the dwarf that he is the stronger of the two because the dwarf could not bear his "abysmal thought" [*meinen abgründlichen Gedanken*]" (Eng. 269; Ger. 408). The thought of the eternal return is grounding and groundless, *gründlich* and *abgründlich*, at once. It grounds itself on an absence of ground in the specific sense of the absence of extratemporal gravity-forming archetypes providing the law for the eternal return of all things. The principle of reason of the eternal return is the absence of the principle of reason, the absence of any *logos*, any measure by which things might be said to be "the same."

The final turn knotting together Nietzsche's thought of the eternal return, turning that thought back on itself, is the peculiar hollowing out of the very moment of that thought which results from seeing it too—this moment here and now, the *Augenblick* with all its trivial details, the spider crawling in the moonlight, the moonlight itself—as eternally recurring and as doubled within itself. The moment is, so to speak, its own image. It is haunted by itself as if it were its own uncanny *revenant*. The moment is single, and yet it is imperceptibly doubled within itself. For this moment too returns, or is a returner. "Must not this gateway too have been there before?," asks Zarathustra. "And are not all things knotted together so firmly that this moment draws after it all that is to come? *Therefore*—itself too?" The moment draws all of the future after itself, in a metaleptic reversal. It therefore draws also itself after itself, in all its innumerable future returns, like all those shadow images, one behind the other, on a slightly out-of-focus television screen. This "*also— —sich selber noch*" is the final critical turn drawing the knot tight. At the same time this turn cuts the knot, disperses the lines to the winds, since it makes the moment not presence but the repetition of itself—image, but image of that strange kind which is not the representation of any original presence. The moment is image of itself, *mimique*, simulacrum, doubling itself to infinity. It is for this "reason" that the moment is no impenetrable wall between past and future, but an open gateway across which they face one another in eternal contradiction. The future is the always not yet of the past. The past is the always already of the future. The moment is the tying of the knot, the drawing together of both in the "*also— —sich selber noch.*" If time is the eternal recurrence of the same, that "same" is not controlled by any fixed measure of sameness, but by a reason without reason. This lack is mirrored or expressed in the way past and future are not congruent but "contradict" each other across the moment. *Ziehen*, "to draw," is the key word here. The moment is a contract or gathering that is at the same time the establishment of a division, a fissure, a point of dispersal. All time is drawn through that gateway of itself. The moment draws the past from the fore and the future through from behind, but it draws also itself through its own opening, in a turning inside out like that relation between preface, postface, and text proper discussed above, before, back there on the other side of the gateway of the moment in which we now are.

I claim to have shown, with Nietzsche's help, how the topics of the linguistic moment as catachresis, spatial images for temporality, and the question of grounding are all drawn together as intrinsic strands in a certain way of thinking about the eternal return. The moment as the image of itself is another naming of catachresis, that is, of *Gleichnis* as parable and metaphor bereft of literal ground. This is confirmed in the way my commentary on Nietzsche's parable does not restate it in conceptual terms but only says it again in more metaphors, images, or parabolic likenesses. The linguistic moment seen in this way implicitly folds into itself all those spatial images for time, each of which is one more never successful attempt to *see* the riddle of temporality as it constantly reverses itself, constantly is drawn through that needle's eye of the moment. And the search for grounds finds its groundless ground, its *abgründlich Grund*, in that "abysmal thought" of the eternal return. That thought was waiting there for me (but where is "there"?) until I could get things together and think it again as the final knot drawing all the topics of this book together and yet at the same time casting them adrift once more in the glimpse of thoughts behind thoughts yet to be thought, in the experience of thought itself as the eternal return.

INDEX

INDEX

Library of Congress Cataloging in Publication Data

Miller, J. Hillis (Joseph Hillis), 1928-
The linguistic moment.

Bibliography: p.
Includes index.
1. English poetry—History and criticism.
2. Space and time in literature.   3. Space and
time in language.   4. American poetry—20th century—
History and criticism. I. Title.
PR508.S65M5   1985   821'.009   84-42894
ISBN 0-691-05442-8 (alk. paper)
ISBN 0-691-01439-6 (pbk.)